Five Hundred Hows & Whys
Sightseeing In Beijing
北京旅游五百问

韩荣良　编译

Compiled & translated
by Han Rongliang

朝华出版社
MORNING GLORY PUBLISHERS

Editor：Zhang Xizhu

Five Hundred Hows & Whys

Sightseeing In Beijing

Published by

MORNING GLORY PUBLISHERS

35 Chegongzhuang Xilu，Beijing 100044，China

Distributed by

CHINA INTERNATIONAL BOOK TRADING CORPORATION

35 Chegongzhuang Xilu，Beijing 100044，China

（P.O.Box 399，Beijing，China）

First edition 2000

ISBN 7-5054-0690-6／G·0190

17-CE-3369P　03000

Printed in the people's Republic of China

目 录
(Contents)

编译者：韩荣良

参加编译工作人员：陈继珍　韩志宇

前　言

　　几近三十年来，我一直在中国最具实力的旅行社——中国国际旅行社总社工作。我做过导游，搞过销售，也曾管理过市场部的产品开发和营销工作，但其中也有相当一部分时间是从事旅游资料的编译工作的，因而积累较丰。

　　也许正是因为这个缘故，数年前，我便萌发了一个想法：要是能把北京的主要旅游景点，以一问一答、融实用与趣味性于一体的方式，并用汉文和英文合排形式予以出版发行，那该多好啊！因为这不仅在对外介绍中国的旅游事业，提高北京旅游景点的知名度方面颇有裨益，而且对旅游从业人员和导游人员的培训，提高他们的业务和知识水平方面，也将起到一定的借鉴和启迪作用。与此同时，对于来北京旅游的中外游客，也将不失为一本别具情趣的旅游参考书。

　　如今，经各方人员的大力合作和襄助，《北京旅游五百问》一书终将以中英合排的形式出版面世。对此，我感到由衷的欣慰。因为它的问世，不仅将一偿我多年来之宿愿，而且还有望在新世纪到来之初，使其在中国旅游业的发展中发挥应有的作用，从而稍尽我的绵薄之力。

　　最后，我要借此机会说明的是，在本书的译编过程中，参照了以往中国国际旅行社总社编撰的中文旅游参考资料。在此，我谨向那些在中文资料编辑工作中付出了巨大努力和辛劳的邱海晏、赵峰、梁新、夏玲和陈巧英等同志表示最诚挚和衷心的谢意。

编译者　韩荣良

1

FOREWORD

It's now almost thirty years since I began working in China International Travel Service Head Office (CITS), a leading and powerful enterprise in China's tourism industry. During my almost life – long work I have served as a tour – guide, a salesman in distributing travel products and managed the work of product development and marketing in the Marketing Department of the CITS Head Office. However, during this period I have also dedicated a great deal of time to the translation of travel materials, and so, by and by have amassed a great collection of them.

It is perhaps because of this that an idea came to me some time ago. What a wonderful thing it would be if the major scenic attractions in Beijing could be set down in English in the form of questions and answers and published in dual versions of English and Chinese that integrate things practical and interesting into one book. For this would not only help publicize China's tourism industry and enhance the awareness of these scenic spots of Beijing but also play a role in the training of personnel and guides working in the tourism trade. At the same time it can also serve as a reference book for visitors to Beijing, both foreigners and Chinese alike.

Now, with the great help and cooperation of my partners a book entitled ＜＜Five Hundred Hows and Whys Sightseeing in Beijing＞＞ is about to appear. For this, I feel very happy because this book is not only the realization of my long – cherished wish but can also play a part in the further development of tourism in China so that I can contribute in some small way to the great undertakings that are taking place around the turn of the century.

Finally, I would like to make it clear that the sources for this book were travel materials formerly worked out in Chinese by the CITS Head Office, which I have merely pieced together and put into English. At the time of the publication of this book I would like to extend my sincere and heartfelt thanks to those comrades Qiu Haiyan, Zhao Feng, Liang Xin, Xia Ling and Chen Qiaoying who have exerted great efforts in the compilation of the reference materials in Chinese.

By the translator and editor

北 京 概 述

北京,简称京,是中华人民共和国的首都,是中国共产党中央和中华人民共和国中央人民政府的所在地,也是全国的政治、经济、文化、交通和对外交往的中心。

北京左环沧海,右拥太行,南襟河济而北枕居庸,真可谓形胜甲于天下。北京的总面积为 16,808 平方公里,逾千万人口。下辖 18 个区、县,其中城区和近郊区有东城、西城、崇文、宣武、朝阳、丰台、海淀和石景山 8 个区,远郊有门头沟、顺义、房山和通州 4 个区,还有昌平、大兴、平谷、怀柔、密云和延庆 6 个郊县。北京是个地域辽阔、人杰地灵、物产丰茂之所。

在历史上,北京是中国最悠久的古都和城市之一。自周武王克殷反商,封召公于燕起,迄今已有 3,000 余年的历史。北京旧称蓟,春秋战国时期为燕国都城,辽时建为陪都,称燕京;金代正式建都于此,称为中都;元时名之曰大都;明清时期又称为京师,通称北京。北京作为都城自金代起已有 700 余年的历史,历代劳动人民都在北京这块丰腴的土地上创造了光辉灿烂的人间业绩,留下了绚丽多彩的古物文化。

北京建筑雄伟,古建荟萃。旧有内外两城,均为明代所筑。今城垣虽已不存,但主要门楼犹在,且尚有保存完好、世界上最大的宫殿建筑群故宫及蔚为壮观的天安门城楼,耸峙于城南的天坛和横卧于西北郊的皇家园林颐和园;更有绵亘于延庆、怀柔两郊县之内的八达岭和慕田峪长城,以及昌平县境的明十三陵等建筑。北京,现已成为国内外宾朋游人所向往的游览胜地。天安门广场是北京市的中心,也是世界上最大的广场。人民英雄纪念碑耸立在广场的中央,其南有毛主席纪念堂,东侧为中国革命博物馆和中国历史博物馆,西侧为人民大会堂。天安门广场是每个中外宾朋游人的必到之处。此外，北海、景山、香山等公园及八大处等园林景区，也都不失为景色佳绝、风光旖旎之去处，而无不为中外游人所交口称道。

北京各项事业迅速发展，城市面貌变化日新月异。尤其是1978年中国实行改革开放政策以来，北京已发展成了全国的铁路交通枢纽，国内航空和国际交往的中心，同时也是中国最大的科学文化中心。为方便游人前来北京观光游览，北京已建成了各类档次的宾馆酒店和旅游设施，餐饮服务也都比较完备，市内交通四通八达，现正向着高速化、立交化的方向阔步前进。

北京已经敞开胸怀，随时准备迎接来自五湖四海的宾朋佳客。朋友，如果您没有到过北京的话，难道就不想到那里一游，一睹古都北京之风采？如果您有兴趣，不妨在动身之前或游览之中先浏览一下这本小册子中的有关章节，因为它对您了解北京古往今来的变迁，发思古之悠情，盼中华之腾飞，是会有所启迪和助益的。

A BRIEF INTRODUCTION TO BEIJING

Beijing is the capital of the People's Republic of China, the seat of the Central Committee of the Chinese Communist Party and the Central People's Government of China. It is the political, economic, cultural and communications center of the country as well as that for international exchanges.

With a vast blue sea to the east, the Taihang Mountains on the west, adjacent to the River in the south and the Juyong Pass ranging to the north, Beijing enjoys a splendid terrain and location in China. Covering an area of 16,808 square kilometers with a population of around 11 million, Beijing has 18 districts and counties under its jurisdiction. Among them, the eight districts of Dongcheng, Xicheng, Chongwen, Xuanwu, Chaoyang, Fengtai, Haidian and Shijingshan are in the city proper and the near suburbs; the other four districts of Shunyi, Mengtougou, Fangshan and Tongzhou are in the farther outskirts; and the rest six are the suburban counties of Changping, Daxing, Pinggu, Huairou, Miyun and Yanqing. Beijing covers a vast area. It is a city rich in products and is a city of which its inhabitants can be deservedly proud.

Beijing has historically been one of China's ancient capitals. From the overthrow of the Shang Dynasty (around 16th − 11th century B.C.) by King Wu of the Zhou Dynasty, who enfeoffed Prince Shao to the region of Yan, Beijing has a history of over 3,000 years. Called Ji in ancient times, it was once the capital of the State of Yan in the Spring and Autumn Peri-

6

od (770 - 476 B.C.). Later, in the Liao Dynasty it was the alternate capital, called Yanjing, and in the Jin Dynasty, Beijing was formally made its capital, being called Zhongdu. Renamed Dadu in the Yuan Dynasty, later rendered as Jingshi during the Ming and Qing dynasties, it has come to be known as Beijing, meaning "northern capital". Beijing, as a capital from the Jin dynasty onwards, has already enjoyed a history of over 800 years. The laboring people of previous and ensuing dynasties with their wisdom and hard work have created and left on this piece of land many marvels, splendid cultural relics and objects, and a brilliant legacy of culture.

Many magnificent buildings of classical styles can be found in Beijing, featuring the acme of ancient architecture in China. The city once had double inner and outer city walls built in the Ming Dynasty. Although the walls no longer exist, the most important city gates and towers are still intact. Furthermore, the entire complex of the Imperial Palace, the largest of its kind in the world, known as the Purple Forbidden City, is still intact and well - protected by the state. You will also find the Temple of Heaven standing in the south of the city and the Summer Palace, the former royal summer resort, spreading out in the northwest. The famous Badaling and Mutianyu Sections of the Great Wall still stretch over the mountain ranges in Yanqing and Huairou counties and the Tianshou Mountain area in Changping County is dotted with the 13 Ming Tombs. All these now have become renowned tourist attractions for visitors from all over the country and also the world. The Tian'anmen Square, the largest public square in the world, is the center of Beijing. In its midst towers the Monument to the People's

Heroes and in the south stands the Memorial Hall of Mao Zedong. Flanking the west of the square is the Great Hall of the
People and on the east are the Museum of Chinese History and
the Museum of Chinese Revolution. Tian'anmen Square is
now an essential destination for every visitor, Chinese or foreign, to Beijing. In addition, the Beihai, Jingshan and Xiang-
shan parks as well as the Badachu scenic area are all renowned
tourist attractions in Beijing praised by visitors from all over
the world.

Beijing is a rapidly developing city in many fields and great
changes are taking place with every passing day in city construction. Especially when the policy of reform and opening to
the outside world was introduced in 1978, Beijing has become
the hinge of the national rail network, a center of air — trans-
ports and interchanges between the nations of the world. At
the same time, it is also the biggest center of science and culture in the country. To cater to the needs of visitors to Beijing,
many star — scaled hotels have been put up in Beijing together
with a relatively complete infrastructure in tourism service and
catering business. In addition, transport in the city is very easy
and a new system of expressways linked up with flyovers and
viaducts is being completed.

Beijing is ready with open arms to welcome visitors from
far and wide. So, if you have never been to Beijing, don't you
want to visit the ancient city mingled with a new feature? If
you do, it would be a good idea to read the relevant sections of
this book either before you arrive or during your visit, because
this will help you know more about the city, understand the
changes that have taken place in Beijing from ancient times up

to the present day. Be intrigued by reflecting on things of the past, and look forward to the great advances yet to come in China.

to the present day; he mused and recollecting an album of the
past, and look forward to the inexhaustible, yet to come in
China ...

天 安 门
(Tian'anmen Square and Rostrum)

1. 天安门何时建成？面积有多大？

天安门位于北京市的中心，是中华人民共和国的象征。始建于明永乐十五年（1417 年），最初命名为承天门，即皇城的正门。明末李自成率领的农民起义军进入北京，后来在清兵入关进攻北京交火时，承天门毁于战火。清顺治八年（1651 年）重建后即改名为天安门。

天安门前的广场，其南北长为 800 米，东西宽达 500 米，总面积为 40 公顷，是当今世界上最大的广场。

When was the Tian'anmen Gate built and completed? How large an area does the Tian'anmen Square cover?

Located in the center of the city of Beijing, Tian'anmen is the symbol of the People's Republic of China. Started to be built in 1417, the 15th year of the reign period of Yongle of the Ming Dynasty (1368 – 1644), the gate was formerly called Chengtianmen (Gate of Heavenly Succession), which was the front gate of the Imperial City then. By the end of the Ming Dynasty, the peasant army led by Li Zicheng entered the city of Beijing, but later when the Qing army marched upon Beijing, the Chengtianmen was leveled under the crossfire. It was rebuilt in 1651, the eighth year of the reign period of Shunzhi in Qing with the name changed into "Tian'anmen".

The Tian'anmen Square in front of it, 800 meters from

1

north to south and 500 meters from east to west, covers an area of 40 hectares. Hence the largest square in the world.

2. "承天门"的含义是什么?

承天门是沿用唐代皇城正门的名称,表示皇帝"承天启运","受命于天"。

What is the implication behind the Gate of "Chengtianmen"?

The name of Chengtianmen was taken from that of the front gate of the imperial city in the Tang Dynasty (618 – 907). It simply means that "the emperor started his fortune by acting upon the mandate of the heaven" and "everything he did was to carry out the will of the heaven above."

3. 天安门的基本建筑是怎样的?

天安门城楼建在汉白玉构筑的须弥座上,高 33.7 米。台座是用每块 24 公斤重的大砖砌成的。砖台上建两层重楼大殿,顶上覆盖着金黄彩灿的琉璃瓦,屋脊的两端和前后四条垂脊上均饰有龙、凤等吻兽。城楼东西宽为 9 间,南北进深是 5 间,系用"九五"之数以示帝王之尊严。

What about the architectural structure of the Tian'anmen Gate?

Built on a Sumeru dais of white marble – pieces, the Tian'anmen gate – tower is 33.7 meters high, and the platform was built of large pieces of bricks, each weighing 24 kilograms. Standing on the platform is the two – storeyed hall of double eaves with its gabled roof covered by glistening yellow glazed tiles. At both ends of the roof – ridge, there are four slanting ledges decorated with dragons, phoenixes and some mythical bird – like animal named "Qiwen". The frontage of the hall consists of nine bays from the east to the west and five bays in depth from north to south, adopting the numerals of nine and five to suggest the supreme dignity of an emperor.

4. 天安门的五个门洞(也称"五阙")有何讲究?

进出天安门"五阙"是有严格的等级区分的,中间的门洞只能供皇帝出入,是他出入皇宫的通道,也是显示其威风的地方。皇帝"御驾亲征"前,就要在天安门前祭路;若派大将出征,皇帝也得亲率文武百官,出到天安门前送行并祭旗。另外,在明、清时期,每年冬至皇帝都得去天坛祭天,夏至还要去地坛祭地,均从天安门的中间门洞出入。皇帝的父母进宫,以及皇帝婚娶时迎接新皇后入宫,也都要从中间门洞通过。但对于此门,却有个规定,那便是只能进喜,不准出丧,包括皇帝的丧礼在内,都严禁由天安门进出。

What is the tale about the Five Tunnel Passage of the Tian'anmen Gate?

For getting into and coming out of the Imperial Palace through the Five Tunnel Passages there is a strict set of rules based on a hierarchy system. The gate is a passage for the emperor to get into or go out from the Imperial Palace and the one in the middle is specially reserved for the emperor himself. So the gate is not only a mere passage, but also a place for the emperor to show off his supreme authority. The emperor will hold a sacrificial ceremony here before his setting out on an expedition under his own command, either to fight against an inva-

3

sion or to put down a rebellion. If a general is sent on an expedition, the emperor himself will have to honor the flag together with his officials and officers in front of the Tian'anmen Gate. Aside from all these, emperors of the Ming and Qing dynasties will have to go through the middle gate to offer sacrifices to the heaven on every Winter Solstice in the Temple of Heaven and to the earth on every Summer Solstice in the Temple of Earth. If the parents of the emperor want to get into the Imperial Palace they are permitted to go through the middle passage. The expected queen going to the wedding ceremony will take this passage too. As a strict rule this gate can be used only for admitting things auspicious and happy, but absolutely forbidden for mourning. Even the funeral procession of a demised emperor is not allowed to pass through the Tian'anmen Gate.

5. 天安门城楼是作何用的?

在封建时代,天安门城楼是举行最隆重典礼的地方,如皇帝颁诏,新帝继位或是册封皇后等,都是先在天安门城楼上宣读诏书,然后再诏谕天下的。明、清时期,盛行科举制度,每次举行殿试,须由皇帝亲自主考,得中前三名者称为状元、榜眼、探花。殿试后两天,皇帝就要召见他们,依次传呼他们的姓名,这就叫做"传胪",即挨个唱名传呼,天安门便是"金殿传胪"的地方。

What wss the Tian'anmen Rostrum used for?

In feudal times, ceremonies of great importance, such as promulgating an imperial edict conferring the title of a queen, or announcing a newly enthroned emperor, were all held on the Tian'anmen Rostrum and then made known to the public in the country. During the Ming and Qing dynasties, the Bagu

System of choosing high – ranking officials by way of a palace examination was on vogue, and the examination was carried out under the supervision of the emperor himself. Those who came off the first three were entitled Zhuangyuan (No. 1 scholar of the country), Bangyan and Tanhua (No. 2 and No. 3 scholars), and they would have the honor to be received in audience by the emperor two days after the examination. On that day they would in turn be called in to see the emperor. This is what was then called "Chuanlu" and the very place for doing that "Jindian Chuanlu" was right in the Tian'anmen Rostrum.

6. 何谓"秋审"和"朝审"？

天安门前也是用作"秋审"和"朝审"的地方。明、清两代，每年五月，刑部衙门便把各省判处死刑的囚犯名册汇集起来，呈送皇帝过目。八月中旬，皇帝诏令有关官员在天安门前进行最后判决，这就是所谓"秋审"。在霜降前，对北京刑部监狱里关押的判处死刑的犯人进行审处，就叫"朝审"。

What were the so – called "Autumn Trial" and the "Palace Trial"?

The place in front of the Tian'anmen Gate was a place for holding what was then called "Qiushen" (Autumn trial) and "Chaoshen" (Palace trial). In May during the Ming and Qing dynasties, the Ministry of Punishment would collect from all provinces and regions of the country the name – lists of convicts sentenced to death and submit them to the emperor for his perusal. And then in the middle ten days of autumn, the emperor would call up all officials concerned to make a final judgement of the cases in front of the Tian'anmen Gate. This is what was then called the "Autumn Trial." But those convicts sentenced to death who were jailed in the prisons of the Ministry of Punishment in Beijing would undergo a final judgement before the Frost's Descent. This is, as then said, the "Palace Trial."

7. 天安门前金水河上的七座石桥系作何用?

在天安门前的金水河上跨有7座石拱桥,中间5座统称为外金水桥。正中的一座桥身较宽,从前是供皇帝通行的御道,称为"御路桥"。其左右两座桥称"王公桥",是亲王等通行用的。王公桥两侧的桥谓之"品级桥",是三品以上文武官员通过的桥。紧挨其外侧的两座便是"公生桥",是四品以下官员通行用的桥。

What were the seven stone bridges over the Golden Water Stream in front of the Tian'anmen Gate used for?

Spanning over the Golden Water Stream in front of the Tian'anmen Gate are the seven arched stone bridges. The five in-between are known as the outer "Golden Water Bridge" and the one in the middle which is broader than all others was specially reserved for the emperor to use it alone, hence the name "Yuluqiao" (Imperial Bridge). The two bridges on either side were for princes to go across, called "Wanggongqiao" (royal family bridge). The another two on the farther sides were the bridges for officials and officers at or above the third rank known as "Pinjiqiao" (ranking bridge). And the last two on the still farther sides are called "Gongshengqiao", meaning the bridge for the ordinaries which were for officials and officers below the fourth grade.

8. 金水桥两岸的石狮子有何说头？

金水河两岸的汉白玉石台座上蹲坐着两对汉白玉石狮子，雕刻十分精美。东边的是雄狮，用右爪戏弄绣球；西边的为母狮，以左爪逗弄小狮。左右成对，相互呼应，显得十分生动活泼。桥头右狮的肚子上有个深约寸许的小洞眼，据传是当年八国联军进攻北京天安门时留下的。有人说，当时石狮目睹侵略者的嚣张气焰，义愤填膺，毅然决然地抛下身边的小狮，向着侵略者勇猛扑去，那小洞就是侵略者留下的枪眼。

What is the story about the stone lions on both sides of the Golden Water Stream?

Squatting on the marble – stone dais on both sides of the Golden Water Stream are the two pairs of lions chiseled out of white marble pieces with a very exquisite and delicate workmanship. The two on the east with their paws playing with the embroidered balls are male and the two on the west with their left paws caressing the cubs are female. One echoing the other, the two pairs on both sides of the stream are full of vigor and vitality, suggesting a sense as if they were alive. Taking a careful look at the lion on the right in front of the bridge you'll find a small hole on her belly about one inch deep. This hole, as said, was left over when the eight powers allied forces marched upon Beijing. At that time, the lion, filled with wrath at the ferocity of the invaders, fell bravely upon them, leaving her young cub aside. The small hole on the belly was the hole of a gunshot then.

9. "华表"是怎样演变而来的?

华表在中国有着悠久的历史。远在尧时就已存在,那就是在木柱上绑上一根横木,让老百姓对官吏发表评论,提出看法,以示君主虚心纳谏,这在当时称为"表木"。周代实行井田制,在田界立木以分地界的行列、远近,使人一见便知路程远近,因而也称"邮表"。同时,在许多通衢大道和桥岸两边也设类似的木揭,以此作为认路的标志。随着时代的发展,这类表木就被美化了,渐渐失去了它原来的意义和作用,演变成了一种纯粹的装饰物,成了宫殿建筑艺术中的一个组成部分。

How did the "Huabiao" (ornamental column) come into being?

Tracing far back in history, the "Huabiao", now the ornamental column chiseled out of white marble, came into being a long time ago in the period of Yao (around the end of 22nd century B.C.) in very ancient China. A bar was fastened horizontally onto the top of a wooden pole, a device then for the common people to put something on it to air their views or comments about their headsmen. It is to show that the rulers were modest and ready to take in opinions from the people and the device was then called "biaomu". During the Western Zhou (11th century – 771 B.C.), the well – field system was practiced, and piles were put up in the fields to mark the demarcation lines of different plots of land so that people would be able to find out easily the distance even from faraway. The pile was then called "Youbiao". And the pile was even put up by the side of a main road to serve as a road – sign. However, as time went on, the "Biaomu" was embellished and was thenceforth

8

losing by and by its original function and significance. Finally it became a part of architecture for a pure decoration purpose of a palace.

10. 天安门前的华表是何年建成的？重量是多少？上面有何雕刻？

天安门前的华表,建于明永乐年间(1403－1424 年),距今已有 500 余年的历史。每个华表重为 2 万公斤。华表上端有一承露盘,盘上蹲着个怪兽,叫犼(音吼),传说是龙的九子之一。因其有守望的习性,故总是蹲在华表上面。它微昂着头,面向前方,所以被人们称为"望天犼"。

When was the "Huabiao" in front of the Tian'anmen Gate erected? What's the weight of it and what is carved on it?

Put up in the period of Yongle's reign (1403－1424) in the Ming dynasty (1368－1644), the "Huabiao" in front of the Tian'anmen Gate, each weighing 20,000 kilograms has a history of over 500 years. Atop it is a "Chenglupan" − a tray for receiving falling dew, with a chimera called "Hou" squatting on it. Hou, as said, is one of the nine sons of the dragon. As it has a habit of alertness for over − watching, it is always made to sit on the dew − receiving tray atop an ornamental column. With its head poking slightly upwards and gazing into the distance it is popularly known as "Wangtianhou."

11. 关于天安门前华表上的"望天犼"曾有些什么传说？

据传说称,望天经常注视着皇帝外出时的行为,时刻在劝戒帝王,不要总在外面幸游作乐,废弃朝政。若帝王久出不归,就会说:"国君呀,你不要长期在外游玩了,赶快回来料理国事吧。我们日夜盼着你回来,已是望眼欲穿了。"因此人们就给这两个取了个美名,谓之"望君归"。

What is the tale about the "Wangtianhou" atop the Huabiao in front of the Tian'anmen Gate?

It is said that the Wangtianhou always keeps an eye on how the emperor was behaving himself when he was away from the imperial palace, and often dissuaded him from living a too dissipated and indulgent life in the merry-making. Should the emperor stay away too long the Hou would say: "Your majesty, don't stay away too long. Please hurry back and take care of the state affairs now. We two Hous, with our eyes strained, are looking forward to your return to the palace." Hence the two Hous were euphonically called "Wangjungui" — meaning "expecting the emperor's return".

12. 关于天安门里的"望天犼"又有什么样的传说呢?

在天安门城楼的后边,也有一对同样的华表,不过其方向正好是相反的,承露盘上的犼也面向着北方。这对总是注视着帝王在深宫大院里的所作所为,而且不断提醒帝王说:"君王呀,你不要老是呆在宫中,只顾着与皇后嫔妃们寻欢作乐,快走出去看看人民的苦难吧! 我们盼你出来,已快到望眼欲穿的程度了。"故此人们便把这两个犼称为"望君出"。

What is there to say about the "Wangtianhou" inside the Tian'anmen Gate?

There are a pair of "Huabiao" behind the Tian'anmen Gate. However their direction is just the opposite to those in front of the Tian'anmen Gate with the Wangtianhou on the dew – receiving tray facing the north. They kept an eye on what the emperor was doing in the rows of imperial palaces and always reminded the emperor, saying: "Your majesty, don't always stay in the palace and indulge in merry – making with your queen and concubines. Please come out and get to know the sufferings of the populace. We two Hous, with our eyes wide open, were expecting you to come out." Hence the two Hous are known as "Wangjunchu", meaning "expecting the emperor to come out of the palace."

13. "望君归"和"望君出"所蹲坐的华表石柱又叫何名？该名称说明了什么？

"望君归"和"望君出"所蹲坐的华表石柱又叫"望柱"。在封建社会里，华表石孔"望君归"和"望君出"的传说，充分地反映了人民群众要求勤政廉洁、政治清明的朴素愿望，以及对统治阶级穷奢极欲强烈不满。

What were the two pairs of Huabiao for the squatting chimeras "Wangjungui" and "Wangjunchu" otherwise called? And what does that mean?

The ornamental column "Huabiao" for the squatting chimeras "Wangjungui" and "Wangjunchu" was otherwise called "Wangzhu," the meaning of which is "column of expectation." In the Chinese feudal society, the legend is a full expression of a mere hope from the populace for a diligent and honest government and their strong dissatisfaction with the extremely dissipated life of the ruling class.

14. 天安门广场是怎么来的？

在明、清时期,天安门广场是皇城正门前的广场,亦即是在天安门南面引出的一大片凸字形旷地,藉以衬托并突出天安门的地位。明朝初年,在现今毛主席纪念堂的位置上建起一座砖石结构的门,称为"大明门",清代更名为"大清门",而在满清王朝被推翻以后,又改称为"中华门",还在东西长安街上分别建起了长安左门和长安右门,均为砖石结构。在这三门之间筑起一道红墙围绕,这便形成了当时面积仅为 11 公顷的小小的天安门广场。

How did the Tian'anmen Square come into being?

With a long history behind it, the Tian'anmen Square used to be a piece of land in front of the Imperial Palace during the Ming and Qing dynasties, an open space jetting out towards the south from the Tian'anmen Gate. It was meant to set off the outstanding importance of the Tian'anmen Gate and the Imperial City behind. In the early days of the Ming Dynasty a gate of brick and stone was built right on the site of the present Memorial Hall of Mao Zedong and was then called "Damingmen" – the Gate of the Great Ming. It was renamed as "Daqingmen" – the Gate of the Great Qing in the Qing Dynasty. But when the Qing Empire was toppled, it was again renamed as "Zhonghuamen" (Gate of China). And then afterwards another two gates called "Chang'anzuomen" and "Chang'anyoumen" were added on both sides of the Chang'an Road, also of a brick and stone structure. Encircled with a newly built red wall, the area within the three gates formed a small Tian'anmen Square, a square of mere 11 hectares.

15. 明、清时代的天安门广场是为谁服务的?

在明、清时代,天安门广场是一片禁地,老百姓是绝对不准入内的,任何人都不得向里张望,否则便算是犯了"私窥宫门"之大罪。官员们到了门前,都必须下马步行。由于这些禁令和规定,那时,北京人想从东城往西城去,就得绕道大明门以南或地安门以北,是很不方便的。

东西两边围墙以外,分布着当时的中央衙门。明王朝把五府六部全都集中在天安门广场周围;清代又改设刑部、都察院和大理寺等。百姓们用"东边掌生,西边掌死"来描绘当时广场周围官署林立、府部对峙的情景。另外,明、清时代的朝审、秋审的犯人,都得由长安右门押进广场。他们个个哭泣,仿佛身入虎口;而殿试高中的进士们,则出长安左门去赴顺天府的庆宴。他们个个笑逐颜开,犹如鱼跃龙门。因此,人们又把长安右门叫做"虎门",把长安左门称为"龙门"。无庸讳言,过去的天安门广场是为统治阶级服务的。

Whom did the Tian'anmen Square serve during the Ming and Qing dynasties?

In the Ming and Qing dynasties the Tian'anmen Square was forbidden to common people. No one could even take a look at it. If anyone did, he/she would be deemed as committing a crime of "illegally peeping at the palace gate". When the officials got to the front of the gate they had to get off the horse and proceed on foot into the palace. Should anyone want to go from the east of the city to the west, he had to go round either by the way south of the Damingmen or north of the Gate of Earthly Tranquility. It was a loathsome trouble then.

Lined outside the red wall on the east and west were the

13

government offices called the central "Yamen". In the Ming dynasty, all five offices and six ministries for administration were centered round the Tian'anmen Square. In the Qing dynasty some of the offices were changed into the Ministry of Punishment, Censorial Court and Court of Judicial Review, etc.. Therefore, people used to describe such offices with the saying: "the offices in the east are dealing with the living, while those on the west are manipulating the death." In addition, in the Ming and Qing dynasties, culprits for "palace trial" or "autumn trial" were all escorted into the square through the western gate with everyone weeping and crying as if they were brought to the mouth of a tiger. Yet those scholars who passed the palace examination were all summoned in by the eastern gate to attend a banquet given by the Shuntian Prefecture, everyone beaming with happiness as if they were carps overleapt the dragon gate. Hence the popular saying the "Tiger Gate" for the gate on the west and the "Dragon Gate" on the east. It goes without saying that in the days of old the Tian'anmen Gate was in the service of the feudal ruling class.

16. 在天安门广场上展开过哪些革命活动？

一百多年以来,外国殖民主义者的入侵曾使天安门几度遭到破坏,蒙受耻辱。但是,发生在天安门前的反帝、反封建的斗争却从未停止过:

* 1919 年 5 月 4 日,中国历史上划时代的"五四"运动,就是在天安门广场上爆发的,它打响了中国人民反帝反封建的新民主主义革命的第一炮。

* 1925 年,上海发生"五卅惨案",引发了中国人民反帝斗争的大风暴,北京的爱国群众在天安门广场上集会声援,这里就

14

成了反帝示威活动的中心。

　＊1926年,北京人民于3月18日在天安门广场举行国民大会,反对日本帝国主义的军舰入侵我国,会后参加游行示威的群众惨遭枪杀,酿成了震撼全国的"三一八"惨案。

　＊1935年12月9日,北京的爱国学生在天安门广场举行群众大会,反对日本帝国主义对中国的侵略,反对军警镇压,革命群众与他们进行了英勇不屈的斗争,这便是中国近代史上著名的"一二九"运动。

　＊1947年5月20日,北京的进步学生在天安门广场举行示威,提出"实施政协决议,组织联合政府","反对饥饿,反对内战"等强烈要求,表达了他们要求建设一个新中国的愿望。

　＊1949年10月1日,毛泽东主席在天安门城楼上向全世界庄严宣告"中华人民共和国成立了。中国人民从此站起来了。"同时也宣布了中央人民政府的成立,并升起了第一面五星红旗。在开国大典之日,全市人民群众在天安门广场举行了游行活动,庆祝中国人民革命的伟大胜利,中央首长还检阅了部队。

　＊1976年1月8日,敬爱的周恩来总理与世长辞。人民群众前去天安门广场举行悼念活动,遭到"四人帮"的阻挠破坏。自1月8日至清明节前,整个广场成了悼念周总理的会场和声讨"四人帮"的战场。4月5日,穷凶极恶的"四人帮"在天安门广场上对革命群众进行镇压,激起了广大人民群众的强烈反抗。

What are the revolutionary activities, which have ever been staged in the Tian'anmen Square?

The Tian'anmen Square, due to the invasion of foreign colonialists over the past hundred years, has been trampled underfoot and many a time it has suffered from destruction and humiliation, but the anti – imperialist and anti – feudalistic

15

movements have never ceased:

A. In 1919, the May 4th Movement took place in the Tian'anmen Square. It is an epoch – making event in the modern history of China as it fired the first gun – shot, signaling the beginning of the new democratic revolution staged in China by the Chinese people in their struggle against imperialism and feudalism.

B. In 1925, the "May 30th Massacre in Shanghai" enraged the Chinese people and roused them into action, promising a hurricane in the struggle against imperialism. To support the just struggle, the patriotic people in Beijing held a grand rally in the Tian'anmen Square, thereby making the place a center for the demonstration against imperialism.

C. On 18 March, 1926, the people of Beijing held a rally in the Tian'anmen Square, denouncing the invasion by the Japanese warship into the territorial waters of China, and the mass demonstration afterwards was cruelly suppressed with some of the demonstrators killed. This is the "March 18th Massacre" that shocked the whole Chinese nation.

D. December 9, 1935, the patriotic students in Beijing held a mass rally in the Tian'anmen Square, denouncing the invasion of China by Japanese imperialism and opposing the high – handed suppression of the students' movement by the army and policemen. This is the "December 9th Students' Movement," a famous event in the modern Chinese history.

E. On 20 May, 1947, the progressive students of Beijing staged a demonstration in the Tian'anmen Square, demanding strongly the "implementation of the decisions adopted at the political consultative conference to form a coalition government." Shouting the slogan "oppose hunger and civil war" they expressed in this way their wishes for establishing a new China.

F. On 1 October, 1949, Chairman Mao Zedong, standing on the Tian'anmen Rostrum, solemnly declared to the world that the "People's Republic of China has been founded" and the "Chinese people have ever since stood up." At the same time he also promulgated the establishment of the central people's government and he himself raised the first five – star red flag up into the sky. On the very day inaugurating the founding of the People's Republic of China, the people in Beijing gathered in the Tian'anmen Square holding a grand parade in celebration of the great victory won by the Chinese people in the revolution, and the state leaders reviewed the People's Liberation Army.

G. On 8 January, 1976, Beloved Premier Zhou Enlai passed away. The broad masses of the people in Beijing went to the Tian'anmen Square to mourn for him, but were hindered by the "Gang of Four". However, from that day on, the whole square became a place of convergence in mourning for Premier Zhou, and also a battlefield in denouncing the "Gang of Four". Up to April 5, the atrocious "Gang of Four" instigated a suppression of the masses of people in the Tian'anmen Square, rousing a great indignation and strong opposition from the people to the "Gang of Four."

17. 如今的天安门广场又是怎样的?

天安门广场于 1957 年进行了扩建,占地面积为 40 公顷,可容纳 50 万人。广场北抵天安门之红墙,南达正阳门城楼,西到人民大会堂,东至中国革命博物馆和中国历史博物馆,其南北长880米,东西宽500米,是世界上面积最大的广场。广场的中心矗立着人民英雄纪念碑,其后是毛主席纪念堂。天安门广场位于北京市的中心,距市内几个商业区均较近,如著名的王府井大街、前门和西单,往返交通均很方便。在广场的北面,天安门城楼之西是中山公园,东边则是劳动人民文化宫,那里是人民群众休憩游乐、避暑、学习或锻练身体的良好去处。

What about the Tian'anmen Square in nowadays?

Enlarged in 1957, the Tian'anmen Square in nowadays covers an area of 40 hectares, which may hold 500,000 people at a time. From the red wall of the Tian'anmen Gate in the north to the Zhengyang Gate – the tower of the front gate in the south, it measures some 880 meters, and from the Museum of Chinese Revolution and Chinese History in the east to the Great Hall of the People in the west it is 500 meters. The square is the largest one of its kind in the world. Towering in the center of the square is the Monument to the People's Heroes with Chairman Mao's Memorial Hall right behind it. Situated in the center of the city, the square is also within the walking distance to the downtown areas, such as the well-known Wangfujing Street, the Qianmen (the Front Gate) Street and the Xidan Street. Close by the west of the Tian'anmen Gate is the Zhongshan Park, and by the east is the Cultural Palace of the Working People. All of them prove are ideal places for sightseeing, relaxation, amusements, physical exercises and study, or just for getting away from summer-heat.

人民英雄纪念碑
(The Monument to the People's Heroes)

18. 人民英雄纪念碑是怎么回事？它是哪年建成的？

人民英雄纪念碑建于 1958 年，耸立在天安门广场的中心。它是为纪念自 1840 年以来至解放战争期间，在反对国内外敌人，争取国家独立、民族解放和人民自由幸福的历次斗争中牺牲了的人民英雄而建立的，也是中国自古以来规模最大的纪念碑。碑基占地面积为 3,000 平方米，碑通高 37.94 米，由 17,000 块花岗岩和汉白玉构成。碑体本身为 32 层，由 413 块花岗岩砌成。碑的正面朝北，对着天安门城楼。碑身长 14.7 米，宽为 2.9 米，厚度达 1 米，重 60 吨。碑的正面是毛主席亲笔题写的"人民英雄永垂不朽"八个大字，背面是周恩来总理题的碑文。全部题字均用镏金板镶嵌。碑身下为双层巨座，其上层四周刻着中国人民所喜爱的菊花、荷花、牡丹和百合花，组成了八个花环，表示敬献给革命先烈。下层巨座周围镶嵌着八幅汉白玉大型浮雕，共雕刻了 190 个性格动态迥异的人物形象，向人民群众展示了近百年来惊天动地的革命史。碑座为海棠形，四周两重平台并围有汉白玉栏杆。

What about the Monument to the People's Heroes? When was it erected?

Towering high in the center of the Tian'anmen Square is the Monument to the People's Heroes. It was erected in 1958 in memory of the people's heroes, who laid down their lives in numerous struggles against both domestic and foreign enemies for the national independence and liberation, and for the freedom and happiness of the Chinese people. Being the largest of its kind, the base of the monument covers 3,000 square meters. The Monument built with 17,000 pieces of granite and white marble stands 37.94 meters high with the obelisk itself consisting of 413 pieces of granite in 32 layers. With its frontside facing the north, i.e. opposite the Tian'anmen Rostrum, the obelisk itself is 14.7 meters in height, 2.9 meters in width and 1 meter in thickness, weighing 60 tons. Inscribed on its frontside are such words: "Eternal Glory to the People's Heroes!" autographed by Chairman Mao himself. The inscription at the back is in the handwriting of the late Premier Zhou Enlai with all characters gold-plated. Under the obelisk are the two-layered base of the monument, and the upper layer is carved with chrysanthemums, lotus-flowers, peonies and lilies loved by the Chinese people and they are formed into 8 wreaths in dedication to the revolutionary martyrs. The bottom layer is inlaid with 8 big pieces of white marble carved in relief, depicting 190 figures of all descriptions in a vivid and life-like way. It tells the people a tale about the earth-shaking events ever happened in the Chinese revolution in a time-span of 100 years in the past. The base of the monument is in the shape of the Chinese flowering crabapple, with a double terrace and marble balustrades.

19. 人民英雄纪念碑上的八幅大浮雕都是些什么内容?

1. 描写"鸦片战争"前夕,愤怒的人民群众在广东虎门炮台焚毁鸦片的情景。

2. 表现 1851 年太平天国起义军勇往直前的伟大革命气

慨。

    3. 表现1911年武昌起义攻打两湖总督衙门时的情景。

    4. 描绘"五四"运动的情景。

    5. 描述1925年"五卅"运动的情景。

    6. 表现1927年8月1日南昌起义的情景。

    7. 展现抗日战争的光辉历史。

    8. 展示人民解放军胜利渡过长江,解放全中国的情景。

What are the eight large pieces in relief about in particular?

    A. Before the outbreak of the Opium War, the enraged masses of people are burning the opium at the Humen Fort, Guangdong province.

    B. It depicts the undaunted revolutionary spirit of the uprising army of the Taiping Heavenly Kingdom in 1851, who were surging bravely forward.

    C. It describes the attack on the governor's "Yamen" of Hunan and Hubei at the time of the Wuchang Uprising in 1911.

    D. It shows the "May 4th Movement of 1919."

    E. It shows the "May 30th Movement" of 1925 happened in Shanghai.

    F. It depicts the "August 1st Uprising" in Nanchang in 1927.

    G. It describes the glorious history in the War of Resistance Against Japan.

    H. The victorious crossing of the Yangtze River by the heroic People's Liberation Army and the situation in which the whole China is liberated.

20. 制作人民英雄纪念碑的浮雕用了多少时间?

这些浮雕所表现的主题思想十分明确,构图严谨朴素,人物形象生动逼真,栩栩如生,雕刻艺术精湛,是我国优秀雕塑艺术家和石工们用了 5 年时间才制作出来的精品。

How long did it take to carve out the eight pieces of relief for the Monument to the People's Heroes?

The theme topics of the relief pieces are expressed in a very succinct way. With a simple, yet well-knit composition, the relief figures look vivid and true to life. Chiseled out with a very exquisite and delicate craftsmanship it took the excellent sculptors and masons of the country five years to finish the job.

21. 人民英雄纪念碑的浮雕说明了什么?

人民英雄纪念碑上的浮雕所说明的是,人民英雄们为了反对帝国主义、封建主义及谋求全国的解放而英勇献身,歌颂他们的丰功伟绩,不忘他们为祖国、为人民所做出的贡献。他们的光辉业绩永远鼓舞和激励着后人奋勇前进,为了祖国更加美好的未来去继续努力奋斗。

What do the relief pieces on the Monument to the People's Heroes mean?

The eight pieces of relief on the Monument to the People's Heroes tell the people about the heroic and glorious deeds contributed by the people's heroes in their struggles against imperialism and feudalism for the liberation of China so as to show that the Chinese people will never forget their great contributions to the motherland and people. And their meritorious deeds will forever encourage the latecomers to brave forward for a brighter future of their motherland.

人民大会堂
(The Great Hall of the People)

22. 人民大会堂是何年建成的？ 面积有多大？ 是作何用的？

人民大会堂位于天安门广场西侧，是 1959 年北京的十大建筑之一。1958 年 10 月底破土动工，1959 年建成，历时 11 个月。其建筑面积为 171,800 平方米。人大会堂是全国人民代表大会开会和人大常委会办公的地方，也是党中央、国务院和各人民团体举行政治活动的重要场所。

When was the Great Hall of the People completed? How large a floor space does it cover? And what is it used for?

The Great Hall of the People, located on the west of the Tian'anmen Square, is one of the 10 major buildings completed in 1959 in Beijing. Breaking the earth by the end of October 1958, the project lasted 11 months before its completion in 1959. With a floor space of over 171,800 square meters, the Great Hall of the People is not only the congress hall for the representatives of the National People's Congress to hold meetings and the office for its standing committee, but also a very important place for the Central Committee of the Communist Party of China, the State Council and other people's organizations to conduct their political activities.

23. 人民大会堂的形状是怎样的?

人民大会堂的平面呈"山"字形,正面墙凸凹按"弓"字形分为五组,其南北长 336 米,东西宽 206 米,中央最高点为 46.5 米。四面开门,周围环立大理石柱 132 根,屋檐为黄绿相间的琉璃瓦。花岗石台阶高 10 米。

How does the Great Hall of the People look like in its shape?

The plane figure of the Great Hall of the People looks like a Chinese character "山", meaning "mountain" and its frontage in the shape of another Chinese character "弓" meaning "bow." Measuring some 336 meters from north to south and 206 meters from east to west, the whole building is divided into five sections with its central part towering as high as 46.5 meters. Doors are opened on all four sides, with 132 veranda-porches built of marble and its eaves covered with glazed tiles in yellow and green. The whole building stands on a granite-platform of 10 meters in height.

24. 人民大会堂由哪几部分组成?

人民大会堂主要由三个部分组成:北部是可容纳 5,000 人座席的宴会厅,中部是万人大会堂,南部是人大常委会的办公楼。另外还有会议厅、休息室、办公室 300 多个。其中有以各省、市、自治区及特别行政区命名的会议厅 31 个。它们的布置都反映了各地的地方特色和各民族的独特风格。

How many parts does the Great Hall of the People consist of?

The Great Hall of the People consists mainly of three parts, the part in the north is a banquet hall which can seat 5,000 people; the middle part, a grand auditorium for 10,000 people and the part in the south contains the offices for the Standing Committee of the National People's Congress. In addition there are still over 300 conference halls, lounges and offices, of which 31 are named after different provinces, municipalities, autonomous regions and special administrative regions. The decoration and furnishing in these halls are of a great wonder, featuring unique styles of different ethnic groups throughout the country.

25. 大礼堂可容纳多少人? 有何设施?

大礼堂平面呈弧形,进深为 60 米,中线宽 76 米,高 32 米。有两层挑台,连同底层在内共设有 10,000 个软席座位。每排坐位前都有供书写用的弧形条案,上面装有扩音器、同时可以译成 12 种语言的意译风。主席台面积很大,为 600 平方米,台上可设 300 多个活动座位,并安装了 32 道吊杆和自动机电设备,可供大型歌舞演出。另外,大礼堂内还配有摄影、广播、电视实况转播和声、光、电、空调等设备。

How many people can the grand auditorium house? And what kinds of installations are there in it?

The plane figure of the grand auditorium is in the shape of an arc, which is 60 meters in depth, 76 meters across its central axis and 32 meters high. With the seats on the ground floor, the balcony and the gallery, it has a total seating capacity for 10,000 people at a time. Rows of the curve - lined seats with writing desks in front are equipped with earphones, through which one can pick up an extemporaneous interpretation in any of the 12 languages. The presidium covers a floor space of 600 square meters with over 300 movable seats. Installed with 32 booms, and some automatic apparatuses for strengthening acoustic, lighting effect, it can also be used as a grand stage for shows, for photographing, broadcasting and on - the - spot TV transmission.

26. 大礼堂穹顶上的灯有何说头?

大礼堂的穹顶中心镶着一组大吸顶灯,其中心是宝石般的巨大的五角星灯,放射出 70 道光芒。沿着光芒线的尖端,围着镏金葵花瓣组成的花灯环,外围散布着 500 盏形似满天星斗的灯孔。这种装饰和布局,象征着全国各族人民万众一心,紧密地团结在中国共产党的周围,同时也象征着我们伟大祖国的前途是光辉灿烂的,是美好的。

What do the lights on the arched ceiling of the grand auditorium particularly signify?

Installed on the arched ceiling is a set of lights with a huge diamond - like red star in the center, giving forth some 70 - odd light - beams and round the end of which is a gold - plated ring of hidden lights in the form of a sunflower petals. On the further outer ring are scattered 500 starry lights, symbolizing the people of all ethnic groups of the country unite closely round the Chinese Communist Party and also suggesting an ever - brighter and beautiful future for their motherland.

27. 人大会堂的宴会厅有多大？起何作用？

宴会厅位于人大会堂中央大厅的北部，是国家领导人宴请贵宾的主要场所。宴会厅东西长 102 米，南北宽 76 米，高 15 米，面积为 7,000 多平方米，可容纳 5,000 人的宴会或 10,000 人的酒会。

How large a floor space does the banquet hall have？And what is it used for？

Located to the north of the Grand Auditorium, it is an important place for the state leaders to hold banquets in entertaining distinguished guests. Measuring 102 meters from east to west and 76 meters from north to south with its top as high as 15 meters it covers a floor space of over 7,000 square meters. It can hold a banquet for 5,000 persons or a cocktail party of over 10,000 people.

中国革命博物馆和中国历史博物馆
(Museum of the Chinese Revolution
and National Museum of Chinese History)

28. 中国革命博物馆和中国历史博物馆的建筑结构是怎样的?

两馆位于天安门广场东侧,与人大会堂隔广场而相望,是个合成一体的建筑物。馆南北长 313 米,东西宽 149 米,通高 40 米,总建筑面积达 69,000 平方米。西正门迎面是 12 根巨型方柱式的门廊和两个各高 39 米的大门墩,横额上镶嵌着一个闪闪发光的旗徽。花岗石的台阶宽 140 米,外墙为浅黄色,屋檐系用金黄彩绿的琉璃砖镶成,整座建筑均安上了高大明亮的玻璃窗。中央大厅是两馆的分界线,将其分为互相对称的两部分建筑,南部是中国历史博物馆,北部是中国革命博物馆。

What is the architectural structure of the Museum of the Chinese Revolution and National Museum of Chinese History?

Located on the east of the Tian'anmen Square and opposite the Great Hall of the People with the square in between, the two museums are housed in one integrated building. Measuring 313 meters from north to south and 149 meters from east to west, the building, 40 meters high, covers a floor space of 69,000 square meters. Outside the front gate facing due west is a porch formed by 12 large square stone columns and two gate posts standing 39 meters high on the two huge stone pedestals and fixed on the lintel of the porch is a glistening flag – like emblem. With the granite paved flight of steps measuring as wide as 140 meters and yellowish walls set off by large windows and eaves decorated with glazed tiles in yellow and green colors, the whole complex of building looks very magnificent, spacious and bright. The central hall marks the place of demarcation between the two symmetrical museums. The one on the south is the National Museum of Chinese History and that at the north, the Museum of Chinese Revolution.

29. 两馆是何年建成的？

两馆系于 1958 年 11 月动工兴建,1959 年 8 月建成,历时 10 个月,是 1959 年中北京的十大建筑之一。

When was the building of the two museums completed?

The construction of the two museums started in November 1958; the project was brought to the finish in August 1959 in the 10 months time and it is one of the 10 large construction projects in Beijing in 1959.

30. 中国历史博物馆有多少年的历史？内分几个业务部门？主要用途是什么？

中国历史博物馆已有 70 余年的历史。1912 年在北京国子监成立了历史博物馆筹备处,1918 年迁至故宫午门城楼及东西朝房,1959 年迁至现址。馆内主要业务部门有:陈列部、保管部、群众工作部、美工部、考古部及图书部。

该馆主要是收藏和保管中国古代、近代历史文物,举办陈列展览并进行科学研究的国家博物馆,起着向广大群众进行辩证唯物主义、历史唯物主义和爱国主义教育的作用,也对海外侨胞和国际友人展示介绍中国的悠久历史及文化、艺术、科学等方面的成就。

How old is the National Museum of Chinese History? How many departments are there in it? And what is it mainly used for?

The National Museum of Chinese History has already been in existence for some 70–odd years. In 1912, a preparation office for the establishment of the museum was set up in "Guozijian" (the Imperial College) in Beijing. Later in 1918, it was removed to the annexes on both sides of the Meridian Gate in the Forbidden City. However, it was finally moved into the present Museum of Chinese History in 1959. The museum consists of the following departments: the department in charge of exhibitions, department for the conservation and protection of cultural relics and department for the work of masses, fine art department, archeology department and library.

The museum is the one at the national level, mainly engaged in collection and conservation of historical and cultural relics of both ancient and modern times, holding exhibitions and carrying out scientific researches. By doing so it aims at educating the masses of people in the way of dialectical and historical materialism and patriotism. In addition it is also introducing to overseas Chinese and foreign visitors some achievements gained by the Chinese people in the fields of culture and art, science and technology during the Chinese history of the long past.

31. 中国历史博物馆有几个展览部分？馆内有多少藏品？

按照中国古代历史发展的过程,展馆分为原始社会、奴隶社会和封建社会3个部分。陈列内容从距今170万年前的元谋人起,至公元1840年的鸦片战争前夕止。在奴隶社会和封建社会中,以朝代的先后次序排列。共展出文物资料 9,000 余件,其中绝大部分为 1949 年后的考古发掘品。

馆内收藏文物 30 余万件,藏书 20 多万册,国内报刊数百种,国外书刊资料 2,000 余种,以及百余幅历史地图。展出面积达 8,000 多平方米。

How many parts do the exhibitions in the National Museum of History consist of? And how many pieces of relics are in collection here?

In line with the evolution of history in ancient China the exhibition is divided into three parts: the primitive society, slave society and feudal society. Exhibits range from the Yuanmou Man of some 1.7 million years ago to A.D.1840 prior to the outbreak of the Opium War. That part of exhibition for the slave and feudal societies is laid out in a chronological order of dynasties with some 9,000 – odd pieces of relics and materials, most of which are archeological findings after 1949.

Kept in the museum are some 300,000 pieces of relics, 200,000 copies of books on various subjects, several hundred kinds of Chinese magazines and newspapers, 2,000 – odd foreign publications, magazines, and materials and more than 100 – odd historic maps. The exhibition covers a floor space of some 8,000 square meters.

32. 中国革命博物馆是何时开放的? 主要任务是什么?

1950 年 3 月,在北海团城成立了中央革命博物馆筹备处,1960 年,改名为中国革命博物馆,并迁至现址,1961 年 7 月 1 日起正式对外开放。中国革命博物馆是搜集,收藏和保管中国近代、现代历史文物资料,举办陈列展览,并进行科学研究的国家博物馆,主要收藏中国自 1919 年"五四"运动和 1921 年中国共产党成立以来的革命文物和党史资料,举办以党史和中国革命史为内容的陈列、展览,开展学术研究,向广大人民群众宣传马列主义、毛泽东思想和邓小平理论,宣传党的历史,进行革命传统教育。

When was the Museum of the Chinese Revolution open to public? What is it mainly used for?

In March 1950 a preparation office for the establishment of a central museum of the Chinese revolution was set up at "Tuancheng" (the Round City) in the Beihai Park. Later it was moved here and officially opened to the public on July 1, 1961. The Museum of the Chinese Revolution is a national museum engaged in collecting, conserving and keeping historical relics and materials of modern and contemporary China, holding exhibitions and carrying on scientific researches. It means to collect relics and materials in on the Chinese revolution and the history of the Chinese Communist Party beginning from the May 4th Movement of 1919 and the founding of the Party in 1921 onwards, hold exhibitions about Party history and the Chinese revolution and to carry out the research work so as to pass the theory of Marxism – Leninism, Mao Zedong thought, Deng Xiaoping's theory and the history of the Party onto the broad masses of the people and carry out the education of revolutionary traditions.

33. 中国革命博物馆所属的主要业务部门有哪些?

中国革命博物馆所属的主要业务部门包括:陈列部、保管部、群众工作部、美工部、研究室及图书资料室等。

How many departments for professional work does the Museum of Chinese Revolution mainly have?

It mainly consists of the following departments and divisions: exhibition department, conservation and protection department, mass work department, fine art department, research office and books and materials office.

34. 中国革命博物馆有哪些藏品？

中国革命博物馆的馆藏文物达 12 万件以上,历史照片 8.1 万余张,资料 23 万余册,美术作品 300 多幅。该馆所陈列的基本上是《中国革命史展》,其内容为 1840 年鸦片战争起,至 1949 年中华人民共和国成立时止的一段历史。展出的资料达 4,500 余件。

What historical relics are collected in the Museum of the Chinese Revolution?

Kept in the Museum of Chinese Revolution are more than 120,000 pieces of historical relics, over 81,000 pictures of historical importance, 230,000 copies of materials and 300 – odd works of fine art. On display here are largely some 4,500 exhibits on the Chinese revolution, ranging from the Opium War in 1840 to the founding of the People's Republic of China in 1949.

35. 中国革命博物馆的展出面积是多少？ 主要展出哪些内容？

中国革命博物馆的展出面积为 4,000 平方米。陈列内容以反映民主革命时期的藏品为多,这包括老一辈无产阶级革命家早期从事革命活动的照片,各革命阶段的重大事件留下的重要文献、报刊、手稿及实物等。在馆内还设有关于老一辈革命家的纪念展,这包括有关周恩来、朱德、刘少奇及邓小平等的展览在内。此外,该馆还举办一些临时性的专题展览会。

How large a floor space does the exhibition hall in the Museum of the Chinese Revolution cover? And what are the main exhibitions being held here?

The exhibition hall in this museum covers a floor space of 4,000 square meters and most of the exhibits are about the period of the new democratic revolution. They include the photos telling the revolutionary activities done by veteran revolutionaries of the elder generations, some important documents, newspapers, manuscripts and material objects left over from the great events of historic importance at various stages of the Chinese revolution. In addition, on display here are some exhibitions in memory of our late revolutionary predecessors as Premier Zhou Enlai, Comrade Zhu De, Comrade Liu Shaoqi and Deng Xiaoping and others. Sometimes, exhibitions on some special topics are also held here.

36. 中国革命博物馆的序幕厅里陈列的是什么?

在中国革命博物馆序幕厅里陈列的是:毛泽东主席亲笔题写的"人民的胜利"和孙中山手书的"世界潮流浩浩荡荡,顺之则昌,逆之则亡";另外还有 1949 年 10 月 1 日开国大典时用过的两门礼炮及毛主席亲手升起的中华人民共和国国旗。

What is on display in the entrance hall of the Museum of the Chinese Revolution?

On display at the entrance hall is a streamer "The Victory of the People" autographed by Chairman Mao Zedong. And another by Dr. Sun Yat－sen, which reads: "Vast and mighty in the world is the onward trend like this. Those who are for it will survive and flourish; and those who are against it will perish!" Aside from these, there are still two salute－guns used on the inauguration of the founding of the People's Republic of China and the first national flag hoisted up into the sky by Chairman Mao himself on the very occasion.

毛主席纪念堂

(Chairman Mao Memorial Hall)

37. 毛泽东主席纪念堂是哪年建成的? 其占地面积和建筑面积分别是多少?

毛泽东主席纪念堂位于人民英雄纪念碑的南面,1977 年 5 月建成。其占地面积为 57,000 多平方米,总建筑面积 28,000 平方米。

When was Chairman Mao Zedong's Memorial Hall completed? How large is its ground – coverage and total floor space respectively?

Located on the south of the Monument to the People's Heroes, the Chairman Mao Zedong Memorial Hall was brought to a completion in May 1977. Covering an area of over 57,000 square meters it has a total floor space of 28,000 square meters.

38. 毛主席纪念堂对外开放的有几个厅? 主要是哪几个厅?

毛主席纪念堂有 10 个厅室对外开放,其中主要的开放厅室为:

1. 北大厅。厅的正中是毛主席的汉白玉座像,高 3.45 米。背景是一幅"祖国大地"的绒绣,宽约 24 米,高约 7 米。

2. 瞻仰厅。正中间安放着存有毛泽东遗体的水晶棺,毛泽东身着灰色中山装,身上覆盖着中国共产党党旗,安祥地躺在棺中。

　3. 毛泽东、周恩来、刘少奇、朱德革命业绩纪念室。

　4. 电影厅。参观者可观看毛泽东、周恩来、刘少奇、朱德等革命先辈生平片断的文献纪录片《光辉永存》。

　5. 南大厅。即用于出口的大厅。在大理石墙面上雕刻着毛泽东主席的诗词《满江红》和郭沫若同志的手迹。

How many halls in the Chairman Mao Zedong Memorial Hall are open to the public? What are the major ones of them?

In the Chairman Mao Memorial Hall there are 10 halls open to the public, the major ones of which are as follows:

A. North Hall: In the center of the hall is the statue of Chairman Mao in sitting posture, which, carved out of a piece of white marble, stands 3.45 meters in height. The backdrop is a woolen tapestry The Vast Land Of Our Motherland measuring some 7 by 24 meters.

B. Hall for Paying Homage to the Remains of Chairman Mao: Laid in the center of the hall is a crystal coffin with Chairman Mao's remains lying in it. Dressed in a gray uniform suit his body is covered with the flag of the Communist Party of China.

C. Memorial Rooms dedicated to Chairman Mao Zedong, Zhou Enlai, Liu Shaoqi and Zhu De, where on display is something telling the meritorious deeds and great contributions they made in the Chinese revolution.

D. Movie Hall: Visitors to the hall can watch a documentary film entitled Everlasting Brilliance, which depicts the meritorious deeds and contributions made at different stages by the four great revolutionaries and other forerunners in the Chinese revolution.

E. South Hall: The hall is used for exit. Inscribed on the marble – applied wall of the hall is the poem composed by Chairman Mao to the "Melody of Manjianghong," in Guo Moruo's handwriting.

39. 建造毛主席纪念堂的材料来自何处?

1. 制作明柱用的石材是产于福建省的花岗石。

2. 柱间镶嵌着的是广州石湾制作的花式陶板。

3. 通体建筑所用的贴面是产于青岛的花岗石。

4. 基座两层平台的台帮,是用产于四川大渡河旁的枣红色花岗石砌成的。

5. 四周围绕的万年青花饰栏杆是用产于房山的汉白玉雕凿成的。

6. 北大厅的四根方柱用的是产于江苏无锡的奶油红大理石,而柱端则采用了天山的白色大

理石作为衬托。

7. 北大厅地面所铺的是浙江杭州产的灰色大理石。

8. 水晶棺基座是用泰山黑色花岗岩制作的。

9. 南大厅下边摆着 10 盆五针松,其花盆是用云南特有的绿色彩花大理石制成的。

Where are the building materials for the Chairman Mao Memorial Hall taken from?

A. The yellow granite used for making the pillars are taken from the Fujian Province.

B. The colorfully glazed pieces of ceramics for the inter – column decorations are taken from the Shiwan Town of

Guangdong Province.

C. The granite pieces applied onto the surface of the walls of the whole building are taken from Qingdao, Shandong Province.

D. The granite pieces used on all sides of the two-tiered base are the claret granite taken from the Dadu River, Sichuan Province.

E. The materials for the balustrades and panels round the base with evergreen patterns carved on them are the white marble-pieces from Fangshan County, Beijing.

F. The four square pillars of the north hall, are made of crimsoned marble from Wuxi, Jiangsu Province, are set off with their caps cut out of the white marble pieces from the Tianshan Mountains, Xinjiang Uygur Autonomous Region.

G. The ground floor of the north hall is paved with gray marble pieces taken from Hangzhou, Zhejiang Province.

H. The crystal coffin bier is made of black granite from the Taishan Mountain of Shandong Province.

I. The 10 green pine pots at the lower level of the south hall are made of dark-green marble with natural flower-patterns, a special product of its kind from Yunnan Province.

40. 纪念堂周围的苍松翠柏来自何处?

纪念堂周围的苍松翠柏来自以下几个地方:

北京的油松;青岛的雪松、桧松和白皮松;延安的青松,还有房山的红果树。

Whence came the pine‑trees and cypresses round the Chairman Mao Memorial Hall?

The pine‑trees came from the several places in the country: the Chinese pine from Beijing; the snow pine, Chinese juniper and lace‑bark pine from Qingdao, Shandong Province; the green pine from Yan'an, Shaanxi Province; and the hawthorn tree from Fangshan County of Beijing.

41. 毛主席的水晶棺周围放的是什么东西?

摆放在毛主席水晶棺周围的是四季常青的君子兰及玻璃栏杆。

What is laid there round the crystal coffin for the remains of Chairman Mao?

Placed round the crystal coffin for the remains of Chairman Mao is the evergreen scarlet kafirlily and the railings made of glass.

42. 在毛主席的水晶棺座四周镶嵌着哪些东西?

在他的棺座四周镶嵌着:金饰的党徽、国徽、军徽,以及毛主席的生卒年份。

What are the inlays on all sides of the bier of the crystal coffin for Chairman Mao's remains?

Inlaid on all sides of the coffin bier is the gilded emblem of the Communist Party of China, the emblem of the People's Republic of China and that of the People's Liberation Army as well as the dates of birth and death of Chairman Mao.

43. 瞻仰大厅正面的汉白玉墙上镶的是什么字?

瞻仰大厅正面的汉白玉墙上镶着 17 个镏金隶书大字:伟大的领袖和导师毛泽东主席永垂不朽。

What are the characters inlaid on the white marble wall in the front of the hall for paying homage to late Chairman Mao?

Inlaid on the front wall of the hall for paying homage to the late Chairman Mao are the 17 gilded Chinese characters in official script, which read: Eternal Glory to the Great Leader and Teacher Chairman Mao Zedong.

44. 毛主席纪念堂南北大门两侧的群雕有多高,其含义是什么?

纪念堂两侧的群雕像高度均为 8.7 米,系歌颂中国人民在中国共产党所领导的新民主主义革命中取得的丰功伟绩,歌颂社会主义革命和社会主义建设的伟大胜利,也表现了全国各族人民将继续努力,在党中央领导下将革命进行到底的决心。

How high are the sculptures in front of the entrance and exit gates of the Memorial Hall for late Chairman Mao Zedong?

All standing 8.7 meters high, the sculptures on both sides of the memorial hall, mean to eulogize the great achievements scored by the Chinese people under the leadership of the Chinese Communist Party in the new democratic revolution, and the great victory won in the socialist revolution and construction, and also to show that the people of all ethnic groups in

China are determined to carry the revolution through to the end under the leadership of the central committee of the Party.

正阳门城楼
(Zhengyang Gate – tower)

45. 正阳门是哪年建成的？有何用处？

旧北京的内城有 12 个城门，正阳门是其中之一，为内城的正门。该门建于明永乐十八年(1420 年)，是北京存留下来的历史最久的城门之一，据说建城用的城砖大部分是由山东临清的名窑烧制的。正阳门在当年是北京全城的最高建筑，其工艺水平在北京的城门楼中最为精湛。正阳门取名的含意为"圣主当阳，日至中天，万国瞻仰"，在封建时代是仅供皇帝御驾出入的地方。

When was the Zhengyang Gate – tower built? And what was it used for?

Built in 1420, the 18th year of the Yongle reign period in the Ming dynasty, the Zhengyang Gate, one of the 12 gates along the inner city wall then, was the front gate of the city of Beijing. It is one of the city gates left over from the longest past. Most of the bricks used for the city construction were as said taken from the then famous kilns of Linqing County, Shandong Province. As the highest building in the city of Beijing then, the tower of the gate enjoyed the most exquisite workmanship in the building technique of all the city gates at the time. The name of the gate was to suggest, "the emperor, representing the supreme authority under heaven, is like the midday sun in the sky, who ought to receive the respects from all the countries around." In feudal society the gate was a passage of entry and exit reserved for the emperor himself alone.

46. 正阳门在建筑方面有哪些特点及传说?

正阳门在建筑上,除楼体本身外,后面还挑出个檐子来。下面是有关该檐子来龙去脉的一段神奇而有趣的传说:在建造箭楼的当时,皇帝发现楼顶太小,与楼身不配,于是便下令要在一个月之内进行重建,否则,工匠们便要遭杀身之祸。正当大家愁容满面,一筹莫展之际,忽然从外面走来了一个衣衫褴褛的老木匠,他手中端着一碟咸菜,请求人们给他添盐,人们为此而感到纳闷,于是便七嘴八舌地议论开了。其中一名工匠忽然灵机一动,说:"老木匠几次让我们给他添盐,莫非是在暗示我们给这个箭楼也添个大檐吧?"大家由此得到了启发,于是便开始研究、计划和施工。箭楼添上了这个重檐,整个建筑显得高大雄伟,且美丽而壮观。

What special features does the Zhengyang Gate have in its architectural structure? And what's the legend about it?

The Zhengyang Gate, apart from the main tower itself, had an eave added onto it from behind at the time of its construction. A mystical legend about it goes like this:

At the time when the arrow tower was going to be completed, the emperor found it out on an inspection tour that the tower top was a bit too small to match the principal part of the building. An imperial edict was then issued to have it rebuilt within a time – limit of one month or the workers would incur a disaster of being decapitated. Everybody, wearing a worried frown, was at the wit's end. One day came an old carpenter in rags and tatters. He, a dish of pickles in hand, was asking

46

them to add pinches of salt into it. Feeling puzzled they started to talk about it. Hitting upon an idea all of a sudden, one of the workmen exclaimed "Several times, the old carpenter asked us to add 'salt' into his plate, would this mean he's indicating us to add a big 'eave' "(in Chinese the pronunciation of 'eave' is just the same as that for 'salt'). Enlightened from it, the workers set to make a study of it, working out a plan and began the construction of it. The arrow tower with this double eaves added onto it looked very splendid, beautiful and magnificent.

47. 你们知道这传说中的老木匠是谁吗? 它说明了什么?

这位传说中的老木匠就是我国古代所说的著名工匠鲁班在显圣呢! 当然,这箭楼的重檐是建筑工匠们的伟大创造,而通过这段神话故事的渲染,更加鲜明生动地歌颂了劳动人民的聪明智慧及创造才能。

Who is that legendary old carpenter? And what does the story mean?

The old carpenter is none other than Lu Ban, who, as a very well – known one in Chinese legendary tales in ancient times, is making his presence and power felt. The double eave that was added onto the principal part of the arrow – tower, are of course a wonderful creation of the builders. However, set off by a mystical story, it is to sing the praises of the intelligence and wisdom of the masses of working people in a more vivid and life – like way.

48. 正阳门城楼的历史与现状情况若何？

正阳门城楼在 1900 年八国联军进攻北京时，被其炮火所击而焚毁。以后虽经重修，但却伤了元气而难比以往。此后又因解放前长时间无人善加管理，年久失修，加上风吹日晒、雨淋剥蚀，油彩脱落，楼顶杂草丛生，成了燕雀营巢栖息之所，正阳门业已失去了它昔日之光辉。中华人民共和国成立以后，人民政府非常重视对文物古迹的保护和修复工作，曾对正阳门城楼进行了多次修缮。后来又在建毛主席纪念堂的同时，将城楼作了彻底翻新，使其显得更加金碧辉煌，巍伟壮观。

What is the past and present of the Zhengyang Gate?

At the time when the eight powers allied forces encroached upon Beijing in 1900, the tower of the Zhengyang Gate was destroyed under the gunfire. Though renovated later, it had been sapped of its original shape and vigor. Left almost unattended for quite a long time before liberation in a state of disrepair, and also due to weathering and water – erosion, the colored paints were already flaking off. The top of the building, overgrown with grass, was reduced to be a mere sanctuary of birds and sparrows. The tower had already lost its splendor of the past. After the founding of the People's Republic of China, the people's government has been paying a great attention to the protection and conservation of cultural relics and historical sites. The Zhengyang Gate has for several times been repaired. Later when the Chairman Mao Memorial Hall was under construction, the whole building once again underwent a thorough renovation, thereby making it look even more splendid and magnificent.

万里长城
(The Great Wall)

49. 长城简介。

　　万里长城是中国古代最伟大的建筑工程,其规模之巨大,工程之艰难,堪称人类历史上的一大奇迹。长城是中华民族的骄傲,是中国古老文化和悠久历史的象征。它经历了数千年风霜雨雪的洗礼,目睹了无数朝代的更迭和人世沧桑的变迁,而今仍傲然屹立于世界的东方。今天,长城作为军事防御工程,用以抵御外来的骚扰侵略,业已成为历史。然而,它却起到了联结中国人民和世界各国人民之间友谊之桥的作用。当登月的宇航员从飞船上遥望地球时,他们用肉眼所能看到的地球上最清晰可见的人造工程,便是中国的万里长城。在北京地区之内可供人们游览观赏的长城有三处:一段是蜿蜒于延庆县境内的八达岭长城以及昌平县境内的居庸关,另一段便是盘旋在怀柔县境内的慕田峪长城。

Brief introduction to the Great Wall.

　　The Great Wall, so far as its gigantic scale and difficulties in the construction are concerned, is beyond doubt a civil engineering project, the greatest of its kind in ancient China. It can certainly be regarded as one of the great wonders ever wrought in the history of mankind. The Great Wall, a glory of the Chinese nation, is the symbol of the ancient culture and the long – standing history of China. Baptized by nature for thousands of years, the Great Wall has witnessed the rises and falls

50

of innumerable dynasties and changes on the earth, yet is still ranging proudly in the east of the world. Today, the Great Wall, however, as a military defence work against harassment and invasion from without, has become things of the past, yet instead it is playing a role in bridging up the friendship between the Chinese people and the people of the rest of the world. When the spacemen looked down with naked eyes onto the earth from the spaceship, the man – made project on the earth that could be clearly discerned is none other than the Great Wall of China. In the area of Beijing, there are three sections of the Great Wall for visitors to enjoy. One is the Great Wall at Badaling that snakes in Yanqing County, the Juyong Pass in Changping County, and still the other that twists and turns in the Huairou County is the Great Wall at Mutianyu.

50. 长城位于何方？为何称之为"万里长城",其实际长度究竟有多长？

长城逶迤曲折于中国的北方,东起渤海之滨山海关的老龙头,西至甘肃省的嘉峪关,途中穿越河北、北京、山西、内蒙古、宁夏、甘肃等三省二市和两个自治区,其长度在万里以上,故名"万里长城",但其实际长度为 6,300 余公里,约合 12,700 多华里。若把以往历代修建的长城总计起来,其长途可达 10 万公里以上。除上述一些省、市、自治区保留有长城外,山东、河南、湖南和湖北等地也都保留有部分长城的遗迹,其中以内蒙古自治区境内所保存的长城为最长,据初步调查表明,其长度约为 30,000 余里。

Which part of China does the Great Wall lie? Why is it called the "Ten Thousand Li Long Wall" and what is its actual length?

The Great Wall, snaking along the north of China with its starting point from the Old Dragon Head of the Shanhai Pass at the seaside in the east, stretches westwards over a distance of 10,000 li. It crosses three provinces, two municipality and two autonomous regions of Hebei, Beijing, Tianjin, Shanxi, Inner Mongolia and Ningxia to end at the Jiayu Pass in Gansu Province in the west, its actual length totaling about 6,300 kilometers, an equivalent of about 3,915 miles. Putting together the walls of suchlike built in various dynasties in ancient China the total length of the Great Wall can be up to more than 100,000 li (about 31,075 miles). Except the Great Wall existing in the aforesaid provinces, municipality and autonomous regions, traces of walls as suchlike can also be found in the provinces of Shandong, Henan, Hunan and Hubei and some other places. However, in all these provinces and regions, the walls found in the Inner Mongolia Autonomous Region stretch the longest of them all, measuring approximately 30,000 li, an equivalent to 9,323 miles.

51. 在中国历史上有哪几个朝代曾大举修筑过长城？

在中国历史上，秦朝、汉朝和明朝都曾大举修筑过长城，我们今天所看到的长城，大部分是明代的工程。

In which dynasties had the Great Wall been constructed and reconstructed on a large scale in the history of China?

In the history of China, large–scale construction and reconstruction of the Great Wall were carried out in the Qin (221 – 207 B.C.), Han (206 B.C. – A.D. 220) and Ming (1368 – 1644) dynasties. The Great Wall seen at present is largely the great engineering work wrought in the Ming Dynasty.

52. 中国古代为什么要修长城呢?

公元前 475 - 221 年,中国历史进入了诸侯纷争的战国时代,诸侯国为了互相防御,都在各自的领地上修建了城墙。而当时地处北方的秦、赵、燕三国,为了防御北方匈奴奴隶主的骚扰,便在其北部修筑了高大的城墙和堡垒要塞,这就形成了万里长城的前身。公元前 221 年,秦始皇击败了其余六个诸侯国,统一了全国。为了防止匈奴的南下侵扰,他派大将军蒙恬,统兵 30 万人,驱逐匈奴于漠北以外;与此同时,他还命令将原来秦、赵燕三国在北方所修建的长城进行连接、加固并延长,遂构成了"万里长城"。继秦皇朝以后历代的封建王朝都曾对长城进行过维修和重筑,其中工程规模最大的当数明朝(1368 - 1644 年)了。

在明朝灭元以后,蒙古贵族退回了漠北草原,但仍经常不断地南下骚扰;同时在东北又有女真政权在逐渐崛起,这对明王朝来说便构成了两个不可小视的威胁。因此,明太祖朱元璋登基伊始便将修建长城作为当务之急来处理。在立国之初(1368年),他就派大将军徐达开始了对长城的修建工作,以后历代仍继续修筑,于 1500 年中叶后完成了对万里长城的全部修建工作,历时近 200 年之久。现在的长城就是在以往秦长城基础上修建而成的明长城,也就是我们今天所看到的万里长城。

Why was it necessary to build the Great Wall in ancient China?

During the time of 475－221 B.C. China had already entered the Warring States period. To defend themselves and against the infringement from the neighboring states all the principal states had the walls built in the bordering areas of their territories. And to ward off the harassment by the Huns (an ancient ethnic group in China) from the north, the three states of Qin, Zhao and Yan had high walls and fortresses built along their northern frontiers. This is the primitive type of the present day great wall. In 221 B.C., the first emperor of the Qin Dynasty succeeded in unifying the whole China by conquering the six other rival states. To prevent the Huns from encroachment, he dispatched an army of 300,000 strong headed by a famous general by the name of Meng Tian to oust the Huns beyond the northern arid area. At the same time an imperial edict was issued to link up into one the sections of walls built by the former states of Qin, Zhao and Yan along the northern borders, thereby forming a long wall, known as the "10,000 li Long Wall". The succeeding dynasties after the Qin kept on the work of maintenance and repairs or having a part reconstructed again and again. The project carried out in the Ming Dynasty was the greatest on scale of all others in the olden days of China.

The feudal nobles of the Yuan Dynasty (1271－1368) when subjugated by the Ming withdrew to the grassland beyond the northern arid areas, but still they kept on harassing the north borders of the great Ming Empire. Apart from that there grew stronger another ethnic tribe called "Nüzhen" in the northeast. These two forces formed a no small threat to the newly founded Ming Dynasty. Therefore, in the very year immediately after the founding of the dynasty, Zhu Yuanzhang, the founder took the reconstruction of the Great Wall as of first importance. He had Xu Da, a famous general sent to supervise the rebuilding of the wall. With his ensuing generations to carry on the work the project lasted for about 200 years to finish after the middle of A.D. 1500. The Great Wall we see now is the very one rebuilt in the Ming Dynasty on the basis of that left over from the Qin dynasty.

53. 秦长城、汉长城（又称外长城）和明长城各有哪些特点？

1.秦长城：公元前221年，秦始皇统一中国以后，军事方面的重点由中原转到了北方。在同匈奴奴隶主政权进行的战争中，秦始皇派大将蒙恬率领30万大军，进攻并收复了当时被匈奴占领的黄河河套地区。但为了进一步巩固战果，有效地防御匈奴的侵犯，就开始大规模修筑长城，把从前秦、赵、燕三国所修的长城连接起来，并进行加固延长，于是便形成了一条西起甘肃岷县，东至河北辽东，长达一万多华里的城墙，长城的新增部分几乎等于原有长城长度的一半以上。从此，长城——这一古代历史上的伟大建筑工程，便以其无可比拟的雄姿巍然屹立在中国的大地上了。秦长城的修建，为而后历代对长城的修建工作奠定了一个坚实的基础。

2.汉长城（又称外长城）：是在西汉时的汉武帝时代（前140－89年）修筑的。汉武帝在位期间，曾派大将卫青、霍去病率领大军将匈奴逐至漠北。他在对匈奴的战争中发现，秦长城在对敌斗争中是个行之有效的防御工事，因而，除了对原有的长城加以利用和修缮之外，为达到"不叫胡马度阴山"的目的，又在阴山

55

以北修筑了一道"外长城"。从地理位置上讲,"外长城"尚在今长城以北千余华里的地方,它东起今天辽东半岛的鸭绿江畔,西至现在的天山脚下,全长近两万华里,是中国古代所建筑的最长的长城。不过,它并不像"秦长城"、"明长城"那么坚固高大,因而只能起到遮挡敌兵视线,使其疑惑畏进,并藉以阻止敌人骑兵突袭的作用。明以前的长城,无论是"秦长城",还是"汉长城",在用料上均是以土、石、木材和瓦件等为主。一般都是就地取材,或凿石垒墙,或取土夯筑;而在沙漠地带,则用沙子和石子,杂以芦草和柳枝层层叠压而成。

3. 明长城:明朝的开国皇帝朱元璋,为了解除元残余势力的骚扰和新崛起的女真政权的威胁,从洪武元年(1368 年)开始,就在秦长城的基础上展开了工程浩大的修建工作。整个工程历时近 200 年,终于修成了一条长达一万二千多华里、享誉中外的长城。明朝修筑的长城,在质量上比前朝有了很大的提高,大量使用的是砖石结构的建筑,且在许多重要地段上不仅用砖石垒砌,还用石灰填缝,使整个墙体十分平整坚固,因而至今保存较完好。另外,明朝还在沿长城一线设立了"九边"重镇,即辽东镇、蓟州镇、宣府镇、大同镇、太原镇、榆林镇、宁夏镇、固原镇和甘肃镇,还有"内三关"即居庸关、倒马关、紫荆关,以及"外三关",即雁门关、宁武关和偏头关。

What special features do the Great Walls of the Qin, of the Han (the Outer Great Wall) and of the Ming respectively have?

A. The Great Wall of the Qin: After the unification of China the first emperor of the Qin (Qin Shi Huang Di) shifted his attention in the military field from the central part to the north of China. In his wars against the slave – owners of the Huns, he dispatched an army of over 300,000 strong headed by

56

a famous general Meng Tian to recover the area occupied by the Huns – nowadays the Great Bend of the Yellow River. To make further an effective defence against the harassment from the Huns he started the construction of the Great Wall on a large scale by joining up the walls formerly built by the states of Qin, Yan and Zhao. He also had it extended, thereby forming a wall of well over 10,000 li—the wall, with its starting point in Mianxian County, Gansu Province in the west, snaked all the way along to dip into the sea at the Liaodong Peninsular in the east. The newly built part measured well over the original walls put together. From then on, the Great Wall, the gigantic civil – engineering project in ancient China, has been stretching magnificently on the Chinese soil and laid a foundation for the reconstruction in the succeeding dynasties.

B. The Great Wall of the Han (or the Outer Great Wall): It was built in the reign of Emperor Wudi (140 – 87 B.C.) of the Western Han Dynasty (206 B.C. – A.D.23). Sent by the emperor, the powerful army headed by the two famous generals – Wei Qing and Huo Qubing drove the Huns to the northern arid areas. With the experience drawn from the wars, the emperor found out that the Great Wall was an effective means of defence. Therefore, in addition to the work of maintaining and exploiting the Great Wall of the Qin, he, to ward the Huns off, had another wall (the Outer Wall) built beyond the Yinshan Mountains, about 500 kilometers north of the Qin Great Wall. Geographically speaking, the Han Great Wall, starting from the Yalu River in the very east of the Liaodong Peninsular, extended some 20,000 li (about 7,830 miles) westwards to end at the foot of the Tianshan Mountains. Nevertheless, the wall, which is not as high and wide as that one of the Qin or of the Ming, could only be used to block the view of the enemy, thereby making them feel puzzled and misled or to prevent the enemy cavalries from making surprise attacks. However, the walls built before the Ming Dynasty, either of the Qin or of the Han, are all built mainly of materials such as earth, stone − pieces, wood and tiles, etc., were taken from nearby areas and put up in a way by cutting out of rocky mountain or built with pounded earth. In the deserts ramparts were piled up even with sand, gravel, reeds and willow − sprigs mixed together.

C. As to the Great Wall of Ming, Zhu Yuanzhang, the founder of the Ming Dynasty, started the reconstruction of the Great Wall on the basis of the Qin Walls immediately after he assumed his reign in 1368. In this way he tried to prevent the remnant forces of the Yuan from harassing and the booming ethnic tribe of "Nuzhen" in the northeast from making threats to the newly founded Ming Dynasty. The work continued about 200 years, and finally it came to an end with a wall measuring well over 12,000 li. A number of important sections built of bricks and stones were done in fine masonry and the wall − seams were filled up with lime and mortar for its reinforcement. The Great Wall done in the Ming Dynasty is much better in quality than the previous ones and still remains in good shape now. In addition, nine strategic towns, namely Liaodong, Jizhou, Xuanfu, Datong, Taiyuan, Yulin, Ningxia, Guyuan and Gansu towns, were disposed all along the wall. In addition, three more inner passes as Juyong, Daoma and Zijin passes together with another three more outer passes as

58

Yanmen, Ningwu and Piantou passes were built for the purpose of strengthening defence.

54. 长城的历史作用何在?

长城这项工程浩繁的防御墙体,在中国的古代历史上是曾起过重要作用的。因为中国自古以来就是个多民族的国家,在历史发展的进程中,各民族在经济和文化方面的发展很不平衡,尤其是到了秦汉以后,北方的游牧民族常常南下骚扰和破坏中原先进的经济和文化。所以汉民族便筑起了长城,这对保护中原地区先进的经济文化免遭侵扰破坏,确是起过积极的作用的。

今天,长城作为一种防御工事,业已完成了它的历史使命。但是作为中国古代的文化象征,作为中国古代工程技术的伟大成就,它还将长期屹立人间,显示中华民族的悠久历史,表现中国古代劳动者的坚强毅力和聪明才智。长城永远是中华民族的象征和骄傲。

What is the role played by the Great Wall in the history of China?

The Great Wall – a gigantic defensive project, has played an important role in Chinese history. Ever since ancient times, China has been a multi – ethnic country with an unevenly developed culture and economy among different ethnic groups in the evolution of history. After the Qin and Han dynasties, the backward nomadic tribes in the north often set harassment on, and undermined the advanced culture and economy of, the central China. To prevent the advanced civilization from being destroyed, the Han people built this Great Wall, which played a very active role in the protection of the ancient Chinese civilization

59

Today, the Great Wall, as a means of defence, has already fulfilled its historic mission. However, the Great Wall, as a symbol of China's ancient culture, will remain proudly on the Chinese soil for a long time to come. Because it epitomizes the great achievements in the field of civil engineering and building technique in ancient China, and it tells in a vivid way the long history, the strong will - power, creative wisdom and talent of the Chinese laboring people. The Great Wall is a real glory and pride of the Chinese nation.

55. 万里长城是怎样修筑起来的？

长城时而盘绕于崇山峻岭之巅，时而穿越于大漠瀚海之中，在中华大地上蜿蜒起伏万余华里。在中国古代，要在崇山峻岭之巅，陡谷斜坡之间，乃至荒漠瀚海地区，修建如此浩大壮观的工程，实在是不易的。而且当时的施工条件十分艰巨，既无机械，也乏必要的工具，就连担砖运土，除可役使毛驴、山羊等爬山牲畜外，全部劳动均得依靠人力，其艰难之程度，实在是难以想象的。以秦代为例，据称秦始皇在修筑长城时，使用了近百万劳动力，占当时全国劳动力总数的五分之一，筑城大军主要由军队、民夫和犯人组成，他们是在刀剑和皮鞭的逼迫下从事繁重劳动的。明朝万历十年(公元 1582 年)的一块石碑上，记载了明时修筑长城的情景：当时是采用守军和民夫分段包干的办法进行的，必须用几千名军兵，再加上众多的民夫才能修起 70 多丈(约合 240 米左右)长的一小段长城来。

长城所过之处，多为高山险谷、大漠草原。整个长城就是依山势地形的不同采用不同的方法修筑的：如遇有突兀险峰，就在山体外侧包砌石块；穿越河谷深壑，便利用地形的陡坎和崖岸筑墙。明长城的墙体是使用大量的砖石垒砌而成的，墙体内部用黄土石子充填，顶部则用方砖铺砌，工程质量大大提高，所以，从山海关到嘉峪关这段由明代整修过的长城,至今大部保存仍较完好。"筑工筑土一万里",巍巍长城凝聚着中华民族的坚强毅力和聪明才智,也渗透着古代劳动人民的血汗,体现了中华民族的伟大,寄托着他们不朽的骄傲。

How was the Great Wall built?

Twisting and turning up mountains and down valleys, the Great Wall, is really a marvelous civil – engineering project in ancient times. At the time relying solely on the manpower with no help of machinery at all, except such animals like donkeys and goats which were used to carry stone and earth up hills and down dales, it was really an unimaginably difficult job to carry out such a huge project. Take the Great Wall of the Qin for instance, records have it that almost one million laborers (about 1/5 of all the manpower in the country then) were conscripted and dispatched to the working site for the project. Army – men, conscripted laborers and prisoners under the threat of swords and whips did all heavy jobs. A stone stele inscribed in 1582 – the 10th year of the Wanli reign period of the Ming Dynasty has it that the work was being carried out section by section within a certain time limit by the garrison army together with the laborers. To fulfil the assigned job, a mere section of about 250 meters had to be done by thousands of army – men and a great number of forced laborers.

Dancing up hills and down dales, crossing deserts and grasslands the walls were built in different ways according to the varied terrain and topography. When going over steep ridges and peaks, pieces of stone and bricks had to be applied onto the faces of them, but when passing by streams or valleys, walls had to be built along abrupt banks or cliffs. The engineering work done in the Ming dynasty used a lot of flagstones on the outside and filled the insides with bits of rock and earth while the top of it was covered up by layers of large pieces of bricks. The wall built in this way was much better in quality than the ones of the previous dynasties. Therefore, a greater part of the reconstructed wall in the Ming Dynasty, extending from the Shanhai Pass to the Jiayu Pass, has been up to now still in good conditions. The magnificent Great Wall, an earthwork with a length of well over 10,000 li, embodies the wisdom and strong will‐power of the Chinese people, the glory and greatness of the nation.

56. 为什么要修"外长城"？试述外长城的简况。

"外长城"远在距今长城千里之遥的北方。它东起黑龙江省的鸭绿江畔，向西行经内蒙古自治区，蒙古人民共和国，直抵今天新疆维吾尔自治区境内的天山山麓，全长近 2 万华里，系我国古代修筑的最长的长城。但是"外长城"并不象今天所存之长城那么宽阔、高大，容不下士兵在上面作战，只能起到遮挡敌兵视线的作用，使其疑惑畏进，同时也能用以阻挡敌骑的突然袭击。为什么要修外长城呢？这里要讲一段历史。

西汉以来，漠北匈奴族经常越过长城南下，深入中原滋扰。西汉初年，特别是汉高祖刘邦去世以后，吕后等统治者始终对匈奴南侵屈辱退让，致使他们胆子越来越大，就连长城也显得形同虚设了。到汉武帝临朝执政时，他采取主动出击的策略，派大将卫青、霍去病率大军进攻匈奴，把他们赶到了漠北。从对匈奴的战争中，武帝发现长城是个行之有效的防御工事，于是就对秦长城一面加以修缮利用，一面又在阴山以北修起了一条"外长城"，籍以加强防御。

Why must the "Outer Great Wall" be built? Please say something in brief about it?

Lying over a distance of 500 kilometers farther north of the present Great Wall, the Outer Great Wall starts from the Yalu River of the Heilongjiang province in the east. It runs westwards through the Inner Mongolian Autonomous Region, and the People's Republic of Mongolia to wind up by the foothills of the Tianshan Mountain in the Xinjiang Uygur Autonomous Region. Measuring a length of about 20,000 li (around 7,830 miles) it is the longest wall ever built of all times in ancient China. However, the Outer Wall is not as high and wide as the existing wall as you see today. It could not be used for fighting but only for screening off the view in order to puzzle and mislead the enemy. It could also be used to prevent the enemy cavalry from making a surprised attack. Why must the Outer Great Wall be built? It has a historical tale to tell.

Ever since the Western Han Dynasty (206 B.C. − A.D. 24), the Huns beyond the northern arid land crossing the Great Wall had harassed the central China time and again. However, in the early days of the Western Han, as a group of officials with Queen Lü in the lead advocated the policy of concession and compromise the Huns had become more and more avaricious and the Great Wall, though still there, seemed to be of no use. When Emperor Wudi came to power, a policy was adopted to take the offensive. He dispatched a strong army under the command of Generals Wei Qing and Huo Qubing to drive the Huns out to the northern arid land. Out from the ex-

perience gained in the battles the emperor learnt that the Great
Wall was an effective means of defence. So he, while keeping
on renovating and making use of the existing Great Wall of the
Qin, made a decision to have another wall, the Outer Great
Wall built beyond the north of the Yinshan Mountains.

57. 中国最北部的古长城在那里?

在大青山以北的蒙古草原上,有一道绵亘数千里的古长城,
当地人叫它"边墙",蒙古语叫"开勒门"。多年的风化,使它成为
高出地面一二米、宽四米的土岗,每隔半里有个城垛化成的圆土
包,隔一里有座方城圈。当地的牧民只知道它西起包头附近,并
说1965年他们曾沿着它从达茂草原一直走到千里之外的东乌
珠穆沁旗,在向东就不知到哪儿了。

著名的历史学家翦伯赞在《内蒙古考古》一文中提到过这道
古长城,认为它是汉武帝时修建的,据《史记.匈奴传》的记载,
太初四年,"汉使光禄徐自为出五原数百里、远者千余里,筑城障
列亭至庐朐"。城即城墙;障是屏障;亭是堡垒、烽火台的总称。
五原和庐朐是地名,五原在今包头附近的五原县东;庐朐是今呼
伦贝尔盟的额尔古纳河。如此说来,这道建于公元前101年的
汉长城,就是中国境内最北部的长城了。

Where lies the northernmost Great Wall of China?

Lying on the vast expanse of the Mongolian grassland to
the north of the Daqing Mountain is an ancient wall stretching
thousands li long. The locals call it "Frontier Wall," or "Kaile-
men" in Mongolian language. Through years after years of
weathering and erosion it has left with an earthen ridge of only
one or two meters high above the ground with a width of four
meters. At every one fourth of a kilometer there is an earth

mound, ruins of battlements, and at every half a kilometer there is a square fortress. The local herdsmen know only that the wall starts from somewhere near the city of Baotou in the west. And they said that once in 1965 they traveled from the Damao grassland all the way along to East Wuzhumuqing Banner, and they don't know where it leads to.

As mentioned in an article "Archeological diggings in Inner Mongolia" by Jian Bozan, a noted historian the stretch of the ancient wall was built in the reign of Emperor Wudi of the Western Han Dynasty. According to the record of the "Commentary of Xiongnu" in the book entitled the Records of History: In 101 B.C., the fourth year of the Taichu reign period, "A Han envoy by the name of Xu Ziwei went as far as hundreds of li and the farthermost even thousand Li away to build cities with barriers and towers from Wuyuan to Luqu". Here the city in ancient times meant the walls, the barriers, the battlements, and towers, the beacon towers. Wuyuan and Luqu were the names of two places. Wuyuan was in the east of the present-day Wuyuan County, near Baotou, and Luqu the E'erguna River in present-day Hulunbei'er Banner. Hence the wall built in 101 B.C. is the very northernmost Great Wall of China.

58. 长城的守军总共有多少？

这是一个经常碰到，但又难以回答的问题。然而可以肯定的是：在不同的朝代，乃至同一朝代的不同时期，守军的数目也不尽相同。依明代长城的驻军情况来看，可以想见这个数目是相当不小的。据记载，仅居庸关一地的守军就多达到 5,000－6,000 人。"北门锁钥"以外不远的岔道城（已在修官厅水库时

拆除),原为八达岭守军的前哨指挥所,那里的守军也达 700 -
800 人之多。

How many soldiers in total were garrisoned along the Great Wall?

This is a question, which is often mentioned yet very hard to answer, really a hard nut to crack. Surely different dynasties or even the same dynasty at different times had varied numbers of soldiers sent in garrison here. Take the case of the Ming Dynasty for instance: the soldiers disposed along the Great Wall were in a considerable number. Records have it that the army garrisoned at the Juyong Pass alone reached more than 5, 000 in number. The soldiers disposed at Chadaocheng of the Beimensuoyao (a lock - out beyond the northern pass - gate, which was demolished when the Guanting Reservoir was constructed), formerly a forward post for the soldiers garrisoned at Badaling, came to a total of 700 - 800 in number.

59. 万里长城是由谁来组织修建的?

从前,有一首歌谣是这样说的:"万里长城呀,在北方...何人造?两千年前秦始皇。"而在史籍之中,称秦始皇"南修五岭,北筑长城"者,更可谓比比皆是。于是便留给后人一个印象,似乎偌大的一座长城,完全成事于秦始皇一人之手。其实这是不够确切的说法。诚如所知,在秦始皇统一六国以前,各个诸候国都是修筑了长城的。秦国在秦昭王时期也修筑了自己的长城,其城址就在赵、燕长城以西,如今的陕西省一带。秦始皇统一中国以后,其军事重点便由中原转移到了北方。在与匈奴奴隶主政权进行的战争中,秦始皇派大将蒙恬率 30 万大军逐匈奴于漠

66

北,此后又用了 10 年的时间来修长城。所谓修筑,也就是将旧有的秦、赵、燕等地的长城加以修葺,并连接起来。如此说来,是否就贬低了秦王朝修筑长城的功劳呢? 不! 因为万里长城若是从头筑起,断非三十万人的十年之功所能成就得了的。即使是在旧有城墙的基础上,要在长达万里之遥的距离之内对旧城加以修葺,并增筑连接,最后形成一条延伸万里有余的雄伟长城,其工程也是十分艰巨而伟大的。而秦始皇作为这一巨大工程的组织者,其功劳也是很大而难与比拟的。且在长城两字之前冠以"万里"的字样,也正是秦始皇治下的杰作。所以把万里长城与秦始皇的名字相提并论,也是不无道理的;而今天我门所见的长城,其规模及基础也是在秦代奠定的。

Who organized the construction of the Great Wall?

A folk – ballad goes like this: "the Great Wall in the north...who had it built? The first emperor of the Qin Dynasty (Qinshihuang) around 2,000 years ago." And you can find more such sayings in the historical records. "While keeping on strengthening the defence works along the Five Ranges down in the south, Emperor Qinshihuang stepped up the efforts in the construction of the Great Wall in the north," thus leaving people an impression as if the gigantic project were done by the emperor himself alone. Actually this is not quite true. As known to everybody the principal states before the Qin all had their own walls built and the State of Qin did it too in the reign period of King Zhao. The site of the wall was somewhere in the nowadays areas of Shaanxi Province to the west of the walls built by the states of Zhao and Yan. After the unification of China, the First Emperor of Qin shifted his attention in the military field from the central part to the north of China. In the wars against the slave – owners of the Huns, he dispatched an army of 300,000 strong commanded by General Meng Tian to drive the Huns out to the northern arid land. Then he again spent 10 years in the construction of the Great Wall. What was said about the building of the Great Wall simply meant to repair the walls formerly built by the states of Qin, Zhao and Yan, and had them joined up by adding some new and extended parts. Does that mean to belittle the contributions made by Emperor Qinshihuang in the building of the Great Wall? By no means, because it would have been impossible for an army of 300,000 strong to completely build the Great Wall in a period of 10 years. Even though it was just to repair or renovate some parts on the basis of the old walls and had them extended, to bring a wall of 10, 000 li to a finish would still be an unimaginable difficult job. However, in this project, the First Emperor of Qin, as an organizer, made tremendous contributions. Moreover, the name of "Wan Li Chang Cheng" first recorded in the Chinese history was also a masterpiece done in the period of his reign. No wonder the Great Wall is always mentioned in the same breath with the name of Emperor Qinshihuang. He was really a great man of the time. Anyhow the Great Wall you see today was built on the very foundation that was laid in the Qin Dynasty.

60. 中国历史上最早的长城是何时修建的?

按照比较通行的说法,中国历史上最早的长城,修建于公元前 5 世纪的战国时期。可事实上现有的资料已经表明:长城早在中国历史上的西周时期就出现了。《诗经》上有此说法:"王命南仲,城彼朔方。"这里所说的是指"宣王中兴"时期,即公元前 9

世纪的事。当时,周宣王用兵,把西戎和严允两大部落赶出了国境。据史学家们所作的考证称:这里所说的"城",即是所谓长城一类的防御工事;而所称"朔方",具体所指便是如今的河套一带地区,亦即后来秦、汉两朝的朔方郡。由此可知,中国历史上最早的长城,出现于公元前 9 世纪,比通行的说法还要早 400 余年。

When was the oldest section of the Great Wall built?

According to a popular saying the oldest section of the Great Wall of China was built in the Warring States Period around the fifth century B. C.. But historical records have it that the earliest one came into being as early as the Western Zhou Period (around 11th century — 770 B. C.). The Book of Odes reads:" an order was given by the King to have the 'city' built in the north." This happened in the rejuvenating time of King Xuan, around the ninth century B. C., when the King succeeded in driving the two nomadic tribes — Xirong and Yanyun — out of his territory. According to the historians the so–called "city" here meant the defensive works like walls and the "north," the areas around the present day "Great Bend of the Yellow River", or the Northern Prefecture set up by the Qin and Han dynasties later. Hence we can come to a conclusion that the initial Great Wall of China came into being in around the ninth century B. C., 400 years earlier than what was said popularly among the people.

61. 八达岭位于北京的何方? 距北京城有多远? 海拔高度是多少?

八达岭横卧于北京的西北方,距城约 70 余公里,平均海拔高度为 600 米,最高点是 800 米。

To which direction of Beijing does the Badaling Section of the Great Wall Lie? How far is it from the city? And what is its elevation?

Stretching along the northwest of Beijing the Badaling Section of the Great Wall is some 70 kilometers away from the city. It averages 600 meters above sea level with its highest peak towering 800 meters.

62. 八达岭地名的由来如何?

八达岭的所在地叫军都山,是通往延庆、宣化、张家口、大同、永宁以及四海的交通汇集点,道路四通八达,故名八达岭。八达岭隧道工程现已贯通,隧道全长 1095 米,是一条双向三车道的隧道,它的贯通,使由北京市内前往八达岭的时间大大缩短,过去约需 2 小时的时间,现在只要 1 小时就足够了。

Whence came the name of Badaling?

The place where lies the Badaling Section of the Great Wall is called the Jundu Mountain. As a hub of communication it leads to Yanqing, Xuanhua, Zhangjiakou, Datong, Yongning and Sihai in all directions, hence the name of Badaling. The project of the tunnel leading to Badaling has now come to an end. It's a dual – way tunnel of three lanes, totaling 1,095 meters long. The tunnel has greatly shortened the time from the city proper of Beijing to Badaling. Formerly it took about two hours drive to cover the distance and is now reduced to one hour only.

70

63. 请问八达岭长城的建筑结构有何特色?

八达岭长城依山而筑,其高低宽窄不一,墙高平均为 7.5 米,墙基宽达 6.5 米,顶宽约为 5.8 米,可容纳 5 匹战马或 10 行士兵同时并进。城墙的下边是条石台基,上砌砖墙,墙身内部用碎石及黄土填充,墙顶地面铺设古代方砖,内侧是宇墙,外侧为垛口,下端筑有射孔,供了望和射击之用。为了防御的需要,分别在山脊的高地,城墙的转角或险要地段筑有堡垒式的城台。城台有高低之分,高的叫敌楼,是供守望和住宿用的;矮的称墙台,乃巡逻放哨之所。原来上面还有建筑物,可供士兵休息,但这些建筑物业已不复存在,然地基至今仍是完好的。

Can you say something in brief about the special features in the architectural structure of the Great Wall at Badaling?

Built along the huge mountain ranges with varied widths and heights, the Great Wall at Badaling averages 7.5 meters in height, 6.5 meters in width at its base and 5.6 meters on its top, which is possible for 5 horses or 10 soldiers to go abreast forward. The bottom of the wall is laid up with rock – blocks, whereas the middle and upper parts are built of large pieces of bricks with the insides filled up with stones and earth and the top covered up with large pieces of rectangular bricks. There are parapets along the inside wall and the wall outside is topped with crenellated battlements for shooting and keeping a watch over the enemy. To strengthen the defence, beacons and watchtowers of various sizes were built at commanding points, the larger and higher ones being used for keeping an eye on the enemy, and the lower and smaller ones only for standing sentry and patrols. In the past there were still some other built – ups along the wall for soldiers to take a rest. They are gone now, but their terraced bases are still well kept up to now.

64. 何谓"关沟"？它在什么地方？

从北京去八达岭的路上,过了南口便进入了一条峡谷,长城的重要关口之一,居庸关就座落其中,峡谷也就因之而称为"关沟"。"四十里关沟",其实并没有四十里,但在这条不长不短的峡谷中,却有着四重关隘,七十二景。在登上长城以前,若能身临其境,先在谷中作半日游,亦不失为一种饶有兴味之举。

What does that "Pass Valley" mean? And where does it lie?

On the way from the city proper of Beijing to Badaling, you'll get into a valley after passing through the town of Nankou. As the Juyong Pass, one of the important passes along the Great Wall, is located in the valley, hence the name "Pass Valley." The so-called "40-li Pass Valley", is actually not long enough as that. However, in this not very long valley are dotted with four pass-gates and 72 scenic spots. What a fun to make a half-day tour in it before going to climb the Great Wall.

65. 请你谈一谈"弥勒听琴"石像的由来？

"弥勒听琴"石像所在的地方,原为石佛寺,曾是关沟的一处要冲所在,当时真可谓骡马驼队,不绝于途;同时,这里也是关沟中的一处胜景。因其挨近"弹琴峡",寺内又琢有弥勒石像,故有弥勒听琴之美谈。但遗憾的是:此寺已毁于八国联军之手。

Whence comes the stone carving "Maitreya Buddha Listening to Lyre - Playing"?

The place where stands the Stone - Buddha used to be the site for the Stone - Buddha Temple. As a hub of communications in the valley it was once a place of importance, crowded with draught - beasts and carts waiting to pass by. It was one of the scenic spots too. Located near the "Lyre Playing Valley" with the Maitreya Buddha carved on the cliff in the temple, hence the name "Maitreya Buddha Listening to Lyre Playing". What a pity the temple was destroyed by the eight powers allied forces.

66. 请你讲一下"望京石"的来历如何?

"望京石"是在"居庸外镇"前不远处的一块长7米,高2米的巨石。据说在1900年八国联军进攻北京时,慈禧太后惶惶然逃出北京,路过这里,顿生留恋之意,就站在这块巨石上回首遥望北京城,因而就叫"望京石"。

Please say something about how the "Expecting Beijing Rock" comes about?

Not far away from the "Outer Garrison Post of the Juyong Pass" lies a large block of rock two meters high and seven meters long. In 1900, when the eight powers allied forces occupied Beijing, Empress Dowager Cixi hastily ran away from Beijing. On the way she suddenly hit upon a nostalgic idea: she wanted to see the city once again. She got on this big rock to take a look at Beijing in the distance, hence the name, the "Expecting Beijing Rock".

67. 云台建于哪一个朝代？有何用处及艺术价值？

云台建于元朝至正五年(1345年)，台面上原建有3座石塔，称为过街塔。塔毁以后又在原址建一寺庙，明正统四年重修寺庙时更名为"泰安寺"，但该寺于清康熙四十一年被烧毁，于是仅留下了这座云台。它的艺术价值在于券门内的石雕，即其顶中和两壁上的四大天王石像，以及石壁上用梵文、藏文、八思文(蒙文)、维吾尔文、汉文和西夏文雕刻的《陀罗尼经咒》和《造塔功德记》等经文。这些雕刻，刻工精细，姿态传神，具有极高的艺术价值，同时也是研究中国古代文字的重要参考实物。云台属于全国重点文物保护单位。

In which dynasty was that Cloud Terrace built? What was it for and what is its artistic value?

The Cloud Terrace was built of white marble in 1345, the fifth year in the reign period of Zhizheng of the Yuan Dynasty. On the terrace there used to have three stone pagodas, called the "Crossing Street Pagoda". When the pagodas were later destroyed a temple was built on the very site. During its renovation in 1440, the fourth year in the Zhengtong reign in the Ming, it was renamed the "Tai'an Temple". However the temple was brought down in a fire in 1703, the 41st year in the Kangxi reign in the Qing, thus leaving only a terrace there until now. Its artistic value was embodied in the marvelous carvings in relief on the facade and walls of the arched gate – the four celestial guardians and the stone inscriptions of Buddhist sutra 'Daturascrolls' and a record in eulogy of the merits done in the building of the pagodas. They were done in Sanskrit, Tibetan, Basi (a kind of Mongolian script), Uygur, Chinese and Western Xia scripts. All of them are of a very high artistic value, and the exquisite workmanship and vividness in carving have left us a very good piece of data material, an important reference for the study of the ancient Chinese scripts. Now the Cloud Terrace is listed as one of the cultural relics under the protection of the state.

68. 烽火台的用途是什么？

烽火台设在长城内外群山之间的制高点上，这是古代用以传递警讯敌情的设施。每当遇有警讯，如在白天，便点燃狼粪，因其所产生的烟雾腾空不散，很远便能望见；夜则举明火为号。明代还以敌军的众寡来确定烟火的堆数。例如，成化二年（1466年）有这样的规定：来敌人数在 100 人左右的，举 1 烟，同时鸣炮 1 响；人数在 500 左右者，举 2 烟并鸣 2 炮；1,000 人以上，3 烟 3 炮；5,000 人以上为 4 烟 4 炮；10,000 人以上为 5 烟 5 炮。这样，指挥官闻讯以后，不仅知道敌人从何而来，而且知道来了多少。凭此便能作出正确的部署，指挥军队迎敌和增援。

What was the beacon tower used for?

At the commanding points along the mountain ranges both inside and outside the Great Wall, beacon towers were built for signaling warnings. Whenever there was an alarm, dried wolf – duns were burnt in daytime on tower – tops. As the smoke rising up wouldn't disperse in the air, it can be seen from a distance even from faraway, but torches were lit at night instead. However, the number of signals to be used in the Ming dynasty was decided according to the number of the approaching enemy. For example, in 1466, the second year in the Chenghua reign period, the regulations were given as follows: if the approaching enemy was around a hundred, one signal warning would be lit with one gun − shot fired at the same time. If the coming enemy numbered around 500, 2 signals with 2 shots fired; then 3 signals with 3 shots for over 1, 000; and 4 signals with 4 shots for more than 5,000; and 5 plus 5 for that of over 10,000 in number. In this way the commanders would know not only where the enemy was approaching but also the number of them, thereby making it possible for them to dispose the defence and reinforcement in a correct way.

69. 请简述一下秦始皇其人如何?

秦始皇生于公元前 259 年,卒于前 210 年。公元前 246 年,秦始皇的父亲去世,由他继位。因其年幼,由其父的大臣吕不韦参与护政,公元前 238 年,吕不韦被逐出政坛,秦始皇开始亲自执政。为稳定秦朝的统治,他于公元前 230 年,发动了统一战争,先后用了 10 年的时间,于公元前 210 年吞灭了燕、赵、韩、魏、齐、楚等六国,最终实现了全国的统一,建立了中央集权制的国家,还制订了法律,统一了货币、度量衡和文字。为加强防御,秦始皇还花了 10 年的时间,组织动员了近百万人,把以前各国分段的城墙加以连接和加固,形成了横贯东西万余里的长城,也便奠定了今天所见的万里长城的基础。他所采取的一系列措施为统一的巩固、经济文化的发展,都起到了一定的推动作用,也为尔后中国两千余年的封建政权打下了基础。

Please say something about Emperor Qinshihuang, the first emperor of the Qin Dynasty?

Born in 259 B. C., Emperor Qingshihuang, died in 210 B.C.. He succeeded the throne when his father passed away in

246 B.C.. As he was too young to do the administration himself, Lü Buhui, the Prime Minister of his father's helped him in the ruling. However in 238 B.C., Lü was ousted from the court and the young emperor took over the power to do the ruling himself. To stabilize his political regime, he started the war of unification of the country beginning from the year of 230 B.C.. Spending 10 years on end in it, he succeeded in conquering the other six states of Yan, Zhao, Han, Wei, Qi and Chu and finally realized the unification of the country. For the purpose of strengthening the newly founded empire, he adopted a series of measures by establishing a centralized state – power, working out a set of laws and unifying the currency, weights and measures and the Chinese characters. In addition, mobilizing hundreds of thousands of laboring people in the country he joined up the walls formerly built by various states, to form a wall that extended over 10,000 li from east to west on the vast land of China, thus laying a foundation for the present day Great Wall of China. All the rules and measures he adopted have played an important role in strengthening the unification of the country, and pushing forward its economic and cultural development. It also provided a solid base for establishing later a feudal rule of over 2,000 years in Chinese history.

70. 请简述一下"孟姜女哭长城"的故事好吗？

说起长城，人们都会不约而同地把它和在我国广为流传的"孟姜女哭长城"的民间故事联系起来。据称在秦始皇执政期间，为了国家的安全而修筑长城，他征集了上百万劳力，投入了很长的时间，在全国展开了这一声势浩大的工程。众所周知，长城是修筑在地势险峻的山脊之上和深谷之间的，工程浩大而又艰险，参加施工的人们不知受尽了多少艰辛，牺牲了多少生命。孟姜女的丈夫万喜良便是其中之一。传说他婚后的第三天便被绳捆索绑而去。孟姜女目睹统治者的残暴，心痛丈夫的遭遇，她为此哭得死去活来；然而万喜良一去3年，杳无音信。在一个寒冬腊月的夜晚，孟姜女忽得一梦，见丈夫破门而入，进门便喊道："快关门啊，冻死我啦!"她从梦中惊醒过来，惦念着丈夫的生死，心中万分忧虑，无比悲伤。于是她便下定了决心，要给丈夫送去御寒的衣服。经过一番准备，数日之后，孟姜女便告别了爹娘，踏上了迢迢千里的寻夫之路。一路上，她受尽了千辛万苦，但为了打听到丈夫的下落，她置一切艰辛苦难于度外，历经磨难，终于到达了长城脚下，筑起的长城果然雄伟壮观，像一条巨龙绵延起伏于群山深壑之中。当时，长城还在继续修建着，民夫们均在严密的监督下从事极为繁重的劳动。他们吃穿未比牛马，个个骨瘦如柴。孟姜女逢人便问，打听自己丈夫的下落，但一直没有找到，日日忧心如焚。后来一位工头告诉她，万喜良已在数月前死去了，且其尸骨已填进了城墙。这一消息犹如晴天霹雳，使她感到悲痛万分，号啕大哭，不省人事。凡听到这哭声的人们无不为之伤感落泪。孟姜女守在长城脚下，一连数日，痛哭不止，她哭着哭着，忽然间，耳边传来地动山摇的一声巨响，雄伟的长城突然崩开了一个40里长的缺口。在烟雾消散之后，民夫们的累累白骨便暴露于泥土碎石之间。这时，孟姜女忍住悲恸，擦干眼泪，辨认出了丈夫的尸骨，细心收殓以后，便怀着对横征暴敛、腐败昏庸的统治者的刻骨仇恨投海自尽了。后人为了歌颂这位传说中的善良妇女的高尚品德，便在山海关外修建了一座姜女庙。与此同时，后人也留下了一副脍炙人口，然又叫人难于捉摸的对联："海水朝朝朝朝朝朝朝落，浮云长长长长长长长消。"

藉此以描述山海关一带风景如画、海天一色的壮丽景象。

Would you please tell us the tale about the "Lady Meng Jiang crying over the Great Wall"?

When the Great Wall is mentioned it seems often and spontaneously to go along with the tale, "Lady Meng Jiang Crying Over the Great Wall", which has always been on the lips of the people. When Emperor Qingshihuang came to power, he, to strengthen his rule over the country spent 10 years in the construction of the Great Wall by conscripting more than one million laborers for the gigantic project. Built along the steep mountain ranges and across the deep chasms, this huge project was surely a strenuous job and a sternly hard work for those who took part in it. Wan Xiliang, the husband of Lady Meng Jiang happened to be one of them. According to a popular saying he was seized to serve as a forced laborer only three days after their marriage. Lady Meng Jiang, witnessing the atrocity of the ruthless rulers, cried her heart out over the maltreatment to her husband. Three years has passes after her husband was taken away, there was no news of him at all. One cold winter night the lady dreamt the return of his husband. He broke into the door shivering all over. He called out: "Shut the door at once, I'm frozen to death!" Startled she woke up from her dream, worrying with a melancholy heart over her husband. She made up her mind to go to look for her husband. With everything prepared a few days later, she, bidding farewell to her parents, set out for the Great Wall. In order to get any possible news of her husband, she defied all difficulties and hardships on the way and finally arrived at the foot of the wall, which, like a huge dragon dancing over the mountain ranges, looked really magnificent. It was still under construction then. The forced laborers, toiling under a strict supervision, lived a beast life. Lady Meng Jiang asked almost everyone she happened to meet about her husband, but failed again and again to get the news of him. Finally she came across a foreman who informed her of the sad news that her husband already died three months ago and the corpse was already filled into the cavity of the wall. Undoubtedly the news proved to be a bolt from the blue for her. Sorrow stricken she cried and cried. Exhausted, she finally fell into a swoon. Everybody at the site shed sympathetic tears for her. But still she stayed there crying until suddenly she heard a loud crash, telling the collapse of a section of the wall of 20 kilometers long, thus exposing behind a whirling dust heaps of skeletons amidst the earth and stones. Restraining her sorrowfulness with a strong willpower, the lady sorted out the bones of her husband. After a careful burial she plunged herself into the sea with the utmost hatred for the ruthless oppression and utterly corruption of the feudal rulers. To keep the kind – hearted lady in legend in memory, a temple was later built nearby the Shanhai Pass at the eastern end of the Great Wall. However at the same time, some scholar also wrote a tasteful yet unimaginable couplet on the temple doorposts to describe the magnificent beauty of the landscape in the area. The couplet reads like this:

The sea – tide flows in. It flows early in the morning and ebbs and thus it repeats in a constant way,

The floating clouds gather. They keep on gathering and always gather up and fall apart night and day.

71. 请你谈一谈京张铁路及其总设计师詹天佑的情况好吗?

在前往八达岭的路上,我们会穿越京张铁路。该路修建于1905年,是中国自行设计、修筑的第一条铁路。它的总设计师,便是中国铁路史上素享盛名的詹天佑工程师。在整个工程的设计与施工过程中,詹天佑不畏艰险,翻山越岭,亲自测量定点,设计绘图。为取得可靠的第一手资料,他常常骑上毛驴外出访问农民,向他们讨教,了解情况。在施工中,他慨然面对外国人的冷嘲热讽,毫不动摇。依靠自己一丝不苟的正确设计,并集工人们的智慧,终于克服了当时技术落后的困难,完成贯通了从居庸关到八达岭两个最艰巨的隧道工程。在施工技术方面,他大胆采用了"人"字形铁路线,改用了自动挂钩,并采用两辆机车并从的大马力牵引法,让一辆机车在前边拉,另一辆在后边推,使火车顺利地爬上并通过了八达岭陡坡。这是詹天佑在中国铁路工程上作出的一大创举。京张铁路于1909年9月实现了通车,比预定计划提前了两年,还节约了工程费用28万两白银。

詹天佑(1861-1919年)出生于广东南海县,他自幼酷爱机械。1872年,当他还是11岁的幼童时,就与其他29名中国幼童被派到美国留学。在9年的学习期间,他先后读完了小学和中学,并以优异的成绩考入了美国耶鲁大学的土木工程系的铁路专修科,于1881年学成回国。詹天佑把自己毕生的精力献给了中国的铁路建设事业。在他逝世后不久,中国工程学会就在青龙桥旁建立了他的全身铜像,以缅怀这位中国铁路建筑史上杰出的工程师。1982年5月,铁道部在青龙桥边新筑了詹天佑夫妇墓,后又在八达岭修建了詹天佑纪念馆。

Would you please say something about the Beijing – Zhangjiakou Railway and its Chief – designer Zhan Tianyou?

On the way to Badaling you'll go across the Beijing – Zhangjiakou Railway. Starting to be built in 1905 it is the first railway designed and constructed by China itself, its chief – designer being none other than Zhan Tianyou – a famous engineer in China. In the whole process of designing and field – work of the project Zhan Tianyou, climbing up hills and down dales in defiance of all difficulties and dangers, made the survey and worked out the plan all by himself. In order to get the first – hand and reliable materials he often went out alone on donkey back, calling on the people nearby to make investigations. Facing all sorts of mockery from aliens in the course of construction he overcame all difficulties incurred from the backward technologies. Relying solely on his own correct design and pooling of wisdom from the workers, he succeeded in completing the most difficult part of the project – the two tunnels leading from the Juyong Pass to Badaling. Resorting to the way in constructing "人 – shaped" railway in his design and a device of automatic coupling and using one engine to pull the train at the head and another to push at the back – end, he finally succeeded in making the train climbing onto the steep slope at Badaling. This is a great invention, a marvelous creation by Zhan Tianyou in China's railway engineering. The Beijing – Zhangjiakou Railway was brought to a completion in September 1909, two years ahead of the scheduled time, which meant a saving of 280,000 taels of silver from the expenditure put aside for the railroad building.

82

Zhan Tianyou (1861 – 1919), a native of Nanhai county, Guangdong Province, took a liking in machinery in his childhood. In 1872, when he was only a child of 11 years old, he was sent together with other 29 children of his age to study in America. Spending nine years there finishing his study in the elementary and high schools he was enrolled with excellent results into the railroad engineering faculty of the civil – engineering department of the Yale University. He returned to China in 1881 when he finished his study. Zhan Tianyou dedicated his whole life to the railroad construction in China. Soon after his death the Chinese Engineering Society erected a bronze statue for him at the Qinglongqiao Railway Station in memory of his outstanding contributions. In May 1982 the Ministry of Railways built a new tomb for Zhan Tianyou and his wife by the Qinglong Bridge. Later the Zhan Tianyou Memorial Hall was built and opened to the public at Badaling.

72. 你能讲一下关于穆桂英点将台的传说吗？

从居庸关到八达岭铁道交叉口的中间,可见一巨大而平坦的岩石横卧于河滩上,石面上可见痕迹似的足印,据传这是当年飒爽英姿的女将穆桂英在巨石上点将出征时留下的。

有关杨家将的传说,在关沟一带流传甚广。杨家将的老一辈杨业,在戏曲中称为杨继业或杨令公,是北宋时期的名将。他当年与契丹作战时的主要战场,在今山西省代县的雁门关内外。后来他的儿子杨六郎、孙媳穆桂英等亦都在那里戍边,关沟一带素来未曾作过辽宋的战场,但后人为了表示对爱国英雄杨家将的敬慕与怀念之情,因而便留下了许多有关杨家将的故事和传说。由于这些故事在民间流传甚广,久而久之,这里也就成了辽宋之间频频交兵的古战场了。

Can you tell in brief about the "Legendary Commanding Terrace on Which Mu Guiying, the Heroine General, Disposed Her Troops"?

Lying by the side of the brook in the middle of the stretch from the Juyong Pass to the cross section of the railroad to Badaling, there is a huge block of rock with a smooth and flat top, on which you'll find some seemingly footprints. It is said that this is the very rock on which the Heroine General Mu Guiying ever stood and disposed her troops for expeditions, thus leaving her footprints on it.

The story about the Yang Family Generals has been very popular among the people along the "Pass Valley." Yang Ye, alias Yang Jiye or Yang Linggong as addressed very often in operas, the elder general of the Yang Family, was a famous general in the Northern Song Dynasty. When he was engaged in battles with the nomadic tribe Qidan (Khitan) the main battlefield was somewhere around the Yanmen Pass in nowadays Daixian County, Shanxi Province. Later, Yang Liulang, his son and Mu Guiying, wife of his grandson, were fighting there too. Actually the Pass Valley has never been the battlefield between the Liao and Song dynasties in history. However, to show respect for the patriotic heroes of the Yang Family Generals and keep them in memory, many tales and legends about them have been passed on. As these stories have been on the lips of the people for quite a long time, the "Pass Valley" has also become a said battlefield between the Liao and Song dynasties in ancient China.

73. 请问"居庸叠翠"为何意?

在由北京前往八达岭的路上,过了南口,即进入一条峡谷,长城的重要关隘之一居庸关便雄居其中,峡谷因而得名"关沟"。这条所谓长"四十里关沟",其实仅为三十华里。峡谷两旁重峦叠翠,树木蓊郁,春来山花烂漫,景色十分瑰丽。远在八百年前的金代,这里就被列为燕京八景之一,称为"居庸叠翠"。居庸关长城现已修复,并已于 1998 年元月 1 日正式对游客开放,城楼也已于 3 月 28 日正式对游人开放,这就为"居庸叠翠"增添了许多迷人的景色。

Can you explain what is the so – called "Piling Verdure overt the Juyong Pass"?

On the way from Beijing to Badaling when passing by the town of Nankou, you'll enter a valley, where the Juyong Pass, one of the important and magnificent passes along the Great Wall is located. Hence, the name "Pass Valley." Ranging along the sides of the "20 – kilometer valley," which is actually a little over 15 kilometers, are towering mountain ridges clad in green and studded with various kinds of wild flowers, presenting picturesque scenery. As far back as the Jin Dynasty (1115 – 1234) this place was listed as one of the "Eight Renowned Scenic Spots in Yanjing," known as the "Piling Verdure over the Juyong Pass." The renovation of the Great Wall at the Juyong Pass was completed and it was opened to the public on January 1, 1998, The towers on the wall were open to visitors on Mar. 28, 1998. Thus adding much beauty to the already enchanting scenes of the "Piling Verdure over the Juyong Pass".

74. 慕田峪长城位于北京何方？修建于何时？何时对外开放？

慕田峪长城横卧于北京东北部的怀柔县境内，全长 2250 米，海拔高度为 535 米，长城上筑有敌楼 17 座。这里是北京境内第二个长城旅游区，山下有缆车直通山顶，日游客接待量约为 20,000 人。

怀柔县境内的长城始建于南北朝的南齐(479－502 年)时期，晚唐时曾进行过一些修补，明朝又作了改建和扩建。1983 年 12 月至 1984 年 8 月又对慕田峪长城进行了全面整修，并于 1986 年 4 月正式对外开放，供中外游人畅游观览。

In which direction does the Mutianyu Section of the Great Wall lie in Beijing? When was it first built and opened to the public?

To the northeast of Beijing in Huairou County, the Mutianyu Section of the Great Wall measures 2,250 meters in length, with an elevation of 535 meters. Studded all along the wall are 17 turreted－fortresses, and the section is accessible by cable cars from below. Known as another section of the Great Wall in Beijing, it is able to receive 20,000 visitors daily. First being built during the period of the Southern Qi (479－502) in Northern and Southern dynasties, this section of the wall was once repaired in the late Tang Dynasty and again renovated and expanded in the Ming Dynasty. Restored to its original shape from December 1983 to August 1984 the Mutianyu Section of the Great Wall was opened to the public in April 1986.

75. 你能介绍一下慕田峪长城上的鸳鸯松和珍珠泉吗?

在慕田峪西北的小山顶上有一株古松,其主干拔地而起,忽又一分为二,但奇异的是:其中一枝为马尾松,而另一枝为油松,所以当地人称它为"鸳鸯松"。

珍珠泉在龙潭以西的山沟中,现已砌成方池,池底不断有水上冒,状如珍珠,故名珍珠泉。据检验,该泉富含二氧化碳,极有利用价值。因珍珠泉与慕田峪长城游览区相去不远,现已被县经济开发区利用来制作矿泉水了。

Could you say something about the "Mandarin – Duck Pine" and the "Pearl Spring" at the Mutianyu Section of the Great Wall?

Standing on the hill – top to the northwest of the Great Wall at Mutianyu is an old pine tree, from which you'll see two branches of different pine trees growing on the same trunk, one being the masson pine and the other the Chinese pine. What a strange thing! Hence the name the "Mandarin – Duck – Pine."

Located to the west of the Dragon Pool in the valley is the Pearl Spring, now a squarely – laid pond. As the water bubbling up from its bottom looks very much like little pearls, the people call it the "Pearl Spring." Chemical analysis determines that the spring water can be of good to health as it is full of carbon dioxide. Since it is located in the tourist area of the Great Wall at Mutianyu, the spring water is now used by the Huairou Economic Development Corp. to make "Pearl Spring Brand" mineral water.

76. 请阐述一下戚继光在修筑慕田峪长城中所作的贡献好吗?

到慕田峪长城去游览的人们,往往都会联想起戚继光,因为他是明代曾经驻守过京畿一带的一位著名爱国将领。明嘉靖年间(1522－1566年),戚继光曾在今北京东北的蓟州一带驻守。当时他尚是个年刚20出头的小官,并不十分引人注目。十数年后,亦即明隆庆元年(1567年),当他在海防前线立下赫赫战功,成为名将之后再次北上,便名声大振了。

1550年,历史上发生了震惊京畿的"庚戌之变"。蒙古族的俺答汗率领其部下,攻宣化,走蓟州,入古北口,围顺义,逼通州,过密云,取良乡,如入无人之境,眼看着北京已陷于重围,似有即刻被占领之危险,这使整个京华大为震惊,但俺答汗实际上仅在京畿周围掠夺了大量财物,而后即便退去。这就是明史上所谓的"庚戌之变"。但自此以后,俺答汗常常举兵南下,多次到蓟州、昌平一带掠夺骚扰。为保京师安宁,当时明朝的统治者曾接二连三,十余次撤换过率兵戍守的大将。杀的杀了,关的也关了,但均无际于事,未能扭转当时的被动局面。在这种情势下,戚继光奉调至京,担起重任。开始的时候,他只管蓟州、昌平一带属下的军事训练;不久就担任镇守总兵之职,统帅并指挥军队作战。

戚继光坐镇北方16年,北方安全无恙。论其功绩,那是多方面的:在军事训练上,他制订了一整套办法,著名的《练兵记实》就是他在北方练兵过程中写就的;他的另一重要贡献便是重修长城。在该项工程中,他一方面组织力量加高加宽原有的长城,还在要塞之处加修了重墙,另一方面则在山海关到昌平之间的长城上建起了1,200多座敌楼。过去的长城规模较小,既不能有效地掩护士兵作战,也不能较好地储存军火粮草。敌楼建成后,士兵不仅可以安全固守,还可随时出击,大大地增强了战

斗力。长城上敌楼的建筑自此为始。此外,在对慕田峪长城的
开发利用中,还在城墙脚下发现了大量的石雷。

**Could you say something about the contributions made by
the famous General Qi Jiguang in the reconstruction of the
Great Wall at Mutianyu?**

When visiting the Great Wall at Mutianyu, you can not
but be reminded of Qi Jiguang, a famous patriotic general in
the later half of the Ming dynasty (1368 – 1644). During the
Jiajing reign period (1522 – 1566) Qi Jiguang once garrisoned
in Jizhou to the northeast of the present day Beijing. As a
young man 20 and a petty officer in the rank and file he cut no
figure at that time. A decade or so later in 1567, the 1st year
under the reign of Longqing in the same dynasty he stood out a
prominent general when he, having scored many victories in
the coastal areas, was once again called back for the defence of
the areas around Beijing.

The story goes back to the year of 1550. At that time the
Mongolian tribes headed by Anda encroached upon Xuanhua
and Jizhou, broke through the Gubeikou Pass, and besieged
Shunyi, clamped down on Tongzhou and trespassed by Miyun
to seize Liangxiang as if they would soon break into Beijing.
But actually Anda and his men withdrew away with a big loot-
ing of the area. This is what the people called the "Incident of
1550" in the historical records of the Ming Dynasty. From
then on, Anda often set his troops upon Jizhou and Changping
and harassed the area. Although over dozens of garrison commanders were changed, jailed or killed, none of them could do
a bit setting check on the harassing tribes. Under such circum-

stances, Qi Jiguang was transferred to Beijing, to be in charge of military training in Jizhou and Changping areas. Soon afterwards he was promoted to be the garrison commander, commanding his troops in battle.

During the 16 years in his terms of office the northern area remained unharmed and peaceful. Speaking of Qi Jiguang made many merits and achievements in his life: first he worked out a whole set of methods in military training, which were included in A Record of Military Training jotted down in the military training course. Second he started the reconstruction of the Great Wall in the area. On the one hand, he organized an adequate labor force to reinforce the original wall by building it higher and wider, and even with some important parts along the wall to be doubled; and on the other hand, he had 1,200 turreted − fortresses built along the wall from the Shanhaiguan to Changping. The Great Wall, being of a small scale in the past, could neither be used to screen off the soldiers to put up a defence in an effective way, nor could it be used for storing ammunition and fodder or other supplies. The construction of the fortresses offered the soldiers not only enough alleyways to move along but also a solid works of defence to rely on, thereby greatly reinforcing the combat strength. Fortresses were started to be built along the wall during Qi Jiguang's terms of office, and in addition, a great number of stone − mines were unearthed during the exploration of the Section of the Great Wall at Mutianyu.

77. 请讲一讲关于慕田峪长城上昭雪碑的故事好吗？

明万历十年(1582年)以后的一段时间里,因宰相张居正的病逝,朝中斗争渐趋激烈,由张居正调来的名将戚继光亦遭排斥。万历二十一年(1593年)以后,权相严嵩专政,朝政腐败,边庭吃紧。为了加强京师的防御,燕山长城的加固维修工程又在继续进行了,因而不得不起用一些过去戚继光部下的有用之才。但严嵩一党实行的是顺我则昌,逆我则亡的政策,一旦发现异己即便罗织罪名,加以陷害。

在加强慕田峪长城防御的过程中,一位原在戚继光部下任职的守备,被调来负责加固长城防御的修建工程。该守备精明强干,通晓兵法,他发现慕田峪长城地区的山势地形非常复杂,原长城一线外侧曲折起伏的山岭颇多,敌人极易隐蔽潜行直至长城脚下。为解决这一难题,必须向长城外侧修筑一个前哨纵深工事。于是,该守备便做好了方案预算报到了兵部。兵部中严嵩的心腹便伺机向该守备勒索贿赂,但他是多年在戚继光手下供职的廉洁奉公之人,那肯向那些狐群狗党折节行贿呢! 这一兵部官员便暗下了害人之心。当工程完工时,他聚集了一帮亲信爪牙,以前往慕田峪检查为名,硬说这位守备把长城的走向定错了位,诬陷他故意如此安排,企图中饱私囊,还罗织种种罪名,将这位廉洁奉公的守备杀害了。这一冤案,直到十余年以后,严嵩倒了台才得以昭雪。事实上,这段长城的走向不仅没错,而且在用料和工程质量上,完全符合节约而又坚固耐用的原则。为表彰这位守备的功绩,特在这段长城尽头处的敌楼内立碑昭雪。这块昭雪碑一直保存了300余年,可惜的是现已荡然无存了。

Could you tell the story of "whence came the 'Redressing Stone – stele' at the Mutianyu Section of the Great Wall"?

After the 10th year of the Wanli reign period (1573 – 1620), there came a period of severe internal strife in the imperial court of the Ming Dynasty when the then well – known prime minister Zhang Juzheng died of illness. The famous general Qi Jiguang was also expelled from his post due to the fact the late prime minister recommended him. After the 21st year of the Wanli reign (1593), due to arbitrary dictatorship of Yan Song, the then crafty and influential prime minister, the political affairs in the court went from bad to worse in corruption and the situation in the frontier areas was very intense. To strengthen the defence of the capital city, the reconstruction and reinforcement of the Great Wall along the Yanshan Mountain Range were once again taken up. Therefore, a number of talented men and engineer formerly under Qi Jiguang had again to be reinstated. However, the brutal practice of "those who submit will prosper while those who resist shall perish" by those of the Yan Song's party would tolerate no dissidents. Once found out, persecution following flame – ups would immediately be inflicted upon them.

In the course of strengthening the defence along the Great Wall at Mutianyu, an officer formerly a junior under Qi Jiguang was again appointed to be responsible for the project. Intelligent and capable as he was he knew the military strategy by heart. When seeing that the terrain outside the Great Wall at Mutianyu was full of ups and downs, which would offer the enemy an easy access under cover right up to the foot of the wall, he decided to build an in – depth outpost so as to overcome the plausible trouble. A plan worked out together with a budget was submitted to the state military department for authorization. But an official, a henchman of Yan Song was in his way trying to extort bribe out of it. The officer in question, having been trained for many years under Qi Jiguang's guidance and honest in performing his duty, refused to commit it. Enraged, the official, committed this to heart, was determined to seek a chance to persecute him in secrecy. When the project was nearing its end, the official, went to the worksite with his lackeys, to make an inspection of the project. On the pretext that the run of the wall was out of correct position and that the officer in charge did it by intention in order to feather his own nest, he put him to death by giving him the ill name. Not until a decade of years later when that influential Prime Minister Yan Song was toppled, had the wronged case been redressed. Actually, the run of the wall was not only totally right in position, but the quality of it and the materials used for the construction were utterly in principle of thriftiness and the wall was very strong and solid. To cite the great dead of this honest soul, a stone－stele was erected within a watchtower at the end of that section of the Great Wall. Three hundred years have gone by since the erection of the tablet, but alas, it has now gone nobody knows where to our great pity!

78. 请问长城上的敌楼、垛口和堡子是作何用的？

敌楼：这是为了解除守城士卒的日晒雨淋之苦，并能凭此以抗击来犯之敌，便于储存武器弹药而设的。

垛口：墙体上头或两侧伸出的部分谓之垛，借以隐蔽、防御敌方的箭及枪炮的袭击；凹陷的部分叫做口，用于窥视敌方的活动，并向敌人射击。

堡子：在长城内外较为平缓的地区均建有"堡子"，系供当年戍卒们畜养战马之用，故当地人们称之为"马圈"。

What were the fortresses, crenellated battlements and walled-in courtyards used for?

Fortress: fortresses were used by the defending troops to take shelter from the wind, rain and heat, fight and check the enemy's advance, and store arms and ammunition.

Crenellated battlements: the parts projecting upwards on both sides of the wall-top are called the crenels, which can be used for cover, defend and shield off attacks by arrows and gun-shots from the enemy. The dented parts are used to shoot and keep eyes on the movement of the enemy.

Walled-in courtyards: studded along the gentle slopes inside and outside the Great Wall, you'll find some ruins of the walled-in courtyards. The garrison soldiers at that time used to raise and keep horses here. They were also called by the local people as "stables".

79. 你能说一说有关长城嘉峪关的情况吗?

嘉峪关雄居于甘肃省河西走廊的西端,北依马鬃山,而南临巍巍的祁连山,扼交通之要冲,地势十分险要,是万里长城西端的雄关重镇,也是明代所筑万里长城的西部终点,素有"天下第一雄关"之称。

嘉峪关建于明洪武五年(1372年)至今已有600余年的历史。其关城呈梯形,周长733米,城墙高10米,面积为30,000多平方米,西边筑有瓮城,城楼两相对称。登高望远,长城若巨龙般蜿蜒曲折于戈壁旱海之中。茫茫大漠,南山积雪,一览无余,瑰丽景色,尽收眼底。

Could you say something about the Jiayu Pass of the Great Wall?

The Jiayu Pass towers magnificently at the western end of the Hexi Corridor in Gansu Province with the Mazong Mountains in the north and the Qilian Mountains down to the south. Striding right at a communication hinge it is a strategic pass at the western end of the "10,000 – li Wall" built in the Ming Dynasty, hence the name "No. 1 Magnificent Pass under Heaven."

Built in 1372, the fifth year under the reign of Hongwu in the Ming the pass has stood there for more than 600 years. Covering an area of over 30,000 square meters it has a trapezoid gate – tower and the city wall measures 733 meters in circumference and 10 meters in height. Built symmetrically with a jarred city at the western side it is easy to lure the enemy in and hit them behind the closed gates. With the wall snaking along the boundless desert, a panoramic view on the city – tower presents a great vista of a vast expanse of the Gobi Desert with snow – capped mountains looming around in the distance.

80. 你能讲一下关于"爱我中华,修我长城"的活动吗?

万里长城是中华民族的象征,也是中华民族的骄傲。"爱我中华,修我长城"是一项全国人民的大行动。自 1984 年北京晚报社、八达岭特区办事处和北京日报社等单位联合发起"爱我中华,修我长城"的社会赞助活动以来,得到了党和国家领导人的关怀和支持,也得到了来自全国各界人士的热情支持和赞助。已故的邓小平同志及其他同志还为这次活动题了词。仅 1984 年一年就收到了赞助金额近 300 万元。瑞典、日本、加拿大、美国、法国、德国、丹麦和澳大利亚等十几个国家的友好人士也都慷慨解囊,出资相助。

至 1984 年 9 月底,"爱我中华,修我长城"社会赞助的第一、二期工程——修复八达岭长城北七、北八城台及北六至北八城台之间的城墙工程业已胜利完成。新修复的长城经有关部门的验收,不仅工程合格,而且恢复了长城的本来面貌。现在,国内外的宾客游人,已可登临海拔高度为 887.5 米的北八城台,俯瞰八达岭长城之全貌,一如登高望远,抚今思昔之宿愿了。

第 3 期工程始于 1984 年 10 月,这包括修复八达岭长城北九、十两座城台和在怀柔县境内的慕田峪长城的 3 座城楼。现在,居庸关的长城也已修复,并于 1998 年 1 月 1 日正式对游人开放。长城的修复工作还会不断进行下去,为了能使更多人参加这一有意义的活动,个人赞助款的下限由原来的 100 元降为 10 元。凡赞助出资 20 万元,修复一座城台的个人,可在城台上单独立碑,以表纪念。

Could you say something in brief about the activities of "Love China and Reconstruct the Great Wall"?

The Great Wall is a symbol and glory of the Chinese nation. The activity of "Love China and Reconstruct the Great Wall" has now pooled into a joint action of the Chinese people throughout the country. The social donation activity for "Love China and Reconstruct the Great Wall" called forth jointly by the Beijing Evening News, the Administration Office of the Badaling Special Area and the Beijing Daily in 1984 has won great concern and support from the leaders of the Party and state. enthusiastic support and sponsorship from persons of all walks of life in China. Our late Comrade Deng Xiaoping and other leaders wrote their inscriptions for the activity. By the end of 1984 we had gathered in a donation amounting to three million yuan. Besides, friendly personages from over a dozen foreign countries like Sweden, Japan, Canada, America, France, Germany, Denmark and Australia also helped a lot in a generous way.

Up to the end of September 1984, both first and second phases of the project funded by the society for the restoration of No. 7 and No. 8 walled terraces, and the wall between No 6 and No 8 terraces along the north section of the Great Wall at Badaling had been completed. The renovated parts of the wall are not only up to the required standard, but also utterly in line with the original feature. Climbing from the northern side all the way up to No. 8 terrace of 887. 5 meters high visitors at home and abroad can get a bird's-eye view of the Great Wall at Badaling, thereby realizing their cherishing wishes of reviewing the past and looking far into the future.

Started from October 1984, the third phase of the project includes the restoration of Nos. 9 and 10 terraces along the north section of the Great Wall at Badaling and the three watch —towers on the Great Wall at Mutianyu in Huairou County. Up to now the Great Wall at the Juyong Pass has been renovated and opened to the public on January 1, 1998. The restoration work of the Great Wall will go on continuously. To get more people take a part in this significant activity the amount for personal sponsorship is now lowered from a minimum of 100 yuan to 10 yuan. anyone who gives a donation amounting to 200,000 yuan for restoring one walled terrace may have a personal tablet erected on the terrace in his or her honor.

明十三陵
(The Ming Tombs)

81. 请你叙述一下明十三陵的简况好吗?

明十三陵位于北京西北郊昌平县境内的天寿山南麓,整个陵区面积达 40 平方公里。这里埋葬着明朝的 13 位皇帝。自公元 1409 年,朱棣建造长陵始,至 1644 年明王朝灭亡,十三陵的营造工程历经 200 余年的时间而从未间断。

公元 1407 年,朱棣派了礼部尚书和一位精通风水的术士到北京地区寻找"吉址",以为万年计。而十三陵所在的地区,山间明堂广大,水土丰厚,是个好地方。且这里的地名也颇贴切,山名黄土山,"黄"乃帝王之本色,而"土"实为江山社稷之根本。朱棣对此感到十分满意,故将此地定为陵区。

明朝共有 16 个皇帝,除朱元璋埋在南京的"孝陵",建文帝朱允炆不知所终,还有景泰帝朱祁钰葬于北京西郊金山外,其余十三个皇帝全都埋葬在这里,因而通称为"十三陵"。

各个陵墓,除面积大小及建造方面的繁简有别外,其建筑布局、规划等规格基本相同。平面均呈长方形,建筑自白石桥起,依此分列陵门、碑亭、祾恩门、祾恩殿、明楼和宝城等等。十三陵以地面建筑宏伟的长陵和已发掘的地下宫殿定陵而著称,是北京著名的游览胜地之一。

Could you tell us something about the Ming Tombs?

Located at the southern foot of the Tianshou mountains in Changping County in the western suburban areas of Beijing, the Ming Tombs cover an area of 40 square kilometers with 13

Ming emperors buried here. Ever since 1409 when Emperor Zhu Di started building his tomb here till the fall of the Ming Dynasty in 1644 the construction of the imperial tombs had been going on ceaselessly, lasting a period of over 200 years.

In 1407, a certain minister of rites and a master geomancer were sent by Zhu Di to find an "Auspicious Area" in the surroundings of Beijing, which was to be used as a site for his eternal repose. Since the area, where the tombs are located now is a sunny and spacious area, fertile and rich in produce, it is considered to be an ideal one. Furthermore, the mountain here used to be called "Huangtu" mountain it is very apt for the location of the royal tombs. As "Huangtu" in Chinese meant for yellow earth, with yellow being the color symbolizing the royal family and the earth the very foundation for the whole royal edifice, Zhu Di was greatly satisfied with it. Thus the area was chosen to be the location for the Ming Tombs.

There are 16 emperors in the Ming Dynasty as known to many people. With the exception of Zhu Yuanzhang, the founder of the Ming Dynasty who was buried in the Xiaoling Mausoleum in Nanjing, Zhu Yunwen, the Emperor Jianwen who disappeared and Zhu Qiyu, the Emperor Jingtai who was buried at Jinshan Hill in the western suburbs of Beijing, all other 13 Ming emperors were buried in this tomb area, hence the area being called the 13 Ming Tombs.

Though different in size and complexity of the structure, all 13 tombs are by and large alike as to the plan and layout. The whole plan is in rectangular shape, in which with the white marble bridge as the start of a tomb area, all other buildings were built alike along an axis to have first an entrance gate, followed by a tablet tower, a sacrificial gate and hall, a tomb tower and a few underground vaults. With the Changling Tomb renowned for its magnificent buildings and the Dingling for its wonderful excavations, the area of the Ming Tombs has now become one of the most famous tourist attractions in Beijing.

82. 明朝的皇陵共有几处?

明朝共有四处皇陵。第一处在今安徽的泗县,即所谓"祖陵",那里埋葬着明朝开国皇帝朱元璋的祖父母,但这座陵墓到清初已被洪泽湖的湖水淹没了。第二处在安徽凤阳,称为"皇陵",埋葬着朱元璋的父母亲。第三处即为南京的孝陵,埋葬着朱元璋本人。

明朝从第三个皇帝永乐帝朱棣起,大多都埋葬在今北京昌平县的天寿山陵园中,也便是今天的十三陵,是为第四处皇陵。只有第七个景泰帝朱祁钰被埋葬在北京西郊的金山上。

明朝还有一处严格来讲不能算作皇陵的皇陵,这便是明嘉靖皇帝父母的陵。该陵在今湖北省钟祥市治内。嘉靖帝朱厚被立为皇帝登基后,即尊其父母为太上皇和太后,并为他们建了陵园。

How many tomb areas does the Ming Dynasty have?

There are four tomb areas in the Ming Dynasty: First the "Ancestral Tomb" area located in Sixian County, Anhui Province, where Zhu Yuanzhang's grand-parents are buried, but the tomb was already submerged in the Hongze Lake in the early days of the Qing Dynasty. Secondly the "Imperial Tomb" in Fengyang County, Anhui. It is the tomb for Zhu Yuanzhang's father and mother, and thirdly, the Xiaoling

Mausoleum in Nanjing, the burial place for Zhu Yuanzhang himself.

Starting from Zhu Di, the third emperor of the Ming, almost all the emperors of the Ming Dynasty, with the exception of Zhu Qiyu, the seventh emperor of the Ming who was alone buried at the Jinshan Hill in the western suburbs of Beijing, were buried in the tomb area at the foot of the Tianshou Mountain in Changping County, Beijing, forming the fourth royal tomb area of the Ming Dynasty.

There is still another royal tomb area of the Ming Dynasty, which, strictly speaking, should not be regarded as a royal tomb area of the Ming Dynasty, that is the tomb for the father and mother of Zhu Houcong, Emperor Jiajing. When Jiajing was appointed as heir prince and later enthroned, he made his father the emperor's father and his mother, consort dowager, and had a tomb built for his parents, which is located in nowadays Zhongxiang City, Hubei Province.

83.十三陵墓的顺序是如何排列的?

陵名	姓名	年号	庙号	在位	终年	备注
长陵	朱棣	永乐	成祖	22 年	65 岁	
献陵	朱高炽	洪熙	仁宗	1 年	48 岁	
景陵	朱瞻基	宣德	宣宗	10 年	38 岁	
裕陵	朱祁镇	正统、天顺	英宗	14 年、8 年	38 岁	中有景泰帝
茂陵	朱见深	成化	宪宗	23 年	41 岁	
泰陵	朱佑樘	弘治	孝宗	18 年	36 岁	
康陵	朱厚照	正德	武宗	16 年	31 岁	
永陵	朱厚熜	嘉靖	世宗	45 年	60 岁	
昭陵	朱载垕	隆庆	穆宗	6 年	36 岁	
定陵	朱翊钧	万历	神宗	48 年	58 岁	
庆陵	朱常洛	泰昌	光宗	29 天	33 岁	
德陵	朱由校	天启	熹宗	7 年	23 岁	
思陵	朱由检	崇祯	思宗	17 年	35 岁	

附:

孝陵	朱元璋	洪武	太祖	31 年	71 岁	陵在南京
	朱允炆	建文	惠帝			下落不明
景泰陵	朱祁钰	景泰	景帝	8 年	30 岁	西郊金山

102

In what order are the 13 tombs of the Ming dynasty arranged?

Tomb Name	Emperor's Name	Title of Reign	Title of Shrine	Duration of Reign	Age of Demise	Remarks
Chang ling	Zhu Di	Yongle	Chengzu	22 years	65	
Xianling	Zhu Gaozhi	Hongxi	Renzong	1 year	48	
Jingling	Zhu Zhanji	Xuande	Xuan-zong	10 years	38	
Yuling	Zhu Qizhen	Zhengtong Tianshun	Ying-zong	14 years 8 years	38	With Jingtai in between
Maoling	Zhu Jianshen	Chenghua	Xian-zong	23 years	41	
Tailing	Zhu Youtang	Hongzhi	Xiao-zong	18 years	36	
Kangling	Zhu Houzhao	Zhengde	Wuzong	16 years	31	
Yong ling	Zhu Houcong	Jiajing	Shizong	45 years	60	
Zhaoling	Zhu Zaihou	Longqing	Muzong	6 years	36	
Dingling	Zhu Yijun	Wanli	Shen-zong	48 years	58	
Qingling	Zhu Changluo	Taichang	Guang zong	29 days	33	
Deling	Zhu Youxiao	Tianqi	Xizong	7 years	23	
Siling	Zhu Youjian	Chongzhen	Sizong	17 years	35	

Appended Table:

Xiaoling	Zhu Yuanzhang	Hongwu	Taizu	31 years	71	Tomb in Nanjing
No tomb	Zhu Yunwen	Jianwen	Huidi			Nobody knows anywhere
Jingtailing	Zhu Qiyu	Jingtai	Jingdi	8 years	30	Jinshan in the western Suburbs

84. 明代共有几个皇帝和几个年号？

明朝共有 16 个皇帝，17 个年号，其起因如下：

公元 1449 年，明朝第六个皇帝朱祁镇（年号正统）在位期间，发生了一场与北方少数民族的战争。为显示其实力，他御驾亲征，结果被打败了，他自己也成了俘虏。于是朝廷便立其弟朱祁钰为帝，改年号为景泰。但一年以后，朱祁镇又被放了回来，七年后发动了一次宫廷政变，史称"夺门之变"，废其弟，而他本人又再次登上了皇位，改国号为"天顺"。

How many emperors did the Ming Dynasty have? **And how many titles of reign did they use**?

There were altogether 16 emperors with 17 titles of reign in the Ming dynasty. How could it come about? The reason is as follows:

It happened in 1449 during the reign of Zhu Qizhen, the sixth emperor of the dynasty whose title of reign was "Zhengtong," the Ming emperor had a battle with a minority tribe in the north. To show his real power the emperor commanded the army in person to the battle. However, he was defeated and was taken a captive. Not long afterwards, the imperial court made his brother Zhu Qiyu the emperor, changing the title of reign into "Jingtai." However, Zhu Qizhen the captured emperor was set free a year later and returned to Beijing. Seven years later he staged a coup in the court and abrogated his brother. It is known in Chinese history as the "Coup of Seizing the Gate." After that, Zhu Qizhen resumed the throne and changed again the title of his reign into "Tianshun".

85. 明朝是否仍有殉葬制度?

明朝初年依然存在着用活人殉葬的制度。明朝前期的四个皇帝,即洪武、永乐、洪熙和宣德都曾用活人作过殉葬,亦即南京的孝陵、十三陵中的长陵、献陵和景陵。据记载,长陵用了16个嫔妃作殉葬,献陵的殉葬是5个嫔妃,而景陵则用了10个。陵园中所谓"东井"、"西井"者即是埋葬殉葬者的地方。"东井"在德陵的馒头山之南,"西井"在定陵的西北。这种墓窟只是一种砖穴,棺椁直接放入穴中,好似下井一样,故称之为"井"。直到天顺末年(1464年),朱祁镇临死前才下令废除了用活人殉葬的制度。他的儿子朱见深临死之前也有同样的遗嘱。

Was there still any institution of burying the living for the dead in the Ming Dynasty?

There was still the institution of burying the living for the dead in the early days of the Ming dynasty. The first four emperors, Hongwu, Yongle, Hongxi and Xuande all used the living to be buried for the dead in the close vicinity of their tombs, namely the Xiaoling Mausoleum in Nanjing, Changling, Xianling and Jingling in the Ming Tombs' area in Beijing. The record has it that 16 concubines were buried for the dead in the tomb of Changling, 5 in Xianling and 10 in Jingling. You may well be told the "Eastern Well" and the "Western Well" in the Ming Tombs area, which are actually the places for burying the living for the dead. The "Eastern Well" is to the south of the Mantou Hill by the side of the Deling Tomb and the "Western Well" to the northwest of the Tomb of Dingling. The tomb cavity for burying the living is built of bricks and the coffin was laid directly into it as if it were put into a well. Hence the name "well." This institution was not abolished until 1464 before the end of the reign of Tianshun. According to Zhu Qizhen's will his son Zhu Jianshen reiterated it before his death.

86. 明朝的殉葬人是怎么决定的?

殉葬人是由新君为已故的皇帝圈定的,其主要对象是妃子和宫女。被圈定人的名单在宫中公布后,皇宫里的人要向她们道贺。殉葬者本人经过一番梳妆打扮之后,就去参加一次宴席。该宴席是在指定的房内举办的,殉葬者吃完后即便集体上吊死去,然后装殓起来,埋到皇陵附近的"井"中。

How was the living to be buried for the dead sorted out in the Ming Dynasty?

The livings buried for the demised emperor were singled out by the newly enthroned emperor mainly from among concubines and court maids. When the sorted - out ones were announced others would offer their congratulations on them. And after decking themselves out a bit they would go to a designated room to attend a feast. When this was over, they had to commit suicide by hanging themselves in a collective way and were buried in the "Well" by the tomb of the deceased emperor.

87. 皇帝死后,皇后是否也要陪葬?

皇帝死后,皇后是不必陪葬的,因为皇后本身也是个至高无上者,不能作为殉葬者一起陪葬。如果皇后先死,据说是先将她埋葬在别的地方,待皇帝死后再一起合葬于皇陵之中。

Will the queen be buried together for the deceased emperor?

No, the queen was not required to be buried for the demised emperor as the queen herself is also considered as one of the supreme. Therefore, she should not be buried together with the deceased. However, if the queen died before the emperor she would, as said, be buried somewhere else first and then when the emperor died they would be buried together in the imperial tomb.

88. 请你讲一下皇帝的葬仪是怎样进行的?

皇帝死后,礼部拟出一份葬仪单,上面列明了葬仪应行的仪式和全部过程。

皇帝所用的棺木叫"梓宫"。起先放在宫中,出丧下葬的前一天,才在午门外设"大升舆",这是一种运载灵柩的工具,随之即按照图式陈列全部仪仗。从这一天起,就由嗣皇帝率领后妃、皇子及众大臣等身穿孝服,举行葬礼。在下葬的前夕举行"辞奠"礼,意为即将告别。在下葬的当天,举行"启奠"和"祖奠"礼,表示经此祭奠后就要启行了。此时就在棺木上加上彩帏,随之便用"龙",亦称"小杠",一种轻便的运灵工具抬往午门,在这里再行"遣奠"礼,这就算作送行了。嗣皇帝只送到这里,不再出午门,此后便由王子和诸王等送往陵园。

棺木抬到午门后即换成"大升舆",再抬往端门。继之,太子将捧着用白绢制成的"神帛",前往太庙(今劳动人民文化宫)行"辞祖"礼,然后出德胜门前往天寿山陵园。从德胜门到陵园的途中,如土城、清河及沙河等处均设有"祭坛",由勋戚(世袭的功臣和皇亲)、大臣、僧道及耆老(乡绅)分别致祭,一般穷苦的百姓是不能参加的。

棺木送至陵园后,先存放在享殿中,行"安神"礼,待预定的下葬时刻一到,还得行一次"迁奠"礼后才开始把棺木往地宫(亦称"玄宫")里抬,到地宫门(又称皇堂门)外,还要举行赠礼,即是将"谥册"、"宝印"和"冥器"以及陪葬衣饰等物摆放在里面,然后关上地宫大门,再在地宫前行一次"享"礼。至此,一套繁琐的葬仪才告结束。

Could you say something about how the funeral rites for the deceased emperor were carried out?

After the death of the emperor, burial rites with detailed procedures as to what to do and how to do would be worked out by the Office of Rites. The coffin for the deceased emperor is called "Zigong", the palace of catalpas, which was firstly to be laid in a palace hall. On the previous day before the burial ceremony, a grand hearse would, based on the set plan, be set up in front of the Meridian Gate with all the articles necessary for the funeral processions displayed in neat order. From this day on sacrificial ceremonies were held with the newly enthroned emperor taking the lead, then followed by files of queens, concubines, the emperor's sons and daughters and the vassals in white. On the eve of the day before the burial, a sacrificial ceremony would be held for the people to pay their last respects to the demised emperor. On the very day of the burial, a ritual ceremony for offering a "Departing Sacrifice" and also a "Sacrifice to the Ancestors" would be held to announce the immediate departure of the funeral processions. At the same time the bier would be shrouded in colored curtains and be carried on an easy hearse, named "Longchun"or "Xiaogang" to the Meridian Gate and a final farewell sacrifice would be held here to show the immediate parting of the deceased. Since the new emperor went no farther than the Meridian Gate, the funeral processions would be accompanied by other sons of the dead, princes and officials all the way to the tomb area.

The coffin would be shifted onto the grand hearse after being carried to the Meridian Gate. However, when the bier approaches the Duanmen the crown prince, would, white silk piece in hand, go to the ancestral temple to bid farewell to the ancestors. Afterwards, the funeral procession would go, by the way through the Deshengmen Gate, slowly to the tomb area located at the foot of the Tianshou Mountains. Along the way from Deshengmen to the tomb area a number of sacrificial altars were set up at such places as Tucheng, Qinghe, and Shahe for the relatives of the royal families, hereditary families with meritorious deeds, officials, monks and Taoist priests and country – squires to pay homage to the deceased emperor, but no populace was permitted to join in.

When the coffin arrived at the tomb area, it would first be laid in the Hall of Sacrifice with a ceremony being held here to appease the gods. When the burial time came the coffin would be carried into the underground palace (also called Xuangong) with another sacrificial ceremony being held prior to the removal of the coffin. However, before entering the gate (also called Huangtangmen) of the underground palace, another ceremony for offering "posthumous register", "imperial seal" and some other burial articles and clothes would again be held outside. After that the door of the underground vaults would be closed with another ritual held for offering sacrifice in front of it, thus putting an end to the over – elaborated funeral rituals

109

for a demised emperor.

89. 明朝迁都北京以后共有 14 个皇帝,为何明陵中仅有 13 座陵墓呢?

事情发生在明正统十四年(1449 年),在一次对北方少数民族瓦剌部的征战中,明英宗于土木堡被掳去。皇太后及群臣遂拥立其弟朱祁钰为帝,号景泰。景泰帝在位 8 年,曾在十三陵陵区内营建寿陵。英宗被放回来后,发动了"夺门之变",复辟了帝位,改年号为"天顺"。天顺元年,英宗废掉了景泰帝,并毁了其寿陵。景泰死后,就以亲王之礼将他葬到了西郊的金山上。因此,明朝迁都北京后,虽有 14 个皇帝,而这里只有 13 座陵墓。但到了成化十一年(1475 年),明宪宗恢复景泰帝号,将其墓扩建为皇陵。

After the capital of the Ming Dynasty was moved from Nanjing to Beijing, 14 emperors ever ruled here. Why were there only 13 tombs in the Ming Tombs area?

It happened in 1449, the 14th year of Zhengtong's reign when Emperor Yingzong was taken a captive in an expedition against the minority tribe Waci at Tumubao. Then, the empress dowager and some officials made his younger brother Zhu Qiyu the new emperor, naming the title of his reign "Jingtai". During the eight years of his reign, a tomb called Shouling was built in the tomb area. However, Yingzong staged a "coup of seizing the gate" several years after his return to the capital and resumed the throne, changing the title of his reign into "Tianshun". At the same time he abrogated Jingtai and had his tomb "Shouling" destroyed. After the death of Jingtai, he was buried at the Jinshan Hill in the western suburbs, treating him

110

as a prince. That's why there are only 13 tombs in the Ming Tombs area but it has 14 emperors after the removal of the Ming capital from Nanjing to Beijing. Nevertheless, in 1475, the 11th year of the Xianzong's reign, the emperor redressed him as Emperor Jingtai and had his tomb enlarged to the size and scale of that of an emperor.

90. 新帝是否一继位便开始修陵?

在民间,确有皇帝一继位便开始修陵之说,但实际情况并非都是如此。就十三陵的情况来看,长陵、永陵和定陵都是在皇帝还较年轻时就修完的。而有的皇帝生前并未修陵,例如献陵、裕陵和茂陵,都是在皇帝死了以后才匆匆修建起来的。

Is it the case that the tomb would soon be built after a new emperor ascended the throne?

Folk saying goes like this that a tomb would be built as soon as a new emperor ascended the throne. But actually it's not the fact. Take the 13 Ming Tombs area for instance, Changling, Yongling and Dingling were built when the emperors were relatively young, but some of the emperors did not do it during their lifetime. Xianling, Yuling and Maoling were all built hastily after the emperors passed away.

91. 十三陵的陵墓中是否都有地下宫殿呢?

古代人是讲迷信的,封建统治者们认为他们死后仍是统治者,所以要有豪华的住宅,死后还要用人殉葬,以便在冥中仍侍候他们。废止人殉制度后,还要以木俑来替代。秦始皇陵前的兵马俑,就是他死后仍在指挥着一个庞大军队的真实写照。从文献中看,也都有修建地下宫殿的类似记载。因此我们可以认为:十三陵的每座陵墓都是建有地下宫殿的,所不同的仅是规模大小不一罢了。

Do all 13 tombs in the Ming Tombs area have their underground palaces?

The people in ancient China were very superstitious and feudal rulers held that they were still ruling in the netherworld after their death. That is why they still wanted to live in luxurious palaces and to be waited upon by the living buried for them. After the institution of burying the living for the dead was abolished, wooden figurines were used instead. The terra — cotta warriors and horses in front of the tomb for Emperor Qinshihuang is a very true case, describing that he was still commanding a huge army even after his death. Besides, the historical records also have similar writings about the building of underground palaces. Therefore, we may believe that every tomb in the Ming Tombs area has its own underground palaces and the only difference lies in their size and scale.

92. 十三陵修陵用的各种物料都从何而来?

十三陵修陵所用的各种物料都是向各地摊派的。从文献上看,其所用之木料来自河南、河北、京西和湖北襄阳等地;砖是由江苏、山东和河北等地烧制的;而琉璃瓦则是由京城专设琉璃厂烧制而成的。

Where did all the materials for the building of the Ming Tombs come from?

The materials for the building of the tombs were apportioned to various places for contribution. The record has it that the wooden materials were taken from Henan, Hebei, north Beijing and Xiangyang of Hubei Province. Bricks were fired in Jiangsu, Shandong and Hebei, and the glazed tiles were made in the special kilns here in Beijing.

93. 陵区前的石牌坊是何时建造的? 有什么作用?

这座石牌坊建于明嘉靖十九年(1540 年),它是陵区的起点,是作为宣扬封建帝皇的功德而设置的,同时也起着标志物的作用。

When was that marble memorial archway at the entrance of the Ming Tombs area erected? And what's that used for?

Erected in 1540, the 19th year under the reign of Jiajing in the Ming dynasty, the marble memorial archway was erected to cite the meritorious and virtuous deeds of the feudal rulers. As a starting point, it is a symbol of the tomb area.

94. 可否讲一下华表的演变过程及其用途是怎样的?

华表,也称"恒表",它有着悠久的历史。在尧舜时期称为"谤木",是供人们在上面书写谏言、评论时政的。《淮南子·主术篇》中说:"尧置敢谏之鼓,舜立诽谤之木,何也? 答曰:今华表木也……或谓之表木,以表王者纳谏也。"又因这种"谤木"多设于交通要道之处,也起到认路的标志物的作用。随着历史的演进,华表又多设置在桥梁、宫殿、城垣或陵墓前,作为标志,后来就演变为建筑物旁的装饰品了。

设置在陵墓前的称"墓表",多系石造,柱身上一般均雕刻有蟠龙等纹饰,顶端为云板或蹲兽。那蹲兽名叫"望天",据称天安门华表上那两对蹲兽,其中门里的一对为"望君出",而门前的一对则称之为"望君归"。

How did the "Huabiao" (ornamental column) come into being? And what's that used for?

Tracing far back in history, "Huabiao", or "Hengbiao", was known as "Bangmu", a wooden column for people to write their opinions on the political affairs in the Yao and Shun period. As said in an article in the book of "Huainanzi", Yao set up drums for the people to make their complaints and Shun wooden columns to air their views and comments. This is the way the rulers in ancient China tried to gather opinions from the common people. As these columns were usually put up at crossroads or communications hubs, they also served as road-signs. However, as time went on, "Huabiao" tended to be erected by bridges, city gates and at the entrance of palaces or tomb-areas, hence a purely ornamental piece.

The one standing at the entrance of a tomb area is called "Mubiao," usually made of white marble pieces with curling dragons carved on it and topped with a carved stone plate or a squatting chimera called "Hou". It is said that of the two pairs of crouching chimeras atop the "Huabiao" inside and outside the Tian'anmen Gate, the one inside the Tian'anmen Gate is called "Wangjunchu," which means expecting the emperor's coming out from the palace, and the other in front of the Tian' anmen Gate is called "Wangjungui", meaning awaiting the emperor's return.

95. 神路上的碑亭是何时建起的？碑文的主要内容是什么？

此碑亭是明宣德十年十月（1435 年）建成的。亭中立一

114

穹碑,高三丈有余,龙首龟趺,称为"大明长陵神功圣德碑"。碑文长达 3,000 余字,为仁宗朱高炽所撰,其主要内容为成祖本纪。碑的背面刻有清康熙皇帝写的《哀明陵三十韵》;东侧记载着乾隆年间修缮明陵所用去的费用;西侧为嘉庆御笔,指出了明朝灭亡的原因。

When was the tablet tower at the entrance of the Sacred Way to the Ming Tombs area built? What's the gist of the inscriptions on the tablet?

The tablet tower, set up in 1435, the 10th year under the reign of Xuande of the Ming dynasty, houses a tablet which, standing on a tortoise pedestal, measures about 10 meters in height. It is called the tablet "To the Superb Merits and Virtues of the Demised Resting in the Tomb of Changling of the Ming Dynasty." The inscription on the front is written by Emperor Renzong, Zhu Gaochi, totaling 3,000 words. It tells the life – story of Emperor Chengzu. Inscribed at the back of the tablet is a "30 – line Lament over the Tombs of the Ming Dynasty" composed by Emperor Kangxi of the Qing dynasty and the eastern side records the expenses spent in repairing the Ming Tombs in the reign period of Emperor Qianlong. And the inscription on the western side written by Emperor Jiaqing himself, tells why the Ming Dynasty was destroyed.

96. 许多石碑均以龟为底座,这是为什么?

中国古代的神话传说称:龙生 9 子,各有其能,其中一子极善负重,名叫"赑屃",通常叫它龟。古代封建帝皇均自称为"真龙天子"。作为龙子的龟,又有负重的特别能耐,它为已经故去的老子去驮碑,乃是天经地义的尽孝道之事。还有一种说法是:

碑是用来为帝皇歌功颂德的,乃传世之物,而龟有千年之寿,以它驮碑,含有长久之意。

Many tablets use tortoises as pedestals, why is it so?

A mythological tale in ancient China goes like this: the dragon had nine sons, each having its own special ability and skill. One of them who was good at carrying heavy loads was called "Bixi", commonly known as "tortoise." In the days of old, feudal emperors all styled themselves as "real dragon", and the tortoise, as son of the dragon, was made to carry the tablet for his late father, was a thing of filial piety. However, another legend has it that the tablet, erected to eulogize the meritorious and virtuous deeds of emperors, is a hereditary objet that will go down from generation to generation for a long time to come. The tortoise, an animal enjoying a long life as of over 1,000 years, is a symbol of longevity. Therefore, it augurs well for the tortoise to bear the tablet.

97. 石像生前的两个石柱究竟起何作用?

陵前设石柱起源于汉朝,多设置于石兽之前,是仪仗开始的标志。只有明孝陵将石柱放在石兽和石像之间。

What's the use of the pair of stone columns leading the stone animals and figures along the spirit way of the Ming Tombs?

To put up stone columns in front of the tomb area was first introduced in the Han dynasty and some columns were usually made to stand at the head of the lines of stone animals, indicating the beginning of a tomb area. Only the stone columns at the Mingxiao Tomb in Nanjing stand between the stone animals and figures.

98. 陵前放置石像生起源于何时？有何意义？

陵前放置石像生的做法自秦汉以来就有了,那是为了表示帝王的威严和身份而设置的,也有守卫陵寝、避邪之含意。

When did the practice of putting up stone animals and figures in front of a tomb area start? And what does it signify?

The practice of putting up stone animals and figures in front of a tomb area started as early as the Qin and Han periods in Chinese history. It was used to show the supreme authority and dignity of the emperors, guard the tomb and ward off the evil spirits.

99. 这组石像生共有多少个？为何要放置这几种石像？

这组石像生共为 24 座,包括 12 石人:4 个勋臣、4 个文臣和 4 个武臣;石兽 12 对:分别是马、骐麟、象、獬豸、狮子、骆驼,各两坐两立。勋臣、文臣和武臣代表生前的文武百官,表示帝王的威严。狮子性猛,吼声极大,置于陵前能起到扶正压邪的作用;獬豸是传说中的异兽,头生一角,专触行为不端之人,表示善辨邪正之意;骐麟是传说中的异兽,是吉祥的象征。而马、骆驼及象都是当时不可缺少的交通运输工具,为皇陵前所必备之动物。

How many stone animals and figures are there in this group here? And why should these animals and figures be put up here?

The group consists altogether of 24 carved stone pieces including 12 stone figures of 4 officials with meritorious deeds, 4 officials and 4 generals. And the other 12 pairs of stone animals are the horses, elk – like chimeras (Qilin), elephants, unicorns (Xiezhi), lions and camels, each of them having two pairs with one pair in squatting posture and the other standing. The stone figures represent trains of officials and generals, showing the supreme authority and dignity of the emperor. As to the animals, the fierce lion bellowing very loudly in front of a tomb area, ward off the evil spirits. The unicorn is as said also a kind of chimera with only one horn at its forehead, with which it pierces only those dishonorable fellows, and the elk, another kind of strange animal, a symbol of auspiciousness. As to the horses, camels and elephants they are indispensable means of transportation, absolutely necessary for an imperial tomb area.

100. 为什么要在陵区内建造棂星门？

棂星门设置在不同的地方,其用意便有所不同。孔庙前设此门,含有招贤纳士之意;但陵墓前设此门,则称为"天门",意即过了此门,便可升上天界。

Why should a Lingxing Gate be built in a tomb area?

The Lingxing Gate (a latticed gate of a rectangular shape) put up in different places has different meanings. If it is put up in front of a Confucius temple it means to call in the virtuous and capable; if put up in front of a tomb it is called the "Heavenly Gate," which means once a person get through the gate he'll be able to ascend to heaven.

101. 长陵大殿建于何时？现存部分是原来的建筑吗？

长陵大殿，即恩殿，始建于明永乐七年(1409 年)，至宣德二年(1427 年)才建成。大殿面阔 9 间，进深 5 间，总面积为 1,956.44 平方米。现存大殿的梁架、大柱均系原有建筑。清康熙皇帝在其《哀明陵三十韵》中提到：“栋柱如旧椽木朽，檐瓦落地狐兔走，以其初建功力观，未修岂数百年久。”乾隆时曾对明十三陵进行过一次重修，花费白银 286,000 两。解放后，人民政府十分重视对历史文物的保护修缮工作，曾重新加以整修，并在建筑物上安装了避雷针。

When was the Grand Hall of the Changling Tomb built? Is the existing one that of the original?

The grand hall in the Changling Tomb area is the Great Sacrificial Hall, the construction of which started in 1409, the seventh year under the reign of Yongle and was finished in 1427, the second year under the reign of Xuande in the Ming dynasty. The hall, with nine – bays in width and five bays in depth, covers a total floor space of 1,956. 44 square meters. The existing crossbeams and columns of the hall are the original ones. About this Emperor Qianlong once mentioned in his "Thirty Lines' Lament over the Ming Tombs" like this: "Though the cross – beams and columns are still there, the rafters are gone. With eaves and tiles fallen onto the ground the foxes and hares make their lairs here. Judging from its original workmanship, how could it come to such a state of dilapidation within a lapse of only a little over hundred years." During the Qianlong reign period in the Qing the Ming Tombs had once undergone a repair, costing a total of 280,000 taels of silver. And then after liberation the people's government, paying a great attention to the preservation and protection of historical sites and cultural relics, has once again repaired the tomb, with a lightning rod installed onto the building.

102. 长陵大殿里的楠木大柱是从何地搞来的?

楠木分为大叶楠、小叶楠、乌楠、香楠、花楠和金丝楠木等数种,以金丝楠木为最名贵。恩殿的 60 根大柱是用金丝楠木制做的。这种楠木多产于四川、湖广、江西等地的深山老林之中。永乐四年,明成祖朱棣曾命礼部尚书宋礼、兵部左侍郎古朴、吏部左侍郎师逵去四川、江西、湖广等地督办采木。永乐十年,朱棣再次命宋礼前往四川采木。

像恩殿所用的这种大楠木,多系数百年才长成的。采伐这种木材,是十分艰辛和危险的。深山峡谷,多虎豹蛇蝎,又常有恶性传染病流行,采伐人往往有去无回,因而当地对伐木人所处的境况常有"入山一千,出山五百"之说。

木材的运输也很困难,大木伐下后,要等待山洪将它们冲出深山,然后经水路二、三年才能从千里之外运到京城附近的通州张家湾;再由那里转运至北京的神木厂,在那里加工成材后方能送往工地使用。可想而知,为了采运这些大楠木做柱子,是要以百姓们付出血汗和生命为代价的。

Where did the Nanmu wood for the columns of the Great Sacrificial Hall of the Changling Tomb come from?

The nanmu wood (phoebe zhennan) has several kinds, such as: the nanmu of broad and small foliage, of black and fragrant and some other kinds. But the best among them is that called Jinsi nanmu (gold – thread nanmu), a sort of wood of a very fine xylem. Growing in the deep mountain forests of

120

Sichuan, Hubei, Hunan and Jiangxi, the 60 columns for the Sacrificial Hall of the Changling Tomb are made of this kind of nanmu wood. Acting upon the imperial order by Emperor Zhu Di, Song Li, minister of the Board of Rites, Gu Po, vice-minister of the Board of Military Affairs and Shi Kui, vice-minister of the Board of Personnel were sent out to the aforesaid regions to take in the wood in the fourth year of Yongle reign period. And to make sure for the supply Song Li was dispatched again to Sichuan to buy the timber in the tenth year of the Yongle reign period.

The nanmu wood, big as that used for the building of the Great Sacrificial Hall in the Changling Tomb, normally takes several hundred years to grow to the size and the lumbering of it was very difficult and dangerous then. As the deep mountain valleys were the usual haunts of leopards and tigers and virulent with infectious diseases, the laborers were often easy to get in but difficult to return. About this the locals of Sichuan had a saying like this: "Enter the mountains by a thousand but no more than half will be able to come out."

When these giant trees were felled, they had to be carried down by mountain torrents. Afterwards it took two to three years to raft them to a wharf by Tongzhou. Then from there again they were transported to the sacred lumber works to be processed before being sent for use at the work – site. The lumbering and rafting of the nanmu wood meant to cost a great deal of lives and blood of the laboring people.

103. 长陵里埋葬的是哪个皇帝和皇后？

长陵里埋葬的是明朝第三个皇帝朱棣（年号永乐，庙号成祖)及其皇后徐氏。明成祖在位 22 年,是本朝皇帝中较有作为的一个。永乐十九年,他将都城由南京迁至北京,这一举措就颇具远见卓识,因为这对保卫边疆、巩固国防,是具有重要意义的。他也很重视文化方面的建设,他称帝后不久,即命翰林院学士解缙等为首,召天下文人三千,开始编写《永乐大典》,积五年之功而告成,共为 22,877 卷,凡例目录 60 卷。在航海方面,成祖曾于永乐三年至而二十二年,派三保太监郑和六下西洋,遍历亚、非大小 30 余国,是中国历史上规模最大、范围最广的一次出使活动。郑和下西洋,促进了与这些国家和地区的经济及文化交流,扩大了中国在世界上的影响。此外,朱棣还采取了一系列措施,进一步巩固了中央集权制的统治,为明王朝的发展奠定了基础。

Which emperor and queen of the Ming Dynasty were buried in the Tomb of Changling?

Buried together with his Queen née Xu in the Tomb of Changling is the third Emperor Zhu Di of the Ming dynasty, whose title of reign is Yongle and that of shrine Shenzong. During the 22 years of his reign he was, comparatively speaking, an emperor with some achievements. For instance, on the 19th year of his reign he decided to move his capital from Nanjing to Beijing. The move itself was in some way an expression of far – sightedness, because it was of great importance to strengthening national defence and guarding frontier areas. He also attached great importance to culture. Soon after he ascended the throne, an order was given to have Xian Jin, an academic scholar, be in charge of compiling the Great Encyclopedia of Yongle's Times by pooling in the efforts of over 3,000 scholars of the country. And it was finished in five years time with a total of 22,877 volumes in texts, apart from the 60 volumes of catalogue and notes. During the period from the third year to the 22nd year of his reign, Zheng He, also known as E-unuch Sanbao, sent by the emperor, had for six times been on board across the sea to over 30 countries in Asia and Africa. It was a diplomatic mission on an ever larger and broader scale in Chinese history. Zheng's mission abroad had greatly promoted the development of relationships between China and those countries in the fields of economic and cultural exchanges and enhanced the reputation and influence of China in the world. In addition, Zhu Di also adopted a series of measures in strengthening the centralization of state power, thereby laying a solid foundation for the development of the Ming Empire.

104. 听说有的陵内有两个甚至三个皇后,这是为什么?

十三陵陵区内埋葬的皇帝是 13 个,但却有 23 个皇后及 1 个贵妃。为什么会有这么多皇后呢? 在封建时代里,母以子为贵,儿子当了皇帝,其母亲就要追封为皇太后。例如:英宗的贵妃周氏生宪宗;宪宗的宫女纪氏生孝宗,妃子邵氏生献帝(世宗之父);世宗嫔女杜氏生穆宗,宫女李氏生神宗;神宗宫女王氏生光宗;光宗的宫女王氏生熹宗,淑女刘氏生思宗。她们都是在儿子当了皇帝以后才被封为皇太后的,随后再合葬或迁入各陵中。这种一陵多后的情况,也是明朝中期以后宫廷生活日趋奢靡荒淫的一种写照。

It is as said there were two or even three queens buried together with an emperor in one tomb, why is it so?

Buried in the Ming Tombs area were the 13 emperors, 23 queens and one imperial concubine of the Ming. How did it

123

happen that there were so many queens here? In China's feudal times, the status of a woman in the royal family would be raised when she had an heir prince son. After her son became the new emperor she would subsequently be endowed with the title of empress dowager. For example, the imperial concubine Zhou of Emperor Yingzong gave birth to Xiaozong, Concubine Shao to Xiandi, father of Shizong. Yet concubine Tu of Shizong gave birth to Muzong and his maid－in－waiting Li to Shenzong. The maid－in－waiting Wang of Shenzong to Guangzong, the maid－in－waiting Wang of Guangzong to Xizong and Lady Liu to Sizong. All of them were subsequently entitled the "empress dowager" when their sons became emperors. They were buried or removed to their respective imperial tomb. The fact, one tomb having two or more queens, reveals in a way the ever more dissolute life in the imperial court after the middle period of the Ming Dynasty.

105. 据说为给皇陵保密,陵墓修完以后,修陵的工匠都将被处死,有这回事吗?

自秦汉以来,就有这种传说。明代的皇陵有许多地面建筑,地下宫殿也都修建在地面建筑的中轴线上,加之十三陵周围有墙,且驻守着保卫皇陵的许多军队,这样兴师动众的事还有什么秘密可言呢!此外,修陵的工程非常浩大,所需之工匠民夫动辄上万。陵墓修完以后,要把这么多人一个不留,全都杀死也是不可能的。

Is it true that all tomb－builders were killed after the completion of a tomb in order to keep it a secret?

It is so said ever since the Qin and Han period. However,

124

each imperial tomb of the Ming Dynasty has a number of buildings on the ground and the tomb – vaults built correspondingly
along the central axis underneath. For the sake of safety the
tombs were walled in and heavily guarded by soldiers. Besides,
the project of tomb – construction was on such a large scale,
requiring tens of thousands of laborers. So how could there be
any secret to be kept? Moreover, it was impossible to kill so
many tomb – builders at a time without letting a single one slip
away.

106. 你能简述一下有关定陵的情况吗？

定陵是明朝第十三个皇帝神宗(年号万历)朱翊钧和两个皇
后孝端及孝靖的陵墓。朱翊钧 10 岁继位,58 岁逝世,在位共 48
年,是明朝历史上在位执政时间最长的皇帝。定陵的修建始于
公元 1584 年,历时 6 年,至公元 1590 年竣工,耗银 800 万两,占
地面积为 18 万平方米。

定陵的发掘工作是公元 1956 年 5 月开始的。它的发掘揭
开了明陵地宫之谜。地宫全都用坚硬的条石筑成,宫内分前、
中、后三室及左右两殿,总面积为 1,195 平方米。内无梁架,均
为石券拱结构。中殿设三张石雕宝座,后殿棺床上放着三口棺
木。地宫内的出土文物计达 3,000 余件之多。

**Could you say something in brief about the Tomb of Din-
gling?**

Dingling, the Tomb of Stability, is the tomb for Emperor
Shenzong by the name of Zhu Yijun the 13th emperor of the
Ming dynasty, whose title of reign is Wanli. He was buried
here together with his two queens – Xiaoduan and Xiaojing.
Zhu Yijun, ascended the throne at the age of 10 and died at 58

with a reign period of 48 years. Hence he was the emperor who was in power for the longest in the Ming Dynasty. The construction of the Dingling Tomb started in 1584. It took six years to complete the project in 1590, covering an area of 180,000 square meters and costing eightmillion taels of silver.

The excavation of Dingling began in May 1956, thus bringing to light the mystery of the underground palaces of the Ming Tombs. Built with hard stone – slabs, the underground palace consists of five beamless vaults, namely the front, the middle and the rear as well as the two on the right and the left, with a floor space of 1,195 square meters. Laid out in the middle vault are three thrones carved out of white marble and the rear hall with the bier holding three coffins for the emperor and his two queens. The archeological findings from the tomb come to a total of over 3,000 pieces.

107. 在修建定陵的工程中,谁是现场施工的负责人? 每日要用多少人工?

定陵的修建是由定国公徐文璧,辅臣申时行负责筹备工作;由兵部尚书张学颜、杨兆负责总督工程,由侍郎何起鸣负责现场督工。据文献记载,修建定陵的用工,每日平均为 2 - 3 万民工。

In the construction of the Tomb of Dingling, who was in charge at the worksite and how many laborers were required daily for the job?

The preparation for the construction of the tomb was carried out by Xu Wenbi, the duke of Dingguo, and his assistant Shen Shixing. The project was implemented under the super-

126

vision of Zhang Xueyan and Yang Zhao, ministers of the ministry of war and He Qiming, vice – minister of war took charge of the work at the worksite. The record has it that it required 200,000 – 300,000 laborers daily for the project.

108. 请问朱翊钧其人究系何等样的一位皇帝？

朱翊钧,年号万历,庙号神宗,是明朝第十三个皇帝。他是个昏庸、残暴、奢侈且荒淫无度的皇帝。在位 48 年,却有过半时间不问朝政。他 10 岁继位,不知世事,全仗大学士张居政辅助。张居政是位有名的政治家,在他辅政期间,对政治、军事、经济等各个方面进行了一系列利国利民的改革。万历十年,张居政病逝。此时已经长大成人的皇帝,非但不缅怀张的功劳,反而信谗抄没了其家产,取消了他所推行的一切改革措施。神宗皇帝的生活,奢侈惊人,仅采办一次珠宝就耗银 2,400 万两。为此,他派出大批矿监税吏,到各地敲诈勒索,扰民滋事。神宗还是个贪杯、残暴的好色之徒,几乎"每饮必醉",而醉后又行凶打人。据文献记载,被他醉后打死的宫人不下千余;此外,他还立十俊,选九嫔,纵容宠幸的郑妃横行于后宫。

Could you tell us what kind of an emperor Zhu Yijun was like?

Zhu Yijun, whose title of reign was Wanli and title of shrine Shenzong, was the 13th emperor of the Ming dynasty. Emperor Wanli was fatuous, cruel and indulged in a luxurious and dissolute life. He ruled the country for 48 years but spent most of his time in merry – making without paying any attention to state affairs. He ascended the throne at the age of 10. As a boy he was ignorant of any mundane affairs. So he had to rely on Grand Academician, Zhang Juzheng. Zhang Juzheng, a famous statesman, carried out in the period of his regency a number of reforms in the political, military and economic fields, which were beneficial to the nation and the people. However, at the 10th year in the reign period of Wanli, Zhang died of illness. At that time the emperor, already a grown – up then, not only failed to cherish the meritorious deeds that Zhang had done, but also had his house searched and his property confiscated. In addition, he abolished all the measures Zhang had taken during the reform. The emperor lived an extravagantly luxurious life. For instance, once he cost 24 million taels of silver to purchase jewels and pearls. To cover the expenses, he sent out a number of mining – controllers and tax – collectors to levy taxes or extort tributes, rousing a great turmoil all over the country. Besides, he was such a heavy drinker that he wouldn't stop drinking without getting muddle – headed. Once drunk he would take fancy in beating palace maids and butlers. The record has it that the number of people put to death in this way came to over 1,000. He also liked to take in a great number of charming young girls from among the people to serve as his concubines or palace maids. A certain imperial concubine Zheng he doted on was given the free rein to run wild in the rear of the palace.

109. 定陵的地面建筑仅存个遗址,这是为什么?

定陵的地面建筑曾数次遭到破坏。明朝末年,李自成率领的农民起义军进攻北京,当路过十三陵时,焚烧了几座坟墓,其中就有定陵。清兵入关时,为达报复之目的,又拆毁了陵区的一些建筑。1914 年,当地豪绅为产权之争而相互陷害,又放火烧了一次。这几次的破坏,使定陵的殿堂建筑全部荡然无存。

Why is it that all buildings on the ground at the Dingling Tomb were left in ruins?

The ground buildings at the Tomb of Dingling were subject to destruction time and again. At the end of the Ming dynasty, when the uprising army led by Li Zicheng passed the tomb area to attack Beijing, some of the Ming Tombs were burnt down, the Tomb of Dingling being one of them. Then later when the Qing army entered the central China some of the tomb buildings on the ground were once again devastated to exact the vengeance. Finally in 1914 when some local tyrants were locked in a strife for rights of property, they set fire on the tombs again, causing destruction to all the tomb-buildings with only the ruins left on the ground.

110. 在发掘明陵时,为什么首先发掘定陵呢?

定陵的发掘工作开始于 1956 年,1958 年正式对外开放。最初曾打算先挖长陵,但因考虑到缺乏经验,就想先挖出个较小一点的陵墓,以便边挖边总结经验。可在全面的勘察过程中,发现定陵的线索比较多,所以就决定先由这里挖起。

但时至今日,尚未对其它各陵进行发掘,这不是因为发掘技术的不足,而是在地下文物挖出之后,如何能使其保持原样不变? 在这个问题尚不能得到妥善解决之前,就不再轻易地去动其它各陵了。

Of all the Ming Tombs in the area, why was the Dingling Tomb the first to be excavated?

The excavation of the Tomb of Dingling started in 1956 and it was formally opened to the public in 1958. According to the initial plan the Tomb of Changling would be excavated first. However, due to the lack of experience, a decision was made to open up a smaller one instead in order to get some experience. In the course of exploration more clues were found for the excavation of the Tomb of Dingling, hence the decision.

But up to now no other tomb has been excavated. This is not because we are short of experience in the excavation, but how to retain the original shape and color of the findings is a problem. Before this problem is solved in a sufficiently better way we won't take it lightly to touch the other tombs any more.

111. 定陵的地下宫殿是如何发现的？

经国家批准，定陵的发掘工作自 1956 年 5 月始。在勘察过程中，考古人员在定陵东南侧的外墙皮脱落处，发现有几层墙砖塌陷下来，并露出了一些砖砌券门的痕迹。后来，在宝城内侧又发现了"隧道门"、"右道"、"宝城中"等字迹。这些发现为定陵的发掘工作提供了十分重要的线索。于是，考古人员便首先在宝城内侧正对券门的地方，开了长 20 米，宽 3.5 米的第一条探沟。发掘了两个月以后，又找到了用砖砌成的两道大墙，这便是隧道。它弯弯曲曲一直延伸到明楼之后。于是便按图索骥，又在明楼后开凿了长 30 米，宽 10 米的第二条探沟，并寻踪开挖至隧道尽头，发现了一块小石碑，上面刻着"此石至金刚墙前皮十六丈深三丈五尺"。依据小石碑的指引，又往西开了第三条探沟，发现在 40 米长的石隧道西头被一道大墙挡住了去路，那就是小石碑上所指示的金刚墙。墙的中间有道上窄下宽、稍向里倾斜的砖缝，原来这就是地下宫殿入口处的金刚门。从动工到找到地宫的入口，整整用了一年的时间。

How was the underground palace of the Dingling Tomb brought to light?

Authorized by the State Council the excavation of the Tomb of Dingling started in May, 1956. During the exploration it was found that at a place on the southeast some mortar pieces on the outside of the tomb – wall were flaking off, exposing signs of a brick – gate collapsed in the inside. Later such traces like a "leading tunnel of the gate," the "right passage" and the "central axis" were further found written on the inside of the tomb – wall. All this offered a very important clue for the tomb excavation. So the archeological workers began to dig the first exploration trench of 20 meters long and 3.5 meters wide. After a work of two months, they found two walls built of bricks leading from the arched gate to the backside of the tablet tower. Then they dug another trench of 30 meters in length and 10 meters in width up to the end. And from there a small tablet was found with an inscription: "From here to the diamond wall is 40 meters with a depth of 11.5 meters." A third trench of 40 meters long was dug according to the tablet, and at the end of it, a large wall was found blocking the way. This was the very aforesaid diamond wall. Revealing on the central part of the wall was something looking like a seam, which, slanting slightly inwards, was narrow on its top but wide at the bottom. This was the diamond gate, the entrance of the underground palace. From the very beginning to the discovery of the entrance to the underground palace it took a whole year's work.

112. 对发掘工作具有重要意义的那块小石碑是谁之所为呢?

小石碑究竟是何人所为,这是很难说清楚的。不过明陵的修建是由兵部、礼部和工部负责的。定陵修完时,神宗尚未死去,所以必须先用土将墓穴封起来。但为以后寻找地宫入口之便,埋下这块小石碑作为标志,也是情理之中的事。

Who set the small stone – tablet that was of great help to the excavation work of the tomb?

It's very hard to tell who did it. However, the building of the Ming tombs was carried out under the supervision of ministers of war, of rites and works. When the Dingling Tomb was completed Emperor Shenzong was still alive. So the tomb cavity and entrance had to be covered up first. However, to make it easier to find the entrance later it was reasonable to lay a small stone – tablet there to show the location of the tomb.

113. 地宫入口处的墙为何称作"金刚墙"?

金刚是从梵文译过来的,含有牢固、锐利、足以摧毁一切的意思。"金刚墙"之称,乃取其牢固不朽之意。

Why is the wall at the entrance of the Underground Palace called the "Diamond Wall"?

What we call "diamond" is a translation from the Sanskrit, meaning something is so solid and sharp that it is good enough to destroy anything against it. The "Diamond Wall" suggests that the wall be very much solidified against decaying.

114. 听说皇陵的陵门内都设有机关暗器,定陵内也有吗?

据文献记载,秦始皇陵的陵门内设有暗器,但他的皇陵至今尚未发掘,到底里面有没有暗器,这就很难说。定陵的陵门内是没有的。

It is said that in royal tombs, there are hidden weapons behind the tomb gates. Is there any found in the Tomb of Dingling?

The historical record has it that there are hidden weapons behind the tomb gate of Emperor Qinshihuang's Mausoleum. But so far the mausoleum has not been excavated, so no one knows whether there's any weapons hidden behind it. However, we can tell for sure that there's not any found in the Tomb of Dingling.

115. 定陵地宫入口的门是如何关闭和打开的?

这是游人非常感兴趣的一个问题。要说清楚如何打开的问题,首先就得说清楚当初是如何关上的。陵墓的大石门是采用倒关的办法闭上的,即是先将两扇石门合过地面的石槽,再将顶门石条立于槽内,然后用一种叫做拐钉钥匙的工具卡住石条,人就抽身出来,再将门从后带上。此时,顶门石正好卡落于门后的凹处,石门就紧紧地关上了。而考古人员在打开石门时,是先用铁丝套住门里面的顶门石,然后顺着门缝插入木板,将顶门石顶立起来,这样宫门就被推开了。因为事先已做好了充分的准备,打开这道门前后仅用了不到 10 分钟的时间。

How was the gate to the underground palace of the Tomb of Dingling closed and opened?

This is a question many Chinese and foreign tourists are interested in. To make it simpler as to how the tomb – gate was opened we have to know first how it was closed in the past. The door was closed from behind with a device, i.e. the two door – leaves were first brought passing the stone – block on the ground, leaving a gap there for the workman to slip out. Then the stone – bolt, known as the "self – acting stone," was made standing onto the block with a specially designed clutch to hold fast the upper – end of it. And finally when the workman started to slip out, the door was shut up behind him. At the same time the bolt fell automatically into the slot cut beforehand on the backside of the two door – leaves, thereby fastening the door tightly from behind. Before opening the door, the archeologists first fastened a wire onto the bolt to prevent it from toppling and then made it standing upright through the gap by pushing it with a plank from outside. The door was thus opened. It took less than 10 minutes to finish the job due to the thorough preparations made beforehand.

116. 地宫里的灯为何称作"长明灯"？

在封建时代,统治者在地宫里安放了巨大的瓷缸,里面装满了香油,并备有灯瓢灯芯,以期点燃以后能长明不灭,照耀他们于地下。实际上,这是不可能的。陵墓一经封上,里面的氧气很快就耗尽了,灯也就自然熄灭了。

Why was the lamp in the underground palace called the "Everlasting Lamp"?

In the feudal times, feudal rulers habitually liked to put large porcelain vats in their underground palaces, filling them up with sesame oil and pewters and wicks as well, hoping that the lamps would be bright forever to light them up in the underground palace. But actually this is impossible. Once the tomb cavity was sealed the oxygen inside would soon be exhausted and the lamplight naturally went out.

117. 门钉为什么会是九排呢？

据称大约是在春秋时代，中国就已有了乘法口诀。那是从一开始乘至九，而九九八十一是最高数字。在中国封建时代里，皇帝的地位至高无上，所以陵门便采用了这个数字。

Why are the doorknobs in nine lines?

It is as said that the rhymes of multiplication had already come into being in around the Spring and Autumn Period in Chinese history, starting from one and goes along to nine. The number nine multiplied by nine gets eighty – one, the highest in numbers. In the feudal society in China the emperors considered they were supreme both in social status and authority, so the number was adopted accordingly for the doorknobs of the tomb – gate.

118. 为什么铺首要取兽头的形状呢？

传说龙生九子而不象龙，但却各有所好。其中一子叫做狻猊，它平生好坐，今佛座狮子便是其像。门上的铺首也就是狻

135

猊,因它嗜坐,便令其看门。

Why are the doorknockers in the shape of an animal's head?

It is as said that the dragon had nine sons but none of them bore any resemblance to the dragon. However, each son had a special skill of his own, and the one by the name of "Suanni" had a habit of sitting without moving around. The lion-like chimera as a ride for Manjusri, the Bodhisattva as you see today is the very animal. The doorknockers are in the shape of "Suanni" too. As Suanni liked to sit there all the time, he was made to keep a watch on the door.

119. 配殿里殉葬用的是童男童女吗?

不是。据记载,明代没有用童男童女殉葬的规定。明初的几个皇帝,是用其嫔妃和宫女殉葬的。从明英宗遗诏废止殉葬后,便改用木俑替代,定陵里出土的就是木俑。

Were the living buried for the dead in the annexed halls the boys and girls?

No, they were not. The record has it that there was no such a rule in the Ming Dynasty as to bury boys and girls for the demised emperor. In the early days of the Ming Dynasty, some emperors had the living buried for the dead, but they were the concubines and maids in the palace. Since Emperor Yingzong abrogated, in his will, the rule of burying the living for the dead, wooden figurines were used instead. Those excavated from the Tomb of Dingling are the wooden figurines.

120. 何谓"金井"、"玉葬"?

皇帝死后,为显示自己身份的高贵,讲究"金井"、"玉葬"。所谓"金井",就是在棺床上留一长方形小孔,把破土修陵时从墓穴中取出的土放一些进去。依据迷信的说法,这样一来,便可起到阴阳结合的作用,对亡人是有好处的。"玉葬"便是在棺椁周围放些玉石,据说这样便可保持尸体不烂。当然,这也是一种毫无科学根据的说法。

What do the "gold – well" and the "jade – burial" really mean?

After the emperor passed away, great attention was paid to the "gold – well" and "jade – burial" in order to show his imperial dignity. The so – called "gold – well" simply meant to leave a small rectangular hole on the coffin – platform, and then put into it a few pinches of earth gathered from breaking the ground of the tomb at the beginning of the project. The superstitious view in feudal times holds it that to do it in this way would make the positive and negative in harmony, thereby favorable to the deceased soul in the nether world. The "jade – burial" meant to put some bits and pieces of jade – stones round the coffin bier, for it would as said prevent the corpse within the coffin from decaying. Surely it is utterly groundless in terms of science.

121. 朱翊钧和两个皇后是同时死去的吗?

不是的。右边的孝靖后姓王,系河北宣化人。初为宫女,16岁时被神宗奸污,封为宫妃、皇贵妃。因她生了长子,遭到来自神宗宠妃郑氏的妒嫉、暗算,47岁就死了,比神宗早死9年。死后按贵妃礼葬于东井,后来她生的儿子当了皇帝,才迁葬至定陵。

左边的孝端后乃浙江余姚人,也为王姓,是朱翊钧的原配皇后。1620 年 4 月死去,比朱翊钧早死 3 个月。那年 10 月,神宗和两个皇后一起被葬入定陵地宫。

Did Emperor Zhu Yijun die at the same time with his two queens?

No, it was not the case. Queen Xiaojing on his right, whose surname was Wang, was a native of Xuanhua County, Hebei Province. She used to be a maid in the court. At the age of sixteen, she was raped by the emperor and then was bestowed the title as Concubine Gong. After she gave birth to a son, the heir prince, she was promoted to be an Imperial Consort. However, persecuted by Concubine Zheng, a great favorite of the emperor, she died early at the age of 47, nine years ahead of the emperor, and buried in the "eastern well" in line with the rites for the imperial concubine. Later when her son ascended the throne she was removed to the right side of the dead emperor in the Tomb of Dingling.

Queen Xiaoduan on the left, whose surname was also Wang, a native from Yuyao County, Zhejiang Province, was the first wife of the emperor. She died in April, 1620, only three months earlier than the emperor himself. In October of the same year Emperor Shenzong was buried together with his two queens in the underground palace of the Dingling Tomb.

122. 定陵地宫里各殿的尺寸分别是多少?

定陵地宫的前殿宽 6 米,长 26 米,高 7.2 米;中殿宽 6 米,长 32 米，高 7.2 米；两配殿都是宽 6 米，长 26 米，高 7.4 米；后殿宽 9.1 米，长 30.1 米，高 9.5 米，总面积为 1,195 平方米。

What is the respective size of the halls in the underground palace of the Tomb of Dingling?

The front hall in the underground palace of the Tomb of Dingling measures 6 meters in width, 26 meters in length and 7.2 meters in height. The middle hall is 6 meters in width, 32 meters in length and 7.2 meters in height. The two annexed halls both measure 6 meters in width, 26 meters in length and 7.4 meters in height while the rear hall is 9.1 meters in width, 30.1 meters in length and 9.5 meters in height. The floor space of these halls totals 1,195 square meters.

123. 凤冠有多重？皇后平时是否戴它呢？

从定陵中出土的凤冠共有四顶,因冠上所饰龙凤数目不等,所以重量也不一样。其中一顶六龙三凤的凤冠,重约 3 公斤。这么重的凤冠,皇后平素是不戴的,只有在朝贺时作为礼冠才戴一下。

How heavy is the phoenix crown? Does the queen wear it normally?

Excavated from the Tomb of Dingling were four phoenix crowns for the queens. As the dragons and phoenixes stuck on the crowns for decoration are not of the same number, their weights are different. One of the crowns with six dragons and three phoenixes on it weighs three kilograms. For such a heavy crown the queen would not wear it in normal time, but wore it on ground occasions.

124. 金冠有多重? 它是怎样制作的?

金冠重900克。其制作程序是用金拔丝,然后自上而下编织,直至冠沿,再将丝头用金箍扣住。冠下的二龙戏珠、龙麟是用缧丝法焊接起来的,显示了一种相当高超的艺术水平。

How heavy is the gold crown? How was it made?

The gold crown weighs about 900 grams. The way of making was like this: the gold must first be drawn into very fine threads, and the knitting was from the top down to the rim till finally to be wound up with a gold ring. At the lower bottom of the crown are the two gold dragons playing with a pearl. The dragon's scales are piled up by way of wielding, requiring a very high artistic level in the craftsmanship.

125. 定陵中出土的丝织品有哪几种? 织物的花纹图案又有几种?

定陵中出土的丝织品有绫、罗、绸、缎、纱、绢及帛等。织物的花纹图案分为大类字面纹样和大类花纹样两种:大类字面纹样的有万寿无疆、洪福齐天、万事大吉、万寿福禄;大类花纹样的有四季花卉、兰桂齐放、岁寒三友、八宝云龙、团龙、团凤、团鹤、暗八仙及柿蒂过肩龙等等。

How many kinds of silk products were excavated from the Dingling Tomb? And how many woven patterns are there on those silk pieces?

From the Tomb of Dingling we have found damask and silk gauze, silk fabrics, satins and sheer as well as thin yet tough silk and other silks, etc.. The patterns on the silk pieces we've found are in general the following two types: one is with Chinese characters, and another with various kinds of flowers. The character patterns mean: boundless longevity, limitless blessing, everything's just fine and long life with happiness and officialdom, etc.. The flower patterns display blossoms of the four seasons, orchids, sweet osmanthus, pine - trees, bamboo and plum - blossoms, clouds, dragons, phoenixes and red - crested cranes, eight immortals and so on.

126. 十三陵修陵所用的砖,为何大多均刻印着文字?

为了修建地宫及皇陵等工程之需,工部要求全国各地烧砖供应,且对所需之砖均有严格要求。为便于检验,规定承办单位和个人要在砖上打印文字,最详细的还有年、月、日,乃至产地、委官、窑户及窑匠的姓名等等。

这些文字的留存,成了研究明史、建筑史的宝贵资料。仅康陵一处,砖的产地就来自河南、山东和江苏各府所属 39 个县。

到了明朝晚期,工部在山东临清设立工部厂,集中烧制,年产砖 100 万块。临清的烧砖历史悠久,烧成的砖质量好,虽经数百年之久而砖形不变。

Why do most of the bricks used in building the Ming Tombs bear some characters?

The Ministry of Works required the whole country to supply high - quality bricks to the construction of the imperial tombs. To make it easier for the check - up, the ministry worked out a set of strict rules: every working - unit or individual should imprint on bricks the date, time and place of production. Some bricks even had to display the name of the official in charge of production and the name of the kiln as well as kiln – artisans.

The words and characters on the bricks have now become valuable materials for the study of the Ming history and of the civil engineering in that period. The rubbings from the bricks used for the building of the Kangling Tomb alone reveal that the bricks used for the building of these tombs came from the 39 counties of Henan, Shandong and Jiangsu provinces.

By the end of the Ming dynasty, the Ministry of Works built kilns in Linqing County, Shandong Province for the special purpose of turning out bricks in a massive way with an annual output of one million pieces. Linqing has a long history in making bricks. The bricks turned out in Linqing are of very high quality, which, even after an endurance of hundreds of years, brook no deformation at all.

127. 为何陵前的这些石碑上都没有字呢?

陵前树起无字碑,仅在唐高宗和武则天的乾陵有此先例。至于十三陵的无字碑,据《世宗实录》载,长、献、景、裕、茂、泰及康七陵门前的碑,均系嘉靖年间先后六年之间建立起来的。要想让一贯懒于问政,专心于得道成仙的嘉靖帝一下子撰就七篇碑文,那自然是办不到的,于是碑就只能空着树起来了。后续的皇帝,因祖宗碑上无字,自己也就难于下笔了。这恐怕就是十三陵前无字碑的由来吧!

Why do all these tablets in front of the tombs bear no inscriptions on them?

The Qianling Mausoleum for Emperor Gaozong and Empress Wu Zetian of the Tang Dynasty took the lead in setting up the wordless tablet. As to the wordless tablets in the Ming Tombs area, the Historical Record of Shizong has it that the tablets in front of the seven tombs of Changling, Xianling, Jingling, Yuling, Maoling, Tailing and Kangling were all put up within the six years during the Jiajing reign period. Emperor Jiajing was lazy in court administration but set his heart all the time on acquiring witchcraft to become an immortal. It was impossible for him to finish writing seven articles for these tablets at a go. Therefore, the tablets could only be left standing there with no inscriptions. The following emperors had to follow his example by setting up wordless tablets in front of their tombs. This is perhaps how the wordless tablets came about in the Ming Tombs area.

128. 历代的陵墓名称上为何都有重名的呢?

历代帝王为其陵墓起名时,均十分讲究喜庆吉祥,所以重名的陵墓颇多,譬如:太祖孝陵与后周武帝之陵名相同;成祖长陵与汉高祖、魏孝文帝陵同;仁宗献陵与唐高祖、金穆宗同;宣宗景陵与魏宣武帝、唐宪宗、金睿宗同;英宗裕陵与金显宗同等等。

Why is it that many royal tombs in different dynasties had the same names?

When giving a name to the imperial tomb, emperors of different dynasties paid great attention to jubilation and auspiciousness. This is why many royal tombs in different dynasties had the same names. For instance, Xiaoling for Ming Taizu had the same name as that for Emperor Wu in later Zhou Dynasty; Changling for Chengzu was same as that for Gaozu of the Western Han and that for Emperor Xiaowen of the Wei

Dynasty. Xianling for Renzong bore the same name as that for Gaozu of the Tang Dynasty and that for Emperor Muzong of the Kin Dynasty. Jingling for Xuanzong was also same as that for Emperor Xuanwu of the Wei Dynasty, Emperor Xianzong of the Tang Dynasty and Ruizong of the Jin Dynasty. And the name of Yuling for Yingzong was same as that for Xianzong of the Kin Dynasty, and so on and so forth.

129. 为什么古代的宫殿、陵墓多红墙黄瓦呢？

红表示胜利、成功等吉庆喜事。黄属土,土乃社稷之本,因而封建帝王均惯用黄色,如皇帝穿黄袍,发出的文告用黄纸书写,称为黄榜;清朝对有功大臣特赐黄马褂等。

Why do many palaces and tombs of ancient times have red walls and yellow tiles?

The red represents auspiciousness and jubilation, suggesting a great victory or success; and yellow is the color of earth, regarded as the altar of the state. So the feudal rulers liked to use things in yellow. For instance: Emperors cloaked themselves in yellow robes and the imperial edicts were written on yellow paper, naming them "Yellow Notices." In the Qing dynasty if a high - ranking official rendered great service he would be bestowed with a yellow sleeveless jacket.

130. 什么叫做"丹陛"？

丹为朱红色,陛系宫殿前的台阶。丹陛就是用红漆涂饰的台阶,也称"丹陛",即是帝王宫殿前的台阶。

What is that called "Danbi"?

"Dan" means scarlet, and "Bi," the flight of steps in front of a palace. So "Danbi" means steps painted in red, or the "Scarlet Steps," the flight of steps in front of the royal palace.

131. 崇祯皇帝吊死煤山后,是谁将其埋葬到十三陵的?

崇祯十七年(1644年)3月19日,由闯王李自成率领的农民起义军攻下北京城,明朝最后一个皇帝崇祯吊死在煤山。李自成进城后,命人将崇祯及其皇后周氏的梓棺送往昌平。此时,官府已无力营葬,昌平吏赵一桂及好义之士孙繁祉、白绅等共捐铜制老钱340千,雇民夫打开田贵妃墓,将崇祯和周氏葬了进去。后至清朝顺治时,特遣工部为崇祯陵修了三间享殿,立了碑记,并筑起了围墙,称"思陵"。思陵原系贵妃陵,是十三陵陵区内最小的一个皇陵。

Who buried Emperor Chongzhen in the Ming Tombs area after he hanged himself at the coal – hill?

On March 19, 1644, the 17th year under the reign of Emperor Chongzhen the uprising army led by Li Zicheng captured the city of Beijing. Emperor Chongzhen, the last emperor of the Ming Dynasty hanged himself at the coal – hill. But when Li Zicheng entered the city he gave the order to had the coffins for the emperor and his queen sent to Changping. At that time the local government was unable to bury the dead emperor. However, a local petty official named Zhao Yigui together with generous esquires Sun Fanzhi and Bai Shen and others pooled in some 340 strings of old copper coins, and they hired a few laborers to have the imperial concubine Tian's tomb opened and put the dead emperor and his queen into it. Later, during the reign period of Emperor Shunzhi in the Qing the Ministry of Works was ordered to have a three-bay sacrificial hall built and a tablet erected for Chongzhen and rounded them up with a wall, naming it "Siling". As the Siling Tomb used to be the tomb for an imperial concubine, it is the smallest one among the thirteen tombs in the Ming Tombs area.

故 宫
(The Imperial Palace)

132. 你能简述一下有关故宫的情况吗？

故宫,也称紫禁城,位于北京市的中心,是明清两朝的皇宫。它是中国现存规模最大、保存最完整的宫殿建筑群,也是世界上最大的宫殿群。

故宫建于 1420 年,五百多年以来,先后有明清两朝的 24 个皇帝在此统治全国。1911 年孙中山领导的辛亥革命推翻了满清皇朝的统治。1925 年,故宫对外开放。解放后分批进行了修缮,现已面貌一新。

故宫占地面积为 72 万平方米,其建筑面积为 15.5 万平方米。共有各类宫室建筑 890 多座,约 9,000 余间房。故宫内珍藏着大量的历史文物及艺术品,因此,它是中国最大的文化艺术博物馆。

Could you say something in brief about the Imperial Palace?

Located in the center of Beijing, the former Imperial Palace, also known as the Purple Forbidden City, was the royal palace for the Ming and Qing dynasties. It is the largest and most well - preserved complex of palaces in China, as well as the largest group of palaces in the world.

During the past 500 years since its completion in 1420, it had been used by the 24 emperors of the Ming and Qing dynasties to rule over the country. The revolution of 1911 led by Dr

Sun Yat-sen brought en end to the Qing government. The Forbidden City became unforbidden and was opened to visitors in 1925. After liberation in 1949, the Imperial Palace underwent renovations part by part, thereby presenting a completely new feature.

Covering an area of 720,000 square meters (about 250 acres), it has a floor space of 155,000 square meters with more than 890 palace buildings containing over 9,000 rooms in various sizes. The palace museum holds a great number of historical and cultural relic as well as precious works of art. Therefore, it is the largest museum of culture and art in China.

133. 紫禁城的城墙有多高、多宽？其南北、东西各长多少？周长又是多少？

紫禁城墙高 10.3 米，上宽 6.8 米，下宽 8.2 米；其墙南北长为 960 米，东西长为 750 米，周长为 3.43 公里。

How high and thick is the wall of the Purple Forbidden City? How long is it from east to west and from north to south? And what is its circumference?

The wall of the Purple Forbidden City stands at 10.3 meters high, 6.8 meters thick on the top and 8.2 meters at the bottom. From east to west, the wall extends 750 meters, and from north to south, 960 meters, with a circumference of 3,430 meters.

134. 谁是故宫建筑过程中著名的设计师呢？

故宫是明清两朝的皇宫，自明永乐三年(1407 年)开始修建，至永乐十八年(1420 年)建成，至今已逾 500 多年的历史。

这个迄今最完整、规模最大且雄伟壮丽的古代宫廷建筑群，莫说在当年动工兴建时实属不易，就是这 500 多年来的维修保固工程，也不知耗费了多少能工巧匠们的心血和殚精竭虑的努力。而在故宫修建工程中，最出类拔萃的一位建筑工程设计师，就得数以木匠为业的雷发达了。

雷发达系江西南康人，其家世代以木工为业。雷幼年时，曾随其父从江西到了南京，在那里所见的宫殿、庙宇和城楼等建筑，或精巧，或雄伟，都曾以好奇之心加以观察，并在其心灵里留下了深刻的印象。稍长，即一面从事木工，一面学会打样，因而不久便成了闻名南京的能工巧匠，时年仅为 30 岁。十年后，清廷修缮宫禁，其中以太和、中和、保和三大殿工程最大，亦最艰巨。雷发达以其杰出的工匠之才被召入京，担负起三大殿的设计修建之责。迄今，经他修缮后的清代故宫仍保持着原有的风貌。自此以后，雷发达的高超技艺得到了清廷的赏识，遂一直在北京供职，担任皇宫的修缮设计工作，直至康熙三十二年（1693年）病逝北京，享年 73 岁。

他死了后，他的儿子雷金玉继承了他的职务，此后一直传到他的后人，至光绪末年的雷廷昌而止。他们祖孙数代，先后参与过的设计工程，除了皇宫以外，还有圆明园、颐和园、静宜园和三山（万寿山、玉泉山及香山）、三海（北海、中海及南海），以及清东陵（在河北省遵化县境内）、西陵（在河北省易县境内）等等。所有这些工程都是当时最艰巨的工程项目，而且图样也出自雷家，实际上，他们就是这方面的权威，因而也就被人们别称为："样子雷"、或"式样雷"及"样房雷"。

Who was the architect of the former Imperial Palace?

The Imperial Palace was the royal palace during the Ming and Qing dynasties. The construction started in 1407, the 3rd year in the reign period of Emperor Yongle in the Ming and

150

was finished in 1420, the 18th year of his reign. It has a history of over 500 years.

The construction of the largest and most magnificent palace was very difficult at that time, and the protection and maintenance alone during the past 500 years has been very difficult too, requiring numerous designers and builders to work their heart out. However, the most outstanding designer was none other than Lei Fada, who used to be a carpenter.

A native in Nankang County, Jiangxi Province Lei was brought up in a carpenter's family. When he was quite young he followed his father to Nanjing, where the beautiful palaces, temples and archways left a deep impression on him. Later, when he grew up he started his career as a carpenter, and meanwhile he learned to do the designing. Not long afterwards, he turned out a cut in his craft when he was only 30 years old. Ten years later, the Qing Court started a large – scale palace construction, and the largest and the most difficult project work was the three main halls – the Hall of Supreme Harmony, the Hall of Complete Harmony and the Hall of Preserving Harmony. Lei Fada, as a well – known carpenter, was summoned to Beijing in charge of designing for the building and renovation of the three main halls. Up to now the Qing palaces built and renovated by him still retained their original features. His superb skill left a very good impression on the Qing Court. From then on he stayed in Beijing dedicating himself to the construction and renovation of the Qing royal palaces. In 1693, the 32nd year in the reign of Emperor Kangxi he died of illness in Beijing at the age of seventy – three.

After his death, his son Lei Jinyu and descendants succeeded him in his career, and it was not until Lei Tingchang that he brought the career to a finish at the end of Guangxu reign period. In addition, the Lei family members were responsible for many other projects too, such as the Yuanmingyuan Garden, Summer Palace, Jingyi Garden, Jingming Garden, Longevity, Jade Fountain and Fragrance Hills, North, Central and South Seas, and the Eastern Qing Tombs in Zunhua County, Hebei Province and the Western Qing Tombs in Yixian County. As these were the most difficult projects at the time with the designs all done by the Leis, the family naturally became an acknowledged authority in the craft, hence being addressed as "Lei the designer," "Lei the shaper" or "Lei the projector."

135. 为什么故宫又称作紫禁城?

封建帝皇居住的宫殿,是不许人民进入或靠近的,周围用一道高大的城墙环绕起来,御林军把守,戒备森严。那时,仅皇帝、皇后、妃子,以及皇族和太监才可以住在里边,所以便称之为"禁城"。

但是为什么又叫做"紫禁城"呢?说法却又不一,一种说法认为:紫禁城的"紫"字与"紫气东来"的"紫"字是同一含意,以祥瑞云气象征帝皇;另一种说法认为:传说天帝是住在天上的"紫宫"里的,而皇帝又自称是"天子",天子住的宫殿就相当于天上的"紫宫",因此便把皇宫也称作紫禁城;还有第三种说法认为:紫禁城的"紫"是指紫微星垣,为皇帝的代称。中国古代天文学家将天上的恒星分作三垣、二十八宿及其它星座。三垣为太微垣、紫微垣和天市垣。"太平天子当中坐,清慎官员四海分"。紫微星垣在三垣的中央,因此称为天子。这后两种说法较为接近。

Why was the Imperial Palace again called the "Purple Forbidden City"?

The former Imperial Palace was forbidden to the public, and in feudal times no access to it was permitted. Surrounded with a high and thick wall, and heavily guarded like a citadel, only emperors, empresses and concubines, the royal families and eunuchs were allowed to live, stay and move around inside the city, hence the name "Forbidden City."

But why was it called the "Purple Forbidden City"? Some said that the word "Purple" was derived from the phrase: "The purple air drifts over from the east," in which the auspicious purple air represented the emperor. Others held that the "Heavenly emperor" lived in the "Purple Palace" in heaven. So the emperor, a self – styled "Son of the Heaven" should live in the "Purple Forbidden City." Still others believed: the word "Purple" was the symbolic color of the North Star, which represented the emperor. In ancient China, astronomers put stars in the heaven into three constellations and 28 lunar mansions. The North Star was the center of cosmic, corresponding to the "Son of the Heaven." Of the above three expressions the latter two seem close to each other.

136. 明朝有多少人参加了故宫的修建工作？工程中所用的木材、石料来自何处？

据记载,明初修建故宫时,曾役使了 10 万工匠和 100 万民夫。木材均由四川、贵州、广西、湖南和云南等省的大山里采伐而来。据称大树砍倒以后,要等到雨季,利用山洪将其从山上冲下来,然后再经江河水路运到北京。石料大都是从北京附近的房山、盘山等地的山上采集来的。

How many people took part in the construction of the Ming Imperial Palace? Whence came the wood and stone materials for it?

A statistic record has it that more than 100,000 artisans and over one million conscripted laborers took part in the construction of the Ming Imperial Palace. The wood materials were taken from the mountains of Sichuan, Guangxi, Guizhou, Hunan and Yunnan. It is said that the trees felled had to be brought down by mountain torrents during rainy seasons, and then were towed to Beijing through waterways. The stone materials was quarried from the nearby hills in Fangshan county and Panshan area.

137. 紫禁城内共有多少个房间?

民间传说称:故宫内有房九千九百九十九间半,并说天上玉帝的皇宫里有房一万间,地下的皇帝不敢僭越,故少半间。那么,这半间房在那里呢? 即指文渊阁楼下西头的那一小间。事实上, 紫禁城内有房屋九千余间,而所谓的半间不过是一种牵强附会的造作而已。文渊阁西头的那一间,其面积虽小,仅能容得一楼梯,但仍是一个整间。因为文渊阁是储藏中国第一部《四库全书》的所在,为了取"天一生水,地六成之,以水克火之意,故文渊阁的房间数便一反紫禁城内房屋均以奇数为间的惯例,采用了不讲对称的偶数——六间。然而,为了布局上的美观,只得把西头的一间造得格外小一些。

How many rooms are there in the Purple Forbidden City?

A popular saying goes like this: there are 9,999 and a half rooms in the Forbidden City and the palace for the Jade Em-

154

peror in the heaven has 10,000 rooms. The emperor on the earth dared not overstep the "emperor in heaven," so the number of rooms in his palace is half a room short. Where is that half room located in the Forbidden City? It refers to the room at the western side of the Wenyuan Pavilion. Though small in size with a space only for a flight of stairs it is still considered as a room. As the Wenyuan Pavilion was the storage for China's first edition of Si Ku Quan Shu (the Imperial Library of Qianlong) the number of rooms in it is an even number of six in contradiction to the usual odd number in all other palace buildings. In this way, it attributes to a Chinese saying:"the heaven the number one to produce water and the earth the sixth to retain it," which means the water will be able to subdue fire so as to keep the storage in safety. However, to make the pavilion look stylish in structure, the room at the western side was designedly made a bit smaller in size.

138. 明、清两代的宫女、太监有多少人？

据说明代末年,在皇宫中的宫女有九千人,太监达十万人。到了清代,虽在数量上有所减少,按定制太监为二千二百六十名,宫女约在三百人以上,但实际上不止此数。另外,每年所要役使的"苏拉",即杂役人员,约在数万人次左右。

How many palace maids and eunuchs were there in the royal palaces during the Ming and Qing dynasties?

It is said that there were more than 9,000 palace maids and over 100,000 eunuchs engaged in service in the royal palace at the end of the Ming dynasty. Though their numbers were greatly reduced in the Qing the fixed number of eunuchs still reached 2,260 and the palace maids over 300. However, the actual numbers were far more than those. For every year, it still needed a supply of scores of thousands of "Sula" (the odd-job man) to do odd jobs in the royal palace.

139. 故宫里的红墙黄瓦是何含意?

故宫建筑所使用的色彩,除了追求外表上的美观外,更为突出的是反映了它的封建政治内容。鲜明的红墙黄瓦色彩,强烈地显示了封建帝皇的"权威"、"尊严"和"富有"。

黄色,自古以来就被统治阶级视为是尊贵的颜色,因为黄色在五行学说中代表了中央的方位,中央属土,而土为黄色。

红色,在中国也一直被人们视为是代表吉祥喜庆的正色,含有庄严幸福的意思。据说早在四、五万年前的山顶洞人就好用红色来装点自己的房屋。

封建皇宫建筑采用黄色琉璃瓦顶,至少在宋代就已开始了。明、清两代更明确了这样的规定:只有皇宫、皇陵或皇帝下令修建的坛庙等建筑,才能使用黄色琉璃瓦为顶。谁违反了这个规定,就会被处以极刑。

故宫因其是帝王居住的地方,所以基本上都采用了黄瓦红墙。但也有少数建筑物采用了黑瓦和绿瓦的,这是因为这些建筑物不是皇帝居住的所在,也有的则是因为封建迷信的缘故。如东华门内的"南三所",是清代皇子所居住的地方,按规定:清代亲王、郡王等高级贵族住宅只能用绿瓦,不得用黄瓦。又如"文渊阁"是黑色,黑色是代表水的颜色。文渊阁是藏书楼,容易起火,使用黑瓦,乃含有以水克火的迷信观念在内。

What do the palatial buildings with purple-red walls and yellow-tile roofs in the Forbidden City mean?

The colors used to apply on the palatial buildings in the

Forbidden City, except for the outside beautification, attributed much more to the feudalistic implications in politics. The purple – red walls in combination with the yellow roofs form a strong and eye – catching contrast, showing the absolute "authority," "supremacy" and "richness" of feudal emperors.

Ever since ancient times, yellow color, has always been regarded by rulers of various dynasties as to denote supremacy. Because in the theory of Five Elements in ancient China, yellow, referring to the earth that occupies the central position, represents supreme royal power in the center.

"Red" in China has as always been mentioned in the same breath with righteousness and auspicious ceremonies, suggesting solemnity and happiness. It is said that even the upper – cave men of 40,000 – 50,000 years ago liked to paint their dwellings in red.

As to the use of yellow – glazed tiles in the construction of royal palaces, it was initiated as early at least as the Song Dynasty. In the Ming and Qing dynasties it was specified that only imperial palaces, tombs for demised emperors and temples or altars built according to imperial edicts could use yellow glazed tiles in the construction. Whoever went against these rules should be put to death without exception.

As the imperial palace was the residence for emperors and his families, the most part was built with the walls painted in red and the roofs covered with yellow glazed – tiles. However, there were still a few palace buildings with black or green tiles. This is because these palace buildings were not used by emperors, and still, it was due to some superstitious reasons. For instance, the three palace buildings located to the south inside the Donghuamen Gate they were the residences for the Qing princes. According to the given rules only green tiles could be used for the Qing high – ranking nobles, such as princes and their like and no yellow tiles should in any case be used. The other example is the Wenyuan Pavilion with black tiles. According to the theory of Five Elements, black represents water. Since the pavilion was meant for storing books, it was easy to catch fire. Therefore, in line with the superstitious idea of the ancients, black tiles were used instead in its construction so as to suggest that it could subdue fire.

140. 故宫的金砖、城砖从何而来？在规格和制作方面有何特点？

金砖:即是明清时期各宫殿内铺地所用的方砖。主要产自苏州各地区。其制作过程是比较复杂的,仅取土一项就要经过掘、运、晒、樵、磨、筛等数道工序;接着还得经过六道工序才能成为制坯的泥,再经过多道工序,历时八个月才能制作成坯;砖坯装窑后还得用草、柴及松枝等烧制 130 天。砖烧成后得另用桐油浸泡,这样铺在地上才能光润耐磨,越磨越亮。据记载,明嘉靖年间,烧 50,000 块砖需花 3 年的时间;清代的每块金砖约合九钱六分白银,在当时可买一石大米,供一名窑工吃 3 个月。砖烧成后送往北京检验,每一块砖都要求使之"敲之有声,断之无孔",官府才算通过检验,予以收下。

城砖:城砖和墙砖是供垒城砌墙用的,其主要产地是山东临清一带。城砖要求长 1.5 尺,宽 7.5 寸,厚 3.6 寸。其质地坚细,色白声响。此外,明清时期也在北京东郊的河西务、广渠门及河南彰德、河北武清仓等地设窑烧砖,以供故宫修建之用。

Whence came the "gold – bricks" and the "city – wall bricks" used in the construction of the Imperial Palace? What is the size and specific feature of a brick in the production?

Gold Bricks: Produced mainly in the area of Suzhou, the square bricks used for paving the ground in the Ming and Qing palace buildings were called "Gold Bricks." The process in the making of a brick was very complicated, requiring over dozens of processes. For instance, to fetch clay alone had so many processes as digging, carrying, sun – baking, grinding and screening, etc. And after that another six processes were required before being made into qualified clay for the adobe. So it took altogether eight months to turn raw materials into a piece of adobe. Then when the adobes were piled into the kiln, straws, firewood and logs of pine – trees were used to fire them for a total of 130 days. After that the bricks have to be soaked in the Tung oil so that they would turn out smooth and wear resisting, and the more they were worn the shiner they would become. A record taken in Emperor Jiajing reign period in the Ming says that at that time it took three years to finish the making of 50,000 bricks. In the Qing Dynasty, it would cost 9.6 grams of silver to turn out a piece of gold brick like that. Then the price was for a picul of rice and three months provision for a kiln – laborer. When finished, the bricks had to be sent to Beijing for quality examination: "It must sound good when being struck and no air – bubbles found inside when broken." Only when they passed the quality examination would the officials in charge finally accept them for the use.

City wall bricks: Used in the building of city walls, they

were mainly produced in the area of Linqing, Shandong Province. As required, the brick must be of 50 cm long, 25 cm wide and 12 cm thick, fine-grained and grayish in color, and they must sound good. Besides, kilns were built to turn out such bricks at Hexiwu and Guangjumen in the eastern suburbs of Beijing, Zhangde in Henan and Wuqing in Hebei so as to make sure for enough supply of bricks for the building and repairing of the Ming and Qing palace buildings.

141. 故宫大门上的门钉有什么用处呢?

在中国古代,为达防御之目的,城门都制作得非常厚实,并在门上加包铁板,用带帽的门钉钉住。北京现存的城门都是这般模样。而宫廷建筑的大门都是加以美化过的,改铜制门钉为镏金。后来,这些门钉便逐渐演变成了一种装饰品了。皇帝走过的门一般均用81个门钉,纵横各九列,取"九"这个数字,表示皇帝是至高无上的。

What's the use of the tacks on the doors of the entrance gate of the Imperial Palace?

In ancient China the device was for the defense purpose. All city doors were usually very thick and solid, wrapped by iron plate for protection. All doors of the city-gates in Beijing were made like this. However, the doors of the royal palaces were embellished with gilded door-tacks to take the place of copper ones. Later, the door-tacks gradually became some sort of ornaments. To put it in general, on the doors of the passages for emperors, 81 door-tacks were used with each line, vertical or horizontal, having nine. Because in ancient China, the number "nine" suggested the supreme power and solemnity of the emperor.

142. 紫禁城宫殿的门槛有何作用?

自古以来,历朝宫殿及民居的门槛都是固定的。从建筑结构上讲,长方形的门框起着支撑的作用,而门槛则是门框的一个不可缺少的组成部分。若没有门槛,就将影响整个建筑结构的稳定性。因此,门槛是不能、也不应该是活动的。在明清两代的500余年间,紫禁城宫殿大门下的门槛也一直是不能活动的。只是到了民国时期,逊清皇室的人员住在紫禁城后半部时,才改成了活动的门槛。

紫禁城内有无数大小不一的门扉,一般每槽都有两扇朱红的门扉,且均设有门槛,大都系用上好的整块木料制成。在后三宫这个以往明清帝后的生活区里,门槛的两头被锯断,并分别在里外均安上了圆铁环,这是为了搬动方便,因为门槛厚实笨重,需要两人才能挪动。另外,在门槛的中部,也有是在两头,里外都安上了铁扣吊,这样一来,两扇大门便可同门槛锁在一起,以保证安全。

What was the role of the threshold for a palace building in the Forbidden City?

Since ancient times, palace thresholds of various dynasties or of houses for civilians have always been made fixed. Structurally speaking, the rectangular doorframes work as a support and the doorsill, an inseparable component part of it. as without a threshold, a structure will not stand firm. Therefore, the doorsill must not be movable. Over the past 500 years in the Ming and Qing dynasties the doorsills for the palace buildings, in the Forbidden City were all securely fixed and immovable. It was not until the period of the Republic of China when the toppled imperial family of the Qing moved to the rear part of the Imperial Palace, were the doorsills there changed into movable ones.

There are many doorways in various sizes in the Forbidden City. However, every door – passage has two red door – leaves and a doorsill made of a whole piece of fine log. Nevertheless, during the Ming and Qing dynasties, quite a number of doorsills in rows of rear courts meant for the living quarters of emperors, empresses and concubines were sawed apart at both ends, and each end was riveted an iron – ring so as to make it easy for removal. Sometimes, iron – buckles were made fixed at the middle both inside and outside the doorsills, or sometimes they were fixed on both ends so that the doors could be fastened very securely.

143. 故宫屋脊上走兽的数目是多少？这说明了什么？

故宫太和殿戗脊上的仙人走兽最多，共 10 个；乾清宫是皇帝居住和处理日常政务的所在，地位仅次于太和殿，因而屋脊上的走兽为 9 个；坤宁宫是皇后的寝宫，小兽为 7 个；东西六宫是嫔妃们的居所，小兽 5 个；至于配殿，则按等级递减，有的仅有一个。除太和殿外，所有屋脊上的走兽数目均为奇数，所减之兽是减后不减前。所以，故宫建筑物屋脊上的走兽数目不同，说明了其居住者在宫内的地位有所不同。

How many chimeras are there on the up – turned ledge of the palace buildings in the Imperial Palace? And what do they actually mean?

The Hall of Supreme Harmony has 10 chimeras, ranking first in all the palace buildings in the Imperial Palace, has the

162

most of them. The Hall of Heavenly Purity, a place for emperors to stay and handle their routine affairs of the state, has nine, next only to the Hall of Supreme Harmony. The Hall of Earthly Tranquility, the residence for empresses has seven animals on the ledge, and only five animals can be seen on the ledges of the six eastern and western palaces, as they were the residential quarters for imperial consorts. As to other less important palace buildings, they hold the fewer animals on their ledges, and you can find only one animal on the ledges of some of the palace buildings. The number of animals on the ledges of all palace buildings is in odd, with the exception of that on the ledges of the Hall of Supreme Harmony. To cut down the animal is from the rear – most forward and not the other way round. Therefore, the difference in the number of animals on the ledges of the palace buildings suggested the different ranks and positions the inhabitants held in the Imperial Palace.

144. 宫殿顶脊上的吻兽及"仙人"走兽有何说头?

吻兽本是屋顶正脊与垂脊相结合的关节,"仙人"走兽原系大木钉,是用来固定瓦脊并防止下滑的一种装置,以后就逐渐演变为单纯的装饰品了。

吻兽:在古代称作鸱吻,或鸱尾,起源于公元一世纪左右的西汉期间。相传鸱是南海中的一种动物,是龙的九个儿子之一,有喷浪成雨之本领。汉以前的重要建筑物上,正脊两端常用凤凰来做装饰。汉武帝时,因为宫殿经常起火而遭焚毁,在建造章宫时,他接受"术士"们的建议,将屋顶的正脊两端枢纽部位装饰成鸱的形状,用以压制火灾,并在鸱吻背上插上一把扇形的剑,以防止其逃脱。以后便代代相传,延续了下来。到了宋代以后,又从带长尾巴的鸱吻逐渐演变为方形的螭兽吻。螭,古代传说

163

为无角的龙，目的仍不外乎是作为防火的龙之意。到了明清两代，使用吻兽的习惯仍保持未改，且形体变得越来越大，称作"正吻"。当时一个重吻达 3,600 多公斤，约值 180 多两银子。

"仙人"走兽："仙人"走兽的来历也颇早，从汉墓出土的冥器上，已可见到一些痕迹，从唐代的敦煌壁画上，也可见到类似的情形。清代根据《大清会典》的规定，除"仙人"外，走兽最多时有10个，太和殿上就是这样的。其自下而上的排列次序为：龙、凤、狮、天马、海马、狻猊、押鱼、獬豸、斗牛及行什。最前端的是骑凤仙人。它们有的是古代传说中的神异动物，如龙、凤、獬豸；有的是凶猛的野兽，如狮、狻猊；有的为水中的怪物，象海马、押鱼；而有的则是优良的骑兽，如天马等等。在设置这些走兽时，也可少于 10 个，一般均为单数。"仙人"据传是齐闵王，因他暴虐无道而走投无路，留下日晒闵王的形象。

据古代传说称，这些小兽均为异兽，都具有一定的象征意义。龙、凤代表着至高无上的尊贵；天马、海象象征着皇家的威德通天入海，广达四方；斗牛、押鱼是海中之异兽，据称能兴云作雨，镇火防灾；狮子是由异域传入的兽中之王，为镇山之宝；狻猊则是中国传说中能食虎豹的猛兽，象征着千山一统，百兽率从；獬豸善辨是非曲直，是皇家所谓"正大光明"、"清平公正"的象征；最后一个小兽的面部很象猴子，古代工匠称之为"行什"，即排行第十，是檐角的压尾兽。檐角上这一行小兽所象征的是皇家的尊贵和吉祥，威德及智慧；同时也具有震慑妖魔、消灾灭祸之含义；此外，它们还具有很强烈的装饰作用，使整个宫殿的造型显得既规格严谨，又富于形式变化，实现了庄重与生动的和谐，宏伟与精巧的统一。

但为何把这些"仙人"走兽装饰在屋脊上呢？其确切含义现已难道其详，但总的说来，除了建筑物的美观装饰外，大概还是出于防火、压邪的迷信观念。

What do the "Wenshou" and "Immortal" chimaras on the roof — ledges of palace buildings signify?

Originally, Wenshou was a joint connecting the main ridge and the four slanting ledges on the roof of a palace building, and the "immortal" chimaras, the large wooden nails used to keep tiles from sliding down. However, as time went by, they gradually became ornamental pieces.

Wenshou: known in ancient times as Chiwen or Chiwei, it originated in the Western Han (206 B.C. – 25 A.D.) as a mythical animal in the South China Sea. As one of the nine sons of the dragon, it was able to gather clouds and produce rain with seawater. Before the Western Han Dynasty the ends of roof — ridges on a palace building of importance were decorated with phoenixes. However, when Emperor Wu of the Han Dynasty was in power, fire often broke out in the palace. Therefore, when the Zhang Palace was being built, suggestions from geomancers were accepted to set bird — like Chiwen at both ends of the main ridge in order to subdue the fire. To prevent Chiwen from escaping, a fan — shaped dagger was stabbed into it from its back, this practice thus being handed down from generation to generation. Nevertheless, after the Song dynasty (960 – 1279) the long — tailed Chiwen was gradually evolved into a chimera "Chi", a mythical dragon — like animal without horns, aiming at preventing fire. The practice was then passed on till the Ming and Qing dynasties when the size of Chiwen, then called "Zhengwen" became larger and larger, the heaviest being over 3,600 kilograms, which cost more than 180 taels of silver.

The "Immortal" chimeras: the origin of them could be traced back to the Western Han Dynasty. And signs of them were found on the burial objects from the Han Tombs, and the same sort of things could also be seen from the murals in the caves of Dunhuang Grottos of the Tang Dynasty. According to the regulations stipulated in Da Qing Hui Dian, a collection of laws and decrees of the Qing dynasty, the chimeras on the ridge, save the foremost immortal, may reach as many as 10, such as the Hall of Supreme Harmony. Lined in order from below upwards they are the dragon, phoenix, lion, heavenly steed, sea horse, Suanni, Yayu, Xiezhi, Douniu, and Hangshi with the "immortal" on phoenix back taking the lead. The "immortal" as said in a popular saying, was the image of the cruel King Min of the Kingdom of Qi, who, having nowhere to go, was finally made to suffer under the scorching sun.

Legend has it that in ancient China, all these chimeras signified something of importance. The dragon and phoenix represented supreme dignity. The heavenly steed and sea horse meant that the influence of the imperial authority could be exerted up into the heaven and down to the deep sea, in a word, anywhere in all directions without hindrance. Douniu and Yayu were mythical sea animals, able to gather clouds and produce rain to prevent fire. The lion, an animal from an exotic land, was the king of all beasts, able to safeguard hills and mountains. Suanni, a legendary and ferocious beast, able to devour tigers and leopards, signified that all mountains around were under unified governance and all beasts at his command. Xiezhi, a chimera, able to tell right from wrong, showed that the imperial court was "Open and Aboveboard", "just and hon-

166

est". The last monkey – like animal, called "Hangshi," was numbered the tenth to wind up the rear. To put all this in a nutshell, these queer animals, apart from the above – mentioned significance, were also very good decorative pieces for the palace buildings, making them look very magnificent yet stylish in structure, a perfect harmony of solemnity and vividness, a unity of something grandiose and exquisite.

We cannot tell for certain why these "immortal" chimeras were made as ornaments on the ledges as to its initial motives. But all in all, aside from the purpose of beautification, they were used to subdue fire and suppress something evil from a superstitious point of view.

145. 紫禁城内的排水系统情况怎样？

紫禁城内中心建筑的三大殿、后三宫的雨水,是利用地面倾斜的明沟来排除的。例如:三大殿的三台,其中心高度为 8.13 米,而台边高度仅为 7.12 米,排水是极为明显的。周围石栏杆的每块栏板底边均有小孔,每根望柱底下都有雕琢精美的石龙头,口内皆有凿通的圆孔,为辅助排水的通道。当大雨如注之时,三重台基上的 1,142 个龙头,亦即千余个排水孔,可将台面的雨水顷刻排尽,构成一幅三台上下千龙吐水的壮观景象。三台上的水泻下后,又利用北高南低的地势向南导水,在本仁、弘义两阁及左、右翼门的台阶下,都砌有白色卷洞,就是为了使雨水南泻时能顺利通过而设置的。然后再穿过东南崇楼台基下的卷洞注入协和门外的内金水河。向西及后三宫的导水,也都采取了同样的方法。

此外,还有许多纵横交错的地下水道,迹象明显的是神武门内内宫墙以北的地面上铺设的石板道。这石板道是地下暗沟的盖板。这条横贯宫城东西的大纬沟,西端通入城隍庙东侧的内金水河;东端经东北城角往南折,尔后注入清史馆院内的内金水河,成为南北方向直接注入内金水河的第一道纵向暗沟。

第二道经沟设在东六宫东面与宁寿宫之间的狭缝里,向南绕过御茶膳房往东,再折向南注入文华殿东面的内金水河。

第三道经沟,由第二道经沟分叉,西穿奉先殿南群房,经西南墙角穿出,自箭亭东侧往南,经文华殿西墙外注入内金水河。

第四条直接注入内金水河的纵沟,自乾清门院内的西南角穿出,横过内右门穿入养心殿南库,然后由南库穿出隆宗门外,折向南至武英殿东面的断虹桥处注入内金水河。

另外,在东一长街、西一长街、东二长街及西二长街等小巷内,都设有短距离的纵沟,这些大小纵沟,分别接通由乾清门内和乾清宫后向东、向西泄水的纬沟和各宫廷院落的纬沟,利用中央高、四周低,北高南低和某些小沟的中间高、两头低的自然落差,将雨水迅速汇总,排入内河,流出宫外。

这些精心设计建造的大小、纵横、明暗的下水道,将整个故宫 90 余个院落,总面积 72 万平方米土地上的雨水通畅迅速排出,这在当时没有精密科学仪器测定的情况下,不能不说是中国建筑史上的一项伟大成就。在建成后的 500 余年间,由于明清两代的不断掏挖、疏通,虽经数千次滂沱大雨的考验,而仍无积水淤塞的记录。

How does the drainage system work in the Forbidden City?

In the Forbidden City, rainwater from the three central main halls and the three rear palaces is drained away by means of slightly declining ground from the center. Take the terrace on which stand the three main halls for instance. It measures 8.13 meters high in the center and only 7.12 meters high by the edges. The device makes rainwater drain away very quickly. At the bottom of the surrounding balustrades are draining holes, and under every decorative stone column there is an exquisitely carved dragon head, and from there you'll find tucked in its mouth a gully hole — an auxiliary draining hole there. Whenever it rains heavily, all 1,142 — dragon — heads on the triple terraces will begin spilling water out of their mouths, forming a wonderful spectacle. And then the water, flowing over the slightly declining ground from north to south, goes down to the culverts built of white stone pieces under the terrace of Benren and Hongyi pavilions, and those under the passage stairs of the side — gates on the left and right. Draining through these sinks towards southeast the water empties into the Inner Golden Water Stream out of the Gate of Harmony. The sinks on the west work the same way as said above and so does the drainage system for the three rear palaces.

Besides, there are still many crisscrossed draining ditches and gullies underground. The most exposed is the one behind the north palace wall inside the Gate of Military Prowess. Covered up on the ground you'll see a walkway paved with stone — slates, but underneath is a grand ditch. Running along the palace wall from east to west, it finally empties into the Inner Golden Water Stream by the eastern side of the Town God Temple in the west of the Forbidden City. Leading to the east, the ditch, passing the northeast corner and then taking a turn towards south, is the first longitudinal hidden ditch pouring directly into the Inner Golden Water Stream in the courtyard of the Museum of the Qing History Books.

The second longitudinal draining ditch stretches underground along the narrow lane between the Six Eastern Palaces and the Palace of Longevity and Quietude. Joining the northern latitudinal draining channel inside the Gate of Military Prowess, it goes southward, passing by the imperial tea preparation house and kitchen, and there turning east and again south to empty into the Inner Golden Water Stream by the eastern side of the Wenhua Hall.

The third latitudinal drain, a branch of the second one, goes westward by the south of the Palace for Paying Homage to Ancestors. And then it goes through a group of buildings towards southwest and again southward to the eastern side of the Arrow Tower to empty into the Inner Golden Water Stream outside the western wall of the Wenhua Hall.

The fourth one, starting from the southwest corner of the yard inside the Gate of Heavenly Purity, goes out through the inner gate on the right into the southern storeroom of the Hall of Mental Cultivation. And then it turns southward from there through the Longzong Gate to empty into the Inner Golden Water Stream at the Broken Rainbow Bridge by the eastern side of the Hall of Military Bravery.

In addition, a number of short gullies can be found along the small lanes by the first and second long streets of the Imperial Palace. All these latitudinal draining ditches in various sizes join those longitudinal ones going out from the Gate and Palace of Heavenly Purity and those out from the other palace courtyards to form a network of underground drainage. They by means of slightly declining ground make rainwater drain away from the palace very quickly.

Designed in a meticulous way without precision instruments, the drainage system in the Forbidden City, which

170

helps drain the rain water away so quickly from over 90 court-yards with an area of more than 250 acres, cannot but be re-garded as a marvelous achievement in the history of Chinese ar-chitectural engineering. Over the past 500 years after the com-pletion of the system, though undergone severe threats by thousands of downpours, yet thanks to the effectiveness of the system and continuous dredging in the Ming and Qing dynas-ties, no staled water or silts have ever been found down in the drainage.

146. 紫禁城内的铜狮子有何作用？

据古籍记载,狮子又名狻猊。《后汉书》及《东观汉记》载,东汉章帝及顺帝时,安息和疏勒国均曾派使者来献狮子。唐朝著名的大书法家虞世南在其所作的《狮子赋》中有"睹目电曜,发声雷响"等句,形容狮子的灵活与凶猛。中国古代早就把狮子的形象用在陵墓、石窟艺术和各种生活用品的装饰上了,例如汉、唐时期的石雕狮子,丝绸之路上发现的对狮纹锦,石窟寺中的文殊菩萨坐骑和各种狮子座,唐代铜镜上的狮子纹,南北朝时印章上的狮子纽、瓷器中的狮子枕及玩具等等。另外,中国民间所广泛流行的狮子舞,也表明了狮子这种动物早已是人们所喜闻乐见的一种动物形象。

明、清两代在紫禁城内陈设铜狮子,不仅是为了炫耀宫廷的豪华,而且也借以显示封建君王的"尊贵"及"威严"。这些铜狮分别陈设于六处,各处均为一对。在中路太和门和乾清门前各有一对;在西六宫,皇帝日常居住和工作的养心殿大门前各有一对、后妃们居住的长春宫前有一对。在外东路,宁寿门(现绘画馆正门)和养心门(现珍宝馆正门)前各有一对。每对狮子,在右边的为母狮,它伸出左脚逗弄小狮,而小狮作仰卧状,口含大狮之爪,把亲昵的母爱体现得淋漓尽致;左边的为公狮,它伸着右腿耍弄绣球,显出十分可爱而勇猛之状。

What's the use of the bronze lions in the Forbidden City?

According to the ancient record the lion was also called Suanni. The historical books Hou Han Shu (History of the Late Han Dynasty) and Dong Guan Han Ji have it that by the reign of emperors Zhang and Shun of the Eastern Han Dynasty (25 – 220 A. D.) lions were brought in by envoys from the States of Anxi and Shule. Yu Shinan, a famous calligrapher of the Tang Dynasty described the animal in his Ode to the Lions: "Its eyesight is like a shaft of lightning and its roaring, a peal of thunder." And in this way the nimble but ferocious beast was vividly brought forth in his writing. In ancient China, lions were used to guard tombs, carved in grottoes and made onto articles for daily use. For example, you can find stone lions of the Han and Tang dynasties, the pieces of brocade with lion patterns discovered on the Silk Road, the lion as a ride for Bodhisattva Manjusri in the Stone Cave Temple, the bronze mirror with lion patterns of the Tang Dynasty, seal with a lion – shaped knob of the Northern and Southern dynasties as well as porcelain pillows and toys. The lion dance prevailing among the Chinese people also tells the fact that lion has long been an animal, and lion dance a form of performing art loved by the people in China.

In the Ming and Qing dynasties, bronze lions were placed in the Forbidden City so as to show the grandeur and magnificence of the Imperial Palace, and "dignity" and "majestic authority" of the feudal rulers. There were altogether six pairs of bronze lions in the palace: They were placed respectively in

172

front of the Gate of Supreme Harmony, Gate of Heavenly Purity, Hall of Mental Cultivation where the emperor resided and handled the routine affairs, Palace of Eternal Spring, the residence for the queen and concubines, Gate of Longevity and Quietude (now the front gate of the painting hall) and Gate of Metal Repose (now the front gate of the treasure hall). For each pair of lions, the one on the right with a cub under its left paw is a female lion, with a lion cub lying on its back with his mother's paw in its mouth, which shows vividly the feminine affection for her young one. The other one on the left playing embroidered ball with his right paw is a male lion. What a lovely yet ferocious animal it is!

147. 紫禁城内的日晷与嘉量作何用处?

在太和殿和乾清宫的露台(亦称丹阶)两侧,陈列着两件历史悠久的文物——日晷和嘉量。它们分列东西,成了露台上的主要陈设。

日晷:在中国很早就发明了,秦汉时期就成了一种应用广泛的计时器。利用太阳投影和地球自转的原理,借指针所生成的阴影来表示时间。在倾角为五十度的晷盘中心,立有一根与盘面垂直的铁针。针的上端指北极,下端指南极。晷盘的上下两面均刻有时辰(清代计时,每个时辰分为八刻,前四刻为初,后四刻为正),上面的时辰由早到晚向左转,下面的时辰向右转。每年春分后看上面的针影,秋分后看下面的针影。紫禁城内的两个日晷系明清期间所置,虽然早就废弃不用,但仍闪烁着古代劳动人民的智慧之光。

嘉量:是中国古代容积的综合标准计量器,因古人称藁谷为禾,而称大禾为嘉禾,故用以秤量禾的器具便称为嘉量。全器共分斛、斗、升、合及龠(音越)五个容量单位。中间较大的一器,其上部为斛,下部为斗;左边一器为升;右边的一器上部为合,下部为龠。依据古制,二龠为合,十合为升,十升为斗,十斗为斛(后改成五斗为一斛)。紫禁城内的两套铜制镀金嘉量,是清代乾隆皇帝依据汉代王莽时期的嘉量形式仿制的,上面镌刻着他写的铭文。

What was the use of the sundial and the imperial grain measures in the Forbidden City?

Displayed on both sides of the open－air scarlet platforms in front of the Hall of Supreme Harmony and Hall of Heavenly Purity are the sundials and the imperial grain measures. As the cultural relics with a long history, they, one on each side, have now become the main ornamental pieces on the platforms.

The Sun Dial (Ri Gui): It is a time－meter invented in ancient China and firstly put into use in the Qin and Han dynasties. Using the projection by the sun and the principle of the rotation of the earth, it tells time by the shadow projected by the handle on the dial－panel. In the center of the sundial with an inclination angle of 50 degrees, stands an iron handle at a right angle. Its upper tip points to the North Pole, and the other end to the South Pole. Both sides of the dial－panel are graduated with a time division of the 12 two－hour periods as done traditionally (in the Qing Dynasty, one period was divided into eight quarters, the first four of which, called "chu", meant the initial, while the latter called "zheng" meant sharp). From morning till night, the shadow of the handle on the upper side of the dial goes anti－clockwise and the handle on the other side, the other way round. Every year after the Vernal Equinox the time is read by the shadow on the upper－

side, and by that on the reverse side after the Autumnal E-quinox. The two sundials in the Forbidden City were put up in the Ming and early Qing period. Though left unused long ago they are still giving forth the brilliance of wisdom of the ancient Chinese people.

The Imperial Grain Measures (Jia Liang): It was a complete set of standard volume measures in ancient China. The Chinese people in the olden days regarded cereal crops as "He" and rice and wheat as "Jiahe," hence its measure the "Jia Liang." The whole set of measures consists of five volume units: Hu, Dou, Sheng, He and Yue. As for the larger one in the middle, the upper part is "Hu", and the lower part "Dou"; that on the left is the "Sheng", and regarding that on the right the upper part is "He", and the lower part "Yue." In accordance with the traditional system, two "Yue" made up a "He," ten "He" a "Sheng", ten "Sheng" a "Dou" and ten "Dou" a "Hu" (but later changed into five "Dou" a "Hu").

With inscriptions by Emperor Qianlong the two sets of grain measures in the Forbidden City made of copper during Qianlong reign (1736 – 1796) are an imitation of that forged under the rule of Wang Mang (9 – 20) by the end of the Western Han Dynasty.

148. 皇帝平时用的厕所在哪里？洗澡的地方在何处？冬天故宫里是如何取暖的？

皇帝在宫里所用的厕所一般为木桶,而在宫外则用皮布。皇帝解手时,由六人撑起帷幄围上,解在皮布里。

皇帝平时在屋里,一般都用木盆洗澡,洗完后,便由太监们用绣龙的手帕帮他自上而下抹干,洗一次澡所用的手帕达数百块之多。

清代到旧历十一月初一,宫中才开始烧暖炕。烧火的地方一般都在房子外边,现已用木板盖起。此外,房间里还设火盆围炉,烧木炭以取暖。

Where was the washroom and bathroom for the emperor? How were the rooms warmed up in winter in the Forbidden City?

The emperor normally used the wooden commode in the palace. If he went out a leather sheet would be used instead. When the emperor wanted to relieve himself, six eunuchs had to screen him off by holding up a curtain around.

The emperor normally took bath in a wooden vat. When he finished eunuchs would dry him by handkerchiefs with dragon – pattern. Therefore, several hundred silk handkerchiefs were required each time.

In the Qing dynasty, the rooms in the Imperial Palace began to be warmed up from the first day of the eleventh lunar month every year. Fire was normally made in a fireplace outside the room, which was covered up with a plank – board now. In addition, enclosed fire – pans were also used in the rooms to burn charcoal with.

149. 所谓"廷杖"是何意思?

廷杖是明代一种独特的刑罚,通俗说,就是皇帝让人用棍棒打臣下的屁股。在封建社会里,所谓"刑不上大夫"之说,并不一定为统治者所奉行。在明代,谁如果违逆了皇上的意图,被批了"逆凛"的时候,就会让"锦衣卫"(即御林军)把他抓起来,押至午门痛打,其中立毙杖下者亦不在少数。

176

行刑地点是在午门前的御路东侧。在午门底下有两处小平房，那就是锦衣卫值勤之处。此外，东西两厢房及禁门下也都站满了禁军校尉，廷杖就是在这样禁卫森严的气氛下进行的。杖打的时候，要把人装在布袋里，打完后再将其举起往地上摔，难怪易于致人于死命。

明朝的廷杖在正德、嘉靖两代使用次数较多。嘉靖号称盛世，但这位皇帝非常反对臣下的进谏，经常责打那些给他提意见的人。他本是以外藩亲王之子入继皇位的，但却非要将其父亲追封为皇帝，于是便在宫廷之内引发了一场轩然大波。一批官员认为这种做法违反了皇家的礼法，于是"君臣争大礼，聚哭左顺门"。可臣下的眼泪反倒激起了皇帝的勃然大怒，"杖五品以下丰熙等官员一百三十四人，死者王思等十七人，于是裹创吮血，填满阶陛，此其最酷者矣。"嘉靖打得最多的是那些御史及给事中一类的"言官"，有一次嘉靖派太监替他祭大庙，有户部给事中张选进谏称，应由武定侯郭勋代祭。嘉靖大怒，"命执选阙下，杖八十，帝出御文华殿听之，每一人行杖毕，辄以报数。杖折者三，拉出已死。帝怒未息。"史家论述，明王朝走向衰亡，实则始于嘉靖。这种拒谏之风的盛行，确是明王朝政治腐败的重要原因之一。

What did that "Tingzhang" mean?

Tingzhang: It was a unique way of punishment practiced in the Ming Dynasty. To put it in a plain way, it meant that the emperor had his vassals cudgeled on their hips. In feudal society, the so – called "Vassals are out of the laws of being punished" was not always abided by the rulers. In the Ming Dynasty, whoever went against the willful wishes of the emperor would immediately be seized by "Jin Yi Wei," the imperial guards and be flogged outside the Meridian Gate. Many of them were even cudgeled to death on the spot.

The place for punishment was in the two small rooms right by the eastern side of the Meridian Gate in the front courtyard, a place for the imperial guards to stay. When a punishment was being executed, both eastern and western annexes and the Meridian Gate were heavily guarded, creating a stern atmosphere. The person was put into a sack before being flogged, and afterwards he would be thudded onto the ground from the air. That is why the culprit was easily put to death. "Tingzhang" was more often used in the Zhengde and Jiajing reign periods. For instance, Jiajing reign was known as the flourishing period in the Ming Dynasty. However the emperor was against whatever advice from his vassals and inflicted punishment as often as not on those who dared to offer proposals. The emperor was the son of a prince before he was crowned, but he insisted that his father should be conferred with the title of emperor, thus rousing a great hubbub among his court officials. A group of officials held that it was a breach of the imperial rules and etiquette, so they "gathered outside Zuoshunmen Gate to reason with the emperor. They prostrated on the ground crying their grievances out." However contrary to their wishes the emperor flew into a rage: He ordered to flog 134 officials under the fifth rank with Feng Xi at the head, of whom, 17 were beaten to death on the spot. The royal court was full of officials covered with blood. What a cruelty! This sort of punishment was resorted to more often than not in the royal court then. And of those beaten by the emperor, most of them were imperial advisers. Historians believe that the Ming Dynasty began to go downhill in the Jiajing reign period. Re-

178

jecting presentations and glossing over errors was one of the manifestations of political corruptness in the Ming Dynasty.

150. 太和、中和及保和三殿的名称各有什么含义?

中文中的"和"是指事物间的协调关系。

太和:意即宇宙间一切事物的相互关系都能得到协调。

中和:"中"之含意为不偏不倚,恰如其分或符合节度的意思。因而"中和"即是说凡事要做到恰如其分,才能使各种关系相互协调,不出偏差。

保和:这就是说要保持住事物之间的协调关系。

What is the implication of the names of the three main halls: the Hall of Supreme Harmony, the Hall of Complete Harmony and the Hall of Preserving Harmony?

"He" in Chinese means the harmonized relation among various things in the world.

"Taihe" (supreme harmony) means that the relations between various things in universe are in perfect harmony.

"Zhonghe" (complete harmony) suggests "mean" or "impartial", i.e. to handle things in a proper and restrained way. Only by doing so, can the relations between the various things be kept in harmony without going astray.

"Baohe" (preserving harmony) denotes to keep in order the harmonized relations already obtained between various things.

151. 午门在明清两代时期作何用处?

午门的用途如下:

1. 午门是皇宫外朝的正门,也是紫禁城的南大门。它突出

179

地体现了皇权至上的构思。午门有三个门,两侧还有左右掖门。中门是供皇帝一人出入的。但在清朝,状元、榜眼、探花所谓三鼎甲在发榜之日是可从中门进入的。此外,皇帝与皇后结婚的那天,皇后也可坐轿由中门进入皇宫。其他文武官员由左门出入,王室宗亲由右门出入,其他较低级的官员则只能从左右掖门出入。

2. 午门中楼左右设有钟鼓楼。皇帝临大朝时,钟鼓齐鸣,祀坛出午门鸣钟,祭太庙击鼓。

3. 每年冬至在此颁布皇帝签发的农历,表示皇帝很重视农事。

4. 午门前还举行向皇帝献俘的仪式。清朝时,把在镇压农民起义和反清势力的战争中抓到的重要俘虏押解到京,向皇帝报功领赏,此谓之"献俘"。

5. 在明朝,午门前还是"廷杖"官吏的地方。文武百官中胆敢冒犯皇帝的尊严者,就有可能被推出午门打屁股,叫做"廷杖"。行刑时,由锦衣卫四人用布袋把犯者兜起来再打。打完了还要举起来往地上摔,因而,即使未被打死,也会被摔死。

What role did the Meridian Gate of the Forbidden City play during the Ming and Qing dynasties?

The Meridian Gate was used in the following circumstances:

1. The Meridian Gate is the outer front gate of the Imperial Palace and also the southern gate of the Forbidden City, suggesting the outstanding supremacy of the imperial power. There are three gateways at the Meridian Gate, including one on the left and the other on the right. The central gate was the passage reserved for the emperor only. However, in the Qing dynasty, the first three outstanding candidates of the imperial

examination (Zhuangyuan, Bangyan and Tanhua) were allowed to go through the central gate into the Forbidden City on the very day when the imperial list of the successful candidates for the examination was announced. The sedan – chair carrying the queen to be can be carried was allowed to go through the central gate into the palace on the wedding day of the emperor and the queen. All other high – ranking officials were permitted to make the entry only by the left gate and the princes or members of the royal family by the right. The rest minor officials could do the entry by the side – gates only.

2. Built on the right and left atop the central part of the Meridian Gate is the Bell and Drum towers. The bell would be sounded and drum beaten when the emperor presided in court. On such occasions, the sacristan would make his exit from the Meridian Gate to sound the bell and beat the drum, with sacrifices offered at the Ancestor's Temple.

3. Every year, the lunar almanac endorsed by the emperor was promulgated here on the day of the Winter Solstice to mean that the emperor attached great importance to agriculture.

4. The ceremony for presenting to the emperor the captives was held here in front of the Meridian Gate. In the Qing dynasty, captives of importance from the war, such as leaders of peasant uprisings or heads of anti – Qing forces were escorted to Beijing and presented to the emperor for merits and awards, this being called "presenting captives".

5. In the Ming dynasty the place in front of the Meridian Gate was also used for punishing top officials, called "Tingzhang." Any official who happened to offend the author-

ity of the emperor would be pushed out of the Meridian Gate to
be cudgeled there by palace guards, some even beaten to death
right on the spot.

152、故宫中的"太和门"有何用途？

太和门：是三大殿的前门,概而言之有如下几种用途：

1．它是明朝皇帝"御门听政",即皇帝在此听取官吏奏事并
作出决策的地方；

2．清朝皇帝去祀坛时出宫至太和门阶下,降舆换辇,即乘一
种带棚盖的车去坛庙祭天地；

3．清朝皇帝在此门举行过宴会；

4．皇帝大婚时纳彩礼、册立、奉迎礼等礼仪都要经过太和
门。

What role did the Gate of Supreme Harmony play in the Forbidden City?

It is the front gate of the three main halls in the Forbidden City.

The gate, to make it short, was used on the following occasions:

1. In the Ming Dynasty, it was a place for the emperor to
hear the reports by his officials and also a place where decisions
were made and issued;

2. In the Qing dynasty, when the emperor was on his
way to offer sacrifices at the altar temples, he would get down
from his carried chair and take a canopied chariot here;

3. It was a place where imperial banquets were thrown
during the Qing dynasty;

4. When the young emperor was going to marry, ceremo-

ny for receiving dower, and conferring the title to queen would be held here, with the procession passing through the gate.

153. 太和殿、中和殿、保和殿各有什么用处?

太和殿的用处是:

1.每年阴历春节,(正月初一)、冬至节、万寿节(皇帝生日),要在这里举行庆典;遇到其它大的庆典或大事件,如皇帝"登极"颁发诏书,公布进士黄榜,以及派遣大将出征等,也要在此举行隆重的仪式。

2.明朝和清初都曾在这里举行过殿试。

中和殿的用处是:

1.太和殿参加大庆典礼以前,先在这里稍事休息,作些准备,听取有关大典的安排回报,还在这里举行受贺仪式的演习及接受执事官的朝拜,然后乘肩舆去太和殿。

2.在祭祀天坛前,皇帝要在此处看祭文。

3.在祭祀先农坛前,皇帝要在这里检查种子、犁等备耕仪式的准备情况。

保和殿的用处是:

1.明朝初期阴历年到来之际,曾在这里宴请群臣及驸马。

2.十八世纪后期起,这里是清朝殿试的固定场所。

3.清朝每年除夕在此宴请蒙古王公大臣。

What roles did the Hall of Supreme Harmony, Hall of Complete Harmony and Hall of Preserving Harmony play?

The Hall of Supreme Harmony:

1. Every year, grand celebrations were held here on the first day of the first lunar month, the day of the Winter Solstice and the birthday of the emperor, known in Chinese as Wan Shou Jie. Other important ceremonies were also conduct-

ed here, such as: the issuing of the imperial edict about the new emperor's enthronement, announcing the list of the successful candidates from the imperial examination and dispatching a general on an expedition.

2. Imperial examinations were held here in the Ming Dynasty and the beginning of the Qing Dynasty.

The Hall of Complete Harmony:

1. Before the emperor went to a grand ceremony to be held in the Hall of Supreme Harmony he would take a short rest here while doing some preparations and listening to the reports concerning the arrangement of the ceremony. Besides, he would also do some practices here for the rites while receiving the respect shown by his officials in charge of the event before he was finally carried on a chair to the spot in the Hall of Supreme Harmony.

2. Every year before the sacrifice was offered at the Temple of Heaven, the emperor would review the sacrificial address here.

3. Before the sacrifice was offered at the Temple of Agriculture, the emperor would hold a ceremony here to make a check on grain – seeds and the plough for the use.

The Hall of Preserving Harmony:

1. In the early days of the Ming Dynasty banquets were thrown here to entertain the emperor's son – in – laws and top officials.

2. In the later period of the 18th century, it was a place for the palace examinations.

3. In the Qing Dynasty, banquet was given here on every New Year's eve for entertaining the Mongolian lords and offi-

cials.

154. 太和殿里的宝座是怎么来的?

太和殿,又称金銮殿,正中设有"须弥座"形式的宝座。宝座的正面和两侧都有陛,即供上下用的木台阶,俗称"搭垛"。宝座上设雕龙髹金大椅,这就是皇帝的御座。椅后设雕龙髹金屏风,左右有宝象、香筒、角端等陈设。在宝座前面陛的左右还有四个香几,上有三足香炉。当皇帝升殿时,炉内焚起檀香,香筒内插藏香,于是整个金銮殿里香烟缭绕,显得格外庄严肃穆。

公元 1915 年,窃国大盗袁世凯篡权称帝以后,把殿内原有乾隆皇帝所题的匾额,及雕龙髹金大椅等物不知挪往何处去了,代之以一个特制的中西结合、不伦不类、椅背极高的大椅,但背后的髹金屏风仍保留了下来。后来,当故宫博物院在 1947 年接收前古物陈列所时,又把袁世凯的这个大椅撤去了,并打算换上原清代所制的龙椅,可始终找不着能与其后屏风协调一致的龙椅。直至 1959 年,依据一张光绪二十六年的旧照片,从存放残破家具的库房中发现了一张合适的雕龙大椅。现在金銮殿里的宝座龙椅就是按其式样修复的。

Whence came the throne chair in the Hall of Supreme Harmony?

The Hall of Supreme Harmony is also called the Throne Hall. In the center of the hall, a throne is set on a platform in the shape of a "Sumeru dais." In the front and also on both sides of the platform, there are flights of steps (called "Bi" or "Daduo" in Chinese) leading to the throne. The gold - gilded throne is carved with dragons, behind which is the screen with dragon pattern. Decorated on the right and left of the throne are such articles as precious elephants, incense - burning tubes

185

and Luduan (a kind of mythical animal), etc. On both sides of the flights of steps in the front are four tables with tripod incense – burners laid on. When the emperor was ascending the throne, sandal wood sticks were burnt in the burners, and incense – sticks in incense – tubes, so that the Throne Hall permeated with wisps of incense – smoke and fragrance seemed more solemn and respectful.

In 1915, when notorious warlord Yuan Shikai usurped the throne, the couplet – boards formerly inscribed by Emperor Qianlong and the throne – chair were moved away. No one knew where they were gone. Only the screen was kept there. Replaced it was a so – called throne, a chair with a high back but a low seat, an ill – combination of the Chinese and western styles. In 1947 when the articles of the former Antiques Exhibition Hall were taken over by the Imperial Palace this chair was removed with an intention to replace it by one made in the Qing dynasty. However, no suitable throne – chair could be found to match the screen behind. It was not until 1959 when an old photo taken in 1900, the 26th year under the reign of Emperor Guangxu was found, that the throne was restored to its former grandeur according to a broken throne – chair discovered from heaps of rubbish from a former storage. The present throne – chair is the very one restored after the model.

155. 宝座前的陈设有何用处? 有何象征意义?

在太和殿内的高台上,光彩夺目的金漆宝座两侧设有成双成对的宝象、角端、仙鹤、香筒(香炉和香亭)四种陈设。台阶上有四个铜胎掐丝珐琅香炉,成一字形排放在硬木贴金的几架之上。这些陈设品,都是燃放檀香用的器皿。每当大典之日,炉中燃起檀香,升起缕缕香烟,伴随着铿锵和鸣的中和韶乐,在宫室中回荡,给殿堂增添了许多神秘色彩。在这些陈设品中,有的是神鸟异兽,有的是仿古礼器,均含有吉祥长寿之意。

太平有象

各式各样,各种质地的象,常常是皇帝宝座旁的陈设品。象,高大威严,身躯粗壮,性情温和,粗大的四蹄直立地上,稳如泰山,象征着社会的安定和皇权的巩固;象上有一宝瓶,盛放着五谷或吉祥之物,表示五谷丰登、吉庆有余等吉祥之意。太和殿宝座旁陈设的是一对铜胎珐琅料石的太平有象,它能通四夷之语,身驮宝瓶而来,给皇帝带来了农业的丰收和社会的太平,因此御名曰:"太平有象"。

甪端

宝座两旁的铜胎珐琅甪端,是中国古代传说中的一种神异之兽,日行一万八千里,通晓四夷之语言。宝座旁放置甪端,表示在位的皇帝乃是圣明之主,因而甪端才捧书而至,护卫在其身旁。

仙鹤

仙鹤也是神鸟,传说能使延年而长寿。仙鹤陈设在宝座旁,是希望皇帝的江山社稷能传至万代,永世长存。

甋式香炉

香炉,作为宫室之中的陈设物已有很长的历史。香炉的形式多种多样,但以仿古代礼器为大宗。有的是仿古代爵杯香炉,仿鬲的狻猊炉,仿鬶的香炉和仿甋的甋式香炉等。在太和殿内宝座台阶前的四个硬木贴金圆几上放置着两对乾隆时代的掐丝珐琅香炉,就是仿古代甋式礼器制作的,炉身勾莲花纹,三象首为足,式样古朴,颜色鲜艳,是美观大方、工艺精湛的艺术品。

盘龙香亭

香筒也是香炉的一种形式,它是清代宫廷内固定的陈设物品之一。香筒,原为在其内放置点燃檀香的香炉,以后逐步发展成为筒式香筒,进而改为亭式香筒,称为香亭。太和殿内陈设的是铜胎掐丝珐琅香亭,筒身上有五爪龙盘绕,亭下盘内燃放檀香。缕缕青烟从带孔的亭身升起,犹如处于云雾缭绕的佛国仙境之中。亭子寓有安定之意,把香炉作为宫廷内的陈设,显示天下大治,国家稳固安定。

What was the use of some sets – out in front of the throne – chair? What do they signify?

On the highly raised platform in the Hall of Supreme Harmony, there set out on both sides of the brightly gilded Throne were pairs of precious elephants, Luduan (a kind of mythical animal), cranes and incense – burners of different types. In front of the platform four incense – burners of filigreed enamel were displayed in line on the hardwood tables covered by gold leaves. All these sets – out are the sandalwood burners. On grand ceremonies, sandalwoods were burnt in them, giving forth spirals of fragrant smoke. Amidst sonorous music, the Hall of Supreme Harmony seemed more solemn and mystical. All of them suggest a sense of auspiciousness and longevity.

Peaceful Elephant

Elephants of all types are as always the sets – out by the side of the throne. Huge yet gentle with four thick legs on the ground, they signify social peace, security and stable rule of royal power. On the back of the elephant there is usually a precious vase containing cereals and auspicious objects, suggesting a rich harvest, happiness and affluence, and having more than enough and to spare. The copper – based enamel elephants were supposed to understand different languages of the neighboring countries. Coming with precious vases on their backs the elephants meant to bring for the emperor rich harvest and peaceful social order, hence endowed by his majesty as the "peaceful elephant."

Luduan

Displayed on both sides of the throne was a pair of "Luduan" made of enameled copper. As a sort of mythical chimera in ancient Chinese fables it was able to travel 9,000 kilometers a day and knew many languages of different countries and regions. The display of "Luduan" by the side of the throne was to show that the emperor was so sagacious and above – board, that even made Luduan to come and stand, holding books by his side.

Crane

The crane is also a kind of mythical bird, said to be able to help prolong people's life. It was to hope that the cranes standing by the throne could help the emperor prolong his rule over the country for a long time to come.

Tripodal Incense Burner

Incense burners, as a kind of setout in the Imperial Palace, can be traced far back into history. They were imitations of bronze wares used for etiquette or ritual purposes in ancient times. Some were imitations of different types of wine jars; some were in the shape of the mythical animal of Suanni; and others, with lotus flowers filigreed on the torso and three elephant heads as pods, were the typical of its kind, a perfect and exquisite work of art in the Hall of Supreme Harmony.

Tubal Pavilion – shaped Burner
with Curling Dragons

The tubal incense burner, a kind of burners, was definitely a fixed setout in the Qing royal palace. The tubal burner was formerly used for burning sandalwoods but was later changed into one of a pavilion style to burn incense sticks with, hence named the tubal pavilion – shaped burner. Made of copper filigreed and enameled, the tubal burner has a five – clawed dragon curling on it, and the plate at the bottom is used to burn sandalwood. With wisps of smoke spiraling up from the burners it suggests an atmosphere of a fairyland looming up in mists and clouds. As the pronuncation of "pavilion" in Chinese is same as that for "stability," the pavilion – shaped burner means that the country is in peace and good order.

156. 箭亭在故宫中是作什么用的? 紫金城内的紫金箭亭有何来历?

箭亭修建于清代,又称紫金箭亭。位于紫禁城南面的一块开阔平地上,它是清代皇帝及其子孙练习骑射的地方。箭亭虽名之曰亭,实质上犹如一座独立的殿堂。箭亭的外观十分引人注目,亭角微翘,屋脊成人字形漫坡,二十根朱漆大柱承托起回廊屋架,减少了中国古代建筑中特有的斗拱重叠的层次,是清代少有的一种建筑形式。最有趣的是,箭亭建筑没有一扇窗户,东西两面是磨砖对缝的墙壁,南北两向为八扇大门,但却南五北三,数不对称,不过看上去却使你感到安排得十分协调。这种独特风格的设计,使箭亭显得格外朴实无华,端壮大方。亭子前后阶石上的浮雕,雕工精美,龙嘴巨开,龙尾耸翘,有浮云环绕其身,若巨龙翱游于海洋上空。亭子前后还放置着清代的两个大铁缸。

乾隆帝修造箭亭,也与他个人平时喜爱骑射有关。他曾向神箭手贝勒允禧学习射箭,骑射技艺十分高超。有一次,他令侍卫引熊来射,但他刚上马,熊突然惊起,他控辔自若,开弓放箭,与侍卫们一起把熊射死。

乾隆帝还把射箭作为应考武举的头等项目,并规定"首场马箭射毡球,二场步射布侯,均发九矢。马射中二矢,步射中三矢为合适;再开弓、舞刀、掇石,以试其勇"。

紫禁城内的箭亭建起后,乾隆和嘉庆皇帝都曾在此射过箭,操演过武艺。每当皇帝及其子孙们在此跑马射箭时,亭前摆起箭靶,八扇大门全部洞开,人站在亭内开弓放箭,列队两旁的武士摇旗呐喊,擂鼓助威,情景十分热闹壮观。

清初规定,经特许在大内骑马的王公大臣,凡入东华门者,一律均在箭亭前面下马。因此箭亭周围的空旷之地,也是当时拴歇马匹的地方。

What was the Arrow Tower used for? Whence came the Purple Gold Arrow Tower in the Forbidden City?

Built in the Qing dynasty the Arrow Tower, also called the Purple Gold Arrow Tower, is located on an open space in the south of the Fengxian Hall (for worshipping ancestors). Used only by the emperor and his off − springs to practice riding and shooting, the Arrow Tower, though called a "tower", is actually a separate building. With a gentle roof and slightly up − turned ledges on 20 vermilion pillars, the building iis a rarely seen architecture in the Qing royal palace. The most interesting is that there is no single window on the Arrow Tower. The eastern and western walls are built of polished bricks. It has eight gates, yet arranged asymmetrically with five gates opened on the south and only three at the north. Uniquely designed, the Arrow Tower is simple, sedate, solemn and graceful. The dragons in relief on the step − stones in the front and at the back of the Arrow Tower are exquisitely carved. With their mouths wide open and their tails upturned the dragons surrounded by clouds look as if they were dancing in the clouds high up above the sea. Besides, there are still two iron cauldrons in the front and at the back of the Arrow Tower.

Why Emperor Qianlong started the building of the Arrow Tower? It had something to do with his personal liking. As he himself took a great fun in riding and shooting, he learned the skill from a "Beile" named Yunxi — a master rider and a sharp shooter — and thoroughly mastered the skill. Once he was out shooting with his entourage, there suddenly came a giant bear. He, rein in hand, shot it dead calm and collected together with his followers.

During Qianlong reign period it was stipulated that if one wanted to become an elite military officer he had to pass through the exam of shooting. The first step was to shoot at a felt – ball on a galloping horse, and the second a bag on foot. And one would get passed with two and three to hit the mark out of nine shoots, and then he would take the tests of prowess by bow drawing, sword playing and stone lifting.

After the completion of the Arrow Tower, Emperor Qianlong and Jiaqing had been here practicing shooting and martial arts. Whenever the emperor and his descendants were here practicing riding and shooting, targets for archery would be set up in front of the Arrow Tower. With the eight gates of the tower opened wide and numerous military men lined on both sides clapping, shouting, and beating drums and gongs, the archers began to shoot from inside the tower. The atmosphere was really thrilling and exciting.

In the early days of Qing, the regulations had it that

princes and high – ranking officials, who were permitted to enter the Forbidden City on horseback, had to get off in front of the Arrow Tower. Therefore, the open ground around the tower was also a place for tethering horses at that time.

157. 清朝末代皇帝溥仪的生平简历如何?

清朝末代皇帝爱新觉罗·溥仪,生于 1906 年,1967 年 10 月 17 日因患肾癌不治而病卒。1908 年,他刚三岁,即登基成了清朝第十个皇帝,年号宣统。1911 年 10 月 12 日,在故宫养心殿由隆裕皇太后主持宣布退位诏书,1924 年被驱逐出宫。离开皇宫后,他曾在日本泡制的伪满州国做傀儡皇帝,1945 年第二次世界大战结束时,被苏联红军俘虏,1950 年回国,经党和政府的教育改造,于 1959 年大赦出狱,此后便从事园林及文史资料的研究工作,编写了《我的前半生》等回忆录。

Could you say something in brief about Pu Yi, the last emperor of the Qing dynasty?

Aisin – Gioro Pu Yi, the last emperor of the Qing Dynasty, was born in 1906 and died of incurable kidney cancer on October 17, 1967. By the end of 1908, he was enthroned as the 10th emperor of the Qing Dynasty at the age of three, the title of his reign being Xuantong. On October 12, 1911, Empress Dowager Longyu, promulgated an imperial edict of his abdication in the Hall of Mental Cultivation of the Forbidden City. Ousted from the palace in 1924 he was afterwards made a puppet emperor of the Bogus Manchuria Regime by the Japanese. By the end of World War II in 1945, the Soviet Red Army took him a captive and he returned to China in 1950. Later under the education of the Party and the Government he was released in an amnesty in 1959. While playing a part in the study of Chinese art of gardening and researches on materials of culture and history, Pu Yi wrote an autobiography entitled From Emperor to Citizen.

158. 清朝慈禧太后的"垂帘听政"是怎么回事?

1861 年,清朝的咸丰皇帝死后,其子载淳(年号同治)登基继位。其时,载淳年幼,依据老皇帝生前的嘱托,由八大臣辅政。但慈禧野心勃勃,发动了一次宫廷政变,从此她就与皇后慈安共同辅政,即共同治理政务之意。但在封建社会里,妇女是不能直接掌权的。所以临朝时,在小皇帝与二太后的宝座之间设置一道黄纱帘。这样,小皇帝表面上看来是在执政,实际上,他只不过是太后的傀儡而已,一切重大的决策,都得由帘子后面的人来作出。这种管理国家政务的形式,在清代历史上称为"垂帘听政"。

1874 年,同治长大成人,开始亲自执政,慈禧不得不撤帘归政。但时间不过一年,由于其子同治患天花(也有说是梅毒),加上慈禧在生活上对他的虐待而致死。1875 年,她又强立年仅 4 岁的载湉(慈禧妹妹的儿子)继位,慈禧再次"垂帘听政"。而在"戊戌变法"失败以后,慈禧索性采取"撤帘训政"了。她让光绪皇帝坐在一边,根本不挂帘子,自己就公开发号施令了。

"垂帘听政"的地点,在故宫的养心殿或颐和园的仁寿殿。

What did the "Ruling behind the curtain" by Empress Dowager Cixi of the Qing Dynasty actually mean?

When Emperor Xianfeng died in 1861, his son Zaizhun succeeded him, being enthroned as the new emperor and the year of his reign called "Tongzhi." As a boy, he had eight ministers assist him according to the will of the deceased emperor. However, ambitious Empress Cixi staged a coup in the palace and began ruling together with Queen Ci'an. As women in feudal times were not allowed to do ruling directly, a yellow gauze screen was hung between the boy emperor and the two empress dowagers. In this way the boy emperor exercised his authority in a seemingly way, but was actually directed like a puppet with all－important decisions made by the two dowagers behind the curtain. This way of running the state affairs was called "ruling behind the curtain" in the history of the Qing Dynasty.

When the boy emperor grew up, Empress Dowager Cixi had to return the power to him. But with the cruel maltreatment in daily life, he died of smallpox (or of syphilis as said otherwise) in less than one year's time. In 1875, Dowager Cixi arbitrarily enthroned Zaitian, the son of her younger sister, a boy of four years old. Thus she once again began her rule behind the screen. After the Reform Movement of 1898 came to a cropper, she, tearing away the curtain, began to rule directly by herself with Emperor Guangxu, an emperor in name, sitting by her side.

The place for "ruling behind the curtain" was in the Hall of Mental Cultivation of the Forbidden City and the Hall of Benevolent Longevity in the Summer Palace.

159. 故宫里那口珍妃井的由来如何?

珍妃是清光绪皇帝的宠妃,她因追随光绪皇帝主张变法而遭致慈禧太后的憎恨。平日里,慈禧对珍妃进行百般虐待。戊戌变法失败之后,珍妃被禁锢在故宫东北角景棋阁后面的小院子内。1900 年,八国联军侵入北京,慈禧决定带着光绪逃走,临走前,她借口"洋人进京,难免污辱",命珍妃投井自杀,即所谓"赐自尽"。但是珍妃始终抗辩不从。最后,慈禧便命二总管太监崔玉桂,将珍妃强行推入贞顺门内的一口井中溺死。事隔一年以后,珍妃的尸体才被打捞上来,葬于西直门外。光绪死后被葬在清西陵的崇陵,同时也将珍妃迁葬于崇陵。从此,这口井便以"珍妃井"而得名。

How did the "Well of Concubine Pearl" in the Forbidden City come about?

Pearl, a favorite concubine of Emperor Guangxu by the end of the Qing dynasty, was deeply hated by Empress Dowager Cixi because she followed Emperor Guangxu advocating the Reform Movement. Normally maltreated in the court by Empress Dowager, she was under house arrest in a small courtyard behind the Jingqi Pavilion located at the northeast corner of the Imperial Palace after the Reform Movement of 1898 came to a cropper. In 1900, when the eight powers allied forces were approaching Beijing, Cixi decided to run away, bringing Emperor Guangxu with her. However, before her leaving, an order was given that the Concubine Pearl should commit suicide on the pretext that "it's unavoidable to be insulted and raped when Beijing is occupied by foreign troops." But Concubine Pearl refused to submit to it. On the order of Cixi she was plunged into the well by Cui Yugui, No. 2 Steward in charge of the eunuchs in the Forbidden City. Her body was retrieved from the well a year later and buried outside the Xizhimen Gate. With the passing away of Emperor Guangxu, she was removed to be buried by his side in the tomb of Chongling at the Western Qing Mausoleum. Hence the name the "Well of

196

Concubine Pearl. "

160. 乾清宫有什么用处?

乾清宫有以下几种用途:

1. 明朝至清初,此宫是皇帝处理日常政务的地方;

2. 清朝雍正以后迁居养心殿,但是皇帝还是经常到此殿选派官吏,批阅奏折,召见臣下、藩臣及策划镇压人民的反抗活动等;

3. 明清两代皇帝死后的灵柩也停放在这里,清朝自顺治至光绪帝的梓宫都停放在乾清宫;

4. 清朝自康熙以后,皇帝不宣布预定太子之名,而由皇帝将指定皇位继承人的名字写好,并用小盒封装好后,置于乾清宫的"正大光明"匾额之后,待皇帝死后,立即打开盒子宣布皇位的继承人。

What was the Hall of Heavenly Purity used for?

The Hall of Heavenly Purity was used in the following ways:

1. From the Ming Dynasty to the early days of Qing, it was the place where emperor resided and handled his routine affairs;

2. During the Yongzheng reign period, he moved to work and stay in the Hall of Mental Cultivation. Occasionally he came here to make appointment of officials, go over memorials to his highness, and grant audiences to his high – ranking officials, envoys from alien lands, and work out strategies and tactics for suppressing the rebellions of the people;

3. In the Ming and Qing dynasties the bier of the deceased emperor was laid up here. In the Qing Dynasty the

biers of emperors from Shunzhi to Guangxu were all laid here in the hall;

4. In the Qing dynasty, from Emperor Kangxi onwards, no pre – nominated heir prince was announced. Instead, the emperor would write down the name of the heir prince, which, locked up and sealed in a small box, would be put behind the Board of "Open and Aboveboard" in the Hall of Heavenly Purity. And when the emperor passed away, the box would be opened and the successor to the throne would be announced right there on the spot.

161. 交泰殿有什么用途呢？

交泰殿的用途为：

1. 皇后过生日时在此殿举行庆祝活动；

2. 公元 1748 年,乾隆皇帝把代表皇权的 25 颗宝玺(皇帝的印章)收存在这里,同时还有自鸣钟和铜壶滴漏等；

3. 清代皇后祭蚕坛之前在此检查仪式的准备情况。

What was the Hall of Union and Peace used for?

The Hall of Union and Peace was used on the following occasions:

1. Celebration was held here on the birthday of the queen;

2. In 1748, Emperor Qianlong put 25 imperial seals here, and the seals were the symbol of the supreme royal power. Besides, it also housed some clocks and a copper clepsydra;

3. In the Qing Dynasty, the ceremonial rites would be checked over here before the queen went out to offer her sacrifices on the altar for silkworms.

162. 坤宁宫的用处是什么?

坤宁宫的用处如下:

1. 明朝时期,坤宁宫是皇后居住的地方,所以又称中宫;

2. 清朝改为祭神的场所,每年正月十日在此祭神,祭神活动的地点在西间;

3. 清代皇帝结婚时还需在坤宁宫的东暖阁先住三天,再移往养心殿,但实际上此宫并不多用。清朝只有康熙、同治和光绪三位皇帝是在这里结婚的,其他都是婚后才当上皇帝的。

What was the Hall of Earthly Tranquility used for?

The Hall of Earthly Tranquility is used in the following ways:

1. In the Ming Dynasty, it was the residence for queen, hence the name "Central Palace."

2. In the Qing Dynasty, it became a place for offering sacrifices to gods. On the tenth day of the first lunar month every year sacrificial rites would be held here in the western room.

3. In the Qing Dynasty, the emperor and queen had to spend the first three days here in the eastern chamber after their marriage before their removal to the Hall of Mental Cultivation. Actually the hall was not used quite often. In the Qing Dynasty, only three emperors, namely Kangxi, Tongzhi and Guangxu, were married here, the rest being enthroned after their marriage.

163. 御花园的情况是怎样的?

御花园始建于明永乐十五年(1417 年),该园呈长方形,东西长 130 米,南北宽 90 余米,总面积为 11,700 多平方米。园内容纳了 20 多种不同风格的建筑,具有浓厚的宫廷气氛。

　　园内主要的建筑及景点包括:堆秀山,浮碧亭,摛藻堂,万春亭,绛雪轩,天一门,钦安殿,连理柏,石子甬道,养鹿苑,养性斋,千秋亭,四神祠,澄瑞亭,位育斋及延辉阁等。

Could you please say something about that Imperial Garden?

　　The construction of the Imperial Garden was in 1417, the 15th year under the reign of Emperor Yongle In a rectangular shape it is 130 meters from east to west and 90 – some meters from north to south with an area of over 11,700 square meters. It contains more than 20 buildings of different types, unfolding a rich atmosphere of an imperial palace.

　　The main buildings and scenic attractions in the garden include: Duixiushan (Rockeries of Piling Prettiness), Fubiting (Pavilion of Floating Verdure), Wanchunting (Arbor of Eternal Spring), Shiziyongdao (Pebbles – patterned Paths), Yangluyuan (Deer Raising Stable), Yangxinzhai (Mental Cultivation Study), Qianqiuting (Pavilion of Eternity) and Sishensi (Four Gods Temple) and so on.

164. 御花园里的钦安殿有何用处?

　　钦安殿是专作供神用的地方。

　　1. 清朝时期在此祀玄武帝,亦即真武大帝。每年立春、立夏、立秋及立冬之际设供案,奉安神牌,由皇帝到天一门与坤宁门之间拈香行礼;

　　2. 阴历七月七日祭牛郎织女,设供案,奉安神牌。由皇帝、皇后、皇贵妃、贵妃及嫔妃等一起到此拈香行礼。

What was Qin'an Hall in the Imperial Garden used for?

The Hall of Qin'an is a place especially reserved for enshrining gods.

1. The God of the North (Zhenwudi) used to be enshrined here in the Qing Dynasty. A table and a tablet of the god would be set up for offering sacrifices to the god at the Beginning of Spring, Summer, Autumn and Winter every year, the days for the four of the 24 solar terms. On these days the emperor would offer incense – sticks and scrape bows to the god between the Tianyi Gate and the Kunning Gate to appease him.

2. On the seventh day of the seventh lunar month every year a table and a tablet for Cowboy and Weaving Girl would be set up to offer sacrifices to them. On that day the emperor, queen, and imperial concubines would offer incense – sticks and scrape bows to Cowboy and Weaving Girl.

165. 养心殿有何用处?

从清代雍正年间起到清末的二百余年间,皇帝多在此居住和进行日常统治活动。

正间是供一些官员在提拔、调动前被领到这里来见皇帝用的,这种礼仪称为引见。书架上放的书都是老皇帝行使统治的经验、教训,是留给小皇帝看的。

西间是皇帝批阅奏折、同军机大臣策划军政活动用的地方。

东间是清末同治、光绪年间,那拉氏慈禧太后在此实施"垂帘听政"的地方。1911 年,清王朝下台的诏书也是在此宣布的。

后殿是皇帝的寝室,顺治、乾隆及同治三位皇帝都是死在该殿内的。

What was the Hall of Mental Cultivation used for?

During the 200 years or so from the reign of Emperor Yongzheng to the end of the Qing dynasty the hall was the place where emperors lived and handled their state affairs.

The room in the middle was used for introducing to the emperor the officials who were to be promoted or transferred. The books on the shelf were the experiences or lessons gained by the previous emperors. They were left to coming emperors to draw lessons from.

The western room was used by the emperor to read memorials, and map out political and military decisions together with grand ministers.

The eastern room was a place for Empress Dowager Cixi to exercise her "ruling behind the curtain" during the reigning periods of Tongzhi and Guangxu, and in 1911 the imperial edict of abdication was also announced from here.

The rear hall was the bedchamber of the emperor. Shunzhi, Qianlong and Tongzhi, the three emperors of the Qing Dynasty all passed away here.

166. 太极殿、长春宫、储秀宫各有什么用处?

太极殿是明清两代后妃们居住的地方。

长春宫是明清两代妃子们居住的地方。清代曾住过皇后,慈禧太后曾在此宫住过。宫中设有宝座,西一间为卧室;西二为书房,案上陈名家小说;东一间为浴室;东二有储物柜供储存物品之用。殿前设有戏台,与体元殿相连。慈禧50岁生日时,常和王公贵妃们在此看戏作乐。

储秀宫是明清两代后妃们居住的地方。慈禧册封为嫔妃时曾在此处住过,1884 年,她 50 岁生日时还在这里搞过庆贺活动。她的儿子同治皇帝就是在储秀宫后的离景轩内出生的。

What were the Taijidian, Changchungong and Chuxiugong used for?

The Hall of Taijidian used to be a residential palace for queens and concubines in the Ming and Qing dynasties.

The Palace of Changchungong used to be a residential palace for concubines in the Ming and Qing dynasties. It once was the palace for queens in the Qing Dynasty. Empress Dowager Cixi, for example, once lived here. In the central room there was a chair for the queen. The room on the western side was the bedchamber and the one further next to it was the study with novels by noted writers. The room on the eastern side was the bathroom, and the one next to it, the storeroom with a wardrobe. Opposite in front of the palace was a theatre connected with the Tiyuan Hall. On her 50th birthday, Empress Dowager Cixi enjoyed operas here with the princes and lords.

The Hall of Chuxiugong used to be a residential palace for queens and concubines in the Ming and Qing dynasties. Empress Dowager Cixi once lived here when she was an attendant in the palace. In 1884, Cixi celebrated her 50th birthday here. Emperor Tongzhi, her son, was born in the Hall of Lijingxuan behind it.

167. 外西路的建筑是供什么用的?

外西路的建筑主要有:

慈宁宫、慈宁宫花园、寿安宫、寿泉宫及英华殿,是供衰老的太后太妃们居住的地方,但也有前朝留下的年轻嫔妃住在这里。

此外,这里还有供佛用的雨华阁和梵宗楼等建筑物。

What were the palace buildings along the outer‑west route used for?

The main buildings along the outer‑west route are:

The Hall of Cininggong with a garden attached to it, the Hall of Shou'angong, the Palace of Shouquangong and the Hall of Yinghuadian. They were the places where elderly queen mothers and concubines lived. Some young concubines or attendants of the former dynasty or emperors also resided here.

Besides, there are still some other buildings such as Yuhuage Pavilion and Fanzonglou Tower.

168. 在西路口的一排房子是作何用的呢?

西路口的一排房子是清朝的军机处所在地,即军机大臣值班的地方。皇帝在养心殿经常与军机大臣策划军政要事,军机大臣即按照皇帝的旨意,在军机处起草并发出种种军政命令。

What was the row of houses by the entrance of the western lane used for?

They used to be the Office of Privy Council for ministers on duty in the Qing Dynasty. As the emperor lived in the Hall of Mental Cultivation, he would often work out decisions on some matters of political and military importance with his ministers here. And then afterwards, abiding by the intention of the emperor, the ministers would map out and promulgate all sorts of imperial edicts at the office.

169. 外东路的一组建筑的用处是什么？

外东路这一组建筑是十八世纪七十年代建造的。乾隆三十七(1772)年时，他打算在自己当满 60 年皇帝后，便让位给儿子，自己做太上皇。所以就开始修建太上皇的宫殿——宁寿宫。整个工程历时 7 年，它包括正殿、寝宫、书房、花园、佛堂和戏楼。现在其中的部分建筑已辟为绘画馆及珍宝馆的陈列室。

What were the palace buildings along the outer – east route used for?

The buildings along the outer – east route was built in the 1770s. The year of 1772 marked the 37th year of Emperor Qianlong's reign. With an intention to quit the throne in favor of his son in the 60th year of his reign, Emperor Qianlong started to build his own residence of Ningshougong Palace for his retired life. Brought to completion in seven years time the palace consisted of a main hall, a residential chamber, a study, a garden, a hall for worshipping Buddha and a theatre as well. Now some of the buildings are used to display treasures, calligraphy and paintings.

170. 铜龙、铜凤象征着什么？有何用处？

龙象征着皇帝，因为在过去，皇帝总是自命为真龙天子。他受命于天，来统治下方的人民。凤象征皇后，古代人们认为凤是一种长生不死、羽毛极美的百鸟之王，以示龙凤含玺。其次，两种动物都是传说中的神兽，因而用来代表皇权。故宫里的铜龙、铜凤实际上是作为香炉用的，其背部有一圆孔，可燃檀香，香烟从嘴部冒出。

What did the brass dragons and phoenixes signify? And what were they used for?

The dragon was the symbol of the emperor. In Chinese history the emperor always styled themselves as the real dragon, and the son of heaven. They were acting upon the mandate of heaven to rule the people down in the world. The phoenix was the symbol of the queen. With very pretty plume all over, people in ancient times deemed it as a bird enjoying a long life, the king of birds. Hence the phoenix was a good match for the dragon.

Both the dragon and phoenix were mythological animals in legend. They were used to represent the royal power. Actually bronze dragons and phoenixes in the former Imperial Palace were used as incense – burners. With round holes on the back to burn sandalwood with smoke emitting from their mouths.

171. 铜龟、铜鹤象征着什么?

龟和鹤的寿命都很长,在古代被视为是代表吉祥的灵物,是一种长寿的象征。

What did the copper tortoise and crane signify?

Both tortoise and crane are animals supposed to be able to enjoy a long life. In ancient China they were deemed as auspicious animals and symbols of a long life.

172. 金提炉有何用处? 珍宝馆里带有凤凰的金脸盆有何用处?

金提炉是清代皇帝、后妃仪仗中的一部分,用以点燃檀香。

206

皇帝出门时,太监手里提着它在前面走。

金脸盆,据说是皇帝的儿子生下来的头三天用它来洗澡的盆。

Where was the use of the gold – warmers? And what was the use of the gold – basins with phoenixes pattern displayed in the Treasure Hall?

The gold – warmer was an article used by the guards of honor of the emperor, queen and concubines in the Qing Dynasty. When the emperor went out, the gold – warmer would be carried in hand by a eunuch at the head of the procession. The gold – basin was used as a bathtub for the newborn son of the emperor during the first three days after he came to the world.

173. 明朝朱棣是如何当上皇帝的?

明朝的第一个皇帝朱元璋在他晚年时,为了巩固自己的统治,几乎杀尽了帮他建功立国的所有的元臣宿将,而后将自己20多个儿子分封各要塞地区为王,掌握各地军权。他认为这样一来,便可以太平无事了。但到了1399年(洪武三十一年),朱元璋死后,因长子朱标早亡,即由其长孙朱允炆继位,改年号为建文。朱允炆上台后不久,便感到其王叔们的权势过大,威胁着自己的统治。于是便与身边的心腹大臣齐泰、黄子澄等一起谋划削藩事宜,即废除藩王的称号,解除其兵权。可当削藩之事威胁到驻守在当今北京地区的燕王、朱元璋的第四子朱棣时,矛盾便激化成了武装冲突。1399年(建文元年),朱棣举兵南下,号称"靖难",意即皇帝受到奸臣的包围遇难,而发兵前去解救皇帝于危难之中。这是一种名为解难、实为夺权的战争。此战打了四年,到1402年,朱棣大军由扬州渡江,攻陷南京。建文帝朱允炆去向不明。1403年，朱棣在南京登上皇位，改年号为永乐。

How did Zhu Di come to be the emperor of the Ming Dynasty?

In his later years, Zhu Yuanzhang, the first emperor of the Ming dynasty, when nearing the late days of his reign, killed almost all his former officials and generals who had supported him in establishing the dynasty. However, in order to strengthen his rule he appointed some 20 – odd of his sons to be the prince governors commanding over the garrisons at various places and regions of strategic importance. He presumed that by doing so his rule over the country could be consolidated, and the country could be in peace forever. Zhu Yuanzhang died in 1399, the 31st year of his reign. As Zhu Biao, his eldest son, died early, his grandson, Zhu Yunwen succeeded him, his reign title being Jianwen. But no sooner had he ascended the throne than he felt a strong threat from his prince uncles, because they were too powerful to be curbed. So putting heads together with Qi Tai and Huang Zhicheng, his two bosom ministers, he worked out a plan to repeal their titles as prince – governors, thereby abrogating their military power. But when this came to clamp down upon Zhu Di, the fourth son of Zhu Yuanzhang, who then was garrisoning in nowadays Beijing, it triggered off an armed clash. In the 1st year of Jainwen reign, Zhu Di marched his army southwards, naming it an "Army of Salvation," which meant that the emperor was under duress by a handful of crafty and fawning court officials, and he was going to retrieve the emperor from the plight. Though for the national salvation in name, the war, which

208

lasted about four years, was actually a war for seizing state power. Crossing the Yangtse River at Yangzhou, the army headed by Zhu Di captured Nanjing in 1402 and since there was nowhere to find Zhu Yunwen, the emperor, Zhi Di ascended the throne in 1403 in Nanjing, changing the title of his reign into Yongle.

174. 明成祖朱棣为何要从南京迁都北京?

燕王朱棣通过"靖难之役"夺取了皇位以后,为了巩固自己的统治,也采取了削藩的政策,以加强中央集权。但又出现了另一个问题,即北方的边防变得十分空虚,蒙古贵族的骑兵不时南下侵扰,对明王朝的北方构成了严重的威胁。朱棣为燕王时,曾多次同元朝的残余势力作战,他在实践中充分地认识到,安定北方对明朝政权的巩固关系十分重大,因此他在称帝后不久就考虑过迁都之事。1406 年,他开始在北京兴建皇宫和城垣。1409年,朱棣在南京称帝后首次回到北京,为了表明他迁都的决心,他还派人在北京选定了陵址。1420 年正式迁都,并改北平为北京。

Why did Zhu Di, the third emperor of the Ming Dynasty, want to move his capital from Nanjing to Beijing?

After he took over the throne by the "War of Salvation," Zhu Di, the former prince of Yan, wanted to strengthen his rule by curbing the power of the local authorities. However, new problems arose − harassed by the cavalries, the remnant forces of the Mongolian nobles, the defense of the northern frontier area was greatly weakened, a serious threat to the Ming empire. When still a Prince Yan, Zhu Di, had many wars or armed clashes with the remnant forces of the former

Yuan Dynasty. He knew well that to appease the northern frontier area was of utmost importance to the consolidation of the rule of the Ming Empire. So he brewed up an idea of moving his capital to the north soon after his ascending the throne. In 1406, he started the building of his palaces and the city walls in Beijing, and 1409 saw his first return to Beijing after he became the emperor in Nanjing. To show his determination in moving his capital to the north, he had his tomb area found in the surrounding areas of Beijing. The capital was officially moved to Beijing in 1420, replacing the name of Beiping with Beijing.

175. 明朝末代皇帝朱由检是如何死的?

公元 1644 年 3 月 18 日,明朝末代皇帝朱由检(年号崇祯),见李自成率领的农民起义军已经打进了北京城,感到走投无路,便仓惶登上景山徘徊观望,回宫后便剑刺了他的女儿,逼死了皇后。到 19 日凌晨,他见皇城已经不保,大势已去,便跑到了煤山(即今景山公园东山)脚下的一棵古槐树下自缢而死。

How did Zhu Youjian, the last emperor of the Ming Dynasty, die?

On March 18, 1644, when learning that the peasant uprising army led by Li Zicheng had already entered Beijing, Zhu Youjian, his reign title being Chongzhen, found no way out. He went up the Coal Hill to cast a blear look over the city. Moving irritably around for a while he then on returned to the palace to kill his own daughter and force the queen to commit suicide. On the following morning, sensing that the palace would soon fall into the hands of the uprising army, he went up the Coal Hill (or Jingshan Park) again, and hanged himself on a locust tree by the eastern hillside.

176. 护城河的宽及周长各为多少？

故宫的护城河宽 52 米, 周长 3,800 米。

What is the width and circumference of the moat round the Forbidden City?

The moat round the Forbidden City is 52 meters in width and over 3,800 meters in circumference.

177. 太和殿前面广场面积是多少？

太和殿前面广场的面积约为 30,000 平方米。

How large is the square in front of the Hall of Supreme Harmony?

The square in front of the Hall of Supreme Harmony covers an area of 30,000 square meters.

178. 太和殿的建筑面积、东西宽、南北纵深及高度各是多少？

太和殿的建筑面积为 2,300 多平方米, 东西之间宽为 64 米, 南北纵深为 37 米, 高为 35 米。

What is the floor space, the width from east to west, and the length from north to south and the height of the Hall of Supreme Harmony?

The Hall of Supreme Harmony covers a floor space of 2,300 square meters with a length of 64 meters from east to west, and 37 meters between north and south. And it stands 35 meters in height.

179. 太和殿内外的松木柱数、高度及直径各是多少?

太和殿内外的松木柱数共有 72 根,每根高度为 12.7 米,直径为 1.06 米。

How many pinewood pillars are there inside and outside the Hall of Supreme Harmony? How high and thick in diameter are they?

There are altogether 72 pinewood pillars both inside and outside the Hall of Supreme Harmony, and each of them stands 12.7 meters high with a diameter of 1.06 meters.

180. 三大殿四周汉白玉石雕栏板望柱及龙首共有多少?

故宫三大殿周围共有汉白玉石雕栏板望柱 1,458 根,龙首数目共为 1,142 个。

How many carved white marble columns are there along the balustrades round the three main halls? And how many dragonheads do they count all round?

There are altogether 1, 458 carved white − marble columns and 1,142 dragonheads around the three main halls in the Forbidden City.

181. 太和殿前的铜炉数目有多少? 铸造年代如何?

太和殿前共有铜炉 18 个,系明嘉靖年间(公元 16 世纪)时铸造。在皇帝举行典礼时,这些铜炉是用来燃烧檀香及松柏枝的。

How many copper - burners are there in front of the Hall of Supreme Harmony and when were they cast?

There are 18 copper - burners in front of the Hall of Supreme Harmony. Cast in the 16th century during the Jiajing reign period in Ming, they were used to burn sandalwood or pine sprigs when grand ceremonies were being held in the imperial palace.

182. 故宫中和殿、保和殿的面积各是多少？高度又各为多少？

故宫中和殿的面积为 583 平方米，保和殿面积为 1,230 平方米，而高度均为 27 米。

What are the respective floor space and the height of the Hall of Complete Harmony and of the Hall of Preserving Harmony?

The floor space of the Hall of Complete Harmony is 583 square meters and that of the Hall of Preserving Harmony 1, 230 square meters with the same height of 27 meters.

183. 故宫内大铜缸的数目是多少？何时铸造？有何用途？

故宫内现有铜缸 231 个，有的是明代铸造的，但也有铸于清代的，铁缸是明代铸造的，鎏金铜缸则铸于清代，当时是为宫内贮水防火之用。每个缸重约两吨，鎏金约一百两。

How many copper cauldrons are there in the Forbidden City? When were they made? And what were they used for?

Now there are 231 copper cauldrons in the Forbidden

City. Some of them were made in the Ming Dynasty, and the others made in the Qing. The iron cauldrons were cast in the Ming Dynasty, and the gilded copper ones were the products of the Qing. They were used as water – tanks for the prevention of fire in the palace. Each cauldron weighs about two tons and the gold applied on the cauldron is about 100 taels.

184. 故宫内铜路灯的数目是多少？何时制作的？

故宫内现共有铜路灯 61 个,它们都是清代制作的。

How many copper lamps along the roads – side are there in the Forbidden City? And when were they made?

Now there are 61 in all copper lamps along the roads – side of the Forbidden City. They were all made in the Qing dynasty.

185. 琉璃起源于何时？使用年代及其烧制地点如何？

琉璃的起源：

琉璃在古代也称"流离",是一种用矿石烧制的半透明体材料,加上铜、铝、锡及硝等不同配料,可以烧制出多种不同的色彩。解放后,在中国出土的战国墓葬品中,就发现有琉璃珠。

琉璃的使用年代：

在汉代以前,琉璃仅被统治阶级用来作为窗扉、屏风、盘碗、剑盒等器物之上的珍贵装饰品。到了北魏初年(公元 5 世纪初),琉璃被大规模地用于宫殿建筑上。隋唐以后,更为普遍地用作砖瓦及各类建筑物的装饰之用,形成了中国古代宫殿、坛庙等建筑的独特材料和风格。

主要烧制地点：

由于琉璃制品基本上是古代封建皇帝及贵族建筑物的专用

214

材料,因此烧制琉璃的地点往往是在各个朝代的京城附近。北魏时,中国第一个烧制琉璃的窑址就是在当时的都城——平城(今山西大同市东)附近;元朝时的窑址在北京和平门外海王村,即现在的琉璃厂;明朝仍用其窑址,以后又扩展到西山门头沟的琉璃渠村等地,直至清代。

When did the colored glaze come into being? When was it used for the first time? And where was it produced?

The making of the colored glaze:

Having different writings of same pronunciation in Chinese, the colored glaze is a kind of translucent material produced by firing a certain sort of ore and adding to it some different ingredients such as copper, aluminum, tin, saltpetre, etc. Glazes ravel various colors. From the burials unearthed after 1949, some glazed beads were discovered from the tombs of the Warring States period.

Before the Han Dynasty, the Chinese people began to use the colored glaze. At that time it was only used by the ruling class as decorations on the gates, windows, screens, plates and bowls, sword – cases, and other treasure articles. It was not until the beginning of the fifth century during the period of the Northern Wei was it widely used on palatial buildings. Later, after the Sui and Tang dynasties it was more popularly used to turn out glazed tiles and bricks for decorations on many buildings of palaces and altar – shrines. Thereby it was a kind of unique building material in ancient China.

As the colored glaze was a kind of building material specially used by feudal emperors and lords on their buildings in ancient times, the places for its production were usually somewhere around the capital cities of different dynasties. The first kiln for making glazes in China was in Pingcheng (nowadays a place to the east of Datong city in Shanxi), the capital city of the Northern Wei Dynasty. The first kiln of the Yuan Dynasty was located in Haiwang Village (now Liulichang Street) near Hepingmen in Beijing, which was still used in the Ming Dynasty and further afterwards extended to Liuliqu Village of Mentougou area in the Qing Dynasty.

186. 藻井和轩辕镜有何解释？

故宫的太和殿、交泰殿及养心殿等殿堂内都有藻井和所谓"轩辕镜"，是中国古代建筑物上的一种传统的装饰处理。

藻井：古代也称天井、绮井或方井等等，仅限用于帝王宫殿、寺庙和贵族府第等所谓尊贵的建筑物上，一般民房是不许用的。它是在建筑物天花板上最重要的部位，如宝座或神像的顶上，做成凹陷似井圈的形状，再在上面刻画种种图案彩纹，即所谓藻文，所以就称作"藻井"。

藻井的中心部位，一般为圆形，叫做"明镜"。在明清时代，往往在明镜部位刻成蟠龙形，所以藻井也叫做"龙井"。关于藻井的来源，则说法不一：有的认为它可能是古代"天窗"的遗迹，尤其是藻井的"明镜部分，就是表示天窗的形象；也有人认为这是原始社会中人们穴居时期，洞顶上入口处的遗迹。当时，洞穴开口处称作"中雷"，不仅可供上下出入和通风透亮，更是举行祭阳的地方。所以后来宫殿坛庙的建筑中都采用藻井，也含有"神圣"的意思。再者，仰望藻井，其形如伞如盖，可显示封建统治者之"尊严"。

关于藻井的文献记载，早在汉代就有了。一般均为圆形、方形或多边形，并饰有各种花纹、雕刻和绘画。

轩辕镜：所谓轩辕镜即是从蟠龙口下垂的悬珠。传说是远古时代轩辕黄帝所造,是中国最早的镜子。但它为什么与藻井联系在一起,其确切的含义尚不清楚,一般的说法是所谓"龙戏珠"的意思,但也有人说这是一种表现"明镜"的手法。

Is there anything to say about the "Coffered Ceilings" and "Xuanyuan Mirror"?

Visitors can find the Caisson Ceiling and the so – called Xuanyuan Mirror at the Hall of Supreme Harmony, Hall of Union and Peace, and Hall of Mental Cultivation in the Forbidden City. It is a sort of traditional treatment to the decorations on buildings in ancient times.

Coffered Ceiling, called the skylight or air – raise in ancient times, was only used on palatial buildings, temples or mansions for reverend lords; no house of civilians was allowed to use it. a concave in the shape of a well was made at the most important part of the ceiling of a building, such as above the sacred seat or a Buddha statue, hence the name "caisson ceiling".

The central part of a caisson is usually round, known as the "bright mirror." During the Ming and Qing dynasties, the part was normally carved with a curling dragon, so the caisson was also addressed as "dragon caisson". As to how the caisson came into being, it has different ways to explain it. Some say it is possibly a leftover of the skylight from ancient times, especially the part of the "bright mirror" which looks very much like the shape of a skylight. Others hold it that it is perhaps an entrance opening of a cave used by primitive men when they were still dwelling in caves. At that time the entrance was called "Zhonglei," which was not only used as a passage but also a skylight or an air – raise. Furthermore it was a place for offering sacrifices to the sun. Therefore, all the palatial buildings and altar – shrines later had caissons suggesting something sacred. Moreover, the caisson, which looks like an umbrella or a canopy from below could help show off "dignity" of feudal rulers.

The record about the caisson could be found in as early as the Han Dynasty. It was round, square or polygonal in shape and decorated with varied patterns, carvings and paintings.

Xianyuan Mirror: It is a suspended string of beads down from the mouth of the curling dragon. Legend has it that it was invented by the Yellow Emperor in remote antiquity. It was the earliest mirror in China. But why was it related to the patterned caisson? Most people say that it means the "dragon is playing with pearls," while the rest hold that it is a means to display the "bright mirror".

187. 请说一说关于三希堂的来历好吗?

公元 1746 年,乾隆皇帝得到了王询的"伯远帖",连同他已得的王羲之的"快雪时晴帖"及王献之的"中秋帖",都藏到了养心殿中西套间的暖阁内,并给这间房起名为"三希堂"。他认为这三种帖是稀世珍宝,并就此作了御批。

Could you say something about how the Hall for Three Rare Treasures came into being?

In 1746, Emperor Qianlong had a chance to lay his hands on the Boyuan Model of Calligraphy by the famous calligrapher Wang Xun. Emperor Qianlong kept it in a suite of the western room in the Hall of Mental Cultivation together with the

218

Kuaixueshiqing Model of Calligraphy by Wang Xizhi and the Zhongqiu Model of Calligraphy by Wang Xianzhi, Wang Xizhi's son, also a famous calligrapher.. Qianlong believed they were rarely treasures, hence the name "Hall of Three Rare Treasures."

香 山
(The Fragrant Hill)

香山公园
(The Fragrant Hill Park)

188. 香山公园位于何处？距北京市区有多远？

香山位于京郊西山的东麓，距北京市区 25 公里，是北京著名的山林公园。

Where lies the Fragrant Hill Park? And how far is it from the city proper of Beijing?

Twenty five kilometers away from the city at the eastern foothill of the Western Hills, the Fragrant Hill Park is a renowned one of all the parks tucked away among the hills in the western suburbs of Beijing.

189. 香山公园的面积有多大？其最高峰的海拔高度是多少？

香山公园的占地面积达 160 公顷，其最高峰的海拔高度为 557 米。

How large an area does the Fragrant Hill Park cover? And what's the elevation of its highest peak?

With its highest peak rising 557 meters above sea level,

220

the Fragrant Hill Park occupies an area of 160 hectares.

190. 香山公园建于何时? 有多少年历史?

远在金大定二十六年(1186 年)时,就在这里为皇帝建"行宫"和香山寺,距今已有 800 余年的历史。以后历代又加以扩建,例如:清乾隆十年(1745 年),香山经大规模的扩建后,便有了 28 景,并定名为静宜园,成为清代京城西部著称于世的"三山五园"之一。

When was the Fragrant Hill Park built? And how long has it been in existence?

As far back as in 1186, the 26th year under the reign of Emperor Dading in the Jin dynasty, the construction of a "temporary palace" for the emperor together with the Fragrant Hill Temple was completed. The succeeding dynasties ever after carried on the job to have it expanded. For instance, in 1745, the 10th year under the reign of Emperor Qianlong in the Qing dynasty, a large - scale expansion started to make the park large enough to contain as many as 28 scenic spots and attractions. Known as Jingyi Garden then, the park became one of the renowned "Three Hills with Five Gardens" of the Qing Dynasty in the western suburbs of Beijing.

191. 清代京西名闻遐迩的"三山五园"所指的是哪里?

所谓"三山五园",它所指的是香山的"静宜园",玉泉山的"静明园",万寿山的"清漪园",还有畅春园和圆明园。

With regard to the "Three Hills And Five Gardens" in the western suburbs of Beijing in the Qing Dynasty, what does that refer to?

The so – called "Three Hills and Five Gardens" refer to the "Jingyi Garden" in the Fragrant Hill, the "Jingming Garden" in the Jade Fountain Hill, the "Qingyi (Clear Ripples) Garden" in the Longevity Hill as well as the "Changchun Garden" and the "Yuanmingyuan Garden."

192. 香山公园曾经受过何种不幸遭遇？

在1860年和1900年帝国主义两次入侵北京时,园内的28景大多为侵略军抢劫和烧毁。继而在军阀、国民党和日伪统治时期,该园又被一些达官显贵,占为私人住宅别墅,年久失修,直至解放前夕,这里留下的只是一片荒凉。1949年后,大部分名胜景点先后得到了重新修建,但因元气大伤,已远不能与以往相比。

What were the unfortunate sufferings the Fragrant Hill Park ever underwent?

In 1860 and 1900 Beijing were twice occupied by the imperialist invaders and most of the 28 scenic spots and attractions in the Fragrant Hill Garden were destroyed by the invading armies. They were set free to plunder at will and set fire to it. Moreover, during the period under the rule of warlords, the Kuomintang and the puppet government controlled by the Japanese invaders, the park was privately occupied by some high – ranking officials and officers as their own villas, thus leaving attended till the liberation of Beijing. After liberation, many of the ruined ones were renovated one after another. Nevertheless, they fall far short as they used to be because the destruction was serious and even vital.

193. "香山"之名是怎么来的?

"香山"一名来自西山顶上的那块巨石,即"乳峰石"。因其形状似"香炉",加之周围常常出现云雾缭绕的动人景象,看来犹如香烟弥漫。因此,人们便称之为"香炉山",简称"香山"。

How was the name the "Fragrant Hill" derived?

The name of the Fragrant Hill was derived from the huge piece of rock at the top of the Western Hills, namely the "Teat Peak Rock." As it looks very much like a censer, often girdled by wisps of spiraling mist as if it were giving out incense — smoke it was called the "Censer Hill." Later, it was shortened as the "Fragrant Hill."

194. 解放后的香山公园有些什么变化?

解放以后,人民政府对香山公园的发展十分关心,在园内栽种了大量的花木果树,还增添了相应的服务设施,如茶座、小吃及小买部等,后来还建了香山饭店。与此同时,还开通了自香山寺至"鬼见愁"的盘山路,后又增建了山脚至"鬼见愁"的缆车,全长 1,400 米,至山顶仅需 18 分钟。

What changes have taken place in the Fragrant Hill Park after liberation?

Since liberation the Government has paid great attention to the development of the Fragrant Hill Park. A great number of flowers and fruit – trees have been planted, and various service facilities have been set up, such as tea－booths, snack and retailers' shops. To offer further convenience to visitors, the Fragrant Hill Hotel was built nearby. At the same time a winding－hill road leading from the Fragrant Hill Temple to the Devil Frowning Peak was opened and also the cable car, 1, 400 meters long, will take you to the summit within 18 minutes.

195. 香山公园里有哪些主要的名胜古迹?

香山公园里的主要名胜古迹分布在北、南、西三个区域,其中主要有眼镜湖、见心斋、昭庙、玉华山庄、西山晴雪、鬼见愁、洪光寺、香山寺和双清别墅等。

What major scenic spots and historical sites does the Fragrant Hill Park have?

The major scenic spots and historical sites are mainly located in the northern, western and southern areas in the Fragrant Hill Park. They are known as the Lake of Spectacles, Tranquil Heart Studio, Bright Temple, Jade Flowers Villa, A Clear Day Snow Scene in the Western Hills, Devil Frowning Peak, Hongguang Temple, Fragrant Hill Temple and Twin Streams Villa and so on.

196. 香山公园附近还有些什么名胜古迹?

在香山公园的附近,主要还有碧云寺、卧佛寺、樱桃沟、玉皇顶、万花山和团城演武厅等名胜古迹。

What other scenic spots and historical sites does the Fragrant Hill Park have in its vicinity?

In the close vicinity of the Fragrant Hill Park, there are the Azure Cloud Temple, Reclining Buddha Temple, Cherry Blossom Valley, Jade Emperor's Summit, Thousand Blossom Hill and the Round City Martial Arts Performance Hall, etc.

197. 香山公园内的眼镜湖其名自何而来?

眼镜湖位于香山公园的北门,那是两个园形的小湖,用一座白石拱桥连接起来。自远望去,犹如一付闪光发亮的眼镜,故取名为"眼镜湖"。湖的北面靠山,上有叠石小洞,洞口有小瀑下注,晃如水帘,故又称之为小水帘洞。

How does the name of the Lake of Spectacles in the Fragrant Hill Park come about?

Lying outside the north gate of the Fragrant Hill Park is a pair of little round lakes, which is linked up by an arched bridge built of white stone – slabs. As it looks very much like a pair of glistening spectacles in a distance, hence the name. By the northern side of the lake there is a small hill with a tiny manmade stone – cave and the entrance of it is screened off by a little cascade, thereby called the "Tiny Water – curtain Cave."

198. 香山著名的"园中之园"在哪里?

见心斋是香山著名的"园中之园",位于眼镜湖的西面。见心斋始建于明代嘉靖年间,是一座具有南国特色的环形庭园式建筑。庭中有半圆形的水池,东、南、西三面为彩廊,连接着正面的三间水榭。这就是见心斋的正厅,中间挂有嘉靖帝书写的七律一首。小院造型别致,环境幽静,池水清澈,游鱼可见,是个悠游休憩的理想之所。

Where does the well – known "Garden Within The Garden" lie in the Fragrant Hill?

Lying to the west of the Lake of Spectacles, the Tranquil Heart Studio is the well known "Garden Within the Garden" in the Fragrant Hill. First built during the period of Emperor Jiajing's reign in the Ming Dynasty this courtyard – style building features the art of architecture in south China. In the courtyard you'll find a semi – circled pond flanked on three sides by a covered and colorfully painted corridor, that joins with a waterside three – bay hall. This is the main hall of the Tranquil Heart Studio and hung in the middle is a septa – syllabic verse composed by Emperor Jiajing. Delicate and exquisite as it is in its architectural structure, the tiny courtyard seems to be tucked away in a secluded spot. With a shoal of fish plying to – and – fro in clear water, the studio is an ideal spot for relaxation and sightseeing.

199. 昭庙建于何时?为什么要建昭庙?其主要建筑是哪些?

昭庙的全称为宗镜大昭之庙,位于见心斋南面。该庙建于乾隆四十五年(1780 年),它是为迎接西藏班禅六世进京而特地建造的一座喇嘛庙。庙宇规模宏大,整个建筑由 3 个主要部分组成:用琉璃砖瓦和汉白玉建成的牌坊,上雕彩云龙纹图案,匾额用汉、满、蒙及藏四种文字书写;主体建筑是藏式虹台,高 3 丈,以砖石为基座,中央部位下凹,天井中立牌,上面用四种文字

226

记述了建庙的缘由;还有便是彩色琉璃塔,塔的上部为七层八角的密檐式建筑,檐端挂有 56 个铜铃,每面龛内均有神像,塔顶置黄色琉璃宝瓶,塔之中部环有白石雕栏,栏下为八面张开的瓦盖,塔基亦为八面,每面均刻有一尊佛像。

When and why was the Bright Temple built? What are the main buildings in it?

Located to the south of the Tranquil Heart Studio, the Grand Bright Temple, built in the 45th year (1780) of Emperor Qianlong's reign in the Qing, is a lama temple which was built up specially for welcoming the sixth Bainqen Lama to Beijing. The temple, spacious in scale, consists mainly of the following three parts: 1. the memorial archway built of white marble pieces and glazed tiles. It is carved with rosy clouds and dragons and the board on it was inscribed in the four scripts of Chinese, Manchu, Mongolian and Tibetan. 2. The main building here is a Tibetan — styled terrace, which, standing about 10 meters high on a brick pedestal is concave in the middle. Erected in its center is a stone — tablet recording in the four scripts about why the terrace was built. 3. There is a seven — storeyed octagonal pagoda built of glazed bricks and tiles. The eaves on the upper part of the pagoda are in compact style with 56 brass — bells hung on their tips. With little shrines housing Buddha figurines on the facades, the pagoda is topped with a precious knob glazed in yellow. Surrounded by balustrades of white marbles in its middle, the underneath of the pagoda is encircled by an octagonal shade covered with tiles. The pedestal of it is also an octahedron with each side having a carved Buddha image.

200. "西山晴雪"是由谁题写的?

"西山晴雪"是著名的"燕京八景"之一,是在金代命名的。清代在此立碑,碑文为乾隆皇帝亲笔所书。这里风景优美,地势开阔,可饱览全园景色。冬季以观雪景为佳,夏季又是纳凉避暑的良好去处,所以后人有诗赞曰:"八景西山晴雪好,夏季避暑亦相宜……"

Who has inscribed the tablet "A Clear Day Snow Scene in the Western Hills"?

"A Clear Day Snow Scene in the Western Hills" is one of the "Eight Scenic Attractions in Yanjing" nominated in the Kin Dynasty, and the tablet was erected in the Qing Dynasty with the inscription autographed by Emperor Qianlong. As the area is pretty and wide open, it is a fine spot for a panoramic view over the garden, enjoying snow scenes in winter and sheltering heat in summer. Therefore, a poem in praise of it goes like this:"Of the Eight Scenic Attractions in Yanjing, a Clear Day Snow Scene in the Western Hills is the best; also it is affable for sheltering away summer heat. . . ."

201. 香山的最高处为什么称为"鬼见愁"?

"鬼见愁"又名乳峰石,位于"西山晴雪"之上。海拔高度为557米,是香山著名的高峰。那里是春游、消夏、赏秋和观雪的绝佳去处。但因山势陡峭,又常吞云吐雾,且攀登十分不易,故有"鬼见愁"之称。

Why is the peak in the Fragrant Hills called the "Devil Frowning Peak"?

The "Devil Frowning Peak," also known as the "Teat Peak Rock," is located above the scenic spot "A Clear Day Snow Scene in the Western Hills." It is a well-known peak of the Fragrant Hill with an elevation of 557 meters. Though it is an excellent place for an outing in spring, sheltering heat in summer, enjoying beautiful scenes in autumn and a snow spectacle in winter, yet the access of it is difficult. As it is very steep and often clad in mist, hence the name the "Devil Frowning Peak".

202. 试述双清别墅的由来,谁曾在那里住过?

在香山寺东南的半山坡上,有一座清静别致的庭院,即为双清别墅。因其院内有两道清清的流泉,"双清"二字便由此而来。这里的环境十分优美,有山有水,相映成趣。院内绿树成荫,正中有一池塘,水上碧莲漂浮,水中游鱼翕忽。池旁建有一座八角小亭,与院内的一棵参天银杏交织成一幅秀丽宁静而又迷人的景色。

此院建于 1917 年,当年河北发大水,督办熊希龄办香山慈幼局,就在此建了一座别墅,始称"双清别墅"。

1949 年 3 月至 11 月,毛泽东主席迁来此地居住,筹划建国大计,并在这里发表了许多重要文件。著名的《七律·人民解放军占领南京》即吟成于这里的八角亭中。建国以后,毛主席仍在这里住了一段时间,直至搬入北京中南海。

Please tell us whence came the Twin – stream Villa? And who once lived here?

Up half the slope to the southeast of the Fragrant Hill Temple there is a nice – looking family – styled courtyard tucked away in a quiet spot. This is the Twin – stream Villa. There are two murmuring springs in the courtyard, hence the name. With hills and brooks around to form an interesting picture, it offers a beautiful environment. In the courtyard there is a little pond shaded in lush green, with water lilies floating on the surface and shoal of fish shuttling freely in the water. With a tiny octagonal arbor by the waterside and an old ginkgo tree towering into the sky, it presents an enchanting and pretty atmosphere here in the seclusion.

Governor Xiong Xiling built the villa in 1917 when he was running a charity office for children here after a flood broke out in Hebei that year.

From March to November, 1949, moving along together with the Central Committee of the Chinese Communist Party, Chairman Mao lived here, working out the program for the founding of the People's Republic of China releasing a great many important documents. A very famous poem "The Capture of Nanjing by the People's Liberation Army" was composed right here in that little arbor. After the founding of the People's Republic of China, Chairman Mao still lived here for some time until he finally moved into Zhongnanhai in Beijing.

203. "玉华山庄"的今昔情况又是怎样的?

"玉华山庄"位于香山公园的中心,原为明清时期的一座古庙。该庙于 1860 年被英法联军烧毁,随后便变成了私人别墅。现为香山公园内的茶点服务部。山庄内亭台高筑,泉水淙淙,古木参天,榕树成行,是游客们休憩、赏景的理想去处。

How was the Jade Flower Villa in the past and how is it at present?

Situated right in the center of the Fragrant Hill Park, the Jade Flower Villa used to be an old temple in the Ming and Qing dynasties. Brought down in a fire in 1860 when the An-glo – French Allied Army was attacking Beijing, it was later turned into a private villa. Now it is a service center offering tea and snacks to visitors to the park. With elegant pavilions on terraces, gurgling springs towering trees and plane – trees lined neatly along, it is an ideal spot for relaxation and enjoying scenic beauties.

204. 香山红叶是否就是枫叶呢?

不是,那是黄栌树叶。香山红叶,名闻中外,是西山风景区中一种奇特景观。香山的黄栌树,是清代乾隆年间开始种植的。经过 200 余年来的培育,现已形成了一个有着 94,000 余株树的黄栌林区。每年深秋的 10 月中旬至 11 月中旬,这里漫山遍野,一片火红,是观赏香山红叶的最佳时节,因而吸引了来自全国各地的许多游客到此一饱眼福。

Are the red leaves in the Fragrant Hills the maple leaves?

No, they are not. They are the leaves of smoke trees (cotinus coggygria). Renowned at home and abroad the red leaves at the Fragrant Hill are a spectacular scene of the Western Hills. The smoke trees were planted here during the Qianlong reign period of the Qing dynasty. Through a careful nurturing of over 200 years, the trees, totaling 94,000, have developed into a forest. Every year from mid – October to mid – November in late fall, the whole area is tinged with red. It is the best season for enjoying the red leaves. So it draws a lot of visitors from all over the country in autumn.

205. 你能简述一下香山饭店的情况吗?

香山饭店位于香山公园内,1982 年正式开始营业。它由美籍华人贝聿铭设计,建筑面积为 36,000 平方米,有 11 个庭院。主园内有一人工湖,另有 18 个景点分别点缀于饭店的各个院内。饭店三面环山,是个领略秋霜红叶盛名之所。

香山饭店有客房 293 套,其中标准间为 262 间,套间 30 套,另有 1 套总统套房。饭店设施一应俱全,客房内备有国际、国内长途直拨电话,小酒巴、中西餐厅及宴会厅 8 个。中餐以川菜、鲁菜、粤菜和宫庭菜为主。另外,其它服务设施,如商店、商务中心、美容院等也都齐全,还有一个可供 6 种语言同声传译的多功能厅。

Could you say something about the Fragrant Hill Hotel?

Located in the Fragrant Hill Park the hotel was put into operation in 1982. Designed by a famous architect, an American Chinese I. M. Pei, the hotel complex consists of 11 courtyards, with a floor space of 36,000 square meters. In the main courtyard, there is an artificial lake. All the 11 courtyards are adorned with 18 scenic attractions of different kinds. Embraced by hills on three sides, the hotel is known for its frosty tints of red in late autumn.

The hotel consists of 262 standard rooms, 30 suites and a

presidential suite. It has every facilities such as DDD and IDD telephone services, mini — bars, eight restaurants and banquet halls serving both western and Chinese dishes. Their Sichuan, Shandong, Guangdong and the imperial court cuisine is very famous. In addition, it has shops, business centers, a beauty parlor and a multi — function hall with earphones able to offer an extemporaneous interpretation in six languages at a time.

碧云寺

（The Azure Cloud Temple）

206. 碧云寺建于何时? 该寺与明代太监有何关系?

碧云寺位于香山公园北门外,寺院建筑十分完整,是西山风景区中一座首屈一指的名刹古寺。该寺始建于元代至元二十六年(1289 年),原名碧云庵。到了明代,御马太监于经看中了这块风景优美、环境清静的风水宝地,就在寺后修建墓穴,以为百年之计,并将庵改为寺。但因不久以后下狱而死去,其愿遂成泡影。后来又有一位叫魏忠贤的太监,在于经的墓穴之上进行扩建,也想死后埋葬于此。但无独有偶,魏因罪发而自缢身死,终令葬身此墓穴的愿望又付之东流。

When was the Azure Cloud Temple built? And what was the original intention of it?

Located outside the north gate of the Fragrant Hill Park, the Azure Cloud Temple, with a complete set of buildings around, is a famous Buddhist temple in the Western Hills. First built in 1289 during the Yuan Dynasty it was originally named the Azure Cloud Convent. However, in the Ming Dynasty, a eunuch by the name of Yu Jing who was in charge of the imperial stable took a liking on this tranquil spot. As it was a place of a picturesque scenery and high geomantic quality, he intended to build behind the temple a tomb for his own eternal rest. At the same time he changed the name of a convent into that of a temple. But not long afterwards, he was jailed and died in prison, his wishes shattered like bubbles. Later, another notorious eunuch named Wei Zhongxian came, trying to enlarge the tomb cavity built by Yu in the hope that he could be buried here after his death. Nevertheless, it was not unique but had its counterpart. He was ordered to hang himself when he was convicted guilty in the first year of Emperor Chongzheng's reign, thus turning his wishful thinking again into a stretch of water eastward flowing.

207. 碧云寺自清代至今有过什么变化?

清乾隆年间,曾大兴土木,为碧云寺增建了"罗汉堂"、"水泉院"及"金刚宝座塔";1954 年,又在这里设立了"孙中山纪念堂"。

寺院的整体布局是沿山势而上的,殿堂层层,依山而筑。自山门至寺顶共为 6 层,300 多级石阶。进山门之前,得先过一座石桥,该桥架于山门之外的绝壁之上,石桥之下为 5 丈多深的沟壑。庙门外四周,古木参天,绿荫蓊郁,一股清泉自寺内冲出,直泻壑底,给人一种爽心舒适之感,是一处游览休憩的理想之所。

What changes have taken place in the Azure Cloud Temple ever since the Qing Dynasty?

During the period of Emperor Qianlong's reign in the Qing Dynasty, a construction project was carried out on a large scale here with an arhat – hall, a spring – water courtyard and a Vajra – seat pagoda built up. Later in 1954, Dr Sun Yat – sen Memorial Hall was set up in the temple.

The layout of the temple was made all along the axis up the slope with rows of halls built one higher up over the other. From the temple gate to the top at the back of it, there are six terraces with more than 300 steps in - between. Before entering the temple gate, you have to cross a stone bridge spanning over a steep cliff with a deep chasm below. Growing on the outside of the temple gate are many old trees towering in lush green, forming a natural shade above. Gushing out from the temple is a clear spill of spring water, which pours right into the bottom as deep as over 10 meters below. Visitors will get a fresh sensation here. Therefore, the Azure Cloud Temple is a very good place for sightseeing or a rest.

208. 碧云寺内的罗汉堂建于何时？内有多少尊罗造像汉？

罗汉堂位于寺内南院,是清乾隆十三年(1748 年)仿照杭州西湖的净慈寺建造的。内有 508 尊罗汉坐像,均系释迦牟尼的弟子,据说这是按照乾隆皇帝钦定的名单和顺序排列的。各罗汉前均立有漆金神牌,上面写有罗汉的名字。乾隆把自己也封为罗汉,名之曰破邪见尊者。

When was the hall of arhats in the Azure Cloud Temple built? And how many statues of arhats do the hall house?

Located in the south courtyard of the Azure Cloud Temple, the hall of arhats was built in 1748, the 13th year under the reign of Emperor Qianlong in the Qing Dynasty and it was an imitation of the Jingci Temple by the West Lake in Hangzhou. Seated in the hall are 508 statues of arhats who are all disciples of Skt. Sakyamuni. Arranged as said in order according to the name - list approved out by Emperor Qianlong every arhat has in its front a gold - painted shrine - board with his name written on it. Among them, Emperor Qianlong is a self - styled arhat by the name of "Doing away with Fallacies."

209. 济公是谁？他在罗汉堂内的什么位置上？

济公即是道济，道济是剃度他的师父为其起的法名，济公或济癫则是他的别称。他是南宋时期的僧人，俗家姓李，浙江临海人。因济公常为民众做好事，佛教徒们便把他神化为罗汉，即所为降龙者是也。他曾出家到杭州灵隐寺，后移住净慈寺。据说，济公来罗汉堂时晚了一步，500 个座位均已占满，只好置身于罗汉堂内的梁上，像高约尺许。

Who is Jigong? Where is he in this hall of arhats?

Jigong or Monk Daoji, is an ordained name given by his master, and Jigong, or insane Monk Ji, is his nickname. Being a monk in the Southern Song Dynasty, he was born in Linhai County Zhejiang Province, and his family name is Li. As he was always doing things beneficial to the populace, the Buddhists deified him an arhat by the name of "Subduing the Dragon." First ordained as a novice in the Lingyin Temple, Hangzhou, he was later shifted to stay in the Jingci Temple. As he came to the hall of arhats a bit late all 500 seats had already been occupied. So he had to sit on the beam instead with his figure minified as of only one third meter in height.

210. 为什么要在碧云寺内设中山纪念堂？

孙中山先生在 1925 年 3 月 12 日病逝于北京，其灵柩曾停放在碧云寺的普明妙觉殿内，后于 1929 年 5 月移至南京紫金山的中山陵安葬，但其衣冠仍封存在金刚宝座塔台基下的拱门内。1954 年，普明妙觉殿进行大整修，并辟为孙中山生平事迹展览室，即纪念堂。

Why was Dr Sun Yat‒sen Memorial Hall set up in the Azure Cloud Temple?

Died on March 12, 1925 in Beijing, the bier of Dr Sun Yat‒sen was laid here in the Hall of Enlightenment and Sensibility in the Azure Cloud Temple. And in May, 1929, it was removed to the mausoleum built for him at the foothills of Purple Mountain in Nanjing, but his clothes and cap were still sealed up in the vault under the platform of the Vajra Seat Pagoda behind the temple. However, the Hall of Enlightenment and Sensibility went over a thorough repair in 1954 and was afterwards turned into Dr Sun Yat‒sen Memorial Hall with his life‒stories on display here.

211. 孙中山纪念堂里陈列着哪些东西？

普明妙觉殿的正厅前檐横匾为孙夫人宋庆龄的手书。正厅中央安放着孙中山先生的半身塑像,背后为朱红漆雕屏风。右侧陈列着孙先生的墨宝遗著;左侧摆放的是苏联政府送来的玻璃棺椁,棺盖为钢质。但因当时孙先生的遗体早在两周以前就已入殓,故未能用上,而陈放于此,留作纪念。厅内左右墙壁上,镶嵌着用汉白玉石雕刻的《孙中山致苏联遗书》的全文。正厅两侧厢房内为孙先生生平事迹展。1990 年又安放了孙中山汉白玉塑像。

What are the things on display in Dr Sun Yat‒sen Memorial Hall?

The horizontal board hung under the frontal eave of the main hall of the Hall of Enlightenment and Sensibility shows the handwriting of Mme Song Qing‒ling. In the center of the hall sits a bust of Dr Sun Yat-sen backed by a carved lacquer screen in red. Displayed on the right are the treasured posthumous works by Dr Sun, and on the left a glass coffin with a steel lid presented by the Government of the USSR. As the coffin arrived too late and the remains of Du Sun had already been coffined two weeks ago, it was not possible to use it any more. So the best way was to leave it on display here. The walls on both sides of the hall are inserted with white marble pieces on which was inscribed with the text in full the posthumous letter addressed to the USSR by Dr Sun Yat-sen written before his death. On display in the two annexes of the main hall is the life story about him and finally in 1990 a white marble statue of him was put on exhibition here.

212. 碧云寺内的金刚宝座塔是怎样一回事呢?

金刚宝座塔建于清乾隆十三年(1748年),本指建于印度菩提伽耶城的释迦悟道成佛之处的纪念塔,塔高34.7米,全部为汉白玉石砌成,是碧云寺的最高点。

塔上有两座小型的喇嘛塔和五座十三层密檐式方塔。整座金刚宝座塔布满着精美绝伦的浮雕,上有大小佛像、天王、力士及龙凤狮象和云纹等,均为传统的藏式雕刻。五塔中,每座塔各代表一尊如来佛,故称为五轮塔。孙中山先生逝世后,其灵柩曾暂停于塔内,后迁往南京安葬,但其生前的衣冠仍封葬于此塔基的拱门里,故该塔又称孙中山先生衣冠冢。

Please say something about the Vajra Seat Pagoda in the Azure Cloud Temple?

Built in the 13th year (1748) of Emperor Qianlong's reign in the Qing dynasty, the Vajra Seat Pagoda used to be a stupa built in the city of Buddhagaya in India, where Skt. Sakyamuni, awaking to the truth, got enlightened to become Buddha. Built all of white marble pieces, the pagoda, 34.7 meters high, is the highest point in the Azure Cloud Temple.

Standing on the platform of the pagoda is the two tiny dagodas and five square pagodas of compact eaves. The whole pagoda is fully covered with exquisite sculptures in relief. Ranging from Buddha figures and figurines, heavenly guardians, muscled warriors, dragons, phoenixes, lions and elephants to decorative cloud patterns, these sculptures are all of traditional Tibetan styles. Of the five pagodas, each represents a Tathagata Buddha, hence being named the Five Wheel Pagoda. When Dr Sun passed away, his coffin was temporarily kept in the pagoda and was later removed to Nanjing. However, his cap and clothes are still sealed in the vault under the platform of the pagoda. Hence the pagoda is also called the pagoda tomb of Dr Sun Yat − sen's personal effects.

213. 碧云寺的水泉院内有"三代树",这有何说头?

所谓三代树指的是院南一棵古老的柏树,由这棵古柏上长出了第二棵柏树,接着又在第二棵柏树上长出了一株白果树。"三代树"接续而生,实乃寺内一大奇观。

What about the "Three Generation Tree" in the Water Fountain Courtyard of the Azure Cloud Temple? Is there anything to say about it?

What we call the "Three Generation Tree" refers to an old cypress tree in the southern courtyard of the temple. Growing on it you'll find another cypress tree and again growing on the second cypress tree is a third tree, a gingko tree. The three trees grow consecutively one on the other, hence the "Three Generation Tree." It is really a spectacle in the Azure Cloud Temple.

卧佛寺
(The Reclining Buddha Temple)

214. 卧佛寺建于何年？为何又称十方普觉寺？

卧佛寺位于西山北面的寿安山南麓,距市区约 20 公里。该寺始建于唐代贞观年间,距今已有 1,300 多年的历史。初名为兜率寺(兜率系梵文音译,意为"妙足"、"知足"),后改名为昭孝寺、洪庆寺、永安寺、十方普觉寺。十方在佛教里系东、西、南、北四方,及其间的东南、西南、东北和西北,再加上、下共十个方位;普觉即是生活在尘世中的人们都能觉醒过来,使芸芸众生皆能领悟佛教的真谛。因为寺内供奉着一尊铜卧佛,故又俗称为卧佛寺。

When was the Reclining Buddha Temple built? Why is it also called the Shifang Pujue Temple?

Located some 20 kilometers from the city at the southern foot of the Shou'an Hill on the north of the Western Hills, the Reclining Buddha Temple was first built in the years of Zhenguan's reign in the Tang Dynasty, tracing over 1,300 years back in history. Named first as the Temple of Douli, a transliteration from a Sanskrit, which means wonderful sufficiency or contentment it was later changed into Zhaoxiao, Hongqing, Yong'an and again Shifang Pujue temple. Shifang in Buddhism means the ten positions, consisting of the four cardinal points of east, south, west and north, the intermediates of southeast, southwest, northeast and northwest plus the above and below; Pujue simply means popular awakening. So Shi-fang Pujue actually means to make all sentient beings in the world awaken to the truth of Buddhism. That's why it is a-gain called the Temple of Universal Awakening. As consecrat-ed in the temple is a bronze Buddha in a state of nirvana, hence the name the Reclining Buddha Temple.

215. 卧佛寺横匾上书有"性月恒明"四字,是何含意?

卧佛寺横匾上所书"性月恒明"四字,意即月亮如佛性,光辉永照。

Inscribed on the horizontal board of the Reclining Buddha Temple is such words as "Xing Yue Heng Ming", what does that really mean?

The four characters of "Xing Yue Heng Ming" inscribed on the horizontal board of the Reclining Buddha Temple mean that the nature of Buddhism is as always bright as that of the moon, which will forever illuminate the mortal world of human beings.

216. 卧佛寺的建筑布局如何? 内有哪些主要建筑?

卧佛寺坐北朝南,由三组并列的院落组成。寺前有一座木牌坊,四柱三楼灰筒瓦顶,其题额为"智光重明"。过了牌坊便是一道长百米缓斜坡,两侧栽种着四行古柏。

其主要建筑有琉璃牌坊、山门殿、天王殿、三世佛殿、卧佛殿及藏经楼等。

How is the layout of the Reclining Buddha Temple? And what are the main buildings in it?

Laid out on an axis from north to south the Reclining Buddha Temple consists of three rows of courtyards and a wooden archway in front of it. The archway has a three tiered roof covered with gray round tiles and is supported on the four pillars. The horizontal board on it is inscribed with four Chinese characters which mean "enlightenment of wisdom and perspicacious understanding". After passing the archway there is a gentle slope of some hundred meters long which is neatly flanked on both sides by four lines of old cypress trees.

The main buildings built along the axis are: an archway built of glazed tiles, the ante – hall of the temple, the Hall of Heavenly Guardians, the Hall for the Buddha of Three Existences, the Hall for the Reclining Buddha and the storage tower for Buddhist scriptures, etc..

217. 卧佛寺的琉璃牌坊是个怎样的建筑?

琉璃牌坊耸立在卧佛寺的山门殿前,是一座四柱七层的琉璃牌坊,颇为壮观美丽,且金碧辉煌。牌坊的正面匾额上书有"同参密藏",背面为"足具精严",均系清代乾隆皇帝御笔。牌坊的后面有一半圆形水池,两侧为钟楼和鼓楼;池上架筑石桥一座,直通山门殿。

What about the glazed archway in the Reclining Buddha Temple?

Standing in front of the ante – hall of the temple is a seven – tiered glazed archway supported on four pillars. It looks beautiful and magnificent and splendidly brilliant. On the frontal board of it is inscribed with such phrase as "Consult together the mystery of Buddhism" and that at the back "the Doctrine of Buddhism is profound and unfathomable", both of which were autographed by Emperor Qianlong of the Qing Dynasty. Passing through the archway you'll find a semi – circled pond with bell and drum towers on both sides, and spanning over the pond is a stone bridge leading all the way to the ante – hall of the temple.

218. 卧佛寺的山门殿内有什么塑像?

山门殿内可见哼、哈二将的塑像,二将又称金刚力士,是佛教中守护庙门的神将。民间传说称:二将之一的哼将,鼻子里能哼出白气;而哈将则能吐出黄气,具有驱逐妖魔,杀灭鬼怪的本领,故俗称哼哈二将。

What is housed there in the ante – hall of the Reclining Buddha Temple?

Standing in the ante – hall are the statues of the two marshals named Heng and Ha, which means the snorter and the blower, respectively. Known as the Buddha's warrior attendants they are the guardians of the temple gate. It is as known very popularly that Heng, the snorter is able to eject two rays of light from his nostrils and Ha, the Blower to blow a great gust of yellow gas out from his mouth. By such means they are able to expel the devils and evil spirits and also eliminate imps and hobgoblins so as to keep the temple in safety, hence nicknamed as Marshals Heng and Ha.

219. 卧佛寺内的四大天王殿中有哪些塑像？

天王殿的正中供奉的是一尊弥勒佛像,他大腹便便,笑容可掬,好似在欢迎各位来宾。看上去他很慈祥,给人一种大慈大悲的感觉。弥勒的后面是韦驮的立像,据说他是因保护释迦佛的佛骨有功而成佛的。殿的两侧各有两尊巨大的塑像,这就是四大天王,即所谓四大金刚,住在须弥山上。四大天王各有一个从者,还有91子。他们显得异常威武,各守一方,确保天下风调雨顺。

What are the statues enshrined in the Hall for Heavenly Guardians in the Reclining Buddha Temple?

Consecrated in the center of the Hall for Heavenly Guardians is a statue of Maitreya Buddha, who with a big belly and wearing an always smiling face, gives visitors and pilgrims to the temple a sense of kindness as if he were offering a warm welcome to them all. Behind him is a statue of Skanda, who, vajra in hand, came to become a Buddha when he succeeded in keeping the remained bones of the Sakyamuni Buddha. On both sides of the hall are the four Heavenly Guardians, nicknamed as the four Diamond Kings (Caturmaharajakayika in Sanskrit), who live in Sumeru mountains. Each of the four guardians has an attendant by his side and besides, they again, having a total of 91 sons, look very powerful and full of prowess. Together with their attendants and sons, the four Heavenly Guardians looking after one of the four cardinal positions they are making it sure to have a favorable weather for crops.

220. 卧佛寺的三佛殿内供奉的是谁的塑像?

卧佛寺的三佛殿内供奉的是三世佛像,关于三世佛有两种不同的说法:其一是过去、现在和未来的三世佛,也即燃灯佛,释迦佛和弥勒佛;其二是三个佛为世界佛,系指东方净琉璃世界的药师佛,娑婆世界的释迦牟尼佛和西方极乐世界的阿弥陀佛。卧佛寺中所供奉的是后述的那种三世佛。此外,殿内两旁还有十八罗汉的彩塑像。

What are the statues enshrined in the Three Buddhas Hall of the Reclining Buddha Temple?

Consecrated in this hall is the Buddha of Three Existences. With this regard there are two different sayings: one is that it's the Buddha of the past, the present and the future, namely the Buddha of Illumination (Dipamkara in Sanskrit), Sakyamuni Buddha and Maitreya Buddha. However, another advocates that it's the Buddha of the following three realms: the Buddha of Pharmacy in the Eastern Pure Glazed World, the Sakyamuni Buddha in the World of Sal Trees and the Amitabha Buddha in the Western Bliss Paradise. But that worshiped in the Reclining Buddha Temple is the latter. Aside from the above – mentioned there are still statues of 18 arhats enshrined on both sides of the hall here.

221. 卧佛及卧佛殿是怎么一回事呢?

卧佛殿系卧佛寺的主体建筑,面阔三间,为绿琉璃瓦黄剪边单檐歇山顶建筑。前檐所书"性月恒明"匾系慈禧手书;殿正面墙上挂一块"得大自存"的横匾,为乾隆手笔。意思是释迦牟尼修道成功,已得到了最大的自由。佛像前置五供八宝,殿左右的玻璃橱内还展存着 11 双黄缎云鞋,为清朝十代皇帝及袁世凯所敬献的贡品。殿外左右各立有一碑,上面所刻为卧佛寺的简历。

殿正中所供奉的为中国现存最大的铜铸卧佛。卧佛初成于唐代,为木雕;元时改铜铸。佛身长 5.2 米,作睡卧状。卧佛身后环立着"十二圆觉"的塑像,即 12 弟子。他们面部表情沉重悲哀,构成一幅释迦牟尼即将涅盘于娑罗树下,向 12 个弟子叮嘱后事的生动情景。

How about the Statue of the Reclining Buddha and the hall for it?

The hall for the Reclining Buddha, with three frontal bays, is the main building in the temple. Covered in green but rimmed with yellow glazed tiles it is a hip - roof building of a single eave. The inscription "Xing Yue Heng Ming" on the horizontal board under the frontal eave of the hall means "having a natural disposition of the moon to give out ever - lasting rays of light" written by Empress Dowager Cixi. Hung over above in the center of the hall is a board of "De Da Zi Cun" autographed by Emperor Qianlong and the inscription suggests that with a profound knowledge in Buddhism one can enjoy a carefree existence of life. As Sakyamuni has succeeded in cultivating himself and got profound attainments so he enjoys a carefree existence to the utmost. Consecrated in front of the Buddha are the sacrificial articles and treasures and displayed in the glass - cases on both sides of the hall are some 11 pairs of sandals of yellow brocade. They are the gifts presented by the ten generations of emperors of the Qing dynasty plus the one by Yuan Shikai, a so - called emperor of 83 days. Erected outside on the right and the left are the stone steles bearing a brief introduction to the temple.

The recumbent copper Buddha is the largest one in China and it was, first a wooden piece carved in the Tang Dynasty, changed later into a copper – cast one in the Yuan Dynasty. Measuring 5.2 meters in length, the Buddha in a nirvana state is surrounded by 12 of his disciples. They, wearing sad faces, pose a vivid picture in which Sakyamuni lying under the sal trees is saying his last words to his disciples before his nirvana.

222. 卧佛寺行宫的布局如何？

卧佛寺行宫由三个院落组成，南侧两院，有假山点缀，小桥流水。行宫的建筑也是采用四合院带回廊的形式，殿宿讲究，环境优雅。北端为莲花池，池畔有彩廊敞轩，山石树木，倒映其中，别有一番情趣。

How is the layout of the temporary imperial palace in the Reclining Buddha Temple?

Consisting of three courtyards the two of them on the south are studded with an artificial hill and a brook of water gurgling away underneath a hunched bridge. The courtyard is built in the style of a quadrangle decorated with a covered corridor and balustrades. Tucked away in a quiet and tasteful environment the residential hall is exquisitely laid out. In the courtyard on the north there is a lotus pond with a colorfully painted corridor and a spacious hall. Clustered around by rockery and shady trees and the reflections in the pond, they present a very tasteful atmosphere ever seen elsewhere.

223. 卧佛寺内的僧舍现作何用?

僧舍原为僧侣们的起居之所,内设六个院落:霁月轩,清凉馆、大禅堂、祖堂和斋堂,均为四合院式的院落。现已辟为别墅,用以接待中外游客。

What are the abodes of monks in the Reclining Buddha Temple used for now?

The abodes used to be the living quarters for the monks of the temple. They spread out in the following six courtyards: the Courtyard of the Clearing Moon Hall, the Courtyard of the Cool and Refreshing Hall, the Courtyard of the Grand Meditation Hall, the Courtyard of the Ancestral Hall and that of the Fasting Hall. All of them are built in a quadrangle style. Now they've been renovated into villas for hosting visitors from both at home and abroad.

樱桃沟
(The Cherry Blossom Valley)

224."樱桃沟"位于何处？其名称从何而来？

"樱桃沟"位于寿安山麓,是一条外广内狭的峡谷。谷口在距香山卧佛寺 500 米之处,因寺中果园以樱桃树最多而命名。前人有讴歌樱桃沟的诗句:"樱桃花万树,春来想灼灼。"樱桃沟便因此而名闻遐迩了。

Where lies the Cherry Blossom Valley? And how is the name derived from?

Located at the foot of the Shou'an Hill it is a valley broad at the mouth but narrow in its depth. With its entrance lying some 500 meters away from the Reclining Buddha Temple in the Western Hills its name is derived from the fact that the valley abounds with cherry trees. In praise of the enchanting scenes there is an ode by an ancient, which goes like this: "Myriad of cherry trees in bloom, the advent of spring brings the flare to the full". It is thus the place becoming known far and near as a scenic area.

225. 樱桃沟的环境怎样？那里有哪些主要景点？

樱桃沟的谷口有一水库,离之不远处的岩壁上有篆文石刻"白鹿仙迹,退谷幽栖"八个大字。这里峰高沟深,背山面阳,气候湿润,花木繁茂,奇石众多,山泉淙淙,是个消夏避暑的绝好去处。

沟中主要景点由：红星桥、鹿岩精舍、退谷亭、一二·九运动纪念亭、水源头、白鹿洞、半天云岭及金鸽子台等。

How is the environment in the Cherry Blossom Valley? And what are the major scenic attractions in the area?

At the entrance of the Cherry Blossom Valley there is a reservoir and over above on the cliff not far from it you'll find an inscription in the seal character style, which reads: the White Deer Retreat — an Immortal's Trace, the Dale of Tranquil Recess — a Seclusion for a Hermit. Spreading out on the sunny side, the place with a high peak at its back and deep chasm down below enjoys an affable climate for many a flowering plants here. With queer rocks around and spring water gurgling along it proves to be an excellent resort for keeping away the heat in summer.

The Major scenic spots in the valley are: the Red Star Bridge, the Deer Cliff Retreat, the Retreat Dale Arbor, the Memorial Tower for December 9th Movement, the Spring Water Head, the White Deer Cave, the Halfway Up Heaven Cloudy Ridge and the Golden Dove Terrace.

226. 樱桃沟的"红星桥"是由谁撰写的？

樱桃沟的"红星桥"三个字是由郭沫若撰写的。这是一座跨溪流的汉白玉精雕石桥，是从端王府迁移而来的。

Who has inscribed the characters the "Red Star Bridge" in the Cherry Blossom Valley?

Mr. Guo Moruo inscribed the "Red Star Bridge". Spanning over a gurgling brook, it is a rickety bridge built of exquisitely carved white marble, which was removed here from the Mansions of Prince Duan.

227. 樱桃沟的"鹿岩精舍"是怎么样呢？

鹿岩精舍是一座石制门楼，额上横刻着"鹿岩精舍"四个字。门外有一坊石碑，上刻"退谷"二字，为清末名士梁启超所书。明末清初文人孙承祥晚年隐居于此，著有《天府广记》一书，并于谷中种松植竹，建造亭台，自号退谷。

How does the Deer Cliff Retreat in the Cherry Blossom Valley look like?

As a stone archway, the horizontal board of it is inscribed with the words "Deer Cliff Retreat" and erected at the entrance is a stone stele with two Chinese characters "Dale of Recess" on it, which was inscribed by Liang Qichao, a celebrity at the end of the Qing Dynasty. A hermit named Sun Chengxiang, a man of letters at the end of the Ming and the beginning of the Qing dynasties used to live here in seclusion. He styled himself Tui Gu (Dale of Recess) wrote a book entitled Tianfu Guangji (Records of Tianfu), and meanwhile he cultivated pine trees and bamboo groves, and had pavilions and arbors built.

228. 樱桃沟花园又怎么样呢？

在《鹿岩精舍》石门之内，就是樱桃沟花园。这是一处环境幽静，而又充满自然野趣的去处。其地势忽而开朗，忽而幽合，沿沟两侧栽种了许多奇花异草，茂林修竹；在绿荫深处还掩映着凉亭茅舍，风景十分优美。著名的地质学家李四光曾在这里的"石桧书巢"、"水流云在之居"等处住过。

How does the Flower Garden of the Cherry Blossom Valley look like?

Spreading out inside the stone archway of the "Deer Cliff Retreat", the garden of the Cherry Blossom Valley enjoys a tranquil environment full of rustic taste. With a terrain now spacious now closed – up, both sides along the valley are planted with a variety of precious flowers and strange herbs, lushly growing trees and bamboo thickets. Dotted in the depth of green are some thatched cottages and arbors with beautiful scenery around. Li Siguang, the well – known late geologist once lived in the "Stone Juniper Study" and "Water Flowing and Cloud Lingering Abode" here in the valley.

229. 樱桃沟花园的水源头有什么特色?

水源头为樱桃沟的溪水之源,其泉水纯净清凉。泉畔有石刻一块,上书"志在山水"四字。另外,在水源头北侧的山坡上还有一石亭,与此一起构成了一幅优美的山水图画。

What are the specific features of the Spring Water Head in the flower garden of the Cherry Blossom Valley?

As the water head of the stream in the Cherry Blossom Valley, the spring water oozing out therefrom is pure and fresh. Erected by its side is a stone stele on which is inscribed with such words as "Devoted to Landscape Beauties". Up onto the northern slope dots a stone arbor, which together with the aforesaid attractions present an enchanting scroll of picturesque painting here in the valley.

230. 樱桃沟花园里的"元宝石"有何说法?

在樱桃沟水源头的石亭以南,有一块巨石挡路,因其石状如元宝,故名。有传说称:清代著名文学家曹雪芹晚年曾在西山一带居住过,他常来此地,酷爱此石,并据此产生了一种神奇的想像,构思出一块"通灵宝玉",将它写进了他的不朽名作《红楼梦》中。

What about that "Ingot Stone" in the flower garden of the Cherry Blossom Valley?

Lying to the south of the Spring Water Head, there is a large block of stone in the way. As it has the shape of a gold ingot, hence the derivation of the name the Ingot Stone. But, a saying goes like this: Cao Xuejin, the well – known man of letters, used to live around here in the Western Hills in his later years, and as he liked the stone very much he often came here for a walk. However, with this stone he stimulated a strange inspiration to describe it as a piece of Precious Jade of Spiritual Understanding, which he put it into his renowned and immortal works of literature A Dream of Red Mansions.

231. 樱桃沟内"白鹿洞"之名又是从何而来的?

白鹿洞的正式名称叫作白鹿岩,这三个字刻在元宝石上。白鹿岩下面有一岩洞,其高2米,深6米,约可容纳20人左右。洞内砌设石床一张,据称辽代有位仙人,乘着白鹿云游到此,因见此地景色佳绝,便住了下来。白鹿岩及白鹿洞便由此而得名。

Whence came the name "White Deer Cave" of the Cherry Blossom Valley?

The White Deer Cave should be actually called the White Deer Cliff and the three characters are inscribed on the Ingot Stone. As under the cliff there is a cave of 2 meters in height and 6 meters in depth, which is big enough to house around 20 persons. In the cave there is a bed built of stone. A story goes like this: during the Liao Dynasty there came an immortal on the back of a white deer. He, having found the place very pleasing, decided to settle down in the cave, hence the derivation of the name the White Deer Cliff and the White Deer Cave.

232. 樱桃沟花园内的"石上柏"是怎么回事?

距元宝石不远处耸峙着一块高约 2 - 3 丈的陡峭巨石,在其缝隙中长着一棵参天大古柏,观之令人惊奇。据传说,曹雪芹曾常游此地,并对这块巨石和柏树产生了极其浓厚的兴趣。在这自然景观的启示下,他终于形成了《红楼梦》中贾宝玉与林黛玉之间缠绵悱恻的"木石姻缘"的奇妙构思。

What about the "Cypress Tree Growing on Rock" in the flower garden of the Cherry Blossom Valley?

Not far away from the Ingot Stone towers a huge rock of over 20 meters high and out from its cleft grows a giant cypress tree of an astonishing height. Cao Xueqin, a famous man of letters used to come, as said, to take a walk around here. And having taken a great liking for the huge rock he got an inspiration from the natural beauty to form in his mind's eye the wonderful plot about the "love affairs of wood and stone". Finally he succeeded in writing a exceedingly sentimental love story between the boy Jia Baoyu and the girl Lin Daiyu as depicted in the famous novel of A Dream of Red Mansions.

233. 樱桃沟花园内"保卫华北"的石刻是何内容?

石刻题刻于 1935 年的"一二·九"运动之际,是由北京和清华两所大学的学生镌刻的。那时,日本帝国主义已经侵占了中国的东北三省,并大有向关内进攻,以达其占领华北、灭亡中国之目的。但是,北京及全国各地的爱国学生们,在中共地下党组织的领导下,在樱桃沟花园举办夏令营活动,进行军事训练,准备参加抗日报国的斗争。

What is the "Safeguarding North China" inscribed on the stele in the flower garden of the Cherry Blossom Valley about?

The inscription was done by the students of Beijing and Qinghua universities at the time of December 9th Movement in 1935. The time was marked by the Japanese invasion of the three northeast provinces of China and its attempt to break into the Great Wall in order to occupy north China and then further subjugate the whole country. However, led by the underground committee of the Chinese Communist Party, the patriotic students of Beijing and other parts of the country held a military training course under the cover of conducting summer camp activities in the flower garden of the Cherry Blossom Valley. And in this way they made themselves ready to join the struggle against the Japanese invasion of China for the defence of the country.

234. 樱桃沟花园内的"一二·九"运动纪念亭建于何时？其主体建筑有何含意？

樱桃沟园内的"一二·九"运动纪念亭建于 1985 年,是首都大中学生为纪念"一二·九"运动 50 周年而自己设计、自己动手、勤工俭学、捐款集资修建的。纪念亭的主体建筑为三个白色三角形建筑物,象征当年军事夏令营帐篷的缩影。三个三角形建筑构成"众"字,意为人民群众与青年学生结合起来,形成众志成城的巨大合力。那大中小三个建筑物表示革命传统代代相传,革命事业后继有人。另外,每个三角形建筑物都有三个足尖,一个顶尖。三个三角形共有 12 个角,但其中有 9 足立地,隐含着"一二·九"之意。

When was the Memorial Tower for December 9th Movement built in the flower garden of the Cherry Blossom Valley? And what does the main structure imply?

Brought to a finish in 1985, the Memorial Tower was designed and built jointly by the students from schools of high learning and middle schools of Beijing. Put up in memory of the 50th anniversary of the December 9th Movement by pooling in the money earned by the students from part – work and part – study, the tower consists of three white triangular buildings to symbolize the tents used during the camping time. The tower, shaped in a Chinese character that means a group of masses of people, suggests the close unity of the students with the broad masses of people and the strength in unity. The difference in size of the three buildings, of which one is smaller than the other, represents that the revolutionary cause, having the late comers to join in, will be carried on from generation to generation. And in addition, the three triangular buildings, with each having three pods down on the ground to make up nine and one point at its top, have twelve angles all told, an implication of December the Ninth.

北京植物园
(Beijing Botanical Garden)

235. 北京植物园建于何时？种植了多少花木？

北京植物园建于 1956 年,现有园林绿地 1,600 亩,栽培露地木本植物 13 万株,露地草本植物 116 种,温室植物 171 种,是一个专门从事植物引种驯化的科研基地,也是进行植物知识教育的科普园地。现为中国北方规模最大的植物园。

When was the Beijing Botanical Garden initiated? How many kinds of plants are cultivated there in the garden?

Initiated in 1956, the Beijing Botanical Garden covers an area of over 100 hectares with more than 130,000 woody plants and 116 species of woody and herbaceous plants growing in the open air and 171 species of plants in greenhouse. The garden is at once a site for scientific research specialized in introducing and domesticating new species of plants and a place for popularizing knowledge of natural science on botany. It is the largest one of its kind in north China.

236. 植物园内有多少松柏区和专类花园？

园内现已建成的有松柏区和十余个专类花园,如:绚秋苑、牡丹园、碧桃园、丁香园、木兰园、集秀园等。在附近有卧佛寺、樱桃沟、曹雪芹纪念堂等,也是景区的组成部分。每年四月中旬至五月初,这里还举办"桃花节赏花会"。

How many areas are there for coniferous trees and special flowers in the garden?

Established in the garden is an area for coniferous trees and a dozen of gardens for special flowers. They are the gardens of: autumn tints, tree - peony, prunus persica var. duplex, lilacs, magnolia and another garden for many other kinds of beautiful flowers. The areas in and around the Reclining Buddha Temple, the Cherry Blossom Valley and the Memorial Hall for Cao Xueqin are also deemed as component parts of the Botanical Garden. Every year a "Festival for Feasting on Peach Blossoms" is held here.

237. 北京植物园内的"绚秋苑"有何特色？

绚秋苑位于植物园内观赏植物区、树桩盆景园及展览温室交接的枢纽地段，面积为 6.16 万平方米，植树 2,000 余株，内建有"秋林绚彩"、"澄湖揽秀"及"写秋坪"等以植物为主题的景区和景点，突出表现了秋色的绚丽。

What specific features are there in the Garden of Autumn Tints of the Beijing Botanical Garden?

Located in a place between the Area for Miniature Tree - roots and the Displaying Greenhouse the Garden of Autumn Tints covers an area of 61,600 square meters with more than 2,000 plants there. Established in the area are such plots as featuring the "Tinges in Autumn Forest", "Charming Scene over a Limpid Lake" and a "Level Ground Painted with Autumn Scenery". They are mainly planted with plants that flourish in fall, giving forth a flare of autumn tints.

238. 植物园内的"牡丹园"有何突出之处?

牡丹园是北京市面积最大、品种最多的牡丹专类花园,同时也种植一些芍药花。该园面积为 7.6 万平方米,栽培牡丹 285 种,约 5,000 余株;芍药 154 种,2,000 余丛。这里的牡丹品种多而且奇,构成了牡丹园的一大特色,成了京华大地上最大的"牡丹王国"。此外,在繁花与松柏丛中还耸立着一尊"牡丹仙子"的汉白玉雕像及大型烧瓷壁画。这里地势起伏,亭台错落,竹柏交翠,多姿多彩,充满了一种诗情画意。

What are the specific features of the "Tree Peony Garden" in the Beijing Botanical Garden?

The "Tree Peony Garden", as the largest with the most varieties of peonies of all peony gardens in Beijing, is also a garden for Chinese herbaceous peonies. Covering a space of over 76,000 square meters it has 285 species with a total of more than 5,000 tree - peonies and 154 species of over 2,000 thickets of herbaceous peonies in it. The garden is known for its various species of peonies of outstanding quality, presenting the largest kingdom of peonies in the area around Beijing. Towering among the densely growing flowers and coniferous trees is a white marble statue named the "Tree Peony Fairy" and also a large porcelain screen of fired murals. With an undulating terrain dotted by pavilions in the midst of lushly growing pine and cypress trees it presents an elegant and colorful picture full of a poetic sense.

239. 植物园中的"碧桃园"主要种植了哪些花卉?

碧桃园建于 80 年代初期,面积为 3.4 万平方米。园内主要收集栽种红、白、粉及洒金等多种花色的碧桃,同时也栽植一些花期比较接近的榆叶梅、连翘及日本樱花。园中草坪面积甚大,借鉴运用了英国风致式园林的风格。

What are the main species of flowers planted in the Garden of Prunuis Persica Var. Duplex?

Established at the beginning of 1980s the garden covers an area of 34,000 square meters and it is planted mainly with red, white and pink prunus persica var. duplex and that of golden – motley color as well. Such flowering plants as prunus triloba, forsythia suspensa and Japanese flowering cherry (prunus senulata) of about the same flowering period are also cultivated here. With a large lawn in it the garden is in the art of gardening an imitation of a British style.

240. 植物园中的"丁香园"里有多少种丁香?

丁香园始建于本世纪 50 年代末,80 年代又加以扩建,现有面积 3.5 万平方米。收集了 22 种丁香的变种,可使花期延长两个月之久。园中草坪甚是宽阔,有"翔鹤"、"嬉鹿"等雕塑点缀其中,显得格外幽雅别致。

How many species of tulips are there in the Garden of Tulips?

Set up at the end of 1950s and expanded in 1980s, the Garden of Tulips covers an area of 35,000 square meters. With a collection 22 variegated species of tulips in the garden, the flowering period can last as long as two months. Having a spacious lawn studded with sculptures of "Gliding Cranes" and "Frolicking Deer", the garden looks even more elegant and tasteful.

241. 植物园中的"木兰园"主要栽种哪些花卉?

木兰园建于本世纪 50 年代末,面积为 0.84 万平方米。这里栽植了最为名贵的白玉兰。此外,园内还建有水池、花坛和绿篱等。

What are the main flowers planted in the Garden of Lily Magnolias?

Built at the end of 1950s the Garden of Lily Magnolias has a space of 8,400 square meters with the most precious species of magnolia denudata cultivated here. Besides, there is a small pond, a flower terrace and a green hedge in the garden.

242. 植物园中的"宿根花卉园"、"集秀园"以及"松柏区"主要种植了哪些花卉树木?

宿根花卉园收集和栽培宿根花卉的专类花卉,面积为 1.44 万平方米。园中栽种鸢尾科、百部科、百合科、菊类及毛茛等宿根花草 60 余种,同时栽有一些如香柏、红枫和竹类等北方少有的植物。

集秀园主要是栽植竹子的专类园,内植竹子 30 余种,有刚竹、甜竹、淡竹和毛竹等。园中央还有池塘及亭台建筑。

松柏区栽植有云杉、雪松、杜松、鹿角松和辅地柏等树种。

What are the main flowers and plants planted in the Gardens of Perennial and biennial root Flowering Plants, the Garden of Varieties of Plants and the Area for Coniferous Trees?

Covering an area of 14,400 square meters the Garden of

Perennial and Biennial Root flowering Plants is a special reserve for such plants of some 60 species as iris, stemona japoni-
ca, liliaceae, chrysanthemums, buttercups. At the same time
there are still some such plants as fragrant cypresses, red maple
and varieties of bamboo that are rare in north China.

The Garden of Varieties of Plants is a special reserve
mainly for the cultivation of bamboo. With some 30 species of
bamboo here they range from phylostachys viridis, phylostachys glauca to phylostachys glauca pubescens etc.

The area for coniferous trees is planted with such trees as
dragon spruce, cedar, eucommia... and some crawling cypresses and so on.

潭柘寺
(The Pool & Cudrania Temple)

243. 潭柘寺位于何处？距北京市区有多远？

潭柘寺又名岫云寺，位于门头沟区潭柘山的山腰里，是北京市郊区最大的一所寺院。距离北京市区约有 45 公里左右。

Where lies the Pool and Cudrania Temple? How far is it away from the city of Beijing?

Nestling at the waist of the Pool and Cudrania Hill in the Mentougou district the Pool and Cudrania Temple (Tan Zhe Si) is also called Xiuyun (Hill and Cloud) Monastery. Located some 45 kilometers away from the city center, the temple is the largest one in the western suburbs of Beijing.

244. 潭柘寺之名从何而来？

潭柘寺因山上有龙潭和柘树而得名，而且该山也称潭柘山，因此，寺也随之而称为潭柘寺。

Why is it called the "Pool and Cudrania Temple"?

The name of the temple is derived from the fact that there is a dragon pool in the hill and the hill is overgrown with cudrania bushes. Furthermore, the hill is also called the Pool and Cudrania Hill, hence the name of the temple.

245. 潭柘寺建于何时?

潭柘寺有着悠久的历史,最早建于晋代(公元 265 - 317 年),自建庙以来,业已历尽 1,700 余个春秋,历史上也曾有"先有潭柘,后有幽州"之说,所以它的历史比起北京城来还要长 800 多年。此后历代均有重建和扩建,其中尤以清代的扩建规模为最大,现存的建筑主要多为明清时期留存下来的。

When was the Pool and Cudrania Temple built?

The temple has a long history and it was first built in the Jin dynasty (265 - 317 A. D.). The temple, ever since its establishment, has already witnessed a vicissitudes of over 1,700 years and a historical saying goes like this: "The Pool and Cudrania Temple came into existence earlier than the Youzhou prefecture". So it enjoys a history of over 800 years longer than that of the city of Beijing. The work of reconstruction and expansion has, of course, been carried out during the dynasties gone by, of which that being done in the Qing dynasty is the largest one in scale. Most of the buildings now in existence are the remains from the Ming and Qing dynasties.

246. 潭柘寺曾有过多少名称?

潭柘寺在晋代称嘉福寺,唐朝叫龙泉寺,金代更名为万寿寺,元时及明清两代又曾多次更名,但以"潭柘寺"流传至今。它的正名究竟叫什么,几乎完全被人们所遗忘,而其俗名"潭柘寺"却流传千古,名闻中外。

How many names has the Pool and Cudrania Temple ever had in its long history?

The temple was first named Jia Fu Si (the Temple of Delightful Happiness) in the Jin dynasty and changed into Long Quan Si (the Temple of Dragon Spring) in Tang period. Later it was again renamed as Wanshou (the Temple of Longevity) in the Kin Dynasty, and changed furthermore several times during the period of Yuan, Ming and Qing dynasties. However, the name that has been passed on and on is the "Pool and Cudrania". Now the name is known to many people far and near, at home and abroad, while its real name has almost gone into oblivion.

247. 潭柘寺在建筑布局上有何特色？

潭柘寺依山势而筑，殿堂逐级而上，参差错落，排列有致，建筑十分宏伟壮观，堪称精美绝伦。潭柘寺的地理位置很好，寺前有山峰作屏障，寺后亦为山所环抱。庙门内外，古木参天，溪水潺潺，幽篁修竹，僧塔如林，是暑夏游玩休憩的理想去处。俗话说："潭柘寺，前有照，后有靠，左右有环抱。"这就更能激起人们来此一游的兴趣与欲望。

What specific features does the Pool and Cudrania Temple have in its layout?

Built along the slope of the hill, the halls of the temple are arranged in a way with one row higher than the other. The temple, sprawling in a fine terrain, is embraced by hills at the back, yet screened off by a peak in front. Dotted around inside and outside the temple are lushly growing trees, bamboo —

thickets and burial stupas for monks, and with brooks of spring water gurgling along, it is really an ideal place for summer excursion. An old saying goes like this: "The Pool and Cudrania Temple has a peak as a screen in front, a hill at the back looking like a back – drop and is embraced by hills on the right and left." Therefore, it charms a lot of people to come here for a visit.

248. 潭柘寺的主要建筑分哪几个部分?

潭柘寺坐北朝南,全寺建筑主要分为三个部分,且主要建筑大都分布在中轴线上,依次为牌楼、山门、天王殿、大雄宝殿、毗卢阁等;东路则有方丈院、延清阁、流杯亭、帝后宫、舍利塔、地藏殿、圆通殿及竹林院等;西路有戒台、观音殿、龙王殿、祖师殿、西南斋、大悲殿和写经室等。

How many parts does the Pool and Cudrania Temple consist of?

Facing south the Pool and Cudrania Temple consists largely of three parts. With the buildings mainly built along the central axis, they are first the archway, the temple gate, the hall of heavenly guardians, the Mahavira hall and the Vairocana pavilion. The buildings along the eastern line are the abbot courtyard, the drifting – cup pavilion, the emperor and queen palace, the stupa, the Hall of Ksitigarbha, the Bodhisattivas' Hall of Manjusri, Avalokitesvara and Samantabhadra and the bamboo – thicket courtyard and so on. And those built along the western line are: the ordination altar, the Hall of Goddess of Mercy, the Hall of Dragon King, the Hall of Ancestral Masters, the southwest study and the hall for scripture

- writing.

249. 潭柘寺外还有哪些建筑？

潭柘寺外还有龙潭、西观音洞、明王殿、歇心殿、安乐堂以及上下塔院等。

What are the other buildings outside the compound of the Pool and Cudrania Temple?

Lying outside the Pool and Cudrania Temple are still the Dragon Pool, the Western Cave of the Goddess of Mercy, the Vidya – raja Hall, the Hall of Heart Repose, the Hall of Peaceful Happiness and the upper and lower pagoda courtyards.

250. 牌楼的结构如何？ 上面有谁的题额？

中轴线的最南端是牌楼，为三间四柱三檐式建筑，顶上覆盖着黄色琉璃瓦，檐下饰有斗拱。牌楼全部都是木质结构，并有彩绘，前额上书有金色大字"翠山章丹泉"，后额所书为"香林净土"，均为康熙手笔。

How does the structure of the archway look like? Who has inscribed the horizontal board on it?

Located at the southern end of the central axis is a stylish archway. It is a tri – tiered building supported on four parallel pillars. Built all of wood pieces painted in color, the top of it is covered with yellow glazed tiles and the lower part is made into mortise and tenon joints. Inscribed on the front board in golden letters is "Hills in green screen off the crimson spring" and that at the back reads, "A pure land tucked away in scented woods." Both were written by Emperor Kangxi of the Qing

Dynasty.

251. 牌楼前有什么古树？有何特色？

牌楼前有两株古松,高 3 米多。夏日来临,枝繁叶茂,相互搭绕,交织成一顶绿色的天棚,遮阳蔽日,可供游人在此休憩纳凉。牌楼下还有一对石狮子,看来颇有威风凛凛之感。

What are the old trees in front of the archway? And what special features do they have?

In front of the archway there are two old pines of a height of over 3 meters. In summer days, their lushly growing branches intertwining one another and their thickly covered green needles forming a natural canopy that shades off the sun – heat, offering visitors a place for enjoying the coolness here. Besides, there is a pair of stone lions at the foot of the archway, suggesting a sense of powerful prowess and bravery.

252. 山门正中悬有谁题写的匾额？

山门面宽三间,有券门三座,全系砖石结构。券脸均为汉白玉石雕花,明间上正中所悬石额系康熙皇帝御笔题写"敕建岫云禅寺"。山门两侧为红院墙,蓝色琉璃瓦,墙上嵌有琉璃大字,左边是"佛日增辉",右边是"法轮常转"。

Who has inscribed on the front board above the entrance gate of the temple?

The entrance gate of the temple is a tri – partitioned building with three arched gates, which were built of stone and brick pieces. Inserted over above the central gate is a stone panel with an inscription by Emperor Kangxi, which reads the

"Hill and Cloud Temple built at the imperial order." The temple gate is joined on both sides by red walls covered with blue – glazed tiles. Inserted on the walls are such big glazed characters: the one on the left reads the "Radiance of Buddhism and the sunshine help strengthen the brightness", and that on the right means the "Dharmacakra (the wheel of law) keeps on turning and will never stop".

253. 潭柘寺的柘树栽于何处？有何用途？

寺门前牌楼西侧栽有几株柘树，是仅留存下来的几株，系供游人观赏之用。以前这里的柘树很多，现已基本绝迹。柘树为桑科小乔木或灌木，其叶可作供养柘蚕之用。柘树在夏季开花，雌雄异株，果实与桑椹相仿，可食，也可用于酿酒，皮和根均可入药。柘树木质非常坚硬，是一种名贵的木材。

Where does the cudrania tree grow in the Pool and Cudrania Temple? And what's the use of it?

On the western side of the archway in front of the temple, there are some cudrania trees, the only ones left for tourists to enjoy. In the past there used to have a lot of cudrania trees growing here, but almost coming to extinction now. Cudrania is a kind of small tree or a bushy plant of the mulberry family, and its leaves can be used to raise silkworms. Flowering in summer it is dioecious and its fruit, looking very much like that of the mulberry, is eatable or can be used for brewery. The bark and roots of it can be used for herbal medicine. With a very hard xylem, it's a kind of very precious timber – wood.

254. 天王殿供奉的是何塑像？

进入山门后的第一个殿便是天王殿。殿正中供奉的是释迦牟尼的弟子弥勒佛的像。两侧供奉四尊高约 3 米的彩塑神像，是四大金刚，又称四大天王，即：怀抱琵琶的东方持国天王；手持宝剑的南方增长天王；西方广目天王，左手托一个多宝珠，右手持蛇；北方多闻天王，左手持一只老鼠，右手拿一把伞。四大天王的脚下均踏着奇形怪状的"八大怪"。

What's the Hall of the Heavenly Guardians used for?

When you get into the temple the first hall behind the temple gate is the Hall of the Heavenly Guardians. Enshrined in the center of the hall is an effigy of Maitreya, a disciple of Sakyamuni. Sculptured on both sides of the hall are the four giants in color called the Heavenly Guardians or Caturmaharaj akayika in Sanskrit, with each measuring about 3 meters in height. The one with a lute in front is called the Guardian in the Eastern Heaven or Dhatarastra. That with a sword in hand is the Guardian of the Southern Heaven or called Virudhaka. And still that with a pearl in his left hand and a snake in his right is known as the Guardian in the Western Heaven or called Virupaksa. And finally that with a mouse in his left hand and an umbrella in his right is known as the Guardian of the Northern Heaven or Vaisramana. Stamped underfoot by the four heavenly guardians are "Eight hobgoblins of all descriptions".

255. 大雄宝殿起何作用？

在大雄宝殿的正中供奉着的是佛祖释迦牟尼的塑像，其背后有佛光，在佛光之上有大鹏金翅鸟、龙女、狮、象、羊、火焰纹等。佛像座落在石质的须弥座上,其左右两侧分别立有阿难陀和伽叶的塑像。这三座佛像均为木质漆金,系清代遗物。

What's the Mahavira Hall used for?

Consecrated in the shrine in the center of the hall is the statue of Sakyamuni, the founder of Buddhism. There is a ring of halo behind him and over above it is decorated with a giant eagle, a dragon – maid, a lion, an elephant, a ram and patterns of flames as well. The Statue of Buddha is sitting on a dais built of stone, and is flanked by his two attendants with Ananda on his right and Mahakasyapa at the left. All three effigies are the wooden sculptures painted in gold and they are the leftovers from the Qing Dynasty.

256. 潭柘寺大雄宝殿的建筑有何特色?

大雄宝殿在天王殿后面,是寺中地位最高的一座大型建筑,面阔五间,歇山重檐,上覆黄琉璃瓦,并带绿条剪边,上下檐均饰有斗拱。大殿的上匾额"大雄宝殿"为赵朴初所书,下匾额的"福海珠轮"是清乾隆皇帝的手迹。殿前有相当宽阔的月台,四周围以石栏。大殿正脊的两端,各有一个系着鎏金长链的碧绿琉璃鸱吻,传说它们是龙所生的九子之一,属水性,能克火,故置于屋脊,以期避免火灾。鸱吻传为元代遗物,据称鸱吻上的四条鎏金鸱链为康熙皇帝的赐品。

What special features does the Mahavira Hall of the Pool and Cudrania Temple have?

Situated behind the Hall of Heavenly Guardians, the Mahavira Hall is a huge building holding the highest status in the temple. With five frontal bays the hall has a hip – roof of double eaves covered with yellow glazed tiles laced in green and rested on mortise and tenon joints. The inscription reading "Mahavira Hall" on the upper plaque was written by Zhao Puchu, a famous Buddhist in China and that on the lower board reading "A Sea of Happiness and the Turning of a Pearl Wheel" autographed by Emperor Qianlong of the Qing dynasty. In front of the hall there is a wide platform with stone balustrades around. At both ends of the roof ridge you'll find a "Chiwen", a mythical bird – like animal tied there with gilded chains. It is said that he is one of the nine sons of the dragon – king, who, betrothed to water by nature, is able to subdue the fire. So he is kept there to prevent the fire from breaking out. The pair of "Chiwen" is the leftovers from the Yuan Dynasty and it is said that the four gilded chains are the alms given by Emperor Kangxi of the Qing Dynasty.

257. 三圣殿两侧的银杏树为何称为"帝王树"？

大雄宝殿之后有三圣殿，在其两侧有两株巨大的银杏树。其中有一棵是辽代栽种的，树龄已在千年以上，但仍枝繁叶茂。树高约 30 米，需 6 人方能合抱。据说康熙皇帝来潭柘寺时，树上新生出了一个侧枝。到了乾隆时期，为表庆贺，皇帝下诏将此树命名为"帝王树"。后因讲究对称之故，便在帝王树的西边栽种了一棵配王树。银杏树也叫白果树，雌雄异株，雌性之树结果，果可食用，也可入药。

Why is the gingko tree here being called the "Imperial Tree"?

Behind the Mahavira Hall there is a hall for the three Bodhisattvas. Towering on both sides of the hall are the two giant gingko trees, one of which, said to have been planted in the Liao Dynasty, has already been here for over 1,000 years. Yet it is still in lush green. Towering about 30 meters high, its trunk is very thick that requires 6 people to embrace it. It is said that the tree had a new branch growing out when Emperor Kangxi paid a visit to the temple. To celebrate this joyous happening an imperial edict was given by Emperor Qianlong to name it the "Imperial Tree". And later to make it a pair in a symmetrical way, another gingko tree was planted on the western side of the hall, being a mate to the "Imperial Tree". As gingko tree is a dioecian the female tree bears fruit, which is eatable and can also be used as an ingredient in Chinese herbal medicine.

258. 毗卢阁是何等样的建筑? 系作何用?

座落在中轴线的终点是一座楼阁式的建筑,面阔七间,山墙两侧有台阶扶梯通往楼上,这便是毗卢阁。阁下层供有木质漆金五方神:右手第一尊是西方阿弥陀佛,表示智慧,第二尊是北方不空成就佛,表示事业有成,中间是法身佛,是大日如来之意,第四尊是东方阿閦佛,表示觉性,第五尊是南生佛,表示福德。阁之东西有配殿,作为展出寺内的珍藏物品之用,如古字画、铜钟、铜器、碑拓、古墓及古建筑等图片,还有塔院内出土的一些文物。毗卢阁内挂有乾隆手书的大匾"圆灵宝镜"。阁上层还供有三世佛,及六角形的须弥座。

What about the Vairocana Pavilion? And what is it used for?

Standing at the back – end of the central axis is a seven – bay building of a pavilion style. On both sides of it there are flights of stairs leading up to the second floor. The building is called "Vairocana Pavilion". Enshrined on the first floor of it are the five wooden statues. Ranging from the east to west they are: the Amitabha Bodhisattva, standing for wisdom; the second one standing for understanding, the third representing the Buddha of the Future; the fourth standing for awakening and the fifth for happiness and virtue. On the eastern and western sides of the pavilion there are some annexes for displaying pieces of relics kept in the temple. They are the old painting and calligraphy scrolls, copper bells and wares, drawings of ancient tombs and buildings as well as some other relics excavated from the pagoda yard of the temple. Hung inside the pavilion is still a placard with an inscription reading "a round, precious and efficacious mirror" written by Emperor Qianlong. And on the second floor you'll find the Buddha statues of the three existences sitting on a hexagonal dais.

259. 潭柘寺内的戒台系作何用?

所谓戒台或戒坛,是供出家的佛教徒受戒之用的地方。前檐悬挂的大横匾上书有"戒坛"二字。殿内设有一座用汉白玉筑成的品字形戒台,上面供奉一尊用松木雕成的释迦牟尼塑像,周围设有绘有彩画的木栏,台上的花木龛内供有一尊接引佛。

What is the Ordination Altar in the Pool and Cudrania Temple used for?

What we call the ordination altar or terrace is used to hold rites for ordaining novices. Hung under the frontal eave of the hall is a large board with writings on it, which read the "Ordination Altar". Sitting on the white marble altar of a convex shape in the hall is a statue of Sakyamuni, sculptured out of a piece of pinewood and round it is a colorfully painted balustrade. Besides, on the altar there is still a carved wooden shrine with a figure of Maitreya Buddha in it.

260. 佛教徒的"三坛大戒"所指究竟是什么?

佛教徒受戒称为"三坛大戒",即所谓沙弥戒、比丘戒(比丘即和尚)和菩萨戒。各种戒的条例略有不同:沙弥戒的戒律共有 10 条;比丘戒的戒律则有 250 条;菩萨戒的戒律则可分为 10 重 48 轻。潭柘寺内的戒台主要是用于受比丘戒的地方。

What does the so‐called three stages of grand ordination rites actually mean?

A person has first to be ordained before he becomes a Buddhist. The first stage of ordination is to be ordained as a Sramanera (or novice), and then to go through the second stage to become a Bhiksu (or monk) and the third stage is to be ordained as a Bodhisattva. However, they have to abide by the respective disciplines or rules. There are ten rules for a novice to abide by, and two hundred and fifty for a monk to stick to. As to the one to become a Bodhisattva he has ten very strict rules and 48 minor ones to adhere to. The ordination altar in the Pool and Cudrania Temple is meant for ordaining monk only.

261. 潭柘寺内的观音殿有何典故?

观音殿在潭柘寺内的最高处,位于一个单独的庭院里。面阔三间,廊下悬挂的金字横匾上书有"莲界慈航"四字,为乾隆皇帝手迹。殿内供奉着观世音菩萨,据说过去有许多朝代的帝王后妃曾来此拜佛进香。其中元世祖忽必烈的女儿妙严公主看中了这块地方，来此出家修行，并每日都来观音殿拜佛颂经。久而久之，她脚下的砖竟留下了一个 30 厘米深的脚印。1592 年，明万历帝的孝定太后把砖带回宫中观赏，后又送回寺内。但原砖被毁，现展陈的为仿制品。

What is the allusion there about the Hall of Goddess of Mercy in the Pool and Cudrania Temple?

Located at the highest point of the temple the Hall of Goddess of Mercy is in a separate courtyard. Consisting of three rooms there is a gilded board hung above the porch gate. The inscription on it, meaning "Ferry of Benevolence in the Realm of Lotuses", was autographed by Emperor Qianlong of the Qing Dynasty. Consecrated in the hall is the Bodhisattva Avalokites'vara. It is said that many emperors, queens and concubines and those of royal families of the past have come here worshipping the Goddess. One who stood out among them is princess Miaoyan, the daughter of Kubilai Khan, who charmed by the fine location of the hall, came here to become a nun, kowtowing everyday to the Goddess of Mercy. So as time went by, the brick she used to stand on was left with a hole of 30 millimeters deep. However, in 1592 the brick was taken to the imperial court by the Queen mother Xiaoding of Emperor Wanli in the Ming Dynasty for her personal appreciation, and was later returned to the temple. What a pity, alas! The original brick has nowhere to find now and on display here is only a replica.

262. 文殊殿内供奉的是何佛像？

潭柘寺内的文殊殿供奉着一尊千手千眼佛，佛像有 4 个头，10 张脸。从脖子开始往上，头依次变小，正面有 4 张脸，左右各有 3 张。佛像有 40 条胳膊，正面有 6 条大臂，两胁各有 16 条小臂。各手心中还刻有一只眼睛，并持有 40 多件法器。

Which Bodhisattva is enshrined in the Manjusri Hall?

Enshrined in the Hall of Manjusri is a statue of Manjusri with thousand hands and thousand eyes. The part from the neck above, having four heads and ten faces, gradually becomes smaller one after the other. The figure has four faces on the front and three on both sides. With a total of 40 arms it has six thick ones in the front, and sixteen smaller ones on each side with an eye carved in each of its palms. Besides, it also carries more than forty pieces of musical instruments in its hands.

263. 潭柘寺的龙王殿内有些什么东西？

在龙王殿的廊檐下悬挂着一条石鱼，原为清康熙年间的制品，长 1.5 米，重 75 公斤。据传石鱼为南海龙宫的一大宝物。现在该殿中所挂的石鱼是复制品，原物已于文化大革命期间被毁。

What is there in the Dragon－king Hall of the Pool and Cudrania Temple?

Hung under the corridor of the Dragon－king Hall is a stone－fish measuring some 1.5 meters in length and weighing 75 kilograms. The original one was cut during the reign period of Emperor Kangxi of the Qing Dynasty. The stone - fish is said to be the precious thing in the Palace of the Dragon King in the South Sea. As the original one was already destroyed during the 10 years of chaos, the so - called Cultural Revolution, this one is only a replica.

264. 潭柘寺内的流杯亭是怎么回事?

流杯亭位于潭柘寺内的行宫院中,这是一组雅致的古代建筑。亭内悬挂着清乾隆皇帝御书的"猗玕亭"横匾一块。亭的台基中间有用汉白玉雕刻的水道,从南看象龙首,由北看又似虎头。若引泉水入水道,水流便经曲折的水道从另一端流出。如将酒杯置于水中,酒杯便会随水漂流,游人可坐在不同的位置上取酒来饮。故此称为流杯亭。

What about that Drifting Cup Pavilion in the Pool and Cudrania Temple?

Standing in the courtyard of the Palace for Temporary Stay, the Drifting Cup Pavilion is a group of ancient buildings of an elegant style. Hung in the pavilion is a board with an inscription done by Emperor Qianlong and on the marble floor of the pavilion is cut with a water channel, the southern end of which looks very much like a dragon head while the northern end the head of a tiger. When spring water is drawn into the channel, it flows twisting and turning to empty only from the other end. When putting a wine cup into the water channel it drifts along with the water. In the meantime, visitors, sitting by the waterside, may pick up the cup to drink while chatting or even chanting poems to their hearts' content. Hence the name the Drifting Cup Pavilion.

265. 流杯亭在北京有几处？

流杯亭在北京共有四处,另外三处分别在:中南海的中海岸,名叫流水音;恭王府的翠锦园中;故宫宁寿宫花园内的碧螺亭中。

How many floating cup pavilions are there in Beijing?

There are four floating cup pavilions in Beijing. Apart from the one in the Pool and Cudrania Temple, the other three are in the following places: the one located on the bank of Zhonghai in Zhongnanhai, is called the "Water Flow Murmuring Pavilion". Another is found in the Cuijing Garden of Prince Gong's Mansions, and still another located in the Biluo Pavilion in the garden of the Ningshou Palace inside the Imperial Palace.

266. 潭柘寺内的万岁宫系作何用处？

万岁宫是清乾隆皇帝到潭柘寺游玩时的住处。另外,寺内还有太后宫。据史料记载,清代的康熙、乾隆帝都曾来这里游玩过,现仍保留有乾隆用过的宝座。

What is that Wansuigong (Palace of Longevity) in the Pool and Cudrania Temple used for?

The palace used to be a residence of temporary stay for Emperor Qianlong when he occasionally paid a visit to the temple. In addition to that there is still a palace for the queen mother in it. The historical record has it that both Kangxi and Qianlong, two emperors of the Qing Dynasty had ever been here for visits, and the precious throne for Emperor Qianlong is still kept here in a very good shape.

267. 潭柘寺内的西观音洞是怎样一回事？内藏何器物？

西观音洞位于潭柘寺西边。洞内泉水清澈见底。山石旁有两眼水井，有一石虎坐于井边。泉之东南有一老虎洞，洞之入口处刻有"神虎"二字。洞口是由数块山石自然形成的，洞中还有疯摩和尚及神虎的塑像。

What about that Western Guanyin Cave in the Pool and Cudrania Temple? And what is kept inside the cave?

Located on the west of the temple, you'll find a pond of limpid water inside the cave and by the side of the stony wall of the cave you'll see two water – wells and a stone tiger crouching by. To the southeast of the spring there is a tiger's cave and inscribed at the entrance are the two Chinese characters reading "Sacred Tiger". The mouth of the cave is naturally formed of a few rock – pieces, and sitting in the cave is a statue of a mentally deranged monk and that of a tiger.

268. 潭柘寺塔院内的塔有何特点？

塔院内有辽、金、明、清时期的和尚墓塔数十座。塔之高度虽都不一，但全部都是砖石结构，规模较大，是北京地区唯一的塔林。

What special features do the Stupas in the stupa – yard of the Pool and Cudrania Temple have?

In the stupa – yard of the Pool and Cudrania Temple there are dozens of stupas for the deceased monks of the temple, which range from the Liao Dynasty all the way down to Kin,

Ming and Qing dynasties. Built all of stone and bricks, the stupas are of different sizes and heights. The scope of the stupa — yard, so far as its number of stupas in it is concerned, can be deemed as the No. 1 stupa — yard in the surrounding areas of Beijing.

戒台寺
(The Ordination Altar Temple)

269. 什么叫做"戒台"?

戒台是佛教寺院中用以向信徒们传授戒律和受戒用的地方,只有在具备相当规模的寺庙里才能设立戒台。

What is an "altar of ordination"?

An altar of ordination is a platform in a Buddhist temple, where the doctrines of Buddhism are being preached among the believers or for a novice to be ordained. However, only a temple of a sizable scale can have such an altar of ordination set up in it.

270. 中国佛教的三大戒台在哪里?

中国佛教寺院中的三大戒台分别为:位于北京西郊的戒台寺,浙江杭州的昭庆寺和福建泉州的开元寺。

Where are the three grand altars of ordination of the Buddhist temples in China located?

The three grand altars of ordination of the Buddhist temples in China are located respectively in the following three temples: the Jie Tai Si (Ordination Altar Temple) in the western suburbs of Beijing; the Zhaoqing Temple in Hangzhou, Zhejiang Province and the Kaiyuan Temple in Quanzhou, Fujian Province.

271. 戒台寺位于北京何处？

戒台寺又名戒坛寺,正式名称为"万寿禅寺",坐落于北京西郊的马鞍山上,距市中心约为35公里。因其寺内有中国佛教寺院里最大的戒台,而称之为戒台寺。1957年被列为北京市第一批文物保护单位,该寺也是京郊著名的旅游景点之一。

Where lies the Ordination Altar Temple in Beijing?

The Ordination Altar Temple (Jie Tai si), alias Jie Tan si, has a formal name called the "Temple of Boundless Longevity". Located at the Saddle Mountain in the western suburbs of Beijing it is 35 kilometers away from the city center. As the temple has an ordination altar, the largest of its kind among all Buddhist temples in China, hence the name Jie Tai Si. The temple, being listed among the first batch of cultural relics under the protection of the Beijing Municipality in 1957, is one of the renowned tourist attractions in the surrounding areas of Beijing.

272. 北京戒台寺建于何年？

北京戒台寺建于唐武德四年(622年),旧称慧聚寺。因辽代有高僧法钧来到寺院讲授戒律,故在此建造了戒台。

When was the Ordination Altar Temple built in Beijing?

The temple was first built in 622, during the reigning period of Emperor Wude in the Tang dynasty, being then called the Temple of Wisdom Accumulation. However, there came in the Liao dynasty a highly accomplished monk by the name of Fajun, who, setting up a pulpit began to preach his Buddhist doctrines, and thenceforth the ordination altar was built here for the purpose.

273. 北京的戒台寺是如何成名的?

在辽代,有一些自愿皈依佛门的人纷纷来寺里学习经文和戒律,此后,再到潭柘寺的楞严坛进行考核,有合格者才准许出家,戒台寺因此便名声大振。自明清及至现今,都曾对戒台寺进行过修葺和扩建,现在的戒台寺更以全新的面貌吸引来自全国的游人及僧人来此游赏或朝山进香。

How did the Ordination Altar Temple of Beijing come to be renowned in the country?

In the Liao Dynasty, a lot of believers in Buddhism flocked here to learn Buddhist scriptures and doctrines in the temple and when finished here they had to pass a test at the Lengyan Altar in the Reclining Buddha Temple. Only those who passed the test could be ordained to be a novice. Thus the temple came to be known in the country. Ever since the Ming and Qing dynasties and even up to now, renovations and expansions in the temple have been carried out on a large scale. Therefore, the Ordination Altar Temple has become a center of gravity that attracts many a tourist to come from all over for a visit and monks here on pilgrims.

274. 现存的北京戒台是什么样呢? 建于何年?

现存的北京戒台是明代建造的,为正方形建筑,每边各长三丈,高一丈有余,共为三层。此台系用汉白玉建造,四周有莲瓣、祥云等图案,刻工非常精美别致。

What does the existing Altar of Ordination in Beijing look like? And when was it built?

The existing Altar of Ordination in Beijing, standing about 3 meters high and square in shape with each side measuring about 10 meters, is built of white marbles in three tiers. Carved on all sides with patterns of lotus petals and auspicious clouds. The craftsmanship of these carvings is very exquisite and nice – looking.

275. 现在的戒台寺是怎样的?

戒台寺坐西朝东,建于山麓的缓坡之上。其正殿为大雄宝殿,前面为天王殿,后面为千佛阁遗址。戒台殿在寺院的西北角院内,殿内还有乾隆皇帝亲笔题的巨匾"树精进幢"。戒台殿的周围有房屋 53 间,原来房内还有 500 尊罗汉塑像,但已经遭到破坏。总之,该寺的殿堂、碑、幢很多,还有叠石假山、松树、古槐,更有宁静舒适的四合院,是个游览休憩的好地方。

How does the Ordination Altar Temple look like now?

Built along a gentle slope the layout of the Ordination Altar Temple faces east with its back – end towards the west. With the Hall of Heavenly Guardians in front, the main structure in the temple is the Mahavira Hall and behind it is a ruined Thousand – Buddha Pavilion. The Hall of the Ordination Altar is located in the northwestern courtyard, and the inscription, which reads "Shu Jing Jin Zhuang" on the large horizontal board hung above in the hall, was autographed by Emperor Qianlong of the Qing Dynasty. The 50 rooms surrounding it had ever been the halls for 500 statues of arhats, but alas, they were ruined a long time ago. The temple has many halls, stone tablets and scripted stone pillars in it in addition to the artificial rockeries, ancient pine and locust trees growing in tranquil quadrangles, thereby making the temple a suitable place for repose and sightseeing.

276. 戒台寺的墓塔主要有哪些？

有辽代两座砖塔,是法钧和尚的衣钵塔和墓塔。在衣钵塔内葬有法钧和尚的衣服等物。戒台寺内还有一石幢,有元代月泉和尚的墓塔,因月泉和尚在寺内当过四年方丈,所以到清末,将其寺外的砖墓塔移到寺内。该墓塔虽小,但却十分别致,有腹盆式八方形的塔基及刻满文字的塔身,在八方形塔顶上,每面均刻有一使乐神,有吹的,也有弹的,形态不一。此外,寺外西面有明代马鞍山护国宝塔,塔身系用汉白玉石雕砌而成,刻有八十八尊佛像。

What are the main stupas for the remains of monks in the Ordination Altar Temple?

Towering in the temple are the two stupas built of bricks in the Liao Dynasty. They are both for the most accomplished monk by the name of Fajun with one being for his mantle and alms bowl as well as some of his clothes and another his remains. Besides, there is another stone stupa in it, which is the stupa for the remains of Monk Yuequan. As he had been the abbot of the temple for some four years during the Yuan Dynasty and for that reason his stupa was removed from the outside to the inside of the temple by the end of the Qing Dynasty. The stupa, though smaller in size, is elegantly built. Aside from these there is still an octahedral platform of a pagoda in the form of an inverted basin and the torso of the pagoda is fully carved with Chinese characters while the top – end of it with some deities playing music and posing different stances. Some of them are playing with flutes and others with percussion instruments in a life – like way. Furthermore, standing to the west outside the temple is the Pagoda for Safeguarding the Empire built at the Saddle Hill in the Ming Dynasty, the torso of which is built of white marbles carved all round with 88 Buddha figures.

277. 戒台寺的千佛阁哪里去了?

解放以前,寺内经常有宗教活动,自 1949 年以后,停止了一切宗教活动,并开辟为公园。1966 年以后,因修理天坛需用木料,故拆除了千佛阁,同时在此期间寺内大部分佛像均毁。80 年代后又重新雕塑了一些佛像供起来。

Where is the Thousand Buddha Pavilion of the Ordination Altar Temple now?

There were quite a lot religious activities in the temple before liberation, but came to a standstill after 1949 when it was opened to the public as a park. However, in 1966 due to the needs of timber for the reparation of the Temple of Heaven the pavilion was brought down and gone with it were many statues. It was only in the late 1980s, were some of the statues got remoulded, and then to be enshrined here again.

278. 戒台五松的名称是什么?

"潭柘以泉胜,戒台以松名"。寺内有著名五棵松,它们是:活动松、自在松、卧龙松、九龙松、抱塔松,合称戒台五松。

What's the respective name of the five pine trees in the Ordination Altar Temple?

It is said that "the Pool and Cudrania Temple is renowned for its springs while the Ordination Altar Temple for the curiously shaped pines." As known to many people, the five well-known pine trees in the temple are the Sensitive Pine, the Unrestrained Pine, the Reclining Dragon Pine, the Nine Dragon Pine and the Embracing Pagoda Pine.

279. 五棵名松各有何特点?

活动松位于千佛阁前,是一棵已有 500 多年历史的古油松。树旁立有乾隆皇帝御题的一方石碑。由于其伞状的大树冠偏向东面,与树干的倾斜方向一致,因而树的重心也便向东偏移,造成重心不稳,只要动其一枝,全树便会摇摆不停,故有活动松之称。

自在松位于寺院前高台阶旁,有 800 余年的历史。

卧龙松位于大雄宝殿后,辽金时代所植,树干弯曲俯伸,"腹部"枕卧于一块剑形石碑上。

九龙松位于戒台寺院前,直径有 2.2 米。

抱塔松位于墓塔边,树龄在千年以上,抱塔松所抱的塔就是辽代高僧法钧和尚的墓塔。

What's the specific feature of each of the five pine trees?

In front of the "Thousand Buddha Pavilion" there is an old Chinese pine of over 500 years, and standing by its side is a stele inscribed by Emperor Qianlong of the Qing Dynasty. As it has a very large canopy slanting slightly towards the east, which coincides with the stem of the tree, so the center of gravity of the tree is unsteady. If you touch one of its branches the whole tree will shake a lot, hence the name the "Sensitive Pine".

The "Unrestrained Pine" is towering without any restriction by the side of a platform in front of the temple and it is already 800 years old.

Planted behind the Mahavira Hall in around the Liao and Kin dynasties the Reclining Dragon Pine features a bending forward tree — stem supporting on a dagger — like stone stele, hence the derivation of the name.

The "Nine Dragon Pine" towers in the front courtyard of the Ordination Altar Temple with a diameter of 2.2 meters.

Located by the side of the burial stupa, the "Embracing Pagoda Pine" is over 1,000 years old. The pagoda it embraces is the very one for the most accomplished monk Fajun of the Liao Dynasty.

280. 清代在戒台寺有过哪些宗教性集"会"？又有哪些小佛殿？

依据文献记载，可以得知当时有许多民间组织起来的各种集"会"，例如"地藏会"、"三元大悲会"、"大悲随心经会"以及"五显财神圣会"等。这些庙"会"在戒台寺内空地上建起了一些小佛殿，如财神殿，娘娘殿、老爷殿、地藏殿等，所有这些均为非正宗的宗教形式在寺内的出现。

What "religious gatherings" were held in the Ordination Altar Temple during the Qing Dynasty? And what are the small shrines in the temple compound?

According to records there had been many religious gatherings held by some non – governmental organizations including the "Gathering for the God of Earth", "Gathering for the Goddess of Mercy", "Gathering for Chanting Prajnaparamitahrdayasutra" as well as "Sacred Gathering for the God of Wealth." With each of these gatherings having a small shrine built in the temple compound in its own memory there are so far many such small shrines here. They are the shrines for the God of Wealth, for the Goddess of Mercy and that of lords and for the God of Earth as well. However, all these shrine halls cropped up in the temple are not the things orthodox in Buddhism.

281. 戒台寺后山上著名的五洞均为何名？

最著名的五洞为：太古洞、观音洞、化阳洞、庞涓洞和孙膑洞。各洞均有景色点缀，如太古洞和观音洞外有一座八角形十一层的小塔；化阳洞右直下百米处有一石龟，若浮于绿波之中；庞涓洞很深，两壁皆为石乳。

What is the respective name of the five well – known caves along the hill – side at the back of the Ordination Altar Temple?

The five well – known caves are the Cave of Remote Antiquity, the Cave of the Goddess of Mercy, the Huayang Cave and the Pangjuan Cave as well as the Sun Bin Cave. Every cave is studded with some scenic attractions including the Cave of Remote Antiquity and the Cave of Goddess of Mercy, which have a small octagonal 11 – storeyed stone pagoda by their side. The Huayang Cave is studded with a tiny stone tortoise lying about a hundred meters away down the side slope, which looks as if it were floating on ripples of a lake. And the Pangjuan Cave known for its depth is a tunnel – like one with quite some stalactites and stalagmites of various descriptions a-long both sides of it.

天　坛
(Temple of Heaven)

282. 天坛建于何时？面积有多大？作何用处？

天坛位于北京城的南端，建于明永乐十八年(1420年)，布局成回字形，墙垣分内外两层。内墙长 3,292 米，外墙长 6,416米，总面积为 2,730,000 平方米，约合 273 公顷。

天坛是明清两代皇帝每年祭天，祈祷五谷丰登的地方。最初祭祀天地均在此处，1530 年在北郊建了地坛，这里才专供祭天之用。

When was the Temple of Heaven built? How large an area does it cover? And what is it used for?

Located in the southern part of the city of Beijing, the Temple of Heaven was built in 1420, the 18th year of Emperor Yongle's reign in the Ming Dynasty. Surrounded by two rings of walls the Temple of Heaven covers an area totaling 2,730,000 square meters, an equivalent to 273 hectares. With the wall from north to south stretching as long as 1,657 meters and that from east to west 1,703 meters, the outer wall is 6,553 meters in circumference while the inner wall measures 4,152 meters in all.

The Temple of Heaven used to be a place where emperors of the Ming and Qing dynasties went twice (and sometimes thrice) a year to do worshipping and offering sacrifices to heaven to pray for good harvests and fine rain. In the past, sacrifices were offered to heaven and earth in one place only. But when the Temple of Earth was built in the north of the city in 1530, the Temple of Heaven was ever since used specially for offering sacrifices to heaven alone.

283. 皇帝每年何时去天坛祭天?

明清两朝,皇帝每年去天坛两次,第一次是在阴历正月十五日,祭祀皇天上帝,为百谷祈雨,典称祀谷礼,即到祈年殿去祈祷五谷丰收;第二次是在冬至到环丘坛去祭天,即祭皇天上帝,奉列祖列宗配祀,以日、月、星、辰、风、雨、雷、云诸神从祀。如遇岁旱,则另举行大雩礼。此外,皇帝还经常在初夏时分去环丘坛求雨。

At what time of the year did the emperor go to the Temple of Heaven to pray for good harvests?

During the Ming and Qing dynasties, emperors went twice a year to the Temple of Heaven, the first time being on the 15th of the first month in the lunar calendar. This time, it was to pray for fine rain and was known in history as a ritual of praying for good harvests; the second time was on the day of the Winter Solstice and this was to offer sacrifices to heaven at the round altar. The sacrifice was offered to the God of Heaven accompanied by the tablets of the ancestors of the royal family and then followed by the gods of the sun, the moon, the stars, the dawn, the wind, the rain, the lightning and the clouds. If in a year of drought another ritual ceremony called "Dayu" would again be held to pray for rain. And apart from all these, some emperors would go at the beginning of summer to the altar to pray for rain.

284. 祈年殿建于何时？何时重修？

祈年殿建于明永乐十八年（1420 年），但该殿自修建以来，已几经变化。最初命名为大祀殿，是一座长方形的大殿；明嘉靖八年（1529 年），改成了三层圆形的大殿，称为大享殿。当时，三层重檐上的瓦是上蓝、中黄、下绿三种颜色。清乾隆十七年（1752 年），才改成三重檐均用一色深蓝的琉璃瓦。光绪十五年（1889 年），此殿为雷火所毁，第二年照原样重建。1972 年，在上次修复的基础上，重修彩绘，使其显得翻然一新。

When was the Hall of Prayer for Good Harvests built and rebuilt?

The Hall of Prayer for Good Harvests has undergone several times of changes since it was first built in 1420, the 18th year under the reign of Emperor Yongle in the Ming Dynasty. At that time the hall was named "Dasidian" – the Hall of Grand Sacrifices and it was rectangular in shape. However, in 1529, the 8th year in the reign of Emperor Jiajing, it was rebuilt into a round one with a roof of three tiers with its name changed to "Daxiangdian" – the Hall of Grand Treatment to Heaven. The roofs of three tiers were decorated in three different colors with the upper one in blue, the middle one in yellow and the lower one in green. Later, in 1752, the 17th year in the reign of Emperor Qianlong of the Qing Dynasty they were all changed into glazed tiles of dark blue. However, lightning destroyed them in 1889, the 15th year in the reign of Emperor Guangxu. It was restored in 1890 in accordance with the original. In 1972, the whole building underwent a thorough renovation with all its paintings redone in the same style as they were done last time.

285. 祈年殿在建筑上有何特色?

祈年殿加上底座共高 38 米,直径为 30 米,共有三重圆形檐子,最高一层的中央为鎏金宝顶。这样高大沉重的建筑物,是用 28 根楠木柱支撑起来的。整个大殿,全系木结构建筑,不仅不用钢筋,且在主要支柱上均不用钉子连接,都以斗拱支架而成,是中国木结建筑的典型之作。

What special features does the Hall of Prayer for Good Harvests enjoy in its architectural style?

Built on a three - tiered platform, the Hall of Prayer for Good Harvests, being of 30 meters in diameter, towers 38 meters high with its eaves fanning out on three tiers, of which the upper one has a gold - plated knob on it. Such a heavy building was supported merely on 28 wooden pillars with no single piece of reinforced concrete at all, and without using a single nail the whole building was brought together by mortise and tenon joints. So it can be deemed as a building of a unique style and a typical wooden structure in the architectural history in China.

286. 祈年殿的圆柱有何象征性?

祈年殿中间的四根柱子叫"龙井柱"每根高 19.2 米,要两个半人才能合抱过来,象征着一年中的四个季节;外围一圈 12 根象征的是一年中的 12 个月;墙内又有 12 根,象征的是一天之中的 12 个时辰;内外檐柱 24 根象征着一年中的 24 个节气;再加上四根龙井柱,共为 28 根,代表了天上的 28 星宿。

What do the pillars of the Hall of Prayer for Good Harvests signify?

The four pillars in the center of the hall, with each pillar standing 19.2 meters high and to be embraced by two and half persons joining hands together, are called "Longjingzhu" – the Dragon Well Pillar. They signify the four seasons of a year. The 12 pillars on the outside symbolize 12 months in a year and another 12 pillars standing in the round wall suggest the 12 two – hour periods of a day. And putting the two 12 pillars together you get 24, they represent the 24 solar terms of a year, and again adding the four in the center of the hall you get 28, that correspond to 28 lunar mansions in the heaven above.

287. 祈年殿内的"龙凤石"起何作用?

龙凤石是祈年殿内铺地石中间的那块圆石,这是一块天然大理石,上面的花纹犹如一条龙与一只凤交绕在一起,故名"龙凤石"。据说大殿顶上的龙凤藻井,就是依据"龙凤石"的自然图案制作的。上下对应,自成一趣。

龙凤石的用处有三:首先它是一种装饰品;第二象征着皇威;第三是皇帝在祈谷时,大致就站在这块"龙凤石"的位置上,面向"皇天上帝"的牌位行礼,也就是说,龙凤石是"皇帝拜位的地方"。

What is the "Dragon and Phoenix Stone" in the Hall of Prayer for Good Harvests used for?

The Dragon and Phoenix Stone, referring to a round stone piece in the center of the Hall of Prayer for Good Harvests, is a piece of natural marble with a pattern that looks very much like a pair of dragon and phoenix intertwining on it. It is said that the decorative pattern on the coffered ceiling is an imitation of the marble piece on the ground, thereby forming a delightful, yet a fine counterpart for that on the above.

The Dragon and Phoenix Stone is used in the following ways: first of all, it is used as decorative piece; secondly a symbol of imperial power and dignity. And thirdly the piece of stone is the very stone where the emperor knelt down to do his worshipping when the ceremony of praying for good harvests was being held here in the hall.

288. 祈年殿院内的东、西两侧殿作何用处?

大殿两边各有一个侧殿,东配殿是专供存放日、月、星、辰牌位,西配殿则为存放风、雨、雷、云等自然神牌位的地方。皇帝在祈谷时,把皇帝的列祖列宗作为配祀,而把自然神的牌位作为从祀。

What are the halls on the east and west of the Hall of Prayer for Good Harvests in the courtyard used for?

On both sides of the Hall of Prayer for Good Harvests there are two annex halls. The one on the east is the hall for safekeeping the tablets of the sun, the moon, the stars and dawn, while that on the west is used for housing the tablets of the wind, the rain, the thunder and the clouds. When the ceremony of praying for good harvests was to be held, the tablets of the emperor's ancestors were made to accompany the tablet of the heavenly god with all other tablets to be followed as their subordinate pieces.

289. 祈年殿中间的宝座和西边的宝座各起什么作用？

祈年殿中间的宝座是放置玉皇大帝的牌位用的；而西边的宝座是供皇帝行礼后休息时坐的。

What are the precious throne in the center and the one by the west side of it in the Hall of Prayer for Good Harvests used for?

The precious throne in the center of the hall is the seat for the tablet of the heavenly god, while the one by the west of it is for the emperor to have a rest when he finishes his praying to heaven for good harvests.

290. 祈年殿内东边的屏风、长桌和座桥有何用处？

这些屏风、长桌和座桥，都是供奉帝王祖先牌位用的地方。

What are the screen, the long table and the seating on the east of the Hall of Prayer for Good Harvests used for?

The screen, the long table and the seating on the east of the hall are used for consecrating the memorial tablets of the emperor's ancestors.

291. 祈年殿后面的殿堂叫什么名字？系作何用？

祈年殿后面的殿堂叫皇极殿，原是放置上帝神位之所，后又作为放置拜天仪式中使用的旌旗、锣鼓等器具之用。

What is the hall behind the Hall of Prayer for Good Harvests called? And what is it used for?

Called "Huangjidian" or the Hall of Imperial Zenith, it

was formerly used for enshrining the tablets of the gods in heaven and later for the safekeeping of banners, streamers, drums and gongs used at the ceremony to pray for good harvests.

292. 皇穹宇的用途和建筑特点是什么?

皇穹宇殿内正面的石台上放置的是玉皇大帝的牌位,两边各有四座石台,过去是放皇帝八代祖宗牌位用的。

皇穹宇是天坛南部的主要建筑,建于明嘉靖九年(1530年),初名泰神殿,后改成今名。原为双重檐,清乾隆十七年(1752年)重建时改为单檐。殿高 19.5 米,直径为 15.6 米。原为八角形,后改成圆形。它用砖木建成,比祈年殿小,但结构与祈年殿基本相同。其特点是藻井较小,顶部无一横梁,殿顶由斗拱支架,下面撑着八根柱子。

What is the Imperial Vault of Heaven used for? And what special features does it have in its architectural style?

Consecrated on the central stone – platform in the Hall of Imperial Vault of Heaven is the tablet of the Jade Emperor, the four stone platforms on both sides are for the tablets of the emperor's ancestors of eight generations in succession.

As a main building in the south of the Temple of Heaven, the Imperial Vault of Heaven was built in 1530, the 9th year in the reign of Emperor Jiajing of the Ming Dynasty. At the very beginning it was called "Taishendian" or the Hall for Pacifying Gods and later changed into the present name. The building, used to have double eaves, was rebuilt into one of a single eave in 1752, the 17th year in the reign of Emperor Qianlong of the Qing Dynasty. The circular hall, standing 19.5 meters high and of 15.6 meters in diameter, used to be an octagonal one in the past. Built of bricks and lumber pieces, the hall, though smaller in size than the Hall of Prayer for Good Harvests, is almost the same as the former in its architectural structure. With a caisson relatively smaller in size, the whole building has no crossbeams at all. The rooftop is made to support on a span – work joining up by mortise and tenon joints which are rested on the eight massive wooden columns.

293. 海漫大道有何用处?

从天坛西边的正门进去,便可见到一条南北走向的高台基,称为丹陛桥,其高 25 米,宽达 28 米,长为 60 米。中间系用汉白玉石铺道,两边用砖垒砌而成,它连结了天坛的祈年殿、皇穹宇、环丘坛三座主要建筑,给人以宏伟壮观之感。此外,此道还被赋于了某种神奇的色彩,象征人间通往天上之路。即到天坛祭天就等于上天,其路途显得那样遥远而漫长。

What is the Danbiqiao in the Temple of Heaven used for?

On entering the compound of the Temple of Heaven from its western front gate, you'll see a raised platform extending from north to south. This is Danbiqiao as usually called by the people. The massive platform, measuring 2.5 meters high, 28 meters wide and 360 meters long. Built of bricks on both sides and white marble pieces paved along the central part, it plays the role of a linkup between the three major buildings. That is to join the Hall of Prayer for Good Harvests in the north, the Imperial Vault of Heaven and the Mound Altar in the south, thereby making it to suggest a sense of magnificence and splendor. Aside from this, it also shows something mystical as if it were a long road, long enough to lead from the world of mortal beings to heaven when the ceremony of praying for good harvests was being held here.

294. 皇穹宇殿外东西两侧的配殿有何用处?

它们的作用与祈年殿旁配殿的用处相同,是供存放日、月、星、辰和风、雨、雷、云等自然神的牌位用的地方。祭天的时候,把牌位搬到环丘坛上去举行仪式,祭奠完毕以后再送回原处存放。

What are the side – halls on both sides of the Imperial Vault of Heaven used for?

Arranged likewise as in the compound of the Hall of Prayer for Good Harvests, the side – halls here are for safe – keeping the tablets of the gods of the sun, the moon, the stars and the dawn as well as those of the wind, the rain, the thunder and clouds. When the sacrifice to heaven was going to be held, the tablets would be moved to the Mound Altar for the ceremonial rites and returned to the same place afterwards.

295. 天坛的建筑为何是圆形的,颜色为何是蓝的?

天坛的主要建筑均呈圆形,因为天是圆的,而天坛是天的象征。晴朗的天空呈蔚蓝色,所以它的颜色也是象征天的。

Why the major buildings in the Temple of Heaven are round in shape with their roofs in blue?

As in ancient China the heaven was deemed round and to symbolize it, the major buildings in the Temple of Heaven were built into round ones, and likewise a clear sky is blue so

306

the roofs of the buildings were correspondingly made the same color to symbolize the sky.

296. 天坛里斋宫的用处是什么?

封建皇帝在祭天前首先要进行三天斋戒,在去天坛祭天的前一天,就住在斋宫里沐浴,以表示对"皇天上帝"的虔诚。斋宫里面,除正殿、宿卫房、典守房和钟楼等建筑外,还有座石亭,里面有个手持书有"斋戒"二字牌子的铜人,名叫"斋戒铜人"。这是为了提醒皇帝,到这里来是斋戒的,这是明洪武十一年(1378年)定的制度。相传这个铜人是仿照唐朝魏征的形象铸造的。

What is the Palace of Abstinence in the Temple of Heaven used for?

In feudal times, emperors had first to do his fasting three days before they went to offer sacrifices in the Temple of Heaven. The day prior to the holding of the sacrificial ceremony, the emperor had to move into the Palace of Abstinence and took a bath there, so as to show his sincere piety for the "god of heaven". In the Palace of Abstinence, apart from the main hall, rooms for guards and attendants to the ceremony and the bell – tower, there is still a stone – pavilion in which stands a brass figure with a tablet of abstinence in hand. The figure is called the "figure of abstinence" which was designed to remind the emperor that he be here for abstinence. The rule was stipulated and handed down ever since 1378, the 11th year in the reign of Emperor Hongwu, the founder of the Ming Dynasty. It is said that the brass figure was a copy of Wei Zheng, the prime minister in the early days of the Tang Dynasty, who was held as a symbol of uprightness and justice.

297. 皇帝去天坛是从哪个门进入的?

过去,天坛只有西边的两个门,现在的北门和东门是民国时期开的,南门更是近几年的事了。因此,皇帝去天坛是进西边靠北的那个门。

By which gate did the emperor get into the Temple of Heaven when he came here for ceremony?

In the past there were only two gates on the west side of the Temple of Heaven. The gate on the north and that on the east were opened during the time of the Republic of China, and the gate on the south was only a matter of recent years. So in the days of old, the emperor normally got into the Temple of Heaven from the gate on the west by north.

298. 为什么天坛南边的围墙是方的,而北边是圆的?

中国古代的传说称"天圆地方"。明嘉靖九年(1530 年)以前,皇帝在此是天地合祭的,所以在北边把围墙修成了圆的,用以象征天,而将南边的围墙筑成方形以象征地。

Why was the compound wall surrounding the Temple of Heaven made square on the south yet semi – circular at the north?

In ancient times the Chinese legend held it that the heaven was round and the earth square. Before 1530, the ninth year of Emperor Jiajing's reign in the Ming Dynasty emperors offered their sacrifices to heaven and the earth at the same time and also in the same place. Therefore, the compound wall was built into a semi – circular one at the north to represent the

308

heaven and square on the south to symbolize the earth.

299. 天坛的九龙柏有多少年的树龄了？

九龙柏是一棵老柏树，其树干纽结纠缠，形状恰似九龙盘绕，故而得名。这棵柏树在建坛之初就已长在这里了，据称其树龄已在八百年以上了。

How old is the Nine Dragon Cypress in the Temple of Heaven?

The Nine Dragon Cypress in the Temple of Heaven is an old cypress tree which has many a spiraling knars intertwining on its trunk, which looks as if there were nine dragons round it, hence the derivation of the name the Nine Dragon Cypress Tree. It is said that the tree was already here at the very beginning of the temple construction, so it has already been here for over 800 years.

300. 回音壁的直径、高及厚度各是多少？

回音壁的直径是 65.1 米，高度为 3.7 米，厚达 90 公分。如果两人分别站在东西墙根，一人靠墙低声说话，另一人就会清晰地听到对方的声音。犹如两人在打电话，煞是有趣。

What is the diameter, height and width of the Echoing Wall in the Temple of Heaven?

The circular Echoing Wall is 65.1 meters in diameter and the wall is 3.7 meters in height with a width of 90 centimeters. If two people stand widely apart by the side of the wall and one of them whispers towards it at one end, another will be able to hear him clearly on the other. It's a very interesting phenomenon as if they were speaking over the phone.

301. 回音壁的原理是什么?

回音壁是一座圆形建筑,结构严密,所用的砖是磨砖对缝的,表面平滑,墙上端又有一圈瓦檐,因而声波不易被砖吸收,也不易从砖墙上部跑掉,只能沿着围墙传播,这就形成了奇特的回音壁。

What's the scientific theory behind the Echoing Wall?

The Echoing Wall is a circular one of a compact structure built of polished bricks and the face of the wall is very smooth. In addition, the wall is capped with an eave, so the sound is neither easy to be absorbed by the wall nor is it possible to slip away from the wall − top above. Such being the case, the sound wave has to go along the wall from one end to the other, thereby producing the echoing effect.

302. 三音石的原理是什么?

三音石中的第一块石头,即靠近皇穹宇的那一块,处在院子的中心,声波的回响同时从墙的各处反射回来,所以只能听见一声回响。但第二块、第三块至墙的距离各不相同,所以声音反射回来的时间也不同,这样就听到了不同次数的回响。

What is the scientific theory behind the Triple Sound Stones?

As the first piece of stone, i.e. the one close − by the Imperial Vault of Heaven, is right in the center of the courtyard and when you stand on it calling, the sound wave comes back from the wall all at once, so you can hear only one echoing sound. But if you stand on the second or third stone you can hear it twice or thrice due to the different distances from the stone to the wall, which require a different time for the sound wave to travel forwards and backwards.

303. 圜丘坛建于何年？

圜丘坛建于明嘉靖九年(1530 年)，清乾隆十四年(1749 年)改建，至今已有二百多年的历史了。

When was the Circular Mound Altar built?

With a history of over 200 years, the Circular Mound Altar was first built in 1530, the ninth year of Emperor Jiajing's reign in the Ming dynasty and was later rebuilt in 1749, the 14th year in the reign of Emperor Qianlong of the Qing dynasty.

304. 圜丘坛的用处和建筑特点是什么？

我们所说的天坛，实际上指的是圜丘坛。在封建时代里，圜丘坛比起祈年殿来还重要，每年冬至那天，皇帝都要登上此坛祭天。圜丘坛是祭天用的，所以砌成了圆形，但又因为是凌空的，所以台上不能建屋，对空而祭，因而称之为"露祭"。

此坛高五米，分为三层，由下而上分别代表地、人、天。上层直径为三十米，中层为五十米，下层达七十米。因古代把天视为阳性，所以坛面、台阶及栏杆所用的石块、栏板的尺度和数目都是阳数，即奇数一、三、五、七、九(九为极阳数)及它们的倍数来计算而定的。坛的上层中心是一块圆石，圆石外第一环砌石九块，第二环为十八块，第三环为二十七块，并依此类推直至九环八十一块为止。中层从第十环九十块起，到十八环一百六十二块止。下层自第十九环一百七十一块起，到最后一环为九的二十七倍,即二百四十三块止。每层有四门,每门的石阶有九级。每层都有雕龙栏杆,栏杆的数目也是九的倍数,上层七十二根,中层一百零八根,而下层则为一百八十根。

What is the Circular Mound Altar used for? And what are the special features in its architectural structure?

When we speak of the Temple of Heaven we are actually referring to the Circular Mound Altar. In feudal times, the altar was in a way a place even more important than the Hall of Prayer for Good Harvests. Every year on the day of the Winter Solstice, the emperor would come to offer sacrifices to heaven on the altar. For this reason, the altar was built into a circular one. Built in open air and with no shelter over it, the sacrificial ceremony was being held right under heaven hence it was called "Luji," or the "open-air offering of sacrifices".

Built in three tiers with a height totaling 5 meters, the bottom tier of the altar represents the earth, the middle one the people and the one on the top the heaven. The top tier is 30 meters in diameter, the middle one 50 meters and the one at the bottom 70 meters, because in ancient times people treated the sun as something positive. The scales and numbers of the stone-slabs used for the altar surface, the flights of steps and the stone railings and panels of the balustrades are all in positive, i. e. in odd numbers, in which nine is the extremity. Therefore, everything made and built here would follow the odd number: one, three, five, seven and nine or their multiples. On the altar you'll find a round piece of stone in the center of the top tier. The first ring round it uses nine pieces of stone-slabs; the second ring 18 pieces and the third ring 27 pieces till the ninth ring using 81 pieces of stone – slabs to finish off the top tier. The middle tier begins from the tenth ring of 90 pieces of stone – slabs to end up in the eighteenth ring of 162 pieces of stone pieces. And the bottom tier starts from the nineteenth ring of 171 pieces of stone – slabs to wind up by 27 times that of the first ring, namely 243 pieces of stone – slabs. With four gates opened on each tier of the altar, every gate has a flight of stair of nine steps. As to the balustrades on each tier, the number of their railings is also the multiples of nine with the upper tier having 72 pieces, the middle one 108 pieces and the bottom tier 180 pieces.

305. 圜丘坛圆心的回音原理是什么？

如果你站在圆心轻声说话,自己听来觉得声音很大。这是因为石面相当平滑,当声音传至等距离的石栏杆后,又同时从四周折射回到石面的中心,使站在圆心里的人听起来感到声波振动很大,是一个自然形成的扩大器。

What is the reason behind the echoing center of the Circular Mound Altar?

Standing in the center of the Mound Altar and whispering to yourself you'll hear a sound much louder than that of your own. This is because the surface of the altar is very smooth. When the sound wave travels to the balustrades of an equal distance around, it turns back all at once in a minute, thereby making the person standing in the center feel the resounding effect produced by the altar, a natural amplifier.

306. 皇帝是怎样祭天的？

祭天前的准备是个复杂的过程：负责祭祀的官员称为大宗伯，事先将拟定好的一份祭祀日程表置于太和殿的案桌上。皇帝下马后站在案前，此时便由大宗伯上前跪奏：x 年 x 月 x 日祭祀安排及祈祷祝词，请皇上过目。皇帝阅视后命执事人将祝词表放到中和殿，然后皇帝登上宝座，百官磕头，依此退出。皇帝在中和殿练习祝词。在祭祀前夕，皇帝身穿礼服、戴冕帽，即礼帽。在故宫的斋宫设斋二日，然后在祭祀的前一天去天坛斋宫设斋，并在环丘坛的东南门外设席棚，称谓御幕，这是皇帝换鞋的地方，在坛门外西侧，设执事官换衣服的地方。祭前还得把献牲用的牛犊等刳净放在燔柴炉的右侧，东南有绿琉璃燎炉，西南设望灯台长竿悬大灯。太和钟（明朝置于斋宫的东西两侧）鸣，皇帝出斋宫，皇帝登坛后钟止。与此同时举火点炉，并把献牲牛犊放在柴上烤，这就叫做燔柴礼；此外还有燎炉八座也与此同时点燃。礼赞官大声朗颂祝词。皇帝带领文武百官依此进香，迎神献礼。皇帝站在正南二台，王公站在三台，其他官员则站在坛南，然后，由执事官引导皇帝及百官登坛献礼，望燎送神。此时，乐队奏乐，并有舞生跳舞。礼毕皇帝返，斋宫鸣钟。

How did the emperor offer sacrifices to heaven?

The preparation of the sacrificial service is like this: the official in charge of offering sacrifices, named "Dazongbo" must work out in advance a plan, in which, it includes a prayer to heaven to be laid on the table in front of the Hall of Supreme Harmony. When the emperor proceeds towards it he must, first getting off the horse, stand in front of the table. At this moment, Dazongbo, the official in charge will kneel down and report to him the plan about the sacrificial ceremony, saying

314

the plan for offering sacrifices to heaven on this day, this month, this year, and the prayer to heaven is ready here for his majesty's perusal. When approved it will be taken to the Hall of Central Harmony. There when the emperor gets onto the throne, the officials around will, kneeling down, kowtow to him and then quit the hall, while the emperor himself will stay on, practicing the ritual proceedings for the ceremony. But by the time of two days prior to the sacrificial service, the emperor will, in ceremonial robe and ritual hat, first go fasting for two days in the Hall of Abstinence located in the forbidden City. And then he will go to the Hall of Abstinence in the Temple of Heaven the day before the sacrificial ceremony begins. Aside from all those mentioned above, a met－booth will be set up at the southeast corner of the altar for the emperor to change his clothes and boots and another to be set up to the west of the altar for the official in charge of the sacrificial service. The calf and other animals for the sacrifice will first be cleaned and then laid by the right side of the oven that is built of green glazed bricks in the southeast corner of the altar. And finally the southwest corner will have a long pole put up with a big lantern on it. When all this done the Bells of Supreme Harmony (installed on both sides of the Hall of Abstinence ever since the Ming Dynasty) are sounded and the emperor starts to come out from the Hall of Abstinence and the bells stop when the emperor has stepped onto the altar. At the time fire will be lit in the ovens, including the other eight temporarily set up for the purpose with the calf and other animals for the sacrifice to be grilled on, this being called "Fanchaili," i. e. the grilling ceremony. While the ceremonial official is chanting aloud the prayer to heaven, the emperor will, heading his retinue, stand due south on the second tier of the altar to offer incense – sticks in turn to welcome the gods from the heaven and offer sacrifices. This finished, the ceremonial official will, to the accompaniment of melodies and dances, begin to lead the emperor onto the altar followed by other officials and officers with their heads up and eyes towards heaven to see the gods off. This being over the emperor will return to the palace to the accompaniment of the pleasant chime of the bell.

307. 皇帝是如何祈谷的?

祈年殿正中为皇帝行礼拜位,靠前大约在地面上天然大理石之处,为致词及接受福胙,代替皇天上帝品尝供神食品的拜位。殿外为陪祀王公的拜位。两旁为奏乐队、舞队及礼官位。台下则为百官拜位。祈年门外东为燎炉。祭日前一天,皇帝到祈谷坛外南门右侧降舆,从祈年门左门进去,先在皇乾殿上香行礼,用龙亭恭请神牌到祈年殿各自的坛位,再由左门出到神库视察祭祀用的献牲物品,尔后返回斋宫。

祀日,皇帝由祈年门左门进入,上左天门的台阶,从祈年殿的左门进入拜位,对着"皇天上帝"的牌位行礼。此时,点燔柴炉迎帝神。皇帝向皇天上帝献玉帛进俎,一连献上三套菜。然后撤馔,送帝神,望燎并奏乐起舞。

How did the emperor pray for good harvests?

The worshipping place for the emperor to pray for good harvests is right in the center of the hall. And a little further from it is the very piece of marble with a pair of dragon and phoenix on it, this is the spot, on which the emperor will kneel down to say his prayers to heaven and taste the offerings on behalf of the heavenly gods. On the two sides outside the hall are the sites for princes to prostrate themselves and still further a- side the spots for the orchestra and dancers and the master of ceremony. Kneeling still farther away in the courtyard are offi- cials and officers. The grilling ovens are set up on the east out- side the Gate of Prayer for Good Harvests. When everything has been well arranged, the emperor will come to the Temple of Heaven the day before the ceremony begins. Descending from his carriage on the right of the Gate of Prayer for Good Harvests he gets into the courtyard by a side gate on the left. After that he will proceed towards the Hall of Imperial Zenith to offer incense — sticks and there he will piously invite the tablets of the heavenly gods to their respective place in the Hall of Prayer for Good Harvests. This being over, he will leave the place by a left gate to check over the offerings prepared in the storeroom and then return to the Hall of Abstinence.

On the very day for holding the prayer ceremony, the em- peror will, getting into the courtyard by a side gate from the left of the Gate of Prayer for Good Harvests. And there follow- ing a flight of steps on the left, he approaches from a left gate towards the worshipping place in the Hall of Prayer for Good Harvests to pay his respects to the tablet of the heavenly god. At the same time fire will be lit in the grill — ovens outside to welcome the gods from the heaven. Silk pieces and courses of dishes will be offered to three rounds before the gods are to be seen off to the accompaniment of music and dances.

雍和宫

(The Yonghegong Lamasery)

308. 雍和宫建于何时及由谁修建？作何用处？

雍和宫是北京著名的喇嘛庙,位于北京东北角,距今已有三百年的历史,但迄今为止仍保持着严格的喇嘛庙风格,是全国的重点文物保护单位之一。

雍和宫初建于清康熙三十三年(1694年),是为其第四子胤禛(世宗雍正)修建的一座华丽的宫邸,当时称为"雍亲王府"。雍正于1723年接帝位后的第三年(1725年)改为行宫,正式改名为"雍和宫"。该宫邸占地99.7亩,约合6.6公顷,有房千余间。

When was the Yonghegong Lamasery built? By whom and what was it used for?

Located in the northeast corner of the city, the Yonghegong is a famous lamasery in Beijing. Though witnessed a vicissitudes of nearly 300 years it has so far still kept a strict style of Lamaism, and is one of the important pieces of cultural relics under the national protection.

Built early as in 1694, the 33rd year in the reign of Emperor Kangxi, this used to be a palace mansion for Prince Yong, his fourth son Yingzheng before his succession to the throne. It was renovated into a palace for his temporary stay and was officially named the "Yonghegong" in 1725, the third year when Prince Yong became the emperor. The palace consists of more than 1,000 rooms, covering an area of over 6.6 hectares.

309. 雍和宫为何改为喇嘛庙?

雍正一生崇信喇嘛教,他经常与德高望重的喇嘛在雍和宫内讲经说道。雍正当了皇帝以后的第一件事,便是通过宗教来笼络少数民族,尤其是信奉喇嘛教的藏蒙两个民族;第二是按清朝的规矩,凡皇帝住过的地方都是"龙潜禁地",除改作庙宇外,不能另作他用。因此他便把原来宫邸中之半改成黄教上院,另一半仍留作行宫,但行宫部分后来被火焚毁,于是就在雍正三年将上院改名为雍和宫。

当雍正于1735年死后,他的梓宫曾在这里停放过,所以又把原来宫内部分主要殿堂上绿色琉璃瓦升格为皇宫宫殿的颜色。雍和宫是在乾隆九年(1744年)正式改成喇嘛庙的。

Why was the Yonghegong being transformed into a lamasery?

During the lifetime of Emperor Yongzheng, he held a firm belief in Lamaism. Before his ascending the throne, interviews or sermons were often held in his palace mansions by inviting some reverend lamas over. After his succession to the throne the first thing he did was to rope in the minority people, especially the Tibetans and Mongols, as they were believers in lama – ism. Secondly in accordance with the rules in the Qing Dynasty, the place where an emperor ever lived was considered as a "dragon – hiding area prohibited from any intrusion" which cannot be used otherwise than being turned into a temple. So decision was made to turn half of it into an upper temple for the Yellow Sect of Lama – ism and the rest still being used as a palace for his temporary stay. However, the part of the palace was later burnt down by fire and the name was changed to "Yonghegong" in 1725, the third year in the reign of emperor Yongzheng of the Qing Dynasty.

Emperor Yongzheng died in 1735. After his passing away his coffin was once laid up here in the lamasery. It was simply because of the fact that some of the building roofs originally in green were upgraded to be in yellow as those in the Imperial Palace. The Yonghegong was officially renamed "Yonghegong Lamasery" in 1744, the 9th year in the reign of Emperor Qianlong of the Qing Dynasty.

310. 雍和宫主要是由哪几幢大殿组成的?

雍和宫的主要建筑物是由五进大殿组成的。第一进为天王殿,第二进是雍和宫的正殿,第三进是永佑殿,第四进是法轮殿,第五进是万福阁,又称大佛殿。这五进大殿,加上它们各自的东西配殿,就构成了雍和宫。

What are the main halls in the Yonghegong Lamasery?

Consisting mainly of the five rows of halls, the first row of the lamasery is the Tianwangdian, the Hall of Heavenly Guardians; the second row the Yonghedian, the Hall of Harmony. It is the main hall of the lamasery. The third is Yongyoudian, the Hall of Eternal Blessing, the fourth the Falundian, the Hall of the Wheel of Buddhist Laws (or Dharmacakra in Sanskrit) and the last the Wanfuge (or alias the Dafolou), the Pavilion of Ten Thousand Happiness (or the Giant Buddha Pavilion). The five rows of buildings built along the axis plus their respective annexes lined on both sides form the present —

311. 雍和宫里的古铜须弥山是这里的原物吗？它有什么说头吗？

这座模型须弥山,是明朝万历年间司礼监的掌印太监冯保所供奉的,但它是由别处移来的。古人称须弥山是一个小世界的中心。在这个小世界的最下层是风轮,其上为水轮,再上为金轮,亦即地轮,再往上更有九山八海,而其中心是须弥山,山顶便是传说中的天堂。顶部下方那些星座的位置,大体上也与天文学上的情况相符合。

Is the Bronze Mount Sumeru an object originally laid here in the Yonghegong Lamasery?

This bronze model of the Mount Sumeru was a gift presented by Feng Bao, who used to be a seal－keeping eunuch in the office of the ritual rites during the reign of Emperor Wanli of the Ming Dynasty, but it was moved here from some other place. About the Mount Sumeru, legend in ancient times has it that it is the center of a small world. In this small world the bottom－most is the wheel of the wind, over it the wheel of the water and still above the wheel of the earth and still further above the 9 mountains and 8 seas, and the Mount Sumeru is right in the center of it. The top of the Mount Sumeru is what is deemed in legend as the "Paradise" and the constellations around its lower part roughly correspond to what have been found in modern astronomy.

312. 雍和宫大殿里供奉的"三世佛"是谁？

这里所供奉的三世佛为:释迦牟尼、迦叶和弥勒。释迦牟尼是佛教的祖师,他在 2,500 年前创立了佛教,称"现在佛"。迦叶佛在他右边,叫做"过去佛",或谓之"燃灯佛"。弥勒佛在释迦的左边,称为"未来佛"。

Who's the Buddha of Three Existences in the main hall of the Yonghegong Lamasery?

They are the Buddha of Sakyamuni, Jaye (or Dipamkara in Sanskrit) and Maitreya. Sakyamuni, the founder of Buddhism, who created the Buddhist doctrine about 2,500 years ago, is the "Buddha of Present Existence". Sitting by his right is Jaye, the "Buddha of Past Existence" and on his left is Maitreya, the "Buddha of the Future".

313. 法轮殿正中供奉的是谁?

法轮殿的正中供奉的是一尊高三丈多的黄教祖师宗喀巴的铜像。佛身高 550 公分。宗喀巴生于明永乐十五年(1417 年),原籍青海湟中县,死于明成化十四年(1478 年)。他是喇嘛教的重大改革者,在其背光处还有他的五个化身像。

Who is consecrated in the center of Falundian – the Hall of the Wheel of Buddhist Laws?

Enshrined right in the center of the hall is a bronze statue of Tsongkhapa, which is 5.5 meters high in sitting posture. As the founder of the Yellow Sect of Lamaism, he was born in 1417 in Huangzhong County, Qinghai Province and died in 1478. He was a great reformer of Lamaism in Tibet. In addition, you'll see the five figurines of his incarnation in the shade of the backside.

314. 雍和宫大殿内的十八罗汉是谁?

他们是释迦牟尼的十八位弟子,受了佛的嘱托,他们将不入涅盘,永远活在世上,宣传佛法,普渡众生。

Who are the 18 arhats in Yonghedian – the Hall of Harmony?

Legend has it that they are the 18 disciples of Sakyamuni. Abiding by the testament of the Buddha they will live on and on and will never fall into a state of nirvana for the sake of preaching the laws of Buddhism so as to save all sentient beings in the world.

315. 大挂毯"大白伞盖"说明了什么?

大白伞盖是释迦牟尼的化身,说明了他以此伞盖庇护众生。

What do the large "White and Green Paras" signify?

According to the theory of Buddhism, paras are the incarnations of the Sakyamuni Buddha, who is using the paras to protect the human beings and extricate them from the sufferings of the world.

316. 雍和宫内的"鼓"和"磬"是作什么用的?

雍和宫内的"鼓"和"磬"是皇帝或大臣进香,或举行较大型的宗教仪式时所敲的法器。

What are the "Drum" and "Chime Bell" in the Yonhegong used for?

They are the musical instruments to be sounded when the

emperor or other high - ranking officials were here to offer incense - sticks, or a religious ceremony of a sizable scale to be held right here in the hall.

317. 五百罗汉山北面玻璃格内的藏文经是谁写的？

玻璃格内藏有两部藏文经，一部为"大白伞盖仪轨经"，另一部是"药师经"，均为乾隆皇帝亲笔手书。

Who has written the sutras in Tibetan that are stored in the glass cases at the north of the 500 Arhats Hill?

There are two golden - lettered sutras kept in the glass cases on the north of the 500 Arhats Hall, one being the sutra of the Buddha of Pharmacy and another about the white paras. Both of them were written by Emperor Qianlong of the Qing Dynasty.

318. 宗喀巴像东西两侧的高台经座是作何用的？

这是 1954 年为达赖、班禅喇嘛到雍和宫讲经而特设的。西侧为达赖喇嘛所用，东侧为班禅额尔德尼所用。

What are the high - raised sutra - stands on both sides of the Statue of Tsongkhapa used for?

They were set up in 1954 for Dalai and Bainchen Lamas when they were here preaching the doctrine of Lamaism. The one on the right is for Dalai and that on the left for Bainchen Erdeni.

319. 雍和宫大殿内藏有多少经书？作何用处？

大殿西墙下存放的为 108 部《大藏经》，东墙下存放的是

207部《续藏经》。《大藏经》藏名为《千珠经》。这些经书是供本殿每年6月6日举行"亮讲会"用的,平时则用其抄本代替。

How many volumes of scriptures are stored in the main hall? And what are they used for?

Along the western side of the main hall stand several bookcases holding 108 volumes of Buddhist scriptures (Dazangjing) and the eastern side 207 volumes of their sequels (Xuzangjing). These Buddhist scriptures are used only for the preaching on every sixth of the sixth month in the lunar calendar and in normal times only copies are used instead.

320. 精致的壁画是何内容?

壁画的内容为"释迦牟尼生记"的一部分。

What are the exquisitely – looking frescoes about?

The frescoes on the walls are about the life – story of the Buddha Sakyamuni, telling how he was born from his mother's armpit and how he later created the Buddhist doctrines and preached them.

321. "长明灯"是作什么用的?

宗喀巴和释迦牟尼像前供放着一个铜制的大灯,名曰"长明灯",或称"续明灯"、"无尽灯",意即佛像之前昼夜长明。

What is the "Everlasting Lamp" used for?

Consecrated in front of the statues of Tsongkhapa and Sakyamuni are the two "Everlasting Lamps" made of copper, or otherwise called the "inexhaustible lamp". It means that it remains bright forever and ever in front of the Buddha.

322. 殿门内侧顶上悬挂的匾榜曰"妙尽无为"是何意思？

"妙尽无为"的意思是"不可思议到了极点就是虚空"。此为乾隆皇帝御笔。

On the inside of the main hall gate there is a board with the inscription "Miao Jin Wu Wei" – the "extremity of wondrousness is nihility" on it, what does it actually mean?

It means "anything that goes to its extremity and becomes inconceivable is nihility," and this was autographed by Emperor Qianlong of the Qing Dynasty.

323. 蟠门内挂的匾榜曰"无量寿轮"是何意思？

"无量寿轮"的含义是"无量寿佛说法流演圆通。"此为乾隆皇帝御笔。

What does the inscription "Wu Liang Shou Lun" – the wheel of eternal life on the board behind the archway gate mean?

The "Wheel of Eternal Life" means that the "preaching by Buddha Amitayus is very profound and fluently flexible". It was autographed by Emperor Qianlong of the Qing Dynasty.

324. 雍和宫内的"戒台楼"和"班禅楼"是作何用的？

"戒台楼"是第六世班禅为乾隆皇帝受戒而建；而"班禅楼"是供六世班禅在为乾隆帝受戒后休息而建的。

What were the Ordination Altar Building and the Bainchen Building in the Yonghegong Lamasery used for?

The Ordination Altar Building was built for the ritual ceremony. It was used to ordain Emperor Qianlong by the sixth Bainchen Lama, and the Bainchen Building was used for him to stay when the ceremony was over.

325. 雍和宫内的"万福阁"(又称大佛楼)供奉谁的像?

"万福阁"是雍和宫内最高的建筑,分为上、中、下三层,阁内供奉的是弥勒佛像,该像从地面至顶部高达 18 米,地下部分 8 米,直径为 3 米,系当今世界上罕见的木雕巨像,它是用一根白檀香木雕刻而成的。

Which Buddha is housed in "Wanfuge" – the Giant Buddha Hall in the Yonghegong Lamasery?

Towering in the Yonghegong Lamasery, Wanfuge, or the Ten Thousand Happiness Hall is the highest building with upper, middle and bottom storeys. Enshrined in it is a giant Buddha of Maitreya standing 18 meters high with a diameter of 3 meters, of which 8 meters are deep underneath. Huge as it is, it's a wooden Buddha rarely seen in the world today.

326. 雕作弥勒佛的巨大白檀木是怎么来的?

据记载这是乾隆十五年(1750 年),西藏第七世达赖喇嘛,为了感谢乾隆皇帝派兵平定叛乱而送的礼品。当时,乾隆正想在雍和宫盖一座大殿,而苦于没有大佛,正好西藏的贡使得知此事,即转告了达赖,后来又想方设法,经由四川给乾隆帝送来了这棵大白檀木。

Whence came the huge trunk of the white sandal wood for making the giant Buddha of Maitreya?

The record has it that in 1750, the 15th year in the reign of Emperor Qianlong, it came as a gift from the 7th Dalai Lama to show his gratitude for the emperor in dispatching the army to put down a rebellion in Tibet. By the time the emperor had it in mind to build a grand hall in the Yonghegong Lamasery, but was then short of a giant Buddha to suit it. However, this was learnt by the envoy from Tibet, who made it known to the Dalai and the sandalwood was later transported laboriously by way of Sichuan to Beijing.

327. 喇嘛教是不是佛教?

喇嘛教是佛教在西藏、蒙古等地的地方宗教形式。公元八世纪,印度的密教传入西藏,汉人地区的大乘教这时也传入西藏,这两教与西藏当地的本教结合而形成了喇嘛教。喇嘛是所谓"上人"、"师长"之意。元朝以后,喇嘛教在西藏有了很大的发展,逐渐形成了政教合一的封建农奴制。

Whether Lamaism is a branch of Buddhism?

Lamaism is the localized form of Buddhism in the regions of Tibet and Mongolia. During the eighth century, the Esoteric Sect of Buddhism found its way into Tibet from India and at the same time the Mahayana (the Great Vehicle) also got into Tibet from the areas of Han nationality. The two sects of Buddhism, combined with the local religion in Tibet, formed the local religion of Lamaism. Lama in Tibetan means "one who's a superior" or "teacher" and Lamaism had gained much headway in Tibet ever since the disintegration of the Yuan dynasty, and by and by when it was combined with politics Lamaism had gradually evolved into a feudal slavery system.

328. 雍和宫内的"四学殿"是怎么回事?

"四学殿"是:

1. 永佑殿东侧的药师殿,那里有大量草药标本,是喇嘛们学习医学的地方;

2. 西边的数学殿是学习天文和地理知识的;

3. 雍和宫大殿东侧的密宗殿,是学习密宗经典之所;

4. 西侧的讲经殿是学习佛教的哲理和章法的地方。

What are the four Study Halls in the Yonghegong Lamasery used for?

The four study halls refer to the following four:

A. The Hall of Medicine: located on the east of Yong youdian, where lamas are able to study medicine by a great collection of herbal specimen in the hall;

B. The Hall of Mathematics: located on the west of the aforesaid hall it is a hall where the study on astronomy and geography are carried out;

C. The hall on the east of the main hall is the one for the study on the scriptures of the Esoteric Sect of Buddhism; and

D. The Scripture Preaching Hall: it is located on the west of the main hall, a hall for the study of the philosophy and the doctrines of Buddhism.

329. 为何把两只大熊的模型也供在雍和宫里?

传说它们是乾隆十九年(1754 年),皇帝由盛京去鄂棱加木打猎时猎获的,其中一只重 900 斤,另一只为 1,000 斤。此外,这里还供着乾隆皇帝当时用过的火枪、七星宝剑以及盔甲、马鞍等。

Why are the two model giant bears displayed in the Yonghegong Lamasery?

It is said that the two giant bears, one weighing 450 kilograms and another 500, were captured by Emperor Qianlong in hunting when he was on his way from Beijing to Elengjiamu in 1754, the 19th year of his reign. Displayed here in the hall are the firelock, the seven - star double - edged sword, the mail and helmet as well as the saddle used then by the emperor.

330. 达赖和班禅其名的由来如何?

达赖和班禅都不是人名,而是喇嘛教的法名,他们俩都是宗喀巴当年的弟子。当宗喀巴死后,便由两人分管西藏,并废除了父子世袭制,采用了转世制,故达赖和班禅的法号一直沿用至今。

How did the religious names of Dalai and Bainchen come about?

Dalai and Bainchen are not the names for a person in particular, but the religious names of Lamaism. Both Dalai and Bainqen lamas were disciples of Tsongkhapa. After his death Tibet was governed separately by Dalai and Bainchen. To replace the ages - old hereditary system from father to son the system of transmigration was introduced ever since, hence the religious names of Dalai and Bainchen used all along up to now.

331. 国家为落实宗教政策,给雍和宫办了哪些事情?

国家于 1980 年招收了一批从内蒙古来的年轻小喇嘛,并由国家拨巨款派古建队对雍和宫进行了重修,使之面目一新,并于 1981 年春重新开放。

What has been done by the state for the Yonghegong Lamasery in order to implement the policy towards the religions in the country?

In 1980, a group of young lamas were taken in from the Inner Mongolia Autonomous Region. The lamasery, after a thorough renovation at an enormous expense from the state, was reopened to the public in the spring of 1981.

颐 和 园
(The Summer Palace)

332. 请谈一下颐和园的情况好吗?

颐和园位于北京的西北郊,距城 15 公里,总面积为 290 公顷,其中水面占四分之三,陆地和山丘约为四分之一。

颐和园是清朝皇家用的避暑行宫,又称夏宫,是中国现存规模最大,保存最为完好的古代园林建筑。该园始建于金贞元元年(1153 年),其后元、明两代曾多次改建,清乾隆时又进行了大规模修建,改称清漪园。1860 年,被英法联军烧毁。1886 年,慈禧太后挪用海军费用进行重建,改名颐和园。1900 年又遭八国联军的破坏,1903 年再度重修。

Could you say something in brief about the Summer Palace?

Spreading out some 15 kilometers away from the city center in the northwestern suburbs of Beijing, the Summer Palace occupies an area of 290 hectares in total, of which three fourths is covered by a pool of water and the rest the land and hills.

Being a summer resort of the Qing royal family the Summer Palace is the most intact, the best preserved and the largest of its kind of the classical gardens in the country. Starting to be built in 1153, the 1st year in the reign of Emperor Zhenyuan the Kin Dynasty, the garden underwent many a time reconstruction and renovation in the Yuan and Ming dynasties. And still later a large – scale reconstruction was again done on it in the period of Emperor Qianlong's reign in the Qing Dynasty, renaming it the "Garden of Crystal Ripples" when completed. In 1860, it was brought down to ashes by the Anglo – French Allied Army, and being rebuilt in 1886 in the hands of Empress Dowager Cixi by embezzling the funds allocated for the building of the navy it was again renamed as the "Summer Palace". However, it was destroyed again in 1900 by the eight powers allied forces and it was rebuilt again in 1903.

333. 颐和园的含意是什么?

颐和园在外文中被译成"夏宫"。中文的意思则另有寓意。在古代,中文中的"颐"表示休息调养,而"和"则指和谐、平安。"颐和"就是说没有人反抗其统治,休息也很舒畅。因而颐和园是"颐养太和,保养元气"的意思。

What's the implication behind the name of "Yiheyuan"?

Versioned in English as the Summer Palace, the name of "Yiheyuan" in Chinese implies something else. In the olden days, the Chinese character "Yi" means to have a rest, and "He" to keep in harmony and peace. To put the two words "Yi" and "He" together is simply to mean that there's no rebellion against the rule of the government, thereby ensuring a good repose. Therefore, the name "Yiheyuan" means a garden in which one can "enjoy a supreme harmony by taking a good care of himself."

334. 颐和园是何时作为公园正式开放的?

1911 年 10 月 12 日,清末隆裕太后被迫宣布退位,但依据

"优待清室条件"之规定,颐和园仍为皇家所有。1911 年,颐和园作为溥仪的皇家私产售票开放。1924 年,溥仪被逐之后,颐和园由北洋军阀统治下的北平市政府接管改为公园。入门券大洋一元,里边各殿另收费用,排云殿为六角,太皇庙收三角。当时从城里到颐和园来玩的,都是些达官贵人,主要的交通工具为毛驴和马车。因而一个人要到颐和园游玩一次,花费约在 500 元大洋,而在当时,一元大洋便可买一袋白面了。

When was the Summer Palace officially opened to the public?

By the end of the Qing Dynasty, Empress Dowager Longyu was forced to promulgate the abdication of the royal power on the 12th of October 1911. However, according to the "terms of offering preferential treatment to the Qing royal family" the Summer Palace would still be kept in the hands of the Qing royal family, while yet to be opened to outside as Puyi's private property by selling admission tickets. In 1924 when Puyi was ousted, the Summer Palace was taken over by the Municipal Government of Beiping then controlled by the northern warlords and changed to be a park for the public. However, it would cost a silver coin to buy a ticket for admission at the entrance and the admission fee for different places in the garden would likewise be charged, ranging from some 30 to 60 cents for each place. Actually, those, who were able to travel on donkeys or chariots to the Summer Palace at the time, were only those lords and nobles. Because for one to pay a visit to the Summer Palace then, it would cost at least 500 silver coins, an equivalent to the price for 500 bagful of wheat - flour.

335. 颐和园是怎样修建起来的？

颐和园所在的地方，早在八百年前的金代就受到了人们的注意。1151年，金朝的第一个皇帝完颜亮把都城迁到北京（即当时的燕京）之后，就看上了这块地方，并于1153年在此设行宫。到了公元1190年，金章宗完颜璟时代，又将离其不远的玉泉山的泉水引来万寿山（即当时的金山）之下，并称这条河为"金水河"。那时这一带有"西山八园"之称，可见这一带已经是初具规模的风景名胜之所了。

据传说称，当时金山上住着一个老头，很懂养生之道。他时而离山很久，时而忽又回到山上，有一次他在山上发现了一块很大的中间凹下去的岩石，凿开一看，原来内藏一个古代石瓮。虽然周围的花纹已模糊不清，但瓮里还藏着几十种东西。于是老头就带着这些东西悠然移居他处，临走时，他把石瓮搬到了山的西边，立下一条谶语云："石瓮徙贫帝里。"到了明嘉靖年间，这个石瓮忽然不见了，而明朝也就果真开始衰败下去了……如此云云。显然，这是一个无稽的传说，含有许多浓厚的迷信成分在内，但是，这个故事在当时却不胫而走，轰动一时，因而竟把金山之名改成了"瓮山"。公元1292年，元代科学家郭守敬奉命在此开凿河道，把昌平一带的泉水引到瓮山之下，形成了一个偌大的水潭，取名为"瓮山泊"，当时人们还称之为"大泊湖"、"西湖"、"西海"，亦即现在的昆明湖。

明孝宗弘治七年（1494年），助圣夫人罗氏在这座山的南面建了一所寺，名曰圆静寺。到了明武宗时（1506－1521年），这里又建起了别墅，把瓮山又重新改称"金山"，而"瓮山泊"也改名为"金海"，在当时统称为"好山园"。

明熹宗时（1623年），皇家密探锦衣卫首领宦官魏忠贤，曾一度将其占为己有。1644年清兵入关后，"好山园"又被改称为"瓮山行宫"。

清乾隆十五年(1751年),高宗皇帝为了庆祝他母亲60岁生日,就于前一年开始了以圆静寺原址为基础的"大报恩延寿寺"主体工程的兴建工作,并把山的名称也改成了"万寿山"。在兴建大报恩延寿寺的同时,"命臣工芟苇废疏导玉泉诸流",把山下的湖泊进行了一番彻底的清理改造,使之成为一"巨浸",同时取汉武帝在长安开凿昆明池之意,把湖的名字改成了"昆明湖"。两者合在一起,统称为"清漪园"。清漪园最后落成于1764年,共用了十五年的时间。原来清朝乾隆年间正在从事东征西伐,所以非常重视练兵。昆明湖修成之后,就在湖的北岸围以石栏,制造了战船,并按期在湖内举行水战演习。

公元1860年,英法联军攻陷北京,园内文物被抢劫一空,清漪园与圆明园同时被毁,只有个别烧不了的建筑物,如铜亭、智慧海及多宝塔才幸免于难。公元1886年,慈禧为了自己的享受,就以光绪的名义,挪用了建设海军的军费八千多万两银子,重建万寿山前山的建筑,工程几乎持续了10年,直至1895年才告竣工,并把园名改成了"颐和园"。光绪26年(1900年),八国联军攻陷北京,侵略军盘踞园内达数月之久,颐和园再一次遭到了严重的破坏,园中建筑被毁,各种珍贵文物几被洗劫一空。后来,慈禧从西安回到北京,不久以后,她不顾国家与民族的灾难,又下令修复颐和园。史书上说,她回京后便大修颐和园,"歌舞无休日,日费四万两",生活之奢靡,达到了穷奢极欲的程度。

Can you say something about how the Summer Palace was being built?

The story about the Summer Palace goes back to the Jin dynasty in Chinese history over 800 years ago. In 1151, when Wanyan Liang, the first emperor of the Jin dynasty moved his capital to Beijing, which was then called Yanjing, he made the place the location of his palace for a short stay – away. In

1190, the period of Emperor Zhangzong, Wanyan Jing's reign, water was drawn from a not-far-away Jade Fountain Hill lying right at the foot of the Longevity Hill, which was then called the Golden Hill, naming the streamlet the Golden Water Stream. The place renowned for its "Eight Courtyards at the Western Hill", had already been developed on a sizable scale.

Legend has it that once there lived in the Golden Hill an old man, who was good at keeping fit by taking a good care of himself. Sometimes he was away from his hamlet for a long time, and sometimes returned all of a sudden. One day he discovered at the middle of the hill a large piece of rock with a concave face in the middle. When cracked open he found an old stone-jar inside. Though the lines on the outside were indiscernible yet contained in the jar were still dozens of articles. Taking them with him he disappeared. Nobody knew where he had gone. However, before his departure he moved the stone-jar to the western side of the hill, labeling it a prophecy, saying that the "removal of the stone-jar foretells the exhaustion of wealth here as a royal capital". Later, the stone-jar suddenly disappeared in the period of Emperor Jiajing's reign of the Ming dynasty and the rule of the Ming soon began to decline... Of course, this is a sheer non-sense, reeking much of a superstitious conception, yet it had roused a great hubbub in the capital. And it was due to this saying that the name of the Golden Hill was changed into the "Stone-jar Hill". In 1292, with Guo Shoujing, a well-known scientist of the time taking the lead, a canal was dug to draw water from the Changping County right to the foot of the Stone-jar Hill, forming there a vast pool. It was then named as the "Stone – jar Pool", or otherwise called the "Vast Pool" or the "West Sea" or again the "West Lake" – the names the present Kunming Lake ever had in the days of old.

In 1494, the seventh year of Emperor Xiaozong's reign in the Ming dynasty a certain Mme Luo built a temple named Yuanjingsi here on the south side of the hill. And afterwards, not until the period of Emperor Wuzong's reign during 1506 – 1521, had a number of villas started to be built here. In due course, the name of the "Stone – jar – Hill" was changed again to "Golden Hill" and the name of the lake the "Golden Lake", or otherwise the "Golden Sea" and the place as a whole were then called the "Pleasant Landscape Garden".

In 1623, during the period of Emperor Xizong's reign, the garden had for a time been usurped by a eunuch named Wei Zhongxian, the head of an organization of secret spies kept by the royal family. And 1644 marked the break – through into the pass by the Qing army into the internal regions and later the name the "Pleasant Landscape Garden" was again changed to be the "Stay – away Palace at the Stone – jar Hill".

In 1751, the 15th year in the reign of Qianlong of the Qing Dynasty, Qianlong, the emperor, in order to celebrate his mother's 60th birthday, started one year ahead of the time a project for the construction of the main body of a temple. It was then called the "Great Temple of Paying Away Gratitude and Wishing for Longevity," which was located on the original site of "Yuanjingsi" – the Tempe of Quietude, changing again the name of the hill into the Hill of Longevity.

During the time when the construction of the "Great

Temple of Paying away Gratitude and Wishing for Longevity"
was under way, an order was given to dredge the Jade Fountain Stream and the Lake down at the hillside, thereby giving
it a new look to become a "vast pool". In the meantime, naming the lake "Kunming", the name was derived from the story
that Emperor Wu of the Western Han (206 B.C. – A.D 25)
dug a Kunming Lake in Chang'an. Putting the Longevity Hill
and the Kunming Lake together, it was named the "Garden of
Crystal Ripples". Completed in 1764 it took 15 years to bring
the project to a finish. During the period of Emperor Qianlong's reign, punitive expeditions were often carried out to put
down rebellions and a great attention was set on military training. So when the project of the lake was brought to an end,
stone railings were put up along the northern bank for tying
the war – boats and navy training was held periodically in the
lake.

In 1860, the Anglo – French Allied Army occupied Beijing. The two gardens, the "Garden of Crystal Ripples" and
the "Yuanmingyuan Garden" were reduced to ashes with many
relics robbed away. Only few such buildings as the Bronze
Pavilion, the Sea of Wisdom and the Multi – treasured Pagoda
that were unable to burn escaped from being destroyed by a
hair's breath. In 1886, Empress Dowager Cixi, in order to enjoy herself, started the reconstruction of the buildings in front
of the Longevity Hill by embezzling, in the name of Emperor
Guangxu, 80 million taels of silver then meant for developing
the navy. The project lasted for almost 10 years before it came
to an end in 1895 and renamed it the "Summer Palace". However, in 1900, the 26th year in the reign of Emperor Guangxu,

the eight powers allied forces encroached upon Beijing and stationed for sometime in the Summer Palace, sacking again all precious relics therein. Not long afterwards, Empress Dowager Cixi returned from Xi'an to Beijing and despite the calamities incurred and the sufferings of the people, she gave the order to restore and repair the Summer Palace. The historical record has it that "when Empress Dowager Cixi returned to Beijing she resumed the restoration work in the Summer Palace on a large scale and led a life of extravagance, drowning herself in the enjoyment of songs and dances, which would spend 40,000 taels of silver daily".

336. 清代皇太后及皇帝是乘坐什么交通工具去颐和园的?

据说,当时可以乘坐轿子和马车经陆路去颐和园,也可乘船由水路前往。清廷皇后去颐和园经常走的是水路,从西直门到广源闸,共有六艘御用轮船,三艘停泊在西直门的倚虹堂船坞中。现在这些船只早已残破散失殆尽,只有"永和号"比较完整。"永和号"是 1908 年 5 月日本送给慈禧乘坐的。现在仍停放在石舫附近道边的岸上。

What conveyances did Empress Dowager and Emperor of the Qing dynasty take for going to the Summer Palace?

It is said that the sedan – chairs and chariots were used as conveyances when they went to the Summer Palace by land, but they could do it by water instead, and the Empress Dowager often went there on board a ship. From the Western City Gate (Xizhimen) to the Guangyuan Water – lock, there anchored altogether 6 ships for the royal family to use, of which three were docked in the Yihongtang Shipyard located by the

Western City Gate. Now all of them were broken and lost with the exception of the Ship named Yonghe. It was made in Japan and presented to Empress Dowager Cixi in May 1908 and it is now still lying there by the roadside somewhere behind the Marble Boat.

337. 颐和园仁寿殿的用途是什么?

清乾隆年间,此殿名为勤政殿,是皇帝听政和召见臣僚的地方,1860 年被英法联军烧毁。清光绪十六年(1890 年)重建时,为了迎合慈禧希望长寿的愿望,改名为"仁寿殿"。"仁寿"二字源于《论语》中的"仁者寿"。殿内悬挂的"寿协仁符"金字大匾是慈禧的自我标榜,其意为"执仁政者长寿"。慈禧在颐和园中的时候,就在这个大殿中"垂帘听政"。在殿门上挂一块纱帘的主要目的是,使门外的那些大臣门看不见她的容貌,而她却可以在殿内通过帘子看清楚外面的一切。

慈禧开始垂帘听政之初,她坐在光绪帝的后面,但过了不久,便坐到了宝座的正中,让光绪坐在右边的宝座上。戊戌变法失败之后,她干脆把光绪皇帝软禁起来,自己坐在大殿中发号施令了。

What is the Hall of Benevolent Longevity in the Summer Palace used for?

During the period of Emperor Qianlong's reign, it was called the Hall of Diligent Administration, a place for the emperor to grant audience to his vassals and officials. Burnt down by the Anglo – French Army in 1860, it was reconstructed in 1890, the 16th year in the reign of Emperor Guangxu, and was then renamed the "Hall of Benevolent Longevity" according to the wishes of Empress Dowager Cixi in her expectation of a long life. The two Chinese character "benevolence" and "longevity" are derived from a book entitled Lun Yu (Anecdotes) by Confucius. It means, "One who's benevolent enjoys a long life". The board hung in the hall reads that "Longevity is in Harmony with Benevolence". It is of course a self – praise by Dowager Cixi herself. That is to say "one who advocates benevolent rule enjoys a long life". While staying in the Summer Palace, the Dowager exercised her ruling behind the curtain in the hall. Hanging down a gauze curtain from the door she meant to prevent vassals and officials outside from seeing her, yet she could see from within all those outside very clearly through the screen.

At the very beginning when the Dowager began to rule behind the curtain she sat behind Emperor Guangxu, but by and by she began to sit in the middle of the throne with the emperor sitting by her right. After the failure of the abortive Reformation Movement of 1898 she jailed the emperor and began to rule by herself alone in the hall.

338. 仁寿殿内的金铜炉是作什么用的?

仁寿殿内的镀金铜炉是供冬季取暖用的,炉内烧的是木炭。

What are the gilded bronze – burners in the Hall of Benevolent Longevity used for?

The gilded bronze – burners in the Hall of Benevolent Longevity are for warming up the room in winter with charcoals burning in them.

339. 仁寿殿内的百蝠捧寿图象征着什么?

整幅图仅有一个大寿字,而用蝙蝠作陪衬。在汉语中,"蝠"与"福"谐音,以此衬托"寿"字,象征着慈禧多福多寿之意。上面盖有慈禧大印,说明是其亲笔所书,实际上是经过翰林院加工描写而成的。

What does that hanging with a Chinese character "Longevity" rounded by hundred bats actually mean in the Hall of Benevolent Longevity?

With only one large character "Shou", longevity on the hanging, the character is set off by a hundred bats encircling it. As the pronunciation of the word "bat" in Chinese is homophonic with the word "Fu", meaning "happiness", the bats are used to set off the character "longevity", suggesting that Empress Dowager Cixi would enjoy a long life with much happiness. Imprinted on the hanging with her own seal it is to show that the character was written by herself, but actually it was carefully embellished by somebody of the Imperial Academy.

340. 清朝的慈禧太后究竟是怎样一个人?

慈禧太后本姓叶赫那拉,生于 1835 年阴历十月初十,死于 1908 年阴历十月二十二日。她出生于满族中等官僚家庭,1851 年慈禧 17 岁时选入宫中为秀女。因受皇上宠爱,次年便升为"贵人",后来又升到了"嫔"的地位,1856 年,她生了个男孩而升为妃。1857 年又被封为贵妃。1861 年,咸丰皇帝在热河行宫死去,由其唯一的儿子载淳继承皇位,慈禧又因"母以子贵"而被晋升为西太后。她给自己册封的名字竟然长达十六个字:慈、禧、端、佑、康、颐、昭、豫、庄、诚、寿、恭、钦、献、崇、熙,简称慈禧皇太后。她的儿子登基时年仅 6 岁,年号为"同治",其含意即是共同治理。因此,慈禧得以实行垂帘听政,掌握了清朝的军政大权。

1873 年同治皇帝 18 岁,他此时开始亲政,那拉氏名义上交权,实际上仍在暗中操纵。1874 年同治因重病而死,慈禧便乘机在不久以后逼死了同治的妻子,皇后阿鲁特氏。但因同治无子,慈禧为了继续掌握大权,她不为同治立嗣子,却强立了一个年仅 3 岁,又是姨甥侄儿的载湉,这就是光绪皇帝,从此,她又开始了第二次"垂帘听政"。1861 年,她又害死了东太后慈安,便一人独揽了大权。1898 年,戊戌变法失败以后,慈禧把光绪帝囚禁在南海的瀛台以及颐和园的玉澜堂之中,她就公开"撤帘听政"了。据说慈禧死的前一天,她还设法害死了光绪。

在慈禧统治中国的四十八年中(1861—1908 年),她对外一贯屈辱投降,提出什么"量中华之物力,结与国之欢心",与帝国主义列强签订了许多丧权辱国的不平等条约,如"辛丑条约"、"伊利条约";而对内则残酷镇压人民。义和团运动就是遭到慈禧勾结外国侵略军的镇压而告失败的。她在生活上极端奢侈腐朽,可谓是中国近代史上的一位卖国求荣,而又残暴成性的封建统治者。

What a person was she, the Empress Dowager Cixi of the Qing Dynasty?

Born in a family of a Manchurian middle class official on the 10th of the 10th month in lunar calendar 1835, and died on the 22nd of the 10th month 1908, Empress Dowager Cixi was chosen as a beauty into the royal court at the age of 17 in 1851. Favored by the emperor, her position in the palace was gradually upgraded. In 1856 after she gave birth to a boy she was conferred upon as "concubine" and next year still further to be-

346

come an "imperial concubine". However, in 1861 Emperor Xianfeng died of illness in the Summer Resort in Rehe, the present – day Chengde and his only son Zai Chun succeeded to the throne. Owing to her son's enthronement Cixi was again upgraded to be the Western Empress with her self – styled title consisting of as long as 16 Chinese characters, but shortened as Cixi, the Empress. At that time the little emperor was only 6 years old and his title of reign was called "Tongzhi", meaning to rule jointly. Since then Cixi got the chance to do the "ruling behind the curtain". But by and by, she sought to control all political and military powers of the Qing dynasty.

In 1873, Emperor Tongzhi began to rule by himself when he was a grown – up of 18 years old. But Empress Dowager Cixi, giving up the power only in name, was actually manipulating it behind the curtain. In 1874 the young emperor died of serious illness and soon afterwards his wife, suffering from persecutions, also followed his steps to the nether world. As the demised emperor had no son, the Dowager, in order again to realize her wishes to rule behind the curtain, instead of choosing heir prince, began to support a 3 year old boy, the late emperor's nephew, Zai Tian by name to succeed him, the very Emperor Guangxu. By doing so, Cixi once again began to rule behind the curtain for a second time in her lifetime.

In 1861, Cixi, by hook or by crook, put the Eastern Dowager Ci'an to death, so the power of ruling fell into her own hands alone. After the Reformation Movement of 1898 came a cropper and the emperor was first jailed on the Yingtai Islet in Nanhai and then in the Hall of Jade Ripples in Summer Palace. Cixi, started to rule by herself alone. It is as said that she put the Emperor Guangxu to death the previous day before she breathed her last.

From 1861 to 1908 China was under her rule for some 48 years, during which her usual practice was to prostrate before the imperialist powers, subjugating the country to humiliation. A notorious saying of hers goes like this: "Using China's resources to exchange in return for favors from alien powers". With this as her political and diplomatic norm she, betraying the sovereignty of the country, signed many unequal treaties with foreign powers, such as the "Treaty of 1901" and the "Yili Treaty", etc., while domestically she cruelly suppressed the people. The Boxing Movement of 1900 was put down under the joint suppression with foreign invaders. Besides, she lived quite an extravagant life. In a word, she's a notorious ruler in the modern history of China.

341. 戊戌变法是怎么一回事?

戊戌变法是一次资产阶级改良主义的政治运动。1898 年是戊戌年,光绪皇帝接受了康有为、梁启超、谭嗣同和严复等人的变法主张,从 6 月至 9 月陆续颁布了维新法令,推行新政。但以慈禧为首的守旧派操纵着军政实权,反对变法,于同年 9 月发动了政变,因而变法维新仅搞了 103 天,就被以慈禧为首的保守势力镇压下去了。故"戊戌变法"在中国历史上被称为"百日维新"。

What is that Reform Movement of 1898 about?

It is a political reformist movement of the bourgeoisie. In 1898, Emperor Guangxu, accepting the proposal of reform advocated by Kang Youwei, Liang Qichao, Tan Sitong and Yan

Fu and some others, tried to carry out a new policy, which was going to be brought forward from June to September. But the old liners headed by Empress Dowager Cixi, who with political and military powers in her hands was strongly against the reform movement, staged a coup in September of the same year. The movement, lasting only for 103 days, was put down by the conservatives with the Dowager taking the lead, hence the movement was also called the "Hundred Day Reform Movement" in Chinese history.

342. "玉澜堂"的用途是什么?

玉澜堂是光绪皇帝在颐和园时住宿的地方,沿用的是清漪园时的旧名,据称是因晋朝诗人陆机的诗赋"应泉涌微澜"而得名。但玉澜堂也是个精致的囚笼,是1898年戊戌变法失败后慈禧用以囚禁光绪皇帝的地方。

玉澜堂的东配殿称霞芬室,其东门正对仁寿殿的后门,从这里可去仁寿殿。玉澜堂的西配殿叫藕香榭,其西门外是一座船码头,走出藕香榭便可达昆明湖畔,正殿的后面有门可通宜芸馆。玉澜堂可谓四通八达,但慈禧为了防止光绪帝逃跑或串通活动,就在周围修起了围墙,至今其墙犹存。

在北京,慈禧将光绪皇帝囚禁在两个地方:一个是中南海的瀛台,另一处便是颐和园的玉澜堂。尽管当时光绪被囚禁起来了,但殿内的摆设还是按原样不动,光绪帝只是在行动上没有自由。堂中宝座后挂的匾额上的字是慈禧的手笔,不过她把"复殿"、"留景"的"景"字写错了,可当时谁也不敢指出她的错误,以免招来不测之祸。

What was the "Hall of Jade Ripples" used for?

The "Hall of Jade Ripples" used to be the residence for

Emperor Guangxu in the Summer Palace. It was a name left over from the Garden of Crystal Ripples and the name is said to have been derived from a poem "Jade Spring brings forth gentle ripples" written by Lu Ji, a poet of the Kin Dynasty. As Emperor Guangxu was held in custody here after the failure of the Reform Movement of 1898, it is so to speak an exquisitely decorated jail.

The annex on the east is called "Xiafen Hall" – a room of rosy – glow with its gate opened on the east just opposite the back gate of the Hall of Benevolent Longevity and it is a direct access to the hall. The western annex is named the "Ouxiang Xie", a waterside arbor with lotus – fragrance. There is a pier derived outside its western gate and a step outside will lead you to the waterside of the Kunming Lake. With its back gate leading to the Hall of Yiyun. Surely the "Hall of Jade Ripples" is accessible from all sides of the Summer Palace. However, to prevent Emperor Guangxu from escaping or ganging up to do something undercover, Cixi had a wall built around it, which still remains today.

In Beijing Empress Dowager Cixi jailed Guangxu in two places: the first place is on the Yingtai Islet in Zhongnanhai and another the "Hall of Jade Ripples" in the Summer Palace. Though the emperor was held in custody, the decorations and furnishings of the hall still remained the same as they had been before. The only difference was that the activities of the emperor were restricted there.

The characters "Fudian", meaning rows of halls and "Liujing", the "Lingering Scenery" on the board behind the throne chair were written by Cixi herself, but she did the word "Jing" in a wrong way. However, at that time nobody was brave enough to point out her mistake lest an unexpected misfortune would fall upon him.

343. 慈禧是如何在德和园的大戏堂内看戏的？

清代宫廷的大戏台共盖了四个(还有若干个小的)，这就是故宫内宁寿宫的畅音阁、圆明园的清音阁，承德避暑山庄内的清音阁，还有便是德和园中的大戏台。据说慈禧对这个戏台的兴趣甚浓，竟亲自参加了戏台的设计工作。戏台分上、中、下三层：下层称寿台，中层为禄台，上层叫福台。每层都有供上下场人出用的门。

寿台的天花板上有天井，主要是作为聚音用的。寿台的台板上有地井，地下室有一水井，是为了起共鸣放大作用而设置的。不过，有时候也用以增加舞台布景的效果。如从天井撒下白纸屑表示降雪，或从地井中升起莲花，用作神仙戏的场面；据称在演出神仙戏时，会从天井里飞下"神仙"来，而演出鬼怪戏时，便会由地下钻出"鬼怪"来。

看戏的时侯，慈禧一个人坐在正对着戏台的颐乐殿门内的木坑上，光绪坐在门外的左窗台处，后妃等人则坐在右窗台处。戏台东西两边的走廊用木障分成十二厢，东厢是王公大臣看戏的地方。不过，他们都没有座位，只能坐在大红垫子上看。等一出戏演完之后，再由太监领出去休息。下一出戏开始前，再由太监引进来。看完戏以后，还要向殿上磕头谢恩。而演员们则在演出前和演出后都要穿好戏装，不带须口，向着颐乐殿上磕头。在慈禧祝寿的日子里，这个大戏台的最上层是福禄寿康造型，第二层是八仙过海造型，最底下的一层才是演正戏的地方，有时也会三层同时演出节目相同的吉祥戏。

当时，专管宫廷演戏的部门叫升平署。按照原来的规定，演员必须由内监充任，但到咸丰年间，就开始吸收一些民间知名的演员加入升平署串演。清末的潭鑫培、杨小楼等演员也曾参加过演出。当慈禧搬到颐和园来住的时候，升平署的全班人马亦随之而来，但不住在园内，而是住在东后门外附近的房子里。

慈禧是个戏迷，每次她来到颐和园的第二天就要看戏，而且一连要演好几天。她做寿的前三天和后五天，要一连演出九天的戏。

How did Cixi enjoy operas performed on the grand stage in the Deheyuan?

In the Qing Dynasty the grand stages used by the royal family in palaces, except a few small ones, include the following four: they are the Changyinge (Unimpeded Sound Pavilion) of the Ningshou Palace in the Forbidden City, the Qingyinge (the Clear Voice Pavilion) in the Yuanmingyuan Garden, the Qingyinge in the Summer Resort in Chengde and the Grand Stage in the Deheyuan (Garden of Virtuous Harmony). Empress Dowager Cixi took so great an interest in operas that she herself even participated in the design of the stage. The Grand Stage has three tiers: the bottom stage was called the "Longevity Stage", the middle one the "Stage of Emolument" and the upper one the "Stage of Happiness" with each tier having doors opened to the other. There is a ceiling well on the longevity stage, a device mainly for acoustic effect and on the ground stage there is a well too, a device for resonance. But sometimes they are used to enhance the stage effect, such as scattering scraps of white paper from the ceiling well to symbolize snowflakes or to let fairies fly down from the sky above. And sometimes lotus flowers will rise, or ghosts, monsters and immortals emerge from the ground well underneath to set off the atmosphere on the stage.

While watching performances Empress Dowager Cixi sits herself alone on the wooden kang inside the gate of Yiledian, the Hall of Pleasant Smiles, with Emperor Guangxu sitting by the left window outside the gate, and sitting on the right are the queens and concubines. The corridors on the east and west are partitioned with wooden piles into 12 sections: the sections on the east are reserved for princes, dukes and ministers to enjoy operas there whereas those on the right for Li Lianying, the chief eunuch and his followers and other court officials. However, there are no seats for them to sit on, instead with red – mats as their seats. When an act is over they will follow the eunuch out to have an interval outside and to return before the next opera is about to begin. When the operas are finished they have to make thanks – giving kowtows to Empress Dowager Cixi in the hall. As for the actors, they have to kowtow to the Empress both before and after the performances with their costumes on but without wearing false bears. During the days for celebrating the Dowager's birthday the upper tier is decorated with the symbols of happiness, officialdom, longevity and fitness in health, the middle tier the Eight Immortals Crossing the Sea and the ground stage is used for performances. However, operas of a same plot are sometimes staged on all three floors, this being called the performance of auspiciousness.

The special office in charge for the handling of performances at the time is called Shengpingshu (Office of Peacefulness). According to the regulations formerly laid down, the actors must be chosen from among the eunuchs in the court, but towards the period of Emperor Xianfeng's reign, some well-known actors are allowed to be summoned in from without taking a part in the performance. Tan Xingpei and Yang Xiaolou and some others have ever joined in suchlike performances in the palace. Every year when Dowager Cixi begins to move into the Summer Palace, all personnel from the Office of Peacefulness will follow her there. But they are not permitted to stay in the Summer Palace, instead in houses outside the eastern back gate.

Dowager Cixi is such an opera-fancier that performances of operas lasting several days have to be staged the very next day after her arrival at the Summer Palace. Operas have to be put on three days prior to the celebration of her birthday and another five days after it, lasting altogether nine days in succession.

344. 你能讲一下"乐寿堂"前"青芝岫"的由来吗？

在乐寿堂的庭院里,点缀着一块巨大的山石,叫做青芝岫。该石长 8 米,宽 2 米,高 4 米,其石色青而润,横卧于一个雕刻精美的海浪纹青石座上。每年夏天,当青芝岫被爬山虎浓密的蔓茎覆盖的时候,便显得格外惹人喜爱。

为什么叫做青芝岫呢?据说它的形状很像灵芝,但颜色青而润,故称之为青芝岫。可人们一般又管它叫"败家石"。据说明代有个官僚叫米万钟的,他嗜好奇石成癖。有一次,他在房山发现了这块奇石,想要运往自家的花园——勺园(现北京大学校园)内作为点缀,但费尽钱财,几乎倾家荡产才运到了良乡,只得弃之路旁,故有"败家石"之称。后来,该石被乾隆皇帝发现,下令将其运到了清漪园,并陈设在乐寿堂的前面。

Could you say something about where the Greenish Rock in front of the Hall of Happiness and Longevity came from?

Studded in the courtyard of the Hall of Happiness and Longevity is a big rock called "Qingzhixiu". It is a greenish rock in the shape of a magic fungus. Measuring some 8 meters in length, 2 meters in width and 4 meters in height, and lying on a stone pedestal, which is exquisitely carved with patterns of sea-waves, the rock is very smooth and greenish in color. Every summer, when covered in verdant ivies, it looks even more lovable and attractive.

Why is it called "Qingzhixiu"? It is because it looks very much like a magic fungus, a glossy ganoderma with a greenish and smooth surface. However, it is also known as a "Rock of Misfortune". The story goes like this: A certain official by the name of Mi Wanzhong in the Ming dynasty who has a hobby in collecting rock and stone pieces of all kinds. One day his eyes fell upon this piece of rock in Fangshan County he tried to ship it back to his own garden named "Herbaceous Peony Garden," which is located nowadays in the campus of Beijing University. But no matter how hard he tried the rock was so heavy that he had to give it up by the roadside, somewhere in Liangxiang County. By then he was almost on bankruptcy, thereafter the rock got the name the "Rock of Misfortune". It was later discovered by Emperor Qianlong on his way back to Beijing. He ordered to have it shipped to the "Garden of Crystal Ripples" and laid in front of the Hall of Happiness and Longevity.

345. 颐和园里的乐寿堂有何用处?

乐寿堂的"乐寿"二字源自《论语》的"知者乐,仁者寿"。它是慈禧太后生前长期居住的地方。每年阴历四月初一,慈禧便来到颐和园,住在乐寿堂内,直至十月初十,过完她的生日以后才回到城里去。

堂内共分四室:

1. 东外室:是她用早餐、饮茶的地方;
2. 东内室:是慈禧换衣服和休息的地方;
3. 西外室:她在这里批阅文件奏章、处理政务;
4. 西内室:是她的卧室。

What's the "Hall of Happiness and Longevity" used for in the Summer Palace?

The two Chinese characters "Le" (happiness) and "shou" (longevity) are taken from the "Confucius Anecdotes," which mean "one who's sagacious feels happy and one who's benevolent enjoys a long life". The Hall of Happiness and Longevity, consisting of four rooms, used to be the residence for Empress Dowager Cixi. Every year on the first day of the fourth month in the lunar calendar she moves to the Summer Palace and stays here in the hall, and won't return until the tenth of the tenth month when the celebration of her birthday is over.

The four rooms in the hall are:

A. The eastern outer room is for her to have breakfast, or sip tea;

B. The eastern inner room is used for her to change clothes and have a rest;

C. The western outer room is for her to read official papers and reports and handle political affairs;

D. The western inner room, her bedchamber.

346. 在颐和园里侍候慈禧的人究竟有多少?

在全园有一千多人。仅乐寿堂内就有 48 人,其中有宫女 20 名,太监 20 名,执事女官 8 名。他们平时都在九龙宝座后面的屋子里候差听命。

How many people are engaged in waiting on the Empress Dowager in the Summer Palace?

There are over 1,000 people dancing attendance on the Dowager in the Summer Palace. In the Hall of Happiness and Longevity alone there are 48, of whom 20 are maids – in – waiting, 20 eunuchs of importance and another 8 are the "ladies – in – waiting" by her side, who normally wait in the room behind the precious throne to attend on her.

347. 慈禧在乐寿堂内是怎样用餐的?

乐寿堂不仅是慈禧居住的地方,也是她的用餐之处。一日三餐都在堂内用餐。堂的正中有一个宝座,慈禧吃饭就坐在宝座上,用餐时在她面前临时搭起三张桌子,拼成餐桌。在这三张桌子上要摆 128 种菜,每种菜都用金底银盖的器皿盛着。此外,还有 50 多种主食,仅粥一项就有 30 多种。每餐要耗费白银约为 2.7 公斤,约值小米 5,000 余斤。这 5,000 多斤小米约可供 5,000 个农民吃一整天了。当时老百姓有句民谚:"帝后一席饭,农民半年粮"。

乐寿堂内还有一张慈禧吃点心用的桌子,这也是好有一说的东西:桌子的玻璃板底下雕刻着西湖风景,而且还能养金鱼,使慈禧在大饱口福之际,还能一饱眼福。

人门常说,皇帝用缮的方式是"一吃、二看、三观",就是说皇帝用餐时放了三个桌子,其中一桌是吃的,一桌是看的,还有一桌是供观赏用的。

How does Empress Dowager Cixi have her meals in the Hall of Happiness and Longevity?

The Hall of Happiness and Longevity is used at once as her residence and a place for her to have meals in. Before she starts to enjoy her meals she'll first sit on the precious throne right in the middle of the hall and then three tables will temporarily be set up in front of her and laid on them 128 courses of dishes in gold - bowls with silver lids. In addition there are still more than 50 varieties of staple foods and among them porridge alone comes to over 30 kinds. Every meal she has will cost 2.7 kilograms of silver, which is an equivalent to the price for 2,500 kilograms of millet, a whole day's food for 5,000 farmers then. A folk saying goes like this: "A mere meal for the empress is half a year's ration for a whole family of a farmer."

In the Hall of Happiness and Longevity there is still a table specially made for the Dowager to enjoy her refreshments on it. The reverse - side of the table - glass is carved with the scenery of the West Lake and underneath it is a goldfish pot. While having her refreshments the Dowager can feast her eyes on something pleasing too.

The imperial meal is laid out on three tables: one is for eating, another for feasting eyes on and the other merely for appreciation.

358

348. 乐寿堂里的电灯是何时安装的？

中国最早的电灯之一就在乐寿堂里，这是 1903 年由德国帮着安装的。据说当时园内文昌阁外有一个小型的发电站，是专为颐和园内的电灯供电的。

说起安装电灯一事，还有一则故事好讲呢！八十多年以前，外国商人把发电设备和电料运到北京，想发一笔洋财，没想到慈禧太后却反对安装电灯。这样一来，洋商慌了，便设法重贿了慈禧太后的贴身太监李莲英。当时，李莲英满口答应了下来，让他们先在颐和园内安装了一台发电机，并在乐寿堂上装上了一排电灯。慈禧回宫后，李莲英便向她献媚说："你看这盏灯好不好？你要什么颜色的灯？"慈禧说要"红的"！李莲英便靠着柱子，偷偷地打开了装在柱子上的红灯开关，红灯果然亮了。李莲英又问还想看什么颜色的？慈禧说要蓝的，李马上关掉红灯，打开了蓝灯，蓝灯又亮了。这时慈禧感到惊讶不已，就问这是什么玩艺儿？李便告诉她：这就是电灯，并向她说明了电灯使用起来灵巧、方便且干净的优点，终于使慈禧同意在颐和园内试用电灯了。但普通市民是在 1920 年以后才开始使用电灯的。

When was electric lights installed in the Hall of Happiness and Longevity?

The installation of the electric lamp in the Hall of Happiness and Longevity was of the earliest in China. In 1903, a German merchant installed a power generating set on the outside of the Wenchang Pavilion and it was specially made for the power - supply of the Summer Palace.

Speaking of the installation of electric lights in the Summer Palace, there is a story to tell. About eighty years ago, a foreign merchant shipped the power - generating equipment and its accessories to Beijing, hoping to make a big fortune here. But, contrary to his wishes, Empress Dowager Cixi was not for it. This landed the foreign merchant in a dilemma. However, he finally found a way out by bribing Li Lianying, the dowager's most favored eunuch who agreed to have the power-generating set installed first in the Summer Palace and then electric lights in the Hall of Happiness and Longevity. After this was done in secret, one day when the Dowager returned to the hall Li Lianying tried his best to ingratiate himself with her by showing her the colorful lights. He first switched on a red lamp and then a blue one to her fancy and this made her feel very strange. Only by then the Dowager began to ask what they actually were, and she was told they were electric lights. Li made some further explanations as they were easier to be turned on and cleaner than the other lamps. At last, she was persuaded to have the electric lights installed in the Summer Palace. However, it was only in 1920 that the electric lights were popularly used among the ordinary people in the city.

349. 总管太监李莲英是何许人？他住在颐和园的什么地方？

李莲英是最得慈禧宠爱的一个太监，也是总管太监。慈禧走到哪里，他就跟到哪里，因此，他在颐和园中也有一个固定的住所，即在那一排九间房（原为慈禧的储衣室）的东边一个小院落，名曰"总管院"。

李出身于一个没落的皮革制硝商家庭。后来，他在前门外一家胡同妓院里当美容师，专为妓女梳理各种发型。他心灵手巧，梳成的发型美观多姿。后来逐渐传开，得到了贵族阶层的认可,进而他的美容技艺为皇宫差役所得知。因慈禧爱美,就专请李进宫来为慈禧梳头。李入宫后不久,就得到了慈禧的欢心,青云直上,成了慈禧的心腹,当上了总管太监。所以宫里人称:"皇上是万岁,李莲英是九千岁。"这说明李莲英是当时宫中显赫一时的"实权派"人物。

What a person is Li Lianying, the eunuch chief? Where does he live in the Summer Palace?

As the most favored eunuch of Empress Dowager Cixi, Li Lianying is the chief of eunuch of the Qing Royal Palace. As he'll follow wherever the Dowager goes so he also has a living quarter in the Summer Palace. It is a small courtyard by the eastern side of a row of nine rooms (formerly used for storing Cixi's clothes) behind the Hall of Happiness and Longevity. And the courtyard is also called the "Courtyard for Eunuch Chief".

Born into a family of a declined leather – tanner, Li used to work in a brothel outside the Qianmen Gate, doing hairdressing for prostitutes. As he was deft in doing it in different styles he came to be known first among the nobility and later in the Qing imperial palace. Since the Dowager took a liking in dressing – up Li was summoned into the palace as a personal hairdresser of hers. Soon afterwards he found favor with the Dowager and becoming her henchman ever since. He was promoted to be the chief of eunuch. So the people in the palace described Li in these words: "The emperor is hailed to enjoy a long life of a ten thousand years while Li a long life of nine thousands". That is to say "Li is an influential person with real power in hand in the palace".

350. 长廊的作用和特点是什么？

在中国的庭园建筑中，走廊是联系主要建筑物的一种附属建筑。有挡风雨、蔽日晒和装饰的作用，也是休息的地方。但万寿山前的这条长廊特别长，有 728 米。若把两根柱子之间的每一块地方算作一间的话，这条长廊就有 723 间，这本身就是一个独特而引人瞩目的建筑，人们因而称之为"长廊"。当人们踏入长廊东端的"邀月门"，就进入了一个一眼望不到尽头的走廊，有些地段笔直如线，但有时又曲折回环，宛似游龙。人在其中，恍入画境。加上留佳、寄澜、秋水和清遥等四座八角重檐亭子分布点缀其中，象征着春、夏、秋、冬四季，使长廊显得格外隽秀宜人。

长廊的每根枋梁上均绘有彩画，原有大画八千幅：包括西湖风景、山水人物、花卉翎毛，以及神话传说等历史故事。1959 年国庆十周年前夕，对长廊进行了完整的油饰，还重新绘制了具有民族风格的彩画，大小一起，共为一万四千多幅。

长廊已于 1992 年列入"吉尼斯世界纪录大全"，是世界上最长的长廊；1998 年又申请成为世界文化遗产，联合国教科文组织已派员对此作了考察，并已列入世界文化遗产名录。

What's the use and special features of the Long Corridor in the Summer Palace?

In the gardening architecture in China, corridor is an accessory part, playing a role in joining up main buildings, providing a shade to keep off sunshine and rain, and also a place for having a rest. However, the corridor in front of the Longevity Hill is particularly long, measuring some 728 meters. If you take a section between two posts for a bay it naturally comes to a total of 723 rooms. Therefore, it is popularly known as "Long Corridor", which presents itself an attractive and interesting structure. Stepping into the Moon Inviting Gate at its eastern end, visitors will find an endless corridor ahead of them with some part of it looking straight as a line while the other parts twisting and turning as if they were somewhere in a wonderland. Studded along the corridor are the four octagonal pavilions with double-eaves, which are respectively named as "Liujia" (lingering scenery), "Jilan" (giving expression to orchid), "Qiushui" (autumn dew) and "Qingyao" (clear view), representing the four seasons of a year.

There are paintings on all the beams of the corridor, numbering some 8,000 large ones in the original which depict scenery of the West Lake, landscapes and figures, flowers, fables and legends and stories in history. However in 1959, prior to the 10th anniversary of the founding of the People's Republic of China, all of them were varnished and some repainted in a style featuring the characteristics of the Chinese nation. And afterwards the paintings, putting the large and small ones together, come up to over 14,000 pieces in total.

In 1992, the "Long Corridor" was listed in the "Guinness World Record" as the longest corridor in the world, and in 1998, it was applied to, and now accepted by UNESCO being listed in the World Cultural Heritage List.

351. 谐趣园的用处是什么?

谐趣园又称"园中之园",是乾隆十五年(1750 年)仿照无锡惠山的寄畅园修建的,原名"惠山园",园内一泓碧水,环岸有以巨间游廊连接起来的十三座亭台楼阁。嘉庆十六年(1811 年)重修时,改名为"谐趣园"。慈禧驻园期间,常在园内钓鱼取乐。

谐趣园内的涵远堂全都是用檀香木装饰起来的,慈禧在大戏台看完戏后,就在这里休息睡午觉。园中的眺远斋地势较高,面对墙外的一条通道。据说慈禧每年农历四月初八,就在此地观看老百姓到妙峰山去赶庙会,因而此山也就叫"看会楼"。

What is the Garden of Harmonious Interests used for?

　　The Garden of Harmonious Interests is a "Garden Within the Gardens," originally known as the "Huishan Garden" built in imitation of the Jichang Garden at Huishan in Wuxi in 1750, the 15th year in the reign of Emperor Qianlong of the Qing Dynasty. With a pool of clean water in the pond there are 13 large pavilions and arbors built and connected by a chain of verandas around it. Rebuilt in 1811, the 16th year under the reign of Emperor Jiaqing, the name of the garden was changed to the "Garden of Harmonious Interests". Empress Dowager Cixi used to enjoy herself here when she was staying in the Summer Palace.

　　Decorated with sandalwood the Hanyuan Hall in the garden was a place for the Dowager to have her nap after she finished watching operas in the Grand Stage Courtyard of Virtuous Harmony. The Tiaoyuan Hall (Hall of Looking Into Distance) was built on a hill in the garden and warded off only by a walled walk from the outside. It is said that the place was where Empress Dowager Cixi used to enjoy the throngs of people going to temple-fair at the Miaofeng Hill every 8th of the fourth lunar month. Therefore, the spot was otherwise called the "Hill for Watching Temple Fair".

364

352. 谐趣园的趣味究竟在何处？

声趣：有山泉数股注入荷塘。该山泉的水源，来自昆明湖后湖的东端。谐趣园之所以取如此低洼的地势，主要是为了形成这道水泉，这样便可使谐趣园的水面与湖面形成一、二米的落差，而在这一、二米的落差之中，又运用山石的堆砌，分成了九个层次，川流不息的水声发出高低抑扬，优雅悦耳的琴韵，故在横卧于泉边的一块巨石上，游客可见刻有"玉琴峡"三字。

楼趣：在玉琴峡西侧有座瞩新楼，这座楼从园内侧看是两层，可从外侧看却是一层。

桥趣：谐趣园中共有桥五座，其中以知鱼桥最为著称。它之所以取名为知鱼桥，这里引用了一个典故。战国时代，庄子和惠子在"秋水濠丘"有过一次关于知不知鱼乐的辩论：一个说，鱼儿游得真快乐；另一个则说，你又不是鱼，怎么知道鱼快乐；另一个又反驳道：你不是我，怎么能知道我不知道鱼快乐。这就是以其人之道还治其人之身，用古人的故事为来访的游人增添了许多乐趣。

Where lie the interests of the Garden of Harmonious Interests?

Interest in sounds: There are a few springs joining together to form a brook, which is gurgling into the pond of the garden. The head of the spring is from the eastern end at the back of the Kunming Lake. With the terrain of the garden located at a lower place the aim of doing so is to draw water from the lake to form a drop of two meters between the water level of the Kunming Lake and that of the lotus pond here in the garden. And along the watercourse of the brook, the rockeries are artificially piled into 9 levels so that it can strike a pleasing sound as if it were playing a lute. Inscribed on the large piece of the rock lying by the side of the brook you'll find three Chinese characters reading "Jade Lute Gorge".

Interest in buildings: On the west of the Jade Lute Gorge, there's a building named "New Vista". If you look at it from the inside of the garden you'll find it a building of two storeys but taking a look at it from outside it seems to be a single – storeyed one.

Interest in bridges: In the Garden of Harmonious Interests there are 5 bridges, of which the one called "Knowing the Fish" enjoys a great fame. Why is it called "Knowing the Fish"? The name is derived from an interesting, yet very philosophical debate between Zhuang Zi and Hui Zi at a place called "Qiushuihaoqiu" (the Mound at Autumn Streamlet) during the Warring States Period. The topic is about "how do you know the fish's happy in the stream?" One says "the fish is swimming happily in the water" and the other retorts, "since you are not a fish yourself, how do you know the fish's happy?" And to this the other again rebuts, "since you are not me how can you know I don't know the fish's happy?" From this you can see clearly the two persons pit their wits against each other, each trying hard to prevail over the other by resorting to a norm in Chinese philosophy "Deal with a person as he deals with you". So this story of the ancients has added much interest to the scenic spot here in the garden.

353. 你能简述一下佛香阁的基本情况吗？

佛香阁建筑在高 20 米的石筑台基上,阁高 41 米。以八根坚硬的大铁梨木为擎天大柱,使整个建筑显得高耸入云,是一座艺术价值很高的古典建筑。在乾隆十五年(1750 年)建造大报恩延寿寺的时候,原打算在这里造一座高九层的延寿塔。1758年,当延寿塔修到第八层时,却奉旨停修,不过已修好的八层并未拆除,而改建成了八面三层重檐的佛香阁。1860 年,这座高大的建筑物被英法联军烧毁。现在我们所见的佛香阁是光绪十七年(1891 年)按原样重建起来的,工程于 1894 年竣工,但由于重建时偷工减料,外形已不完全像原来所模仿的"黄鹤楼"了。

佛香阁中原供奉着一尊"接引佛",亦即阿弥陀佛,但已在文化大革命中不翼而飞了。过去,每逢初一、十五,慈禧都要到此烧香礼佛,进行祈祷,希望死后她的灵魂能升上西天佛国。

佛香阁不仅是建筑艺术中的极品,更是一处风光佳绝之地,登上佛香阁,你不仅可以饱览昆明湖上的旖旎风光,而且园外周围数十里之内的瑰丽景色,也可一览无余,尽收眼底。

Could you say something about the Tower of Buddha Fragrance?

Built on a stone platform of 20 meters in height, the Tower of Buddha Fragrance, with 8 tall columns of ferreous mesua supporting it, stands 41 meters high up into the sky and it is a typical architecture of a classical style with a very high artistic value. In 1750, the 15th year of Emperor Qianlong's reign, a tower of 9 storeys high was to be built here when the Great Temple of Paying Away Gratitude and Wishing for Longevity was under construction. However, in 1758 when the project reached its 8th layer an imperial edict was suddenly given to stop the construction and instead on the very site to have it built into a 3 – storeyed octahedron of double – eaves, which was the Tower of Buddha Fragrance. Burnt down by the Anglo – French Army in 1860, the present tower was rebuilt according to the original style in 1891, the 17th year under the reign of Emperor Guangxu and was brought to completion in 1894. But due to the sluggishness in work and the materials for its construction stinted, the tower has lost its original shape, a copy of the "Yellow Crane Tower" as it should have been.

In the tower there used to have a Welcoming Buddha or otherwise called the Amitabha Buddha in it but nobody knows where it had gone during the vandalic Cultural Revolution. On every 1st and 15th of every lunar month in the past Empress Dowager Cixi would come here worshipping and offering incense-sticks to the Buddha in the hope that her soul would be able to ascend to the "Realm of Buddhism" in the western heaven after her passing away.

The Tower of Buddha Fragrance is not only a quaint art piece but also an ideal place to enjoy oneself. On ascending it, you'll not only be able to feast your eyes on the scenery down below on the Kunming Lake but also to have a panoramic view over a great distance around and beyond the Summer Palace.

354. 排云殿有什么用处？

排云殿是慈禧太后在颐和园内的祝寿之地。"排云"二字源自晋代郭璞的游仙诗"神仙排云出,但见金银台"之句。

在明代,圆静寺就建在这块地方。到了清代乾隆年间,就在这里改建了一座大报恩延寿寺。在挪用海军建设费用大修颐和园之同时,慈禧为了庆祝她的六十岁寿辰,就在这里建起了排云殿,作为接受百官朝贺之用。

排云殿中央的九龙宝座,就是慈禧过生日时接受百官朝贺所用的座位。在举行庆典的时侯,光绪跪拜在"万寿无疆"的大匾之下，一品官跪在金水桥前，二品官跪在金水桥上，三品官跪拜在大门外，而三品以下的就只能跪在排云殿门以外。每逢她的生日，慈禧都要大肆挥霍，不仅在园内张灯结彩，还要从紫禁城到颐和园东宫门的沿途设立经坛、戏楼、彩棚点景，在排云门外，还设有中和韶乐、丹陛大乐，以及卤部仪仗等等，可谓极尽穷奢极欲之能事。

排云殿的东配殿叫"芳辉"，西配殿叫"紫宵"；二宫门外的东配殿叫"玉华"，西配殿叫"云锦"，这些都是放礼品用的地方。

What is the Hall of Dispelling Clouds used for?

The Hall of Dispelling Clouds is a place where Empress Dowager Cixi used to celebrate her birthday in the Summer Palace. The two Chinese characters "Pai Yun" (dispelling clouds) are derived from the poem Ode to the Fairyland by Guo Pu, a poet of the Kin Dynasty. It reads like this: "Fairies make their appearance from behind the dispelled clouds and there unveils a paradise of silver and gold".

In the Ming Dynasty, here used to be the former site of the Yuanjing Temple. During the period of Emperor Qianlong's reign in Qing a "Great Temple for Paying — away Gratitude and Wishing for Longevity" was built here on the site. Later when the Summer Palace was renovated and reconstructed by embezzling the funds meant for the building of a navy the Dowager Cixi had the Hall of Dispelling Clouds built here for the celebration of her birthday and also as a place for officials to pay their respects to her.

The nine — dragon throne in the center of the Hall of Dispelling Clouds is the seat for the Dowager Cixi where she would sit for her officials to pay their respects to her. When the birthday ceremony was in progress Emperor Guangxu would be on his knees under the large board of "Longevity," The top – ranking officials would be on their knees outside the hall in front of the Golden – water Bridge whereas those of the 2nd rank to be on their knees just on the bridge. Still those of the 3rd rank would kneel down out of the gate of the courtyard and those under the third outside the Gate of Dispelling Clouds. On every occasion of her birthday she would spend extravagantly not only on colorful lanterns and festoons for decoration in the Summer Palace, but also on setting up scripture – chanting altars, decorated theaters and booths all along the way from the Forbidden City to the eastern gate of the Summer Palace. Aside from all these, guards of honor and bands were called in to line both inside and outside the Gate of Dispelling Clouds in order to make the celebration one of more solemnity and grandeur.

There are annexes on both sides of the Hall of Dispelling Clouds. The one on the east is called "Fanghui" (Fragrant Radiance) and the other on the west called "Zixiao" (Purplish Night), and still there are annexes in the outer courtyard too with the one on the east being named "Yuhua" (Jade Flower) and the other on the west "Yunjin" (Clouding Brocade). All of them are for displaying presents to the Empress Dowager on the day of her birthday celebration.

355. 排云殿里的慈禧画像是由何人、何时画的?

排云殿里的一幅慈禧大型油画像,是 1905 年慈禧 71 岁时,由她的美国干女儿卡尔女士(一说是荷兰女画家休伯特)给画的。为了迎合慈禧希望青春永驻的愿望,她把这位老太太画得像四、五十岁的中年妇女。

Who painted the portrait of Empress Dowager Cixi hung in the Hall of Dispelling Clouds? And when was it being done?

Done by an American paintress, her stepdaughter Karl by name (Another story say that it was done by a Dutch paintress by the name of V. S. Hubert), the large oil painting of Empress Dowager Cixi was portrayed in 1905 when she was already 71 years old. However, to pander to her wishes that she would always remain young, the picture of a 71 − year old woman was deliberately painted to be a woman of 40 to 50 years old.

356. 听鹂馆有什么用处?

听鹂馆建于乾隆年间,1860 年被英法联军烧毁,清光绪十八年(1892 年)又重建。鹂是黄鹂鸟。这种鸟的叫声非常悦耳,人们常用黄鹂的声音形容优美的歌声和乐曲。因为清代帝后在此欣赏戏曲和音乐,所以叫做听鹂馆。听鹂馆的戏楼建于 1892 年,在德和园大戏台未建成之前,艺人就在这座小戏台上为慈禧演戏。

What is the Hall of Listening to Orioles used for?

Built in the period of Emperor Qianlong's reign, it was brought down in a fire by the Anglo − French Army in 1860 and was later rebuilt in 1892, the 18th year of Emperor Guangxu's reign. Oriole is a kind of bird, whose chirping sounds very pleasing, with which people like to match against a sweet and interesting song, or a piece of music. Since emperors and queens of the Qing Dynasty used to enjoy operas or melodies here, so the derivation of the name, the Hall of Listening to Orioles, is quite natural. Because the small stage was built in 1892 before the completion of the grand theater in the Garden of Harmonious Virtues, operas used to be put on here for Empress Dowager Cixi.

357. 石舫的用处和修建的目的是什么？

石舫的船基是明代圆静寺放生台遗址。石舫建于公元 1755 年,船体全部用大理石建成,通长 36 米。原有中式舱楼, 1860 年被英法联军烧毁后,又于光绪十九年(1893 年)模仿翔风火轮建洋式舱楼,并在船体两侧加上两个机轮,名清晏舫。1903 年,慈禧又加盖了一层木结构的洋式层楼,轮窗上镶嵌了五色玻璃,上下楼舱各有大镜一面,可以反射湖里的波光涟漪,坐在镜前,尤如身在湖中飘荡一般。因此慈禧经常在石舫上饮茶作乐,观赏湖光山色。

可是修造这艘"永远不动的船"的主要目的,还是以此来象征清皇朝的政权犹如磐石般坚硬稳固,永远挺立在汪洋大海之中,任凭风吹浪打,而稳如磐石,毫不动摇。

What is the Marble Boat used for? And what's the purpose of building it?

The base for the Marble Boat is a ruined "Platform for Freeing the Caught" of the former Yuanjing Monastery of the Ming Dynasty. Built of the marble pieces in 1755, the hull of the boat measures 36 meters in length. Originally it used to have an awing of Chinese style but was burnt down by the Anglo-French Army in 1860. It was later rebuilt into one of a foreign style in 1893, the 19th year under the reign of Emperor Guangxu in imitation of a steam ship named Xiangfeng with two water – wheelers, one on either side, added onto it and the boat was afterwards renamed "Qingyanfang" (Boat of Pure Banquet). In 1903 Empress Dowager Cixi had another storey of a wooden structure added onto it and decorated with colored pieces of glass. Each floor had a large mirror to reflect the ripples in the lake. Sitting in front of the mirror will give you a sense as if you were floating in the lake. Empress Dowager Cixi often came here sipping tea and enjoying herself on the landscape beauties all round.

However, the purpose of building this immovable boat was to symbolize that the rule of the Qing regime was stable and consolidated as a large piece of rock, which would stand still forever in the vast ocean and would, under no circumstances whatsoever be wavered or toppled.

358. 十七孔桥的建筑特色是什么?

十七孔桥建于公元 1750 年,是一条连接龙王庙和东堤的大石桥,长达 150 米。据称这座桥是仿卢沟桥所建,但比卢沟桥更美。在石桥两旁每一根石栏杆的顶部,都刻有形态各异、栩栩如生的石狮子,大小共为 544 只。

为什么该桥是十七个孔呢? 据说人们从两端的那一头看过去,总是看到正中的一孔,这个孔正好是第九孔。因为九是帝王最喜欢的、最吉利的数字,所以此桥便采用了十七孔。

What is the special feature of the Seventeen Arch Bridge?

Built in 1750, the 17 – Arch Bridge, a large stone bridge of 150 meters in length, is for joining up the eastern causeway and the Dragon Temple in the Kunming Lake. It is said that the bridge is a copy of the Lugouqiao (Marco Polo Bridge), but much prettier than that. Carved on the top of each post of railing on both sides of the bridge are lions of various sizes and descriptions, numbering 544 of them in total.

Why was the bridge being built into 17 arches? It is said that you can see the 9th arch only if you take a look at the bridge from either end of the bridge. As nine is the most lucky and favored number by emperors in Chinese numerals, the bridge was therefore built into a 17 − arch one.

359. 知春亭的名称是从何而来的?

知春亭在玉澜堂之南,昆明湖中一小岛的中央,桥与岸之间有桥相连。知春亭建于乾隆年间,1860 年被英法联军烧毁,光绪时又重建。此亭四面临水,周围种有桃树和垂柳。每年二、三月间,湖水解冻,春天开始到来之前,这里已是桃花映红,柳丝吐绿,最早向人们报道了春天的来临,故起名知春亭。知春亭是观赏湖光山色的极好去处。

Whence came the name of "Pavilion of Promising Spring"?

Located on an islet of the Kunming Lake to the south of the Hall of Jade Ripples, the Pavilion of Promising Spring is linked up with the lakeside walk by a mere bridge. Built in the period of Emperor Qianlong's reign and reduced to ashes by the Anglo − French Army in 1860 it was later rebuilt in the reigning period of Emperor Guangxu. Planted on the islet are a number of weeping willows and peach trees and the pavilion is embraced by water on all sides. Every February and March when the ice begins to melt in the lake peach trees are red in bloom and willows turn green, heralding the earliest advent of spring. Hence the derivation of the name the Pavilion of Promising Spring. Besides, it is also a wonderful place for enjoying the pretty scenery on the lake and hills nearby.

360. 昆明湖东堤的铜牛是作什么用的？

乾隆年间为何要在这里摆一只铜牛呢？那是为了镇压水患。这是中国自古以来的一种风俗习惯。相传这种做法始于夏禹之时，那时每治完一个地方的水患，就铸一只大铁牛沉于河底，他们以为这样就能永远把水患镇压下去了。而到了唐代，人们已不再把铁牛投入河底，而是放置在岸上。到清乾隆皇帝时，他疏浚了昆明湖，加筑了堤岸，当然也不能不放一条牛以镇压水患，于是他便在岸上放置了一只镀金的铜牛，并在它的背上用篆文铸了一篇"金牛铭"记述此事。

不过，遗憾的是，1860 年的英法联军及 1900 年的八国联军侵占北京以后，他们把镀于牛身上的金子全都刮光了。

What is the Bronze Ox on the eastern causeway of the Kunming Lake used for?

The Bronze Ox laid here during the period of Emperor Qianlong's reign was for the purpose of taming the flood. As one of the Chinese traditional customs, the practice is said to have begun ever since Yu the Great of the Xia Dynasty (22nd – 17th century B. C.). Whenever and wherever this Yu the Great finished taming a flood he would sink a very big iron ox onto the river – bed, assuming that the flood could in this way be subdued. Towards the Tang Dynasty the iron ox was no longer sunk into the river but instead to be laid somewhere on the riverbank. When Emperor Qianlong finished dredging the Kunming Lake and built a causeway he couldn't do otherwise but lay a gilded brass ox here in order to tame the flood, and to memorize it a "Golden Ox Inscription" was done on the back of the ox.

However, it's a pity that all gold gilt on the brass ox was scraped away by the Anglo-French Army and the Army of Eight Allied Powers when they occupied Beijing respectively in 1860 and 1900. And thus the gilded ox was reduced to a bare brass one laid here by the lakeside.

361. 龙王庙有什么用处?

龙王庙座落在昆明湖中的南湖岛上,该岛亦称蓬莱岛。原来庙内有金面龙王像,后来久而久之,人们就习惯把它称为龙王庙了。古代习惯在闹过水灾的地方修建龙王庙,请龙王保佑一方免受水患。虽然这是迷信,但也为山水之美平添了许多景色。龙王庙又叫广润灵雨祠。岛上最高的建筑物是龙王庙北侧的涵虚堂,与万寿山排云殿隔湖相望。现在的涵虚堂、龙王庙是慈禧统治时重修的(该堂在乾隆时期称望蟾阁,是模仿黄鹤楼的式样建造的)。那时,帝后们在这里欣赏月下景色,观看湖上水兵们的水战演习。

What is the Temple of Dragon King used for?

Studded in the south of the Kunming Lake, the Temple of Dragon King is located on the Nanhu Islet or alias the Penglai Islet. As there used to have a golden-faced dragon king here in the temple, so it was called the Temple of Dragon King. In ancient times a dragon king temple used to be built wherever a flood had ever happened and the dragon king was prayed to help prevent the area from being flooded. Though this is something superstitious it has added much beauty to the scenery in the surrounding areas. The temple is also known as "Guangrunlingyu" Temple, which means a temple able to bestow a good and universal rain to the mortal world as wished for. Located on the highest spot to the north of the temple is the Hanxu Hall, which is a right opposite of the Hall of Dispelling Clouds on the Longevity Hill across the lake. The present Hanxu Hall and the Temple of Dragon King were built in the period of the Empress Dowager's reign. However, the former hall built in the period of Emperor Qianlong's reign was named "Wangshange Pavilion", the pavilion for enjoying the moon. Built in imitation of the "Yellow Crane Tower", Emperor Qianlong used to enjoy the night scene or review the training of his navy here.

北海公园
(The Beihai Park)

362. 北海公园位于何处? 有多久的历史?

北海公园位于景山公园的西面。早在 11 世纪的中叶,辽代就在这里建立瑶屿(行宫);到了 1179 年,金代又在这块美丽的地方开湖建岛。1922 年,北海被正式辟为公园。

Where is the Beihai Park located? How long has it been in existence?

The Beihai Park is located to the west of the Jingshan Park. The existence of the park can be traced back to the mid – eleventh century about a thousand years ago when a temporary royal residence named "Yaoyu" was first built here during the Liao Dynasty. And later in 1179 the rulers of the Jin dynasty started to dig a lake here, forming an islet in the middle of the lake. The place was opened to the public as a park in 1922.

363. 北海公园的面积有多大?

北海公园的面积共为七十多万平方米,其中水面占去了一半以上。

How large an area does the Beihai Park cover?

The Beihai Park covers a total area of over 700,000 square meters, of which the water surface occupies more than half of it.

364. 北海公园主要由那几个部分组成？平均水深是多少？

北海公园主要由北海和琼岛两个部分组成。湖中平均水深
为2米。

What are the major parts that consist of the Beihai Park?
What's the average depth of water in the lake?

The Beihai Park consists mainly of the two parts: the
Lake of Beihai and the Qionghuadao – the Jade Flowery Islet
with the water to an average depth of 2 meters round it.

365. "北海"原来是作何用处的？

北海原是历代封建帝王的禁苑，即皇家大花园，旧时称"太
液池"，但因其地处故宫西华门以西，故又称西苑。北方习称湖
池为海，到明朝时便有三海之称，即北海、中海和南海，组成太液
池，池上横跨一座用汉白玉石建筑的金鳌玉蛛桥。

What was the Beihai Park originally used for?

The Beihai Park used to be a "Forbidden Garden" for feudal rulers of dynasties in the past, namely the grand garden for
royal families. In the days of old it was called the Lake of
Taiye, or the Western Garden, as it was located outside the
Western Flowery Gate of the Forbidden City. The northerners
habitually like to address a lake as "sea". So up to the Ming
dynasty there were three seas: the North, Middle and South
seas, which, being put together, were then called the "Lake
Taiye." Spanning over the lake was a bridge called "Jin Ao Yu
Dong" – a Golden Tortoise and Jade Rainbow Bridge built of

white marbles.

366. 北海公园的中心点在哪里？有何特点？

北海的园林布局以琼岛为中心,三面环水,有白塔高耸其巅;四周山石玲珑,岛上林木蓊郁;楼阁重重,栉次鳞比,各具特色,富于诗情画意。三海的绚丽景色,在中国历史上早已闻名,如燕京八景中的"琼岛春荫"、"太液晴波"就在北海和中海之内。

另外,北海除内部的建筑,东、南两面用石桥与岸相连,并与其东面的景山、故宫相互辉映,若从北海的西岸向东南眺望,景山在水中的倒影确是十分美观。这体现了中国古代园林建筑艺术中,从园外借景的传统手法,达到了良好的效果。

Where is the central part of the Beihai Park? And what special features does it have?

In the art of gardening the layout of the Beihai Park is centered round the Jade Flowery Islet. Facing waters on three sides the white dagoba thrusts high from among quaintly built rockeries and lush green. With row upon row of stylish buildings and pavilions around, the islet suggests a poetic sense of beautiful paintings. The natural charm of the three seas has long been known in Chinese history. Among the "Eight Well - known Scenic Spots in Yanjing", the "Spring Shades Over the Islet" and the "Shimmering Ripples on Lake Taiye" are located within the area of the Three Seas.

In addition to the buildings in the park, the islet is joined with the shore by two bridges on the east and south, making it a splendid homologue against the Jingshan Park and the Forbidden City to its east and south. If you take a look at them from the western shore of the Beihai Park you'll find the reflection of the Jingshan Park a splendid view in the lake. This represents a high attainment of borrowing the view from outside, a traditional method often resorted to in the Chinese art of gardening.

367. 北海公园里的水来自何方？

北海公园里的水是来自西山玉泉的水，该水经昆明湖南流，到积水潭、什刹海，而后注入"三海"。

Whence comes the water in the Lake of Beihai?

It comes from the Jade Fountain Stream in the western hills. The water first empties into the Kunming Lake and it then flows southward by way of "Jishuitan" – the Water Accumulation Pool and "Shishahai" before it finally pours into the "Three Seas".

368. 北海公园的景区里主要有哪些建筑？

北海公园里的滨岸诸景，主要分布在北海北部水面沿岸，包括桃花山、濠濮涧、画舫斋、先蚕坛、静心斋、西天梵境、九龙壁、大小天经厂、澄观堂、铁影壁、阐富寺、五龙亭、极乐世界、万佛楼和妙相亭等。

What are the main buildings in the scenic area of the Beihai Park?

Most of the buildings in the scenic area of the Beihai Park are disposed along the north lakeside. They are: Taohuashan – the Peach Blossom Hill, Haopujian – the In – between Hao and Pu Brooks, Huafangzhai – the Studio of Colorfully Painted Pleasure Boat, Xiancantan – the Altar of Silkworms, Jingx-

382

inzhai — the Mental Repose Study, Xitianfanjing — the Buddhist Realm of Western Heaven, Jiulongbi — the Nine Dragon Screen, Chengguantang — the Hall of Serene View, Tieyinbi — the Iron Shadow Screen, Chanfusi — the Gospel Preaching Temple, Wulongting — the Five Dragon Pavilions, Jileshijie — the World of Eternal Bliss, Wanfolou — the Tower of Ten Thousand Buddha Figures and Miaoxiangting — the Pavilion of Buddhist Apprehension and so on.

369. 琼岛的石山是由什么石叠成的?

琼岛原来是个湖中土岗,后来才改为用太湖石叠砌而成的石山。

What are the rocks used for piling up the rockeries on the Jade Flowery Islet?

The Jade Flowery Islet used to be an earthen hillock in the lake and later the man — made rockeries piled up on it are the water — eroded rocks from the Lake Tai.

370. 北海内的白塔是哪年建的? 有多高?

白塔建于清顺治八年(1651 年)。该塔由地面至塔顶的高度为 67 米,白塔本身的高度为 35.9 米。

When was the White Dagoba built in the Beihai Park? And how high is it?

The White Dagoba was built in 1651, the 8th year under the reign of Emperor Shunzhi in the early days of the Qing Dynasty. From the ground level to the apex of the Dagoba, it measures 67 meters, of which the Dagoba itself towers 35.9

meters high.

371. 白塔建于北海公园的什么地方？

北海白塔位于白塔山巅，亦即原来所说的琼岛，或琼华岛，后因清代在其上建了白塔，始改称为白塔山。

Where is the White Dagoba located in the Beihai Park?

The White Dagoba was built on top of the White Dagoba Hill, which was formerly known as the Jade Islet, or the Jade Flowery Islet. However, the name was changed in the Qing Dynasty to be the White Dagoba Hill due to the fact that a white dagoba was built upon it.

372. 为什么要建白塔？

白塔为藏式喇嘛塔。当时建塔的意图在借助崇奉佛教，以达巩固清朝统治的目的。顺治八年的建塔碑记云："有西域喇嘛者，欲以佛教阴赞皇猷，请立塔寺，寿国佑民。"

Why must a white dagoba be built here?

The White Dagoba is a Lamaist pagoda of the Tibetan style. The building of the dagoba was intended to consolidate the rule of the Qing regime by advocating Buddhism in the country. In regard with the building of the dagoba in 1651, the inscription on the stele reads: "A Lama from the western region wished to strengthen the rule by way of advocating Buddhism. So he says a white dagoba must be built in order to prolong the life of the country and benefit its people".

373. 白塔曾经历过什么灾难吗?

清康熙年间发生地震,白塔遭到破坏,后又重建。雍正八年重加修葺,历经 11 年才告完成。1976 年的唐山大地震波及北京,白塔顶端再次遭到破坏,又再次修复,使其显得更加耀眼壮观。

What calamity has the White Dagoba ever suffered?

In the period of Emperor Kangxi's reign in the Qing Dynasty an earthquake brought destruction to the White Dagoba. The reconstruction started later in 1730, the 8th year under the reign of Emperor Yongzheng and the whole project was brought to a finish in eleven years. However, later in 1976 another strong earthquake happened again in Tangshan Hebei Province. This did another destruction to its apex and it was later repaired again, thus making it look more splendid as it is now.

374. 在 1976 年修建白塔时发现了什么吗?

在 1976 年修建白塔时,于塔顶木柱上发现放着一个二寸见方的小金盒,盒盖背面刻有一太极图,盒内存有两颗豌豆大小的舍利子,四周用朱砂粉衬托保护着。

What was discovered from the White Dagoba in the course of its reparation in 1976?

From the top of the column supporting the apex of the White Dagoba, a square gold box of around 7 square centimeters was found. Carved on the backside of its lid is a Taiji Diagram and contained in the box are the two bean－like Buddha' s relics (or sarira in Sanskrit) lined all round with cinnabar powder for its protection.

375. 北海中的悦心殿是作什么用的?

悦心殿位于白塔的西南面,"燕景八景"中的"琼岛春荫"原就设在这里。清代皇帝从乾隆到光绪,历朝皇帝游北海时,都曾在此召见大臣和办理政事。殿内有皇帝用的宝座和古玩陈设,园内还有铜鼎、铜缸、铜鹤、铜鹿、铜凤、铜龙等物。另有供皇帝品茶和进早点的御缮房和饽饽房。慈禧时,又在院内增设漆彩画天蓬架子。每年寒冬腊月,皇帝都要来此观赏太液池上的冰嬉。

What is Yuexindian – the Mental Pleasing Hall in the Beihai Park used for?

Yuexindian – the Mental Pleasing Hall is located to the southwest of the White Dagoba, the former location of the "Spring Shades over the Jade Islet", one of the "Eight Well – known Scenic Spots in Yanjing". Emperors from Qianlong to Guangxu had all been here granting audiences to officials or handling political affairs while they were here relaxing in the park. In the hall you'll find a throne – chair, antiques and curios, and still there are some bronze tripods, vans, cranes, deer, phoenix and dragons in the courtyard. In addition you'll be able to find a small sitting room for the emperor to sip tea, and a little kitchen for preparing and serving breakfast here. In the period of Empress Dowager Cixi's reign a painted grillage was set up in the courtyard, where she and the emperor would come every winter to enjoy the ice – sporting feats on the lake Taiye.

376. 静心斋建于何时？面积有多大？有何用途？

静心斋始建于明代,清时曾进行过扩建,面积为 4,700 平方米。原名静清斋,是太液池园中的小园,曾有"乾隆小花园"之称。园内有一排 9 间的厅堂,堂前有莲花池,池边堆叠假山,并有小泉环绕,布局十分精巧。乾隆时,曾有两位著名和尚在此为乾隆讲经;嘉庆、道光、咸丰三朝时,是后妃祭佛、游园休息的地方;慈禧曾亲自绘图修缮,夏季乘小火车到这里来避暑等。静心斋在以往的二百多年中,从未对外开放过。解放后经过整修,于1982 年正式对外开放,作为宴请外宾之所。

When was Jingxinzhai – the Study of Mental Repose built? How large is it? What is it used for?

First built in the Ming dynasty and expanded in Qing, Jingxinzhai – the Study of Mental Repose covers a floor space of 4,700 square meters. Formerly called Jingqingzhai – the Study of Quietude, it used to be a small garden within the Garden of Lake Taiye or the "Mini – garden of Qianlong" as it is otherwise renowned. In the courtyard, there is a row of hall of nine bays and in front of it you'll find a lotus – flower pond rimmed all round by delicately laid – out rockeries and cascades. During the period of Qianlong's reign there had been two famous monks preaching Buddhist scriptures here for the emperor. And later, in the period of Jiaqing, Daoguang and Xianfeng it used to be a place for repose when queens or concubines were here worshipping Buddha or making tours in the park. When it came to the period of Empress Dowager Cixi's reign she herself worked out a plan for its reparation and renovation, and she often came by mini – train to spend her summer days here . Over the past 200 years the place has never been opened to the public and it was not until 1982 when it underwent a thorough renovation, was it opened to the outside for entertaining foreign guests.

377. "琼岛春荫"是怎么一回事？

"琼岛春荫"位于白塔的东北面,那里立有著名的燕京八景之一的"琼岛春荫"石碑。燕京八景始于金代,清乾隆皇帝亲笔题字,制成了八块石碑,分别立于八景之所在地。"琼岛春荫"石碑的正面为"琼岛春荫"四个字,背面为乾隆所题七律诗一首。

What is that "Spring Shades over the Jade Islet" really meant for?

Erected to the northeast of the White Dagoba it is a stone stele inscribed with the words "Spring Shades over the Jade Islet." It is one of the "Eight Well – Known Scenic Spots in Yanjing", which came to be known in the Kin Dynasty. They were made into eight stone steles with Emperor Qianlong's handwriting on them in the Qing dynasty and put up in their respective scenic areas. Inscribed on the front of the tablet are the four Chinese characters "Qiong Dao Chun Ying", which means "Spring Shades Over the Jade Islet" and the reverse side of it is a septa – syllabic regulated verse composed by Emperor Qianlong himself.

378. 阅古楼是作什么用的？

阅古楼的题额是乾隆皇帝的御笔,为两层楼宇,上下各有房25间,左右环抱,成半月形。楼上存放乾隆年间模刻的《三希堂法帖》。"三希"系指王羲之的《快雪时晴帖》、王献之的《中秋帖》

和王珣的《伯远帖》,三帖在当时被称为"希世奇珍"。1747年,乾隆将三王墨迹及魏晋以来的名家墨迹编定为《三希堂法帖》32卷,令人分刻在495块石板上,将所刻石板嵌入阅古楼的墙壁,原帖仍藏于故宫养心殿的三希堂内。

What's that Yuegulou — —the Building for Reading Classics used for?

With the characters on the front board autographed by Emperor Qianlong, Yuegulou is a two-storeyed building of a crescent shape with each floor containing 25 rooms. Stored in the rooms on the upper floor are volumes of Sanxitang (Hall of Three Rarities) Model Calligraphy (referring to the three classic Chinese calligraphic works, namely, the "Kuaixueshiqing Tie" by the famous calligrapher Wang Xizhi, another "Zhongqiu Tie" by Wang Xianzhi and still another "Boyuan Tie" by Wang Xun). They are regarded as the "precious and rare wonders of China". In 1747, Qianlong gave an imperial order to have the calligraphy books by the three Wangs and other famous calligraphy books from the Wei and Jin dynasties onwards put together. And they were compiled into a collection of 32 volumes, naming them the "Model Calligraphy in the Hall of Three Rarities" and also to have them inscribed on 495 pieces of stone steles. They were finally fixed into the walls of the aforesaid building of Yuegulou. However, the original ones of the model calligraphy are still well kept in the "Hall of Mental Cultivation" in the Forbidden City.

379. 漪澜堂是作何用的?

漪澜堂位于白塔山北坡的山脚,这里曾是帝后们登舟泛湖用的码头，乾隆皇帝常常在此垂钓，其他皇帝也曾在此赐宴。漪澜堂西边的道宁斋，曾是清代皇帝和御用文人吟诗诵文之所。现在的漪澜堂已成了以宫廷风味著称的"仿膳"餐厅了。最初，在"仿膳"做小点心的厨师，原是清宫内为慈禧做点心的御厨，那时做出的小烧饼、栗子面窝窝头、豌豆黄等是很出名的，均系仿照清宫御膳房的做法制作的。现在这种技艺已经传给了年轻的一代。

What is that Yilantang – the Hall by Rippling Lake used for?

Located at the north foot of the White Dagoba Hill, the Hall by the Rippling Lake used to be a pier for emperors and queens to board their pleasure boats. Emperor Qianlong often came here angling, and other emperors also often held their banquets here. On the west of the hall is a chamber called Daoningzhai, a place for emperors of the Qing and their bosom men of letters to chant poems.

The hall has now been adapted into a famous restaurant "Fangshan", specialized in serving imperial cuisine. At the very beginning, the chef of the restaurant for preparing deserts was the one who ever worked in the Qing Imperial Kitchen for Empress Dowager Cixi. The little baked cakes, the cone – shaped chestnut dough and the yellowish cakes of peas turned out from the restaurant are greatly appreciated by many people, and all these things are copied from the Qing Imperial Kitchen. Now the art and skill has been passed on down to the young generations.

380. 濠濮涧是作什么用的？

濠濮涧位于北海东岸，由北海引水辗转至此，形成一个内部水池。沿岸有叠石假山，水上架桥，临水有轩室，周围树木蓊郁。相传这里曾是明宣帝与他的后妃及内侍近臣们的饮酒之处。清乾隆帝曾在这里宴请大臣。颐和园未修复前，慈禧夏季常在此避暑听书。

What's that Haopujian – the In – between Hao and Pu Brooks used for?

Located on the north shore of the Beihai Lake, the water in Haopujian is drawn from the lake to form an inner pond here in the courtyard. Along the banks of the brooks you'll see manmade rockeries, arched bridges spanning over them, and chambers facing the water shaded in lush green. It is said this used to be a place for Emperor Xuan of the Ming dynasty, his queen and concubines as well as his liege subjects to drink wine here. Emperor Qianlong of the Qing had ever been here entertaining his high ranking officials, and Empress Dowager Cixi often came to spend her summer days or listen to story – telling before the reparation of the Summer Palace.

381. 画舫斋是作何用的？

画舫斋又称状元府，位于濠濮涧北面，有一座三层的院落，中有水池。画舫斋为临池的正殿，以走廊与配殿相连，廊下有金锦彩绘。清代皇帝常约集名画家进园作画。画舫斋的西套间为慈禧的烟房。东跨院的古柯庭为光绪的住所，其师翁同龢常到此为光绪授读，并留宿于此；得性轩是光绪的寝室。其后院还有奥旷室、以及清叉房、御茶房和饽饽房等。现在的画舫斋已辟为国画展览室。

What's that Huafangzhai － － the Studio of Gaily Painted Pleasure Boat used for?

Located by the north of the Hao Brook the Studio of Gaily Painted Pleasure Boat or otherwise called Zhuangyuanfu, the No. One Scholar's Mansion, is a court consisting of three yards. You'll find a pond in the middle of it and the studio is a main hall by the waterside, which is joined up with annexes by colorfully painted corridors. Emperors called time and again famous painters of the time to do paintings here. The western chambers used to be the smoking rooms for the Dowager Cixi and the east of it is Guketing, the Courtyard of Old Branches. It was once the residence for Emperor Guangxu, in which Weng Tonghe, the tutor of the Emperor often came to give him lectures and stay overnight here, while Dexingxuan, the Studio of Mental Enlightenment was the living room for the Emperor himself. There are still some other rooms in the backyard, which used to be the imperial teahouse and kitchen here. Now the place has been turned into an art gallery.

382. 西天梵境是作什么用的?

西天梵境,南临北海,原为明代西天禅林喇嘛庙,后塌毁。清代重修,现改名。殿前的两块石碑,左边一块刻有全部《金刚经》,右边的刻着全部《药师经》。正殿为大慈真如宝殿,用楠木建成,殿内供三尊三世佛铜像,均高丈五。殿前有天王殿,后为琉璃阁,是一座无梁阁,外面嵌砌五彩琉璃花饰与佛像。西天梵境前有一座琉璃牌坊,亦称"般若祥云"牌楼,与圆明园中的"慈云普护"牌楼是姐妹之作。

392

What's that Xitianfanjing – the Buddha's Realm in the Western Heaven used for?

Facing the North Sea in the south, Xitianfanjing used to be a Lamaist temple by the name of the "Temple of Western Heaven" in the Ming dynasty, but fell apart later. It was rebuilt in Qing and acquired the present name. In front of the hall there are two stone – steles, one bearing the whole text of Vajra Sutra and another the Scripture of Bhaisajya – guru. The main hall, built of nanmu wood, houses the Buddhas of the Three Existences, all being of a height around 5 meters. Further in front of the main hall you'll find a hall of heavenly guardians and at its back a beam – less pavilion, on the outside of which is inserted with glazed flower – patterns and Buddha figures. At the foremost front of the temple there is still an archway named "Banruoxiangyun" which was built of glazed bricks and tiles, an outstanding art – work of a match for that by the name of "Ciyunpuhu" in the Yuanmingyuan Garden.

383. 北海的九龙壁是什么样的?

九龙壁位于西天梵境西侧,建于明代万历年间,为大西天经厂门前的影壁。壁高5米,长27米,厚1.2米,用彩色琉璃砖砌成,两面各有九条蟠龙,戏珠于海水和天空之间,每条蟠龙姿态各异,栩栩如生,光彩照人。此外,壁的正脊、垂脊、瓦筒及陇垂等处,共有大小不一的龙635条。

What does the Nine Dragon Screen in the Beihai Park look like?

Located to the west of the Buddha's Realm in the West-

ern Heaven, the Nine – Dragon Screen was built in the period
of Emperor Wanli's reign in the Ming dynasty. The screen
built of glazed bricks, stands 5 meters high with a length of 27
meters and a thickness of 1.2 meters. Decorated on the screen
are highly glazed curling dragons of nine on each side. Playing
with a pearl and dancing over the sea in the sky, each and every of them poses a very graceful stance and looks vivid and life
– like. Besides, there are also dragon patterns on the main
ridge and the slanting ridges and eave – tiles, totaling 635 in
number.

384. 北海的九龙壁保存得怎么样?

大型而著名的九龙壁在全国共有三块,最大的九龙壁在山
西大同市,保存最好的是北海的九龙壁,还有一块在北京的紫金
城内,已有 200 余年的历史了。

**How is the preservation work of the Nine – Dragon Screen
in the Beihai Park carried out**?

There are 3 large – sized nine dragon screens in the country: the one in Datong, Shanxi Province is the largest, that in
the Beihai Park the best preserved and still another inside the
Forbidden City, all having a history of over 200 years.

385. 铁影壁是作什么用的?

铁影壁是一块火山熔岩凝成的岩石雕刻品,高约 1.92 米,
长为 5.12 米,颜色似铁,檐下两面刻云纹、异兽等,是元代遗留
下来的雕刻艺术文物。铁影壁两面刻有麒麟,在古代人们心目
中是象征吉祥的神话动物。1946 年,铁影壁从德胜门果子市的
一座"护国得胜庵"前移至北海公园内。

What's that Tieyinbi – – the Iron Shadow Screen used for?

The Iron Shadow Screen is a piece of artwork carved out of a hardened lava – piece. Standing 1.92 meters high with a width of 5.12 meters it appears to bear the color of iron with cloud – patterns and chimeras carved on both sides under the eaves. As a piece of cultural relics left over from the Yuan dynasty of some 600 years ago the elk – like animal (Qilin), one on either side, is a mythical chimera symbolizing good luck and happiness in the mind's eye of the people in China's ancient times. The Iron Shadow Screen was moved into the Beihai Park in 1946 from a convent named Huguodesheng'an located at Guozishi (the fruit market) in the surrounding areas of the Deshengmen Gate.

386. 五龙亭的作用是什么?

五龙亭位于北海北岸,建于清顺治八年。在五座亭子中,中间的一座叫龙泽亭,是皇帝垂钓处;东西各有两座方亭,是文武官员陪钓之处。东为澄祥亭,再东为滋香亭;西为涌瑞亭,再西为浮翠亭。

五亭用石桥相连,亭北有一座明代的五孔石桥,系用汉白玉雕成;桥北有汉白玉牌楼,牌楼北面有避暑凉殿。

五龙亭是封建帝皇用于钓鱼、赏月以及观看焰火的地方。每年盛夏,康熙皇帝的祖母,都要来这里消暑纳凉。

What is that Wulongting – – the Five Dragon Pavilions used for?

Located by the north shore of the Beihai Lake, the Five

Dragon Pavilions were built in 1651, the 8th year under the reign of Emperor Shunzhi of the Qing Dynasty. Of the five pavilions, that in the middle, being called the Dragon Pool Pavilion, used to be the angling spot for the emperor and the other four on the east and west were for officials and officers to keep his company. The pavilion right by its east is the one called "Chengxiangting", the Pavilion of Serene Auspiciousness. And the one further on is "Zixiangting," the Pavilion of Permeating Fragrance, while that by its west is named "Yong ruiting," the Pavilion of Gushing Auspiciousness, and the one further west is "Fucuiting," the Pavilion of Floating Verdure.

The Five Dragon Pavilions are linked together by stone bridges, and to the north of the pavilions there is a five－arched bridge built of white marbles in the Ming dynasty and farther north you'll find a white marble archway in front of a summer－resorting hall.

Feudal rulers not only used the Five Dragon Pavilions for angling but also for enjoying the mid－autumn moon and the display of fire－works on festive days. Besides, every summer in the past the Grandmother of Emperor Kangxi would come to spend her summer days here in the garden.

387. "极乐世界"系作何用？面积有多大？

"大西天"是一组宗教建筑群，而"小西天"只是其中的一组建筑，亦称"极乐世界"，或称"观音殿"，位于北海西北。这是乾隆皇帝为孝圣皇太后祝寿祈福而建的，极乐世界是一片相当大的建筑群，总称"小西天"。极乐世界是一座方形亭式建筑，是其中的主要建筑之一，高 25 米，总面积为 1,260 平方米，四周有水渠、石桥，四座琉璃牌楼和四座角亭，还有假山，山上布满了 500

多尊罗汉佛像。

What's that Jileshijie − − the World of Eternal Bliss used for? And how large a space does it cover?

Located at the northwest corner of the Beihai Park, the Great Western Heaven is a large group of architecture for religious purposes. And Jileshijie, the World of Eternal Bliss, which is also called the Small Western Heaven or the Hall of Goddess of Mercy (Bodhisattva Avalokitesvara in Sanskrit), is only a small part of buildings among them. The hall was built during the Qianlong's period in celebration of the Queen − mother Xiaosheng's birthday. The whole Great Western Heaven covers a large area, of which the World of Eternal Bliss is only a main building, a square hall in pavilion style. Standing 25 meters high the hall has a total floor space of 1,260 square meters, surrounded on all sides by creeks with stone bridges spanning over them, and four archways and arbors at the four corners as well. Aside from these, the place still has a man − made rockery with 500 arhats seating around on it.

388. 万佛楼内真供有万尊佛像吗?

万佛楼位于极乐世界的后面,建于 1770 年,俗称万福楼,是乾隆为她母亲做 80 大寿而建的。这是一座用五色琉璃砖砌成的三层楼宇。内墙壁上有大小佛洞一万个,每个洞内供一尊纯金无量寿佛;楼内供铜铸三世佛像。八国联军侵占北京后,殿内万尊金佛和三尊铜佛被劫掠一空。

Is it really the case that there are ten thousand Buddha figures in Wanfolou － － the Tower of Ten Thousand Buddha Figures?

Located at the back of the World of Eternal Bliss, the Tower of Ten Thousand Buddha Figures, commonly known as Wanfulou, the Tower of Ten Thousand Happiness, was built in 1770 by Emperor Qianlong in celebration of the 80th birthday of his mother. The glazed tower of three tiers has ten thousand niches on the insides of the building walls, each containing a small amitayus Buddha of pure gold and also enshrined in the tower were the Brass Buddhas of Three Existences. However, all of them were looted away when the eight powers allied forces occupied Beijing in 1900. Alas, what a pity!

389. 永安桥建于何时？

永安桥位于白塔山南面,是连接白塔山与北海南岸的通道。始建于元初,桥的两端有四柱三楼式木牌坊各一座,均有蓝底金字题额。桥北的牌坊上题"堆云",南端上题"积翠",牌坊外各有一对石狮。

When was the Yong'anqiao - the Eternal Peace Bridge built?

Located to the south of the White Dagoba Hill it works as a passage from the hill to the south shore of the Beihai Lake. First built at the very beginning of the Yuan dynasty, there is a four pillared wooden archway at either end of the bridge. Written on the board of the archway at the north end in golden

398

letters and set off in blue is "Duiyun," the Accumulating Clouds, while on the plaque to the south of the bridge is "Jicui," the Piling Verdure. Besides, there are still pairs of stone lions squatting by the sides of the archways.

390. 北海幼儿园的简况如何？

北海幼儿园位于北海公园的蚕坛。原为北平社会局托儿所,1949 年后改为此名,是北京著名的全托幼儿园之一。该园占地面积 22,000 平方米,建筑面积 7,010 平方米。收托 3 至 6 岁儿童 500 余人。近年来,该园还在试办培智班,从事弱智儿童的培育工作。该园也十分重视电教和其它教育手段相结合的做法,尽力做到课程活泼有趣,以增强教育效果。

How are the things going on in the Beihai Kindergarten?

Located inside the Altar for Silkworms in the Beihai Park the place used to be a kindergarten under the Bureau of Social Affairs of Beiping and was renamed to its present name in 1949. Covering an area of 22,000 square meters, it has a floor space of 7,010 square meters, being one of the well – known full – board kindergartens in Beijing. Enrolled in the kindergarten are some 500 children of 3 to 6 years old under the care of nurses and teachers. In recent years the kindergarten has tried to run a class for some handicapped children. To raise the level of pre – school education and strengthen its effect the kindergarten has paid much attention to the combination of audio – visual teaching with other means in education so as to make its courses more lively and interesting.

391. 北海餐厅何年开业？经营何种风味？

北海餐厅在北海公园内,以经营山东风味菜肴为主。1925年开业,1973年扩建。建筑面积为1,200平方米,内设一个小宴会厅和一个快餐厅。这里制作的小点心富有特色,是很受人们欢迎的,冷点以豌豆黄、云豆卷著称;热点中则以小窝头、肉末烧饼最为有名。

When was the Beihai Restaurant opened in business? And what sort of cuisine does it serve?

Opened in business since 1925 in the Beihai Park, it mainly serves Shandong cuisine. Expanded in 1973 the restaurant has a floor space of 1,200 square meters, housing in it a small banquet hall and a snack restaurant. With some well-known chefs here the restaurant is known in serving famous deserts, and the most tasteful ones served here are the yellowish cakes of peas, rolls of kidney beans, little cone-shaped chestnut flour dough and baked sesame cakes stuffed with chopped meat.

392. 近年来北海公园组织过哪些季节性的活动？

近年来,北海公园于中秋节组织灯展、冬季还有冰灯展。其布置美丽动人,吸引了不少游人前去观赏,场面十分热闹。

What activities are organized from season to season in the Beihai Park during recent years?

In the recent years there have been lantern shows around the Moon Festival days and ice-cut lantern shows in winter. Colorfully decorated and with pretty scenes all round these activities do attract a lot of visitors both at home and abroad, thus presenting an enthusiastic and fascinating atmosphere on the spot.

团　城

（The Round City）

393. 团城位于何处？何年建成？

团城位于北海公园南门西侧，享有"北京城中之城"之称。辽、金时为琼华岛前水中的小屿；元时在此建城廓和仪天殿。明代重修后改为承光殿，同时用砖筑成近似圆形的城台。

Where is the Round City located? And when was it built?

Located by the west of the South Gate of the Beihai Park, the Round City is known as a "City within the City". During the period of Liao and Kin the place was only a small islet in front of the Jade Flowery Islet, but towards the Yuan Dynasty, a hall named Yitiandian – the Hall for Ceremony to Heaven surrounded by a wall was built here. And later adding to it with a terrace the hall was rebuilt and renamed Chengguangdian – the Hall for Inviting the Light in the Ming dynasty.

394. 团城有多高？面积有多大？

团城有 5 米多高，面积约为 4,500 平方米。

How high is the wall of the Round City? And how large an area does it cover?

The wall of the Round City stands more than 5 meters high and the city covers an area of 4,500 square meters.

395. 团城的位置有何优越性？

团城位于故宫、景山、中南海和北海之间。周围风光如画，松柏苍翠，碧瓦朱垣的建筑构成了北京市内最优美的风景区。

What advantage does the location of the Round City enjoy?

Located in the center encircled by the Imperial Palace, the Jingshan Park, the Zhongnanhai and the Beihai Park it enjoys a picturesque scenery all round. Draped in pines and cypresses and studded with red walls and green tiles the Round City boasts of the prettiest scenery in the city of Beijing.

396、团城台上有些什么建筑？

团城的城台上有殿宇及上百间房屋，城池中生长着参天的古松柏。承光殿位于城台的中央，殿前有玉瓮亭。另外，周围还有堂、廊屋、假山及山上的小亭，组成一组环状的园林景色。

What buildings are there on the terrace of the Round City?

On the terrace of the Round City there are halls and houses totaling about a hundred under the canopy of sky – thrusting trees and lacebark pines. Situated in the center of the terrace is the Chengguangdian – the Hall for Inviting the Light with the Jade – jar Pavilion in front of it. Aside from all these things there are still some small halls, annexes and corridors, man – made rockeries with kiosks, forming a group of circular scenic spot of a garden style.

397. 玉瓮究竟是何物？

玉瓮是元始祖忽必烈大宴群臣时盛酒用的酒器。《元史》称之为"渎山大玉海"。明灭元后，玉瓮流失于北京西华门外的真武庙中，道士们用作腌菜缸，清乾隆年间找到，并为其建石亭，储于团城之内。

What is that Yuweng – the Jade – jar really about?

Known as "Dushandayuhai" in the history of the Yuan dynasty the Jade Jar was actually a very large wine – container used by Kubilai Khan, Emperor Shizu of the Yuan Dynasty in entertaining his liege subjects. When the Yuan Dynasty was replaced by the Ming the Jade Jar got lost and nobody knew its whereabouts, but was later recovered in the Zhenwumiao, the Temple of North God by the Western Gate of the Imperial Palace. The Taoists used it for keeping pickles. During the period of Emperor Qianlong's reign in Qing it was removed back to its original place with a pavilion built for its protection.

398. 渎山大玉海有多大？有何特点？

渎山大玉海存放于承光殿前的玉瓮亭中，并为其制作了汉白玉雕花石座，是用缅甸整块玉石雕琢而成的，其高为 0.66 米，周长 5 米，直径 1.5 米，重 3,500 公斤，于公元 1265 年制成。是中国现存最早、形体最大的玉器。

How large is that "Dayuhai" – the large wine container? And what special features does it have?

Seating on a carved pedestal of white marble made specially for it and kept in the Jade – jar Pavilion in front of the

Hall for Inviting the Light, Dayuhai, the large wine container was chopped out of a single piece of dark – green jade from Burma. Standing 0.66 meter high with a diameter of 1.5 meters and a circumference of 5 meters, the Jade Jar weighs 3,500 kilograms, and it is so far the earliest and the biggest single – piece jade carving in China.

399. 渎山大玉海的膛内和外壁雕刻着什么？

乾隆作《玉瓮诗》及其解释,刻于渎山大玉海内壁,并令48位词臣各写一首《玉瓮诗》,刻于亭子的石柱上,外壁上还刻有出没于风浪波涛之中的龙、鱼及其它海兽。

What engravings are there on the inside of the Wine – container and outside on the walls and pillars?

An ode to the Jade – jar and its explanations composed by Emperor Qianlong was inscribed on the inside of the big Wine – container. In addition, the Emperor gave the order that everyone of the 48 nominated poets should, with the Jade – jar as the topic, write a poem about it. Now you can find them engraved on the stone – pillars of the pavilion. Aside from these, carved on the outside of the wall are some curling dragons, varieties of fish and other sea animals in waves.

400. 团城内种了哪些古树？皇帝为其封了何名？

团城内有金代所植的栝子松,距今已有八百多年的树龄,是北京最古老的树木;还有数百年树龄的白皮松两棵、探海松一棵,皆树色苍翠,更加衬托出团城的幽静环境。皇帝曾封栝子松为"遮荫侯"、白皮松为"白袍将军"、探海松为"探海侯"。

**What kind of old trees are growing in the Round City?
And what are the names given to them by the emperor?**

A pine tree is said to have been growing here since the Kin Dynasty about 800 years ago, and is believed to be the oldest one in Beijing. Emperor Qianlong named the tree the "Marquis of Sunshine Shade". The other two trees of several hundred years old here are the lacebark pines, being called "Generals in White Robe" and another pine tree which reclines slightly over the Lake of Beihai, known as the "Marquis of Sea Exploration". With all these trees in lush green the Round City seems to have nestled in a tranquil environment.

401. 承光殿内的玉佛又是怎样一回事?

承光殿位于城台中央,内有木龛一座,供奉着用整块玉石雕琢的白色玉佛一尊,佛像高 1.2 米,头顶及衣褶嵌以红绿宝石。佛像面容慈祥,全身洁白无瑕,光泽清润。

What about the Jade Buddha enshrined in the Hall of Inviting the Light?

Situated in the center of the terrace, the Hall of Inviting the Light houses a wooden shrine with a Jade Buddha in it. The Buddha figure, measuring 1.5 meters high, was chiseled out of a single piece of white jade with red and green gems inserted on the top of its head – piece and along pleats of its drapery. With a kind look the Buddha figure is flawlessly white and very lustrous.

402. 玉佛来自何处？为何其左臂上有一伤痕？

关于玉佛的由来,据说是由清代僧人明宽游历南洋时从缅甸带回来的。其左臂上的一处伤痕,系八国联军在挖凿宝石时用刀砍伤的。

Whence came the Jade Buddha? And how is it that there's a scar on its left arm?

The Jade Buddha is said having been brought back to Beijing from Burma by a mendicant named Ming Kuan of the Qing Dynasty when he went south to study Buddhism. As to the scar left on the Buddha's arm, it is hacked by the eight powers allied forces when they were grabbing for the gems inserted on the Buddha.

景山公园

（The Jingshan Park）

403. 景山公园何年建成？占地面积多少？

景山公园位于故宫北面，在北京城南北中轴线的中心点上。占地面积23万平方米。1949年辟为景山公园。

When was the Jingshan Park built? And how large an area does it cover?

Spreading out to the north of the Imperial Palace on the central point along the north – south axis of Beijing, the Jingshan Park covers an area of 230,000 square meters and was opened as a park to the public in 1949.

404. 景山公园系作何用？为什么又叫煤山？

景山公园在元代仅为一小丘，称青山，因山下堆放过煤，故称煤山。这里风景壮观，是北京市内登高望远，观览全城景色的最佳去处。原为元、明、清三代的皇家御苑。

What's the Jingshan Park used for? And why was the Jingshan otherwise called the Coal Hill?

It used to be a hillock at the very beginning of the Yuan Dynasty and was then called the Green Hill. As the place was once heaped with coal, hence the name Coal Hill. Visitors will find it a superb spot to overlook the picturesque scenery here. Climbing atop the hill you'll get a panoramic view of the city of Beijing, and the best spot for doing it in the city. It used to be an imperial garden during the period of Yuan, Ming and Qing dynasties.

405. 景山有多高? 周长是多少?

景山高度为 43 米,周长为 1,015 米。

How high is the Coal Hill? And how long is its circumference?

The Coal Hill stands some 43 meters high and the hill measures 1,015 meters in circumference.

406. 景山是怎样形成的?

明代永乐年间,清理紫禁城筒子河(即护城河)和太液池南海时,将挖掘出来的泥土堆积在这里,成为大内"镇山",取名万岁山。

How did the Coal Hill come into being?

During the period of Emperor Yongle's reign of the Ming Dynasty the hill was piled up with the earth and mud dug out from the moat round the Imperial Palace and the Lake of Nanhai, thereby forming the hill within the area of the royal palace. It was then named as "Wansuishan," the Hill of Majesty.

407. 景山公园内的绿化情况如何?

景山公园内花卉草坪占地达 1,100 平方米,各种树木近万株。

How is the work of afforestation going on in the Jingshan Park?

Lawns dotted with various kinds of flowers cover 1,100 square meters and trees of different species amount to nearly 10,000 in the park.

408. 景山公园内有哪些主要建筑物?

景山公园有三座园门(景山门、山左里门、山右里门)、绮望楼、五座峰亭(自东向西为观妙亭、周赏亭、万春亭、富览亭、辑芳亭)、寿皇殿、兴庆阁和永思殿等。

What are the main buildings in the Jingshan Park?

The Jingshan Park has three gates: Jingshanmen, the Gate of Jingshan; Shanzuolimen, the Left Inner Gate and Shanyoulimen, the Right Inner Gate. The buildings are Qiwanglou, the Tower of Splendid View; Wuzuofengting, the Five Hilltop Pavilions. Ranging from east to west, the pavilions are called the Guanmiaoting, the Wonder Appreciation Pavilion, Zhoushangting, the All Round View Pavilion, Wanchunting, the All Time Spring Pavilion, Fulanting, the Eye Feasting Pavilion and Jifangting, the Pavilion of Gathering Fragrance. Besides, there are still Shouhuangdian, the Hall of Imperial Longevity; Xingqingge, the Pavilion of Flourishing Happiness and Yongsidian, the Eternal Cherishing Hall and so on.

409. 五座峰亭中曾摆放过什么东西?

五座峰亭中曾摆放过五尊铜佛像,通称五味神。1900 年被八国联军掠走四尊,万春亭(中间最大最高峰上)的一尊,被砍断了左臂,现已无存。

What were the things ever placed in the five hilltop pavilions?

There used to be a brass Buddha in each of the five pavilions. They were commonly known as Wuweishen – the Gods of Five Tastes, In 1900, the Eight Allied Powers looted the four of them away and the largest one enshrined in the All Time Spring Pavilion was unfortunately chopped off an arm, and it disappeared now.

410. 绮望楼系作何用?

绮望楼位于景山大门北面的南北中轴线上,原是清代乾隆年间办官学时供奉孔子牌位的地方,现为展览室和卖品部。该楼为黄色琉璃筒瓦歇山顶、重楼重檐式建筑,面阔五间,进深三间。明间悬的匾额用满汉文书"绮望楼"三字,四周有汉白玉护栏。

What is Qiwanglou – the Tower of Splendid View used for?

Located north of the Jingshan Gate along the north – south axis the tower is built of double – eaves and roofed with yellow glazed tiles. Decorated with white marble balustrades around, the tower is 5 bays wide and 3 bays in depth. Hung above the spacious hall is a horizontal board inscribed in three Chinese characters, reading "Qiwanglou", which was written in Chinese and Manchu scripts. The tower used to be a place for enshrining the Tablet of Confucius when an official academy was opened here during the period of Emperor Qianlong's reign of the Qing Dynasty, but now it is only used for exhibition and a retail shop.

411. 观妙亭是怎么样的?

观妙亭位于最东侧的小山峰上,是一座蓝琉璃筒瓦、重檐圆攒尖顶的建筑。亭内正中有一石须弥座,高一米,二米见方。石座上原摆放铜佛一尊,1900 年被八国联军掠走。

What does Guanmiaoting – the Wonder Appreciation Pavilion look like?

Standing on the eastern end of the Hill the pavilion is a round building with double – eaves of glazed tiles and a cusped roof. Right in the center of the pavilion you'll find a Sumeru dais of one meter high and two meters in square. There used to be a brass Buddha on it, but was looted by the Eight Powers Allied Forces in 1900.

412. 周赏亭是怎么样的?

周赏亭位于景山公园内东起第二座山峰上,是一座绿琉璃筒瓦顶,并以黄琉璃筒瓦剪边的重檐八角攒尖式亭子。有两槽柱子,内外各八根。亭内正中有一石须弥座。

What does that Zhoushangting – the All Round View Pavilion look like?

Standing on the hill next to the Wonder Appreciation Pavilion is the octagonal Round View Pavilion with double – eaves of glazed tiles and a green roof rimmed with yellow. It's supported on the 16 pillars forming inner and outer rings.

There is also a Sumeru dais in the center of the pavilion.

413. 万春亭有何特点？

万春亭位于五亭的正中最高峰、北京古城垣中轴线的中心点上，也是全城的最高点。有黄琉璃筒瓦盖顶和绿琉璃筒瓦剪边，是一座四角攒尖式，三层檐的亭子。有两层柱子，外层每面六根，共 20 根，内层每面 4 根，共 12 根。在亭子正中，原有木质漆金毗卢遮那佛像一尊，带有莲座背光，高约 3 米。莲座下曾有木制须弥座，最下为石制须弥座，为目前仅存之物，佛像等物均被八国联军毁坏。

What special features do Wanchunting – the All Time Spring Pavilion have?

Erected at the highest point, and right in the middle of the five pavilions on the Coal Hill, the pavilion, on the central point of the north – south axis that divides the old city of Beijing into two equal parts, is the highest spot of the old city of Beijing. The pavilion has triple eaves and four up – turned ledges covered with yellow glazed tiles, which are rimmed with green ones. The pavilion has 32 columns, the outer 20 columns with six of them on each side, and the inner 12 columns with four on each side. In the center of the pavilion there used to be a gold – plated wooden statue of Vairocana Buddha, which together with a lotus and having a mandala at the back stands 3 meters in height. Under it there ever had a wooden dais, and another stone dais at the bottommost, which is the only thing in existence now. The Buddha statue and other things are destroyed by the Army of the Eight Allied Powers to our great pity.

414

414. 明崇祯皇帝是如何自缢的?

传说景山东麓山腰处,是明朝末代皇帝崇祯朱由检上吊自缢的地方。1644 年,农民领袖李自成率起义军炮击北京,城外明军纷纷投降。崇祯见势不妙,便砍伤公主,自己跑到景山上一棵槐树下自缢而死。清军入关后,为招降明廷官吏,称此槐为罪槐,以铁链加锁(铁链已被八国联军盗走),并作出规定凡清室皇族成员到此,均要下马步行。原槐树早已枯死,现树系后人补栽。后又加筑短墙维护,并在旁立一石碑,记载崇祯自缢的经过。

How did Chongzhen, the last emperor of the Ming Dynasty, hang himself on the Coal Hill?

It is said that at the eastern end of the Coal Hill, there is a place where Zhu Youjian or Emperor Chongzhen, the last emperor of the Ming Dynasty committed suicide here by hanging himself. The story goes like this: In 1644, the peasant uprising army led by Li Zicheng bombarded the city of Beijing and many soldiers of the Ming outside the city laid down their arms. Sensing the critical situation, Emperor Chongzhen, after slashing the princess, ran all the way to the Coal Hill and committed suicide there by hanging himself on a locust tree. After the Qing army marched into the city of Beijing, they, to rope in the Ming officials and lure them into surrender, labeled the tree the sinister tree and had it locked up with an iron-chain, which was robbed away by the Army of the Eight Allied Powers. The Qing court also set down the rules that the Qing royal family members had to get off their horses when they were passing by the place. The original tree died long ago

415

and the present one is planted later. Now to protect the tree a low brick wall has been built around it with a stone stele erected by its side, which tells how Emperor Chongzhen hanged himself here.

415. 寿皇殿何年建成？有何用处？

寿皇殿位于景山正北,朝南。明代始建,清乾隆年间又重建。外有4柱9层的木牌坊3座,分东、南、西三面,均为黄琉璃筒瓦庑殿顶建筑,门前正中设牌楼式拱券门3座。该殿原为供奉清代历朝皇帝神像,以为祭祖之用。该建筑全部仿照太庙形式建造,整个建筑布局谨严,富丽堂皇,自成一体。民国年间,古物陈列所将所有"御容"收储。现为北京市少年宫。

When was that Shouhuangdian − the Hall of Imperial Longevity built? And what is it used for?

Located due north of the Coal Hill and facing south, the Hall of Imperial Longevity was first built in the Ming Dynasty and rebuilt during the period of Emperor Qianlong's reign of the Qing Dynasty. Erected on three sides of its east, west and south are three four − pillared archways of triple eaves covered with yellow glazed tiles. Right in front of the hall there are three arched gates built in the style of an archway. The hall enshrining the portraits of the deceased Qing emperors was used as a place for offering sacrifices to the imperial ancestors. During the period of the Republic of China, the Institution for Preservation of Cultural Relics put all the portraits of emperors inside for protection. With a well − knit layout the magnificent and splendid architecture is a fine copy of the Ancestral Temple of the Imperial Palace. Now the hall is used for Beijing Children's Palace.

416. 永思殿有何作用?

永思殿位于寿皇殿之东,原是历代皇帝停灵之所,后改为帝后停灵的地方。明代时为帝王习射的去处。

What's that Yongsidian - - the Eternal Cherishing Hall used for?

Located east to Shouhuangdian, the hall was first used for housing the coffins of emperors and later for holding those of emperors and queens. However, in the Ming Dynasty it was a place for emperors to practise archery.

大观园

(The Grand View Garden)

417. 大观园位于北京何处？它是一座什么样的园林？

大观园位于北京市西南隅的护城河畔，原址是明、清两代的皇家菜园，称为"南菜园"。它是一座再现中国古典文学名著《红楼梦》中"大观园"景观的文化公园。1984 年，为拍摄电视剧《红楼梦》，经过各文献专家的商讨，依据作家在书中的描述，采用了中国古典建筑的技法和传统的造园手法建成的。园中的园林植物、山林水系、小品点缀，均忠实于原著的时代风尚和细节描写。《红楼梦》中的大观园是为贾府大小姐元春（被选进皇宫封为皇妃）而建的省亲别墅，既有私家府园的特点，又有皇家苑囿的规格和色彩。

建造大观园的地址原是一片荒地废墟，经过园林艺术家的创造和辛勤劳动，"昔日全无"的废墟便成了"今朝竟有"的美好境界。

Where is the Grand View Garden located in Beijing?

Located by the city moat in the southwest corner of Beijing, the Grand View Garden used to be a vegetable farm for the royal family during the Ming and Qing dynasties. At the time it was known as the South Vegetable Garden. The Grand View Garden is a garden well – known for its cultural connotation, a reproduction of the garden described in the classical novel A Dream of Red Mansions. In 1984, the garden was built to produce the TV play A Dream of Red Mansions. It is built in a style as described by the author in his works and in traditional methods and skills of the Chinese art of gardening discussed and decided by the experts in the study of the classic novel. The plants, hillocks and waters as well as all sorts of decorations in the garden are strictly laid out in accordance with the details and the styles at that time as described in the original works. In A Dream of Red Mansions the Grand View Garden used to be a private garden. It was later conferred with the title of an Imperial Villa for returning home to pay a visit to parents when Yuanchun, the eldest daughter of the Jia Family, was chosen an imperial consort.

The site of the garden used to be a piece of waste land, which, through the wisdom and efforts of horticulturists, has been turned into something superb and a picturesque wonderland shared by visitors from all over the world.

418. 大观园的面积有多大?

大观园占地面积达 13 万平方米,园内建筑面积为 9,270 平方米,开辟水面 24,000 平方米,堆山叠石 2.6 万土石方,庭院景区 5 处,自然景区 3 处,殿宇景区 1 处,佛寺景区 1 处,共有主、副景点 40 余个。

How large an area does the Grand View Garden cover?

The Grand View Garden covers an area of some 130,000 square meters, and the floor space of the buildings in the garden amounts to 9,270 square meters. With the water − surface making up 24,000 square meters, and the earth − work of 26,000 cubic meters for making rockeries and hills the Grand View Garden consists of five gardenized scenic spots, three natural·attractions, an area of buildings and a realm of Buddhism. The total scenic spots in the garden come up to more than forty.

419. 大观园的由来有何特点?

《红楼梦》是中国文学史上的丰碑,作者曹雪芹塑造了贾宝玉和林黛玉两个青年男女栩栩如生的艺术形象,深刻揭示了封建社会内部种种无法克服的矛盾及其必然走向灭亡命运。同时,还运用他那独具的艺术匠心,描绘出一座"天上人间"诸景具备的大观园。应当说,《红楼梦》本身就是一座富丽堂皇的艺术大厦,而大观园是它不可分割的一部分。大观园里的一景一物,都是为烘托人物性格,渲染情节气氛,深化作品主题服务的。

大观园是《红楼梦》中主要人物的重要活动场所。书中引人入胜的情节,均在此地进行。大观园里的古典建筑,曲折奇幻,瑰丽多姿,是无数中外游人钟情憧憬的地方。

What special features does the Grand View Garden have in regard of its origin?

The novel A Dream of Red Mansions is a monumental work in the history of Chinese literature. Portrayed in the novel by the author Cao Xueqin as principal characters are two youngsters, Jia Baoyu, the boy and Lin Daiyu, the girl. By describing the life of the youngsters, the author tried to reveal the innate contradictions in the feudal society, which would ultimately lead to its downfall. With his unique artistic ingenuity he describes the Grand View Garden as an earthly paradise. The novel itself is a splendid mansion of art, and the Grand View Garden constitutes an inalienable part of the whole edifice. Every scenic spot or a thing is designed to set off the character of a person and create the atmosphere for the plot so as to bring out the theme in a more prominent way.

The Grand View Garden is, so to speak, a grand stage for main characters to act. Aside from all these, the classical architecture in the garden, marvelous in its designing concept and picturesque and elegant in style, draws a great number of visitors from both at home and abroad.

420. 大观园的兴建过程怎么样呢?

1984 年,北京市宣武区为美化环境,决定改建南菜园。当时,正值拍摄电视连续剧《红楼梦》制景选址,经双方商定,把制景一次性的需要,变为永久性的园地,以造福人民。于是便决定集资,在南菜园地区兴建北京"大观园"。

这个大观园的总体设计方案,是经过著名的红学家、古典建筑学家、园林艺术家及清史专家会商后制定的。在建筑造型上,力求忠实于原著作《红楼梦》的时代风尚和神韵。采取清代北方园林的建筑风格,兼收南方古典园林的精华,使之既具有北方园林的富丽宏阔,又饱含南方造园艺术的闲寂幽深,给人以气势宏伟,结构精巧之感。最终,大观园以其精湛的艺术魅力,给人以美的遐想和回味无穷的享受。

大观园始建于 1984 年 6 月,1985 年 7 月完成第一期工程;1986 年 10 月,二期工程告竣;第三期工程于 1988 年落成。在修建过程中,得到了国内外人士的大力支持和关注,曾被评为"北京十六景"之一和"首都八十年代十大建筑"之一。

How's the project of the Grand View Garden carried out?

In 1984, a decision was taken by the Xuanwu district of Beijing to transform the area of the south vegetable farm into beautiful environment. At the same time the choice of a site for shooting a TV play A Dream of Red Mansions was underway. An agreement on building the farm into a film – shooting site was signed. The decision would bring happiness to the people around the area of the south vegetable farm and the fund was gathered from among all walks of life.

The overall plan for the project of the Grand View Garden was worked out by concerted efforts of famous experts in the study of the novel A Dream of Red Mansions, architects specialized in classical architecture, horticulturists and historians in the study of the Qing history. As to the style and structure of the buildings to be built, attention has been paid to the fashion and romantic charm as described in the original works. The Grand View Garden, by integrating the architectural style in the north and the essence of classical art of gardening in the south, has both the magnificent features of gardens in the north and the quaint elegance and tranquility of those in the south. Splendidly structured and exquisitely laid out the garden gives an artistic appeal and endless enjoyment to its visitors.

The project of the Grand View Garden was started in June 1984; its first phase of work was finished in July 1985, the second phase in October 1986, and the third to complete the project in 1988. In the course of its construction it has received great support and concern from a great number of people both at home and abroad. The garden has been recommended as "one of the 16 well – known scenic spots in Beijing" and one of "10 major constructions in the 1980s in the capital of Beijing".

421. 大观园里有哪些主要建筑?

大观园里的主要建筑有:园门、曲径通幽、沁芳亭、怡红院、潇湘馆、秋霜斋、滴翠亭、稻香村、暖香坞、藕香榭、红香圃、蓼汀花溆、芦雪庭、紫菱洲、凸碧山庄、凹晶溪馆、栊翠庵、省亲别墅牌坊和顾恩思义殿等。

What are the main buildings in the Grand View Garden?

The main buildings in the Grand View Garden are the Garden Gate, A Winding Path Leading to a Secluded Retreat, the Seeping Fragrance Pavilion, the Happy Red Court, the Bamboo Lodge, the Studio of Autumn Freshness, the Alpinia Park, the Red Rue Studio, the Pear Fragrance Court, the Dripping Emerald Pavilion, the Lotus Fragrance Anchorage, the Sweet Paddy Cottage, the Smartweed Bank & Flowery Harbor, the Purple Caltrop Isle, the Reed Snow Cottage, the Convex Emerald Hall, the Concave Crystal Lodge, the Green Lattice Nunnery, the Warm Scented Arbor, the Archway in front of the House of Reunion and the Hall of Recalling Imperial Favor and Mindful of Duty, and what not.

422. 大观园大门的格式是怎样的?

大观园的大门是五开间的朱红大门,坐北朝南,两旁均有石狮镇守。门栏和窗扉的雕刻非常精细,加上左右两边的白墙,依势蜿蜒,使其显得格外悦目赏心。

What architectural style does the Gate of the Grand View Garden follow?

Facing south, the scarlet garden gate, five bays in width,

is flanked by stone – lions, one on either side. The door sills and window – lattices, which are exquisitely carved and set off by white walls snaking along on both sides, present a beautiful and pleasing scenery to the eyes and minds of visitors.

423. "曲径通幽处"是怎么来的?

进入大门口,便是一座用太湖石堆砌而成的假山,贾宝玉在山口镜面的白石上题有:"曲径通幽处"五个字。这座假山挡住了全园的景色,山上白石奇异,千姿百态,很是风趣。它们纵横拱立,似鬼如兽,似云若仙。而山脚下微露两条羊肠小径,故此处取名"曲径通幽"真是恰到好处,给人以一种神鬼莫测的感觉。

What is the origin of "A Winding Path Leads to a Secluded Retreat"?

On entering the garden gate an artificial rockery piled up with water – eroded limestone from the Lake Tai screens away the view. But on the mirror – like stone above you'll see an inscription "A Winding Path Leads to a Secluded Retreat" worded by Baoyu. Studded with white stone pieces in marvelous shapes and graceful stances some of them looking like beasts and others angels or fairies in misty clouds present visitors quite an interesting picture here. At the foot of the rockery there are two paths meandering into a retreat, evoking from among visitors there a sense of mystery and wonder.

424. 沁芳亭建于何处? 匾额上是谁题的词?

沁芳亭建于大观园的中轴线上。一泓碧水为白石护栏环抱,在池上建有一座 13 孔石桥,凉亭就座落在石桥之上。宝玉所题"沁芳"匾额便挂于亭中,并在亭柱上题七言对联一副:"绕堤柳借三篙翠,隔岸花分一脉香。""沁芳"的含意是水渗透着芳香,而那副对联是围绕着水而写的:水光澄碧,颇似借来了堤上杨柳的翠色;泉水也散发出芬芳的幽香,如同两岸飘来的花香似的,分外醉人。"绕堤"、"隔岸",水在其中,而语中却不带"水"字,是这副对联的绝妙之处,使人回味无穷。

Where is the Seeping Fragrance Pavilion located? And who does the inscription on the plaque?

The Seeping Fragrance Pavilion with balustrades all round is erected on a 13－arched bridge spanning over a stretch of emerald water and on the central axis running through the Grand View Garden. Hung above on the pavilion is a plaque with the words "Seeping Fragrance" inscribed by Baoyu and flanked on both sides by a couplet that reads:

"Willows on the dyke lend their verdancy to three punts;
Flowers on the further shore spare a breath of fragrance."

The Seeping Fragrance Pavilion means that the water is permeated with fragrance and the couplet indicates that it turns green just because it has borrowed the verdancy from the willows on the further shore and also due to this it seeps out delicate fragrance. The couplet, describing the water but without using the word "water", suggests the sense by resorting to "on the dyke" and "on the further shore." Really marvelous touch of a master hand!

425. 沁芳亭在《红楼梦》中起什么作用?

沁芳亭是一座很幽静的凉亭,座落在沁芳桥上,宝玉和黛玉经常在此处幽会。他们在此处度过了时而甜蜜幸福,时而又忧愤悲伤的时光。例如有一天,宝玉坐在沁芳桥畔桃花底下读《会真记》,当读到落红成阵段落之时,忽见风吹桃花,散落得处处皆是,他随即将手中落花抖落池中,显得一片凄凉;黛玉瞧见,触景生情,责怪宝玉不该这样做,沾污了清洁美丽的桃花,不如拿土掩埋,保持桃花的纯洁干净。黛玉常常以落花自况,"独把花锄偷洒泪,洒上空枝见血痕",十分伤感地哭颂出《葬花吟》,以表达她内心数之不尽的郁结缠绵之意,充满了封建社会里"薄命女"的一片愤懑、孤愤和抗议之情。

在曹雪芹的笔下,小说《红楼梦》里的许多故事情节都发生在这里,因而,沁芳亭在《红楼梦》中起着十分重要的作用。

What is the Seeping Fragrance Pavilion used for in the novel A Dream of Red Mansions?

Quiet and secluded, the pavilion is erected on the Seeping Fragrance Bridge, where Baoyu and Daiyu often came trysting. They spend their sweet and happy, yet sometimes grievous hours here. One day when Baoyu, sitting under a peach – tree by the side of the Seeping Fragrance Bridge, was reading the book the "Western Chamber", quite a few flower – petals got falling on him in a gust of wind. He at once shook them off into the pond nearby, leaving before his eyes a pool of misery. Just at the moment Daiyu came over when Baoyu was just reading "Red petals fall in drifts" she got upset and started to blame Baoyu for not having buried them but letting the beautiful flowers besmeared. To prevent the fallen petals from being spoilt Daiyu often got them buried whenever she found them. Comparing herself to the fallen flower – petals, she often recited the following lines of a verse in a melancholy mood:

"Alone, her hoe in hand, her secret tears

Falling like drops of blood on each bare bough."

426

By reciting these lines she poured out the bitterness from the innermost recess of her heart, the grievance and protest from an unlucky girl of the feudal society.

In Cao Xueqin's novel many stories and plots happened in the Seeping Fragrance Pavilion. Therefore, we can say, the pavilion plays a very important role in the novel A Dream of Red Mansions.

426. 贾宝玉的住处为何称为"怡红院"？

怡红院是一座金碧辉煌的大院落,由于贾宝玉爱红色成癖,故称他的住所为"怡红院"。怡红院外粉墙环绕,绿柳周垂。三间垂花低悬的红漆门楼,四面抄手游廊。院中有甬路相连,更有石山点缀;在宽阔的住房前,栽种着阔叶芭蕉、若伞的海棠、挺拔的青松。五间抱厦,飞檐鎏金,上悬"怡红快绿"的匾额,还有雕镂花样的隔扇,使整个庭院显得富丽堂皇,雍容华贵,故而称为"怡红院"。

Why is the living quarter of Jia Baoyu called the "Happy Red Court"?

The Happy Red Court is a splendid and spacious courtyard. As Jia Baoyu took a great fancy in red color, so the name of his residence was called the "Happy Red Court". Enclosed by pink walls with green willows all round the Happy Red Court has three arched gates with door – leaves painted in red. Along the walls inside runs a corridor and the center of the courtyard is adorned with a rockery joined up by cobbled – paths. Planted in front of the spacious hall of the residence are the plantains and multi – petaled crab – apple trees and pines. The five – bayed hall gaily painted have a plaque hung above at the entrance, inscribed with the characters "Happy Red and Delightful Green". The doorposts and windowsills are carved and latticed. So the whole courtyard suggests a scene of splendor and elegance, hence the name the "Happy Red Court".

427. 怡红院里有哪些建筑?

怡红院庭院斜廊直通山顶轩厅,是怡红公子贾宝玉经常邀请众姐妹,共同赏月、吟诗、猜谜作乐的地方。

厅内西面是宝玉的书房,另有晴雯居住的粉红闺帐;房内东面是宝玉的卧室。后院有满架的蔷薇及水池,并在水池上架一白石,供游人往来。石头砌岸,池中碧水澄澈,群鱼畅游其中,显得格外幽静。只有当兄弟姐妹们来此游玩时,才显出一番热闹的景象。

What are the main buildings in the "Happy Red Court"?

In the Happy Red Court, the covered corridor leads all the way up to a small hall on top of the hill. It is a place where Baoyu, the prince of the "Happy Red Court" often came to enjoy the glorious full moon, chant poems, guess riddles or make merry with the girls around him.

The western room is Baoyu's study, and going further inside you'll find a little chamber screened off with a pink curtain of gauze, that's bed-room for Baoyu's maid, Qin Wen; while the eastern room is the bed-room for Baoyu himself. In the backyard you'll find bunches of roses and a small pond with a white stone-slab spanning over it for passers-by. The stone-banked pond, with shoal of fish swimming about in the crystal-clear water, presents an extremely quiet environment. Only when the girls were around here playing, would

428

the atmosphere at the place be enliven and become lively for a while.

428. 怡红院内的匾额"红香绿玉"是谁题的? 后又为何改成"怡红快绿"?

当贾政带着宝玉及其客人初游大观园来到怡红院时,他命宝玉题额,于是宝玉便题了"红香绿玉",体现了"蕉棠两植"的特点(即芭蕉的香,海棠的红)。在元妃幸游大观园后,指出她最喜欢的地方恰与宝玉有所不同,含蓄地透露出"金玉良缘"与"木石前盟"的对立,故将"红香绿玉"改成"怡红快绿",命宝玉为她以"怡红快绿"赋诗。

Who inscribed the plaque with the words "Crimson Fragrance and Green Jade" in the "Happy Red Court"? Why was it later changed to "Happy Red and Delightful Green"?

The first visit to the Grand View Garden was made by Jia Zheng and his lot. When they arrived at the Happy Red Court, he bid his boy Baoyu to give it a name. And accordingly his son had it out with that inscription "Crimson Fragrance and Green Jade", which refers to the special feature of the two plants: the plantain and multi – petaled crabapple tree in the yard. However, when the imperial consort Yuanchun returned to pay a visit to the Grand View Garden later she found out the place she liked most was different from Baoyu. That indicated in allusion that the Golden Jade Happy Marriage was antithetic to the "Solemn Pledge of Love". So she decided to have the original name changed to "Happy Red and Delightful Green", and by using this new inscription as the new theme she bid Baoyu to compose a poem for her.

429.贾宝玉和林黛玉的雅号是什么?

贾宝玉的别号为绛洞花主、富贵闲人、怡红公子,绰号无事忙。贾政、王夫人之子,元春的胞弟,贾府里通称宝二爷。

林黛玉,别号潇湘妃子,绰号多病西施。林如海之女,贾母的外甥女,贾宝玉的姑表妹,贾府里通称为林姑娘。

What are the elegant names for Jia Baoyu and Lin Daiyu?

Jia Baoyu, alias Master of flowers in Red Cavern, the Rich Unoccupied, Prince in Happy Red Court and also nicknamed as Much Ado About Nothing. He is the son of Jia Zheng and Lady Wang, brother of the Imperial Consort Yuanchun, also called the Second Young Master in the Mansions of the Jia family.

Lin Daiyu, alias Queen of Bamboo, also nicknamed as the Delicate Xishi. She is the daughter of Lin Ruhai, grand - daughter - in - law of the Lady Dowager of the Jias, and cousin of Jia Baoyu. She is called Miss Lin in the Mansions of the Jias.

430. 潇湘馆是作什么用的? 里面的布局如何?

潇湘馆是林黛玉在大观园里的住所,馆上边有宝玉所题的匾额"有凤来仪"。凤凰被人们认作是仙禽,它的出现是好事的征兆。另外,古时又多以凤凰比后妃,额题为元春归省而拟。馆内有修舍数间,回廊曲折,翠树摇曳;阶下有石子铺路,弯弯曲曲的小径通向闺房。

院北面有三间小小的房舍,一明两暗,门窗上绘淡绿色的竹千竿。西屋有黛玉的书房,她抚琴的蜡像,紫鹃站立一旁。后窗下摆一张病床;堂屋里放着一张桌子、二张小凳,这里是供人们下棋的地方。东屋是黛玉的卧室。书房与一小亭相衔,形状颇似江南一叶小舟,别具风格。这是黛玉读书、赋诗后休息的地方。亭前一股溪流,汇入环抱潇湘馆的潺潺流水,加上翠绿的细竹,使这个地方显得格外清雅幽静,非常适合黛玉的情趣。

What was that Bamboo Lodge used for? How is it laid out inside?

The Bamboo Lodge is the abode for Lin Daiyu when she moved to live in the Grand View Garden. Above the gate of entrance is a board with an inscription, the place "Where the Phoenix Alights" done by Jia Baoyu. The phoenix is popularly regarded by the Chinese people as a fairy bird, and so her advent promises a good luck. And likewise in ancient times the mystical bird was also referred to as imperial consort and the inscription on the board was written just before Yuanchun, the imperial consort, who returned to pay a visit to her parents. Seen in the Bamboo Lodge are several houses with corridors, a bamboo thicket and cobbled paths zigzagging to a boudoir.

Seen in the north of the courtyard are three houses with one of them opening to the south. Painted on the doors and windows of them are hundreds of bamboo in light green. In the western room, the study for Daiyu, you'll find a wax – figure of Daiyu playing a zither and her maid Zijuan standing by her side. Under the window at the back there lays a bed. Placed in the hall is a table with two stools, a place for them to play chess. The eastern chamber is Daiyu's bedroom and the study is joined up with a small pavilion, the delicate shape of which resembles a small boat seen in the south of the Yangtze. This is a place for her to have a rest after reading books or

431

chanting poems. In front of the pavilion there is a streamlet emptying into the gurgling brook round the Bamboo Lodge, which, set off by green bamboo groves, makes the place seem to be very quiet, yet full of elegance, a place fit for Daiyu's taste.

431. 秋霜斋的作用是什么？

秋霜斋位于大观园内的东北部,这里是探春进园后的住所。院内东侧有晓翠堂,四面出廊,飞檐立柱。园中的姐妹们曾在此互起诗翁别号,依据探春的意思,创办了海棠社,姐妹们争相咏唱白海棠。

探春有三间相连的住所,大理石案上堆放着笔砚和名人书帖。屋内西墙上挂着《烟雨图》,左右挂着对联:"烟霞闲骨骼,泉石野生涯。"其意是:于烟霭云霞之中,养成浪漫洒脱的天性,在涌泉山石之畔,度过幽闲自得的山野村人的生活。

晓翠堂前的石山上建有一座八角凉亭,称"赏月亭",是大观园景观中的制高点之一。该亭白石为栏,朱柱彩檐,登亭眺望,可饱览全园秀丽的景色。

在秋霜斋后院外有一座假山,山顶上建有一清白石"拜台"。是贾母带领大观园众人拜天祭祀、祈求好运的地方。

What was the Studio of Autumn Freshness used for?

Located in the northeast of the Grand View Garden, the Studio of Autumn Freshness is a living quarter for Tanchun when she moved into the Grand View Garden. In the east of the yard there is a hall named "Morn Verdure" with obtrusive eaves and verandas around. The young ladies in the garden, according to the suggestions of Tanchun, organized the Begonia Club and each of them got a name as a poet.

432

There are three inter-linked rooms in the courtyard. Piled on the marble-faced table in the room are some writing brushes, ink-stone and copies of calligraphy model and scrolls of paintings done by noted calligraphers and painters. Hung on the Western Wall is the Picture of Mist and Rain flanked by a couplet which reads:"In mist and rain I loiter my time away; and with rockeries and springs around I'm a hermit to stay." This means: one who lives by rockeries and springs in the mist and rain incurs a habit of a loiterer and enjoys a pastoral and carefree life.

Built on the hillock at the Hall of Morn Verdure is an octagonal kiosk, named Kiosk for Moon Appreciation. Being one of the highest points in the Grand View Garden, the kiosk with painted eaves on red pillars, and surrounded by white-marble railings is a place where one can take a bird's eye view of the whole garden.

At the back of the Studio of Autumn Freshness there is a manmade hill on which a "Worshipping Terrace" is built with green-whitish stones. It is a place where the Lady Dowager of the Jia Family, taking the lead of the whole family, prays to heaven for good luck.

432. 贾探春是何等样的一个人？

贾探春，别号自称"蕉下客"，绰号"玫瑰花"，系贾政和赵姨娘之女，贾府通称三姑娘。她平素喜欢阔朗，充满了一副男子气。她还是大观园内一位精明的女管家，她志高自负，常常自诩为"野客"、"山人"，自命风雅清高，热中于为封建王朝"立出一番事业来"。

What kind a person is Jia Tanchun like?

Jia Tanchun, nicknamed Stranger Under the Plantain and Rose Flower. She is the daughter of Jia Zheng and his concubine Zhao, so she is also called the Third Miss in the Grand Mansion. Being somewhat gallant she's sometimes very boyish and as a shrewd stewardess in the Grand View Garden she's rather pompous, styling herself as a hermit, elegant and above worldly interests, and hanker after creating and establishing something wondrous for the feudal society.

433. 滴翠亭的结构和外观如何？作何用处？

大观园内西角门旁，有一座卧水双层建筑，这便是湖心亭，亦称"滴翠亭"。该亭垂檐四角，四周游廊曲栏，雕窗镂格，下有一泓碧水，与怡红院隔水相望。在亭内举目，可眺望园中佳景。

滴翠亭的一边，有折带桥与岸相连。岸边的垂柳遮荫蔽日，景色十分秀丽，颇有"蓬莱仙境"的意味。南边有一小土丘，丘顶上立有一块山石，镌有"花冢"二字，这里是黛玉葬花的地方。

What does that Dripping Emerald Pavilion look like? And what was it used for in the Grand View Garden?

Near the side - gate in the western corner of the Grand View Garden is a two - storeyed pavilion dotting on the water of the lake, its name is the Dripping Emerald Pavilion. This quadrangular pavilion with slanting eaves has balustrades all round and its windows are delicately latticed and carved. Opposite the Happy Red Court, with a stretch of water in - between, it is a good place in the garden for enjoying the beautiful scenery.

A zigzagging bridge connects it with the shore, which is neatly planted with weeping – willows in lush green. The scenery around is so beautiful that it looks as if it were a Fairyland of Penglai. To the south of it there is a little earth – mound with a stone – tablet on its top, which reads "Flower Mound". It is the place where Daiyu often came to bury the fallen flower – petals she picked up.

434. 稻香村的由来如何？是谁的住所？

绕过山环,便可见黄泥矮墙隐约于绿荫之中,这里面有草顶凉亭和一些茅舍。院外有用桑、榆、槿三种树枝编就的两溜青篱。院后辟有荷塘、稻田,路旁碣石上题曰:"稻香村"。院内北舍,东屋无一彩绘,屋内纸窗木榻,陈设简陋,一洗大观园内的富贵气象,颇似农家田舍风光。

稻香村是李纨进大观园后的住所。李纨,系贾政、王夫人长子媳妇。贾府里通称珠大奶奶。她终生持操守节,有一定的道德修养,被姐妹们推为诗社社长,自起别号"稻香老农"。稻香村充满山野气息,与住所的主人李纨守节寡欲的性格非常协调。

How about the Sweet Paddy Village? Who lived there?

Going round a hillock you'll find a low wall built with brownish adobes, tucked away in a dense green. Encircled are a thatched arbor and several cottages. The outer courtyard is kept off by a double – hedge intertwined of sprigs of mulberry, elm and hibiscus bushes, and behind it there is a lotus – pond and paddies with a stone – tablet by the path, indicating the Sweet Paddy Village. The rooms inside are quite out of ostentation, in which, except for some simple furnishings and papered – windows, only a wooden couch is seen in the room, a

435

purely pastoral life.

The Sweet Paddy Village was the abode for Li Wan in the Grand View Garden. Li Wan, a widow of the elder son of Jia Zheng and Lady Wang, is known in the Mansions as the elder mistress. Fostered by feudal etiquette and rites she kept her chastity all her life long. Self – styled as the "Old Peasant of the Sweet Paddy" she was chosen by the young ladies in the Grand View Garden to be the warden of a poetry party, the Begonia Club. Reeking of a rustic taste, the Sweet Paddy Village proves suitable to her personality in keeping chastity down to the ground.

435. 暖香坞(蓼风轩)是作何用的?

暖香坞又名蓼风轩,是惜春入园后的住所,也是她作画的地方。蓼风轩是惜春的书房,但有时也在这里下棋。

惜春是贾珍的胞妹,贾府里通称为四姑娘。

在惜春卧房门上的匾额上写有"暖香坞"三个字。大观园的小姐、少奶奶们在芦雪亭争着联吟即景诗之后,又在这暖香坞凭着雅兴编制灯谜。

What's the Warm Scented Arbor (or Smartweed Breeze Cot) used for?

The Warm Scented Arbor, also named the Smartweed Breeze Cot, is the lodge for Xichun in the Grand View Garden and is also a place for her to do paintings. The Smartweed Breeze Cot is her study, a place sometimes for her to play chess here.

Xichun, sister of Jia Zhen, is known in the Mansions as the fourth miss.

436

Hung above the gate of her bedroom is a plaque inscribed with the words "Warm Scented Arbor." Since the girls in the Grand View Garden started chanting impromptu poems in the Reed Snow Arbor they had had a get – together here to compose lantern riddles.

436. 藕香榭的作用是什么?

藕香榭建在大观园中轴线以东的池中水上,有正房三间,左右有回廊,四面临水,南面有竹桥跨水与岸相接。亭柱上挂有对联:"芙蓉影破归蓝桨,菱藕香深泻竹桥。"其意是:芙蓉花影摇动起来便知有船要归来,飘满菱花莲藕芳香的水上架着竹桥。这副对联充满了诗情画意。附近植有桂树,每到金秋时分花香四溢。湘云、宝钗在此开海棠诗社,边吃螃蟹,边作菊花诗。贾母二进大观园时,曾让园内女戏子在此处水亭上演习乐曲,借水赏音,格外动听,使人心旷神怡。林黛玉借着咏菊,真实而自然地抒发了自己的内心世界,所作的三首诗被评为最佳之作。

What's the Lotus Fragrance Anchorage used for?

Erected on waters east to the central axis of the Grand View Garden the Lotus Fragrance Anchorage including three frontal rooms with verandas is connected to the shore by a bamboo bridge in the south. Written on the posts of the pavilion is a couplet reading:

Magnolia oars shatter the reflections of lotus;

Water chestnuts and lotus – flowers scent the bamboo – bridge.

That is to say: the twisted image of lotus in the water tells a boat's return, and where their scent permeates over the water one sees a bamboo – bridge. What a poetic scene the couplet unfolds! There are two osmanthus trees nearby, which give forth an intoxicating fragrance. Every fall, Xiangyun and Baochai sponsored a poet – party of the Begonia Club composing poems on chrysanthemum here while having a feast of crabs. Once actresses were sent in to play music for the girls when Lady Dowager who came to visit the Grand View Garden the second time. The girl – poets surrounded by waters while listening to the melodious music, really had a wonderful time, feeling overjoyed and relaxed. At this occasion Lin Daiyu composed three poems on chrysanthemum to expose her innermost feelings, which turned out to be the best to the great appreciation of all.

437. 红香圃的用处是什么?

红香圃系《红楼梦》小说中的"芍药园",是一处以赏花为主的自然风景区。在书中描写的是三间敞厅,而今建成的却是封闭式的,四面装有活动隔扇,夏天将隔扇撤掉,便成为宽敞的大厅,以便乘凉赏花;而到冬天再按上隔扇就成了暖阁。红香圃地势开阔,花木繁茂,是专为观赏芍药而建的。在其东面有蔷薇园、荼蘼架、木香棚,是春夏两季绝好的去处。

What's the Red Rue Garden used for?

The Red Rue Garden is a "Garden of Peonies". As described in the novel of A Dream of Red Mansions, it is a natural scenic spot used mainly for enjoying flowers. The place as said in the novel used to be an open hall of three bays, but is now built into an enclosed one with movable partitions all round. In summer, the partitions can be removed away to make it a spacious hall for enjoying flowers or the cool from the open air, while in winter with the partitions fixed on, it becomes a warm pavilion. With a variety of flowers in surrounding, such as peonies, roses, and other pergolas of green ivies it is a wonderful place both for spring and summer days.

438. 芦雪亭有什么用处?

芦雪亭地处旁山临水的湖滩边,是冬令赏雪的好地方。其建筑简朴,三间屋舍,后窗可供垂钓,有一陌小径穿芦度苇与藕香榭的竹桥相连。

大观园里的脂粉香娃们,在冬日的雪天里欢聚亭中,坐在温暖的地炕上,拥栏赏雪,争联即景诗,好不热闹。他们虽在芦雪亭里吟咏,可是他们的身世遭遇、性格、向往都不一样,在这联欢的盛况之中,早已隐藏着贾府的糜烂衰朽,预示着大观园雪霁之时的更大悲哀!

What's the Reed Snow Arbor used for?

On the brink of the water and backed by the hill the Reed Snow Arbor is a fine spot for enjoying snowscape in winter. Consisting of three rooms the structure of the building is very simple with windows at the back opened for angling, and a zigzagging path through the reed thickets leads to the bamboo - bridge of the Lotus Fragrance Anchorage.

In winter times the girls in the Grand View Garden used to have a get - together here. Sitting on the warmed Kang or leaning over the railings and verandas they enjoyed the falling snowflakes from the sky, while vying with one another in composing impromptu poems on snow, thus making the place livelier than ever. By reciting their poems they exposed their innermost feelings of their grievances in the past and expressed their wishes for a happy future. Through this outward splendor of the Jia Mansions, one can easily sense the innate decadence and weakness in its interior, which foretells an inevitable catastrophe when the "snow" melting away.

439. 蓼汀花溆的外观有何特色?

蓼汀花溆是由巨石堆砌而成的。山石层叠,有石阶盘旋而上。石岸曲折,构成豁朗的港洞。一带清流出于石间,势若游龙,两边石栏上挂着五光十色的水晶玻璃风灯,在岸上的柳树及杏树上装饰着用各种绫绸绢纸和通草做成的花朵,每棵树上还悬挂着无数灯盏,如同一个扑朔迷离的玻璃世界,煞是好看。大观园里的众人也常到此一游。

What special features does the Smartweed Bank and Flowery Harbor have in its appearance?

Piled up with big stones the Smartweed Bank and Flowery Harbor is an artificial rockery with spiraling stone – steps leading up to its top. The winding stone – bank around forms a big cavern underneath and out from it flows a clean spring as if it were a curling dragon snaking along. The stone railings on both sides are decorated with wind – proof lanterns made of colorful glass – pieces and the banks are planted with willows and apricot trees adorned with paper and silk strips, flowers made of rush and a number of decorative lanterns, thereby suggesting a splendid world of labyrinth. The inhabitants in the Grand View Garden often came here for a stroll.

440. 蘅芜院的作用是什么?

蘅芜院是薛宝钗进大观园后的住所。其匾额上书有"蘅芜院"三字,门内迎面便是两组参天拔地的太湖石假山,占据了大半个院落。院中无一棵树木,唯有奇藤异草。院两边是油漆彩绘抄手游廊。五间敞厅,四面出廊,绿窗油壁,非常清雅幽静,这种环境符合居室主人薛宝钗的性格。

What's the Alpinia Park used for?

The Alpinia Park was the abode for Xue Baochai when she moved to stay in the Grand View Garden. Written on the plaque above the gate is the inscription "Alpinia Park," and the gate is confronted with two towering rockeries, which occupy a large part of the courtyard. There is no tree at all in it save some unknown wistarias and plants. On both sides of the courtyard there are colorfully painted corridors. A hall of five bays with porches and green windows makes one feel tranquil and refined. The environment is very apt for the disposition of a person like Xue Baochai.

441. 薛宝钗是个什么样的人?

薛宝钗,别号蘅芜君,薛姨妈之女,宝玉的姨表姐。后嫁于宝玉,贾府里通称宝姑娘。宝钗出身皇商家族,她世情练达,胸有城府,虽有"青云之志",却装作寡语鲜言,安分随时。她对宝玉并不感到满意,但为了当上"宝二奶奶",她便刻意对上逢迎,对下笼络,终于达到了她与宝玉"金玉良缘"结婚之目的。可是她并没有得到爱情生活的幸福,而最终成了封建主义的牺牲品。

What kind of a person is Xue Baochai?

Xue Baochai, alias Lady of Alpinia Park, is the daughter of Aunt Xue, cousin of Baoyu on the maternal side. Known in the Jia Mansions as Miss Bao she later married to Baoyu. Born in a family of doing business for the royal court she 's shrewd and deep, knowing the ropes of the society. Bearing "lofty aspirations," she pretends to be reticent and go along with the prevailing trends of the time. Though not very satisfied with Baoyu, yet wishing to be the mistress of the second young master she tried every means to fawn on the superior and rope in the inferior, and finally realized her wish in marrying to Baoyu. Nevertheless instead of getting happiness in marriage she became a whipping – girl of the feudal society.

442. 缀锦楼的作用是什么？

缀锦楼位于东紫菱洲,是迎春进大观园后的住所。该楼是一座飞檐彩绘的两层楼阁,上下各五间,进门便是曲折游廊,环境异常幽静。楼上横悬一匾,上书"缀锦楼"三字。一楼是迎春的居室,南面是迎春的红帐卧榻,东面是书房。院内的东厢房是丫鬟们的下房。

What's the Variegated Splendor Tower used for?

Located on the Purple Caltrop Isle in the east of the Grand View Garden the Variegated Splendor Tower was the abode for Yingchun when she moved to stay in the garden. The tower with flying eaves is a colorful building of two storeys with each floor consisting of five rooms. On entering the courtyard you'll see corridors winding along, presenting a tranquil atmosphere in its surrounding areas. Hung above the tower gate is a plaque with the inscription "Variegated Splendor Tower." Since the first floor is used for Yingchun's chambers: the room facing the south with a red gauze curtain on is her bed – room and the one facing the east her study, and the annexes in the east of the yard are for her maids.

443. 迎春是怎么样的一个人?

迎春,别名菱洲,绰号二木头,贾赦之女。贾府里通称二姑娘。迎春误嫁了中山狼孙绍祖家,她整天挨打受骂,横遭摧残,从未过上一天的安宁日子。

What kind of a person is Yingchun?

Yingchun, alias Mistress of Caltrop Isle and also nicknamed as No. 2 Wood head, Was the daughter of Jia She, known in the Jia Mansions as Second Miss. Married unhappily to Sun Shaozu, nicknamed Wolf of Zhongshan, she suffered from abuses and beatings day after day had never seen a day of peaceful life.

444. "顾恩思义殿"有何含义? 是谁题的匾额?

"顾恩思义"的含义是:天地造化了博大的慈爱之心,老百姓人人都感恩戴德;皇帝赐予的古往今来的恩泽,使普天之下都得到了恩惠和荣耀。该匾额是元春所题。顾恩思义殿是省亲活动的主要场所,是一座楼台高筑的正殿,两厢各有配殿五间,四廊相接。正殿后的主楼为"大观楼",东面有"缀锦阁",西面是"含芳阁"。三座建筑之间以游廊相连。

What 's the implication behind the Hall of Recalling Imperial Favor and Being Mindful of Duty? Who has inscribed it?

The implication behind the "Hall of Recalling Imperial Favor and Being Mindful of Duty" is that the nature's creation has generously brought the beneficence to the people of the world, and so everyone should feel deeply grateful to it. Since emperors and lords of the past took all mortal beings in the world under their wings and bestowed upon them their great benevolence and glory they should do likewise to them. Inscribed by Yuanchun, the imperial consort, the Hall of Recalling Imperial Favor and Being Mindful of Duty is the main area of activities of the visit paid by the imperial consort Yuanchun to her parents. The main hall towering in the center and two rows of annexes on both sides, each row consisting of five rooms are linked up by four corridors. The building behind the main hall is the Grand View Tower, the Variegated Splendor Tower in the east and the Fragrant Tower in the west: the three building are joined by verandas.

445. 凸碧山庄的作用是什么？

凸碧山庄是一座建于土山上的建筑物,是一个宽敞的大花厅,是贾母率园中众人中秋佳节赏月的地方。众人围坐在桌旁,一起玩击鼓传花取乐。贾母提议:"如此好月,不可不闻笛。"于是她们又欣赏起笛声来。悠扬的笛声一起,令人顿觉烦心解除。但时过不久,在这静夜明月之中,不禁又使人伤感和凄凉起来。

中秋赏月,自古至今不知使人生出了多少思念、追忆和怀想,从心头涌起了多少遐思和憧憬的波澜呵!

What's the Convex Emerald Village used for?

Located on a hillock piled up with earth the Convex Emerald Village is a spacious hall, a place for Lady Dowager to enjoy the glorious full moon on the day of the Mid Autumn Festival together with her family and guests. Sitting round a table they made their merry by passing round a flower to the beating of drum. In the meantime the old lady suggested: "At a moment in such a beautiful and serene night with the bright moon high up in the sky, it's won't be good enough not to have a flute – playing". Soon performers started to play music instruments thus making everyone relieve all cares and anxiety. Nevertheless, the utterly stillness of the moonlighted night quite easily made them feel lonely and despairing.

Ever since ancient times the enjoyment of moonlight in the Mid Autumn Festival night has brought forth from the people mind's eye many reminiscences that leave them much to reflect upon, ponder over or chew with.

446. 凹晶溪馆的作用是什么？

在山坳低洼的近水处有一座矮小的屋宇,这是山庄的退房,因其屋形为"凹"字形,故名凹晶溪馆。它傍山而筑,格外幽静,特为赏月而设。凸碧山庄和凹晶溪馆,这二景均为黛玉所拟,此二处一上一下,一明一暗,一高一矮,一山一水,是为赏月的最佳之处。在凹晶溪馆赏月,可见天上一轮皓月,池中一个月影,观者犹如置身于水晶宫之中一般。

What's the Concave Crystal Lodge used for?

Located on a piece of lowland by the waterside is a small house, a backyard lodge in a style of a hamlet. As the Concave Crystal Lodge is built in the shape of a Chinese character "凹", which means concave, hence the derivation of the name. Since the lodge is specially built by the waterside for enjoying the glorious moon the environment here is extremely serene and quiet. Daiyu drafted the names of the Convex Emerald Hall and the Concave Crystal Lodge. The two places,

445

one being higher, brighter and on the hill while the other lower, shadier and by the water, prove to be extremely suitable. When you enjoy the full moon in the Concave Crystal Lodge you will see a bright moon high up in the sky and the other in the shimmering lake below as though you were landed in a crystal palace.

447. 省亲别墅牌坊在建筑上有何特色？

省亲别墅牌坊，是一座龙蟠螭护、玲珑琢就的玉石牌坊，正上方镌刻着"省亲别墅"四个鎏金大字，左右分别刻写着"芳岸"和"玉津"。玉石牌坊的后面，正上方镌刻着"国恩家庆"左右刻的分别是"云影"、"波光"。玉石牌坊上刻着"天仙宝境"，后来元妃命换了"省亲别墅"。牌坊之西是座大石桥，桥边是通外河的水闸，因其是引沁芳源的水流入，故称"沁芳闸"，桥也称为"沁芳闸桥"。

What special features does the Archway in front of the House of Reunion have in its architectural style?

The Archway of the House of Reunion is built of marble – stones carved with rampant dragons and coiling serpents. Inscribed on the front above are the four gilded characters "Xing Qin Bie Shu", meaning the House of Reunion, and on its right and left sides are carved inscriptions "Fang'an" – the Fragrant Bank and "Yujin" – the Jade Ford. The back of the Archway is carved with the characters "Guo En Jia Qing", meaning Benevolent Rulers, Happy Family, which is matched by "Yun Ying" – Cloud Shades and "Bo Guang" – Shimmering Rays on its right and left sides. The former front inscriptions on the archway were the characters "Tian Xian Bao Jing", meaning the "Precious Fairyland of Immortals," but were later changed into "House of Reunion" upon the order of the imperial consort Yuanchun. To the west of the archway is a stone bridge and the water flows out from a spring called the Seeping Fragrance. By the side of the bridge there is a water − lock controlling the water to flow into a stream outside. Hence the "Seeping Fragrance Lock" and the "Seeping Fragrance Lock Bridge" are given to the water − lock and the bridge respectively.

448. 栊翠庵的作用是什么？

栊翠庵位于大观园西部,隐现于密林深处,花木甚多,环境幽静,是妙玉进园后的住所。北屋为佛殿,上悬匾额"妙音香界",殿内有观音坐像,是她烧香拜佛的地方。东室禅房是妙玉的卧室,也是她参禅修行的场所。

How about the Green Lattice Nunnery?

The nunnery in the west of the Grand View Garden is tucked away in trees and flowers. The quiet place is quite suitable for Miaoyu to live. The house in the north is a Buddha's hall with the plaque inscribed with the words "Miao Yin Xiang Jie", meaning the profundity of supernatural teachings in the realm of Buddhism, and enshrined in the hall is a statue of Goddess of Mercy (Bodhisattva Avalokitesvara in Sanskrit) in a sitting posture. This is the place where Miaoyu did worshipping and burned incense − sticks to the Buddha. The room in the east is her bedchamber and also a place for doing her meditation.

449. 妙玉是怎样的一个人？

妙玉，自称栏外人，系一带发修行的尼姑。她最欣赏宋人范成大的诗句："纵有千年铁门槛，终须一个土馒头。"意思就是：纵然用千年不坏的铁门槛，也挡不住死亡的来临，最终还得埋到坟墓里去。故妙玉自称"蹈于铁槛之外"，做个槛外人。

What kind of a person is Miaoyu?

Miaoyu, self-styled Person beyond the Pile of Mortals, was a nun without having her hair shaved. She appreciated most following lines of a poem by Fan Chengda, a Song poet.

Though there's an iron-threshold of a thousand years,

There must be an earth-mound in front of you.

That is: though the iron-threshold won't be worn away even for a thousand years it cannot resist the inevitable outcome of a person to pass away. No matter who he or she is it will inevitably be buried into a grave. Therefore, Miaoyu styles herself "Person beyond the Pile of Mortals."

450. 你知道大观园中有哪些园？请举例说明之。

在大观园里有：怡红院、潇湘馆等，均为大观园中之园，那是按风景建筑设计的。而正门、省亲别墅则不同，它们是清代宫廷式建筑。

Do you know how many gardens there are in the Grand View Garden? Please name some of them for illustration.

The Happy Red Court and the Bamboo Lodge are the gardens within the Grand View Garden. They are designed and built in the style of a scenic spot, which are different from that of the front gate and the House of Reunion for the latter is done in a palatial style prevailing in the period of the Qing Dynasty.

451. 北京大观园的建筑布局与《红楼梦》的描写过程有何关系?

《红楼梦》描写了宝玉和黛玉之间的爱情和贾府春、夏、秋、冬盛衰的过程,而北京大观园的建筑,也是按春夏秋冬,琴棋书画来设计的,其布局如:蘅芜院"雪洞"是操琴的好地方;潇湘馆"宝鼎烟绿,幽窗指凉",则是下棋的好地方;"温香拂面"的暖香坞正适合惜春作画;"桐剪秋风"的秋霜斋是读书的妙处。同时,大观园里的所有建筑均与居住在那里的主人公的思想感情、性格、遭遇和生活状况等相吻合。

What is the connection there between the architectural layout of the Grand View Garden in Beijing and that as described in the novel of A Dream of Red Mansions?

The novel of A Dream of Red Mansions describes the sad love – story between Baoyu and Daiyu. It runs through the "four seasons" in the rise and fall of the Jia Mansions. And the architecture in the Grand View Garden is likewise laid out and built according to the four seasons of spring, summer, autumn and winter with each having a suitable environment for playing lyre, chess or doing calligraphy and paintings. For instance, the "Snow Cave" in the Alpinia Park is a good place for playing lyre and the Bamboo Lodge known for:

Still green the smoke from tea brewed in a rare tripod,

Yet cold the fingers from chess played by quiet windows.

So it's a good place for playing chess. The Warm Scented

Arbor, known for its "face – caressing warm scent" proves to be a suitable place for Xichun to do her paintings, and the Studio of Autumn Freshness, known for "Autumn Wind Ruffling the Plantain Trees", is a nice spot for study. To take it all in all, the buildings in the Grand View Garden coincide with the feelings, personal characters, experiences and living conditions of the persons living in the Grand View Garden.

北京常识题
(General Knowledge about Beijing)

452.北京市的面积有多大？

北京市面积共为 16,808 平方公里,占全国总面积的 0.175%。

How large an area does the Municipality of Beijing cover?

Covering an area of 16,808 square kilometers, Beijing accounts for 0.175 percent of the whole territory of the country.

453.北京市的海拔高度是多少？

北京市区的海拔高度为 43.71 米。

What is the elevation of the municipality of Beijing?

The elevation of the city of Beijing proper is 43.71 meters above sea level.

454.北京市的年平均气温是多少？

北京市位于北温带,是典型的大陆性季风气候,但气候较为宜人。虽然一年之内四季分明,然而春秋时间较短,冬夏季节则长。全年平均气温为 11.6 摄氏度,7 月份最热,昼夜平均气温为 25.8 摄氏度;1 月份最冷,昼夜平均气温为零下 4.6 摄氏度,全年的最佳气候是在 8、9、10 三个月之间,乃为北京旅游的最佳时节。

What is the annual mean temperature in Beijing?

Located at the North Temperate Zone, Beijing enjoys a typical continental, yet affable monsoon climate. Though it has distinctive four seasons, the time for spring and autumn is relatively short and that for summer and winter is much longer. The yearly mean temperature is 11.6 degrees centigrade (53 degrees Fahrenheit.) The hottest days are in July and the highest temperature averages 25.8 degrees centigrade (or 77 degrees Fahrenheit). The coldest days are in January with a mean temperature at minus 4.6 degrees centigrade (or 23.7 degrees Fahrenheit.) The best season in a year is in August, September and October, when it is ideal for making tours in Beijing.

455. 北京的四季各有多少天? 每个季节各有何种特点?

春季:4 月 1 日至 6 月 4 日,共有 65 天;
夏季:6 月 5 日至 9 月 7 日,计达 95 天;
秋季:9 月 8 日至 10 月 22 日,仅为短暂的 45 天;
冬季:10 月 23 日至次年的 3 月 31 日,共长达 160 天。
特点:春天干燥而多风沙,但由于近年来的植树造林,气候环境已明显改善;夏天炎热多雨;金秋是美丽的,但较短暂;冬季晴朗但较寒冷。

How many days are there in each season in Beijing? What's the specific feature for each of it?

Spring: From Apr.1st to Jun.4th, a total of 65 days;
Summer: From Jun.5th to Sept.7th, 95 days in all;
Autumn: From Sept.8th to Oct.22nd, a mere 45 days;

Winter: From Oct. 23rd to the next Mar. 31st, 160 days;

The specific feature for each season is as follows: Spring is usually dry and windy, sometimes even having sandstorms, but due to the efforts of afforestation in recent years the weather conditions have been much improved; Summer is hot with more rainy days; Autumn spells a pleasant climate though, yet time is very short and only winter lasts longer with a clear but cold weather.

456. 北京市在大多数情况下的最高气温和最低气温是多少?

在通常情况下,北京市的最高气温为 37 - 38 摄氏度,最低气温为零下 16 - 17 摄氏度。

In most cases what is the highest and the lowest temperature in Beijing?

In normal times the highest temperature in Beijing is 37 - 38 degrees centigrade, which is about 98 - 100 degrees Fahrenheit. and the lowest is minus 16 - 17 degrees, that is about 1.4 or minus 0.4 degrees in Fahrenheit.

457. 北京市全年的无霜期共多少天?

北京市全年的无霜期为 180 天。

How many frost - free days are there in a year in the area of Beijing?

In the area of Beijing there are one hundred eighty frost - free days in a year.

458. 北京市全年的平均日照时间是多少?

北京市全年平均日照时间为 2,700 小时。

What is the average sunshine time in a year in Beijing area?

The sunshine time in a year in Beijing averages about 2, 700 hours.

459. 北京城内最热的一天是在什么时候?

北京地区属暖温带湿润季风气候,一年四季分明。进入夏季以后,天气很快就会炎热起来。在一般情况下,最热的月份为七月份,高温天气也大多出现在这个月内。然而,北京城区百余年来最热的一天却出现在 1942 年的 6 月 15 日。这天的温度,据当时多方面的测定表明为摄氏 42.6 度。

What date is the hottest day in Beijing?

Situated in the monsoon climate of the warm temperate zone, Beijing has four distinct seasons in a year. When entering into summer the weather gets hot very quickly. In normal case the hottest weather in a year is in July with most of hot days in the month. However, the hottest day ever appeared in Beijing in about a hundred years time is on the 15th of June 1942, the temperature according to the reports from many aspects concerned having reached as high as 42.6 degrees centigrade.

460. 北京市全年的平均降雨量是多少?

北京市全年的平均降雨量为 644.2 毫米,夏季雨量相对集中,每年 6 - 8 月的平均降雨量约占全年总降雨量的 75%。

What is the annual average precipitation in the area of Beijing?

The annual rainfall in Beijing area averages 644.2 mm., which relatively concentrates in summer. From June to August, the volume of rainfall comes to 75% of its annual precipitation.

461. 北京降雨量最多是在哪年哪月？

七月份是北京地区降雨量最多的月份。据 1784 至 1956 年间的统计材料表明,7 月份平均降水量为 239.1 毫米,约为全年同期平均降水量 636.8 毫米的 1/3 还多。百余年来,北京降水量最多的年月是 1890 年 7 月。这年的全年降水量为 991.9 毫米,而 7 月份的降水量竟多达 825 毫米。

Which month and which year did it have the most rainfall in Beijing?

July is usually the month with the most of rainfalls in the Beijing area. According to the statistics made from 1784 to 1956 the rainfall in July averages 239.1 millimeters, being a little over 1/3 of the annual rainfall of 636.8 millimeters. In the past hundred years or so the month with the most of rainfalls in the Beijing area is in July, 1890. The annual precipitation reached in that year was 991.9 mm., yet with 825 mm. concentrated in July.

462. 流经北京市的主要河流有哪几条？

流经北京市的主要河流有 5 条,它们分别是永定河、潮白河、北运河、拒马河和泃河。

What are the main rivers flowing through the area of Beijing Municipality?

The main rivers that flow through the Beijing area are the following five：Yongding，Chaobai，Juma and Xun rivers and the North Canal as well.

463.北京市有多少个民族？它们所占的比例如何？

北京市有 56 个民族。在全市的总人口中,汉族占 96% 以上,少数民族占 3.8%。

How many nationalities are there in Beijing? What is the proportion?

There are 56 nationalities in Beijing，of which the Han nationality of the people occuries, a proportion of over 96%， while the population of other ethnic groups comes to 3.8% of the total.

464.北京市的家庭平均人口是多少？

北京市每一家庭住户的平均人口为 3.1 人。

What is an average family size in Beijing?

In Beijing，each household as a family has an average of 3.1 persons.

465.北京有多少年的历史？

北京以历史悠久闻名于世,它作为都城已有 800 余年的历史。北京就其历史而言,可上溯到 50 万年前的"北京人"时期,那时,我们的祖先就已繁衍生息在北京周口店一带。三千年前的周朝就已封召公于此,称这里为燕。十二世纪中叶,金朝在北京正式建都。其后历经了元、明、清三代以至今日。北京,除了解放前的大约 40 年时间外,都是全国的政治、经济和文化生活的中心。

How long is the history of Beijing?

Known to the world with its long history, Beijing, as a capital, has already undergone a period of over 800 years. And so far as its history is concerned, it can be traced back to the time of "Peking Men" some 500,000 years ago. At that time, our ancestors already began to live in and around the present day Zhoukoudian area and some 3,000 years ago the Zhou Dynasty then already enfoeffed Prince Shao to this area, calling it Yan. In the middle of the 12th century the Kin Dynasty made it its capital and the ensuing dynasties of Yuan, Ming and Qing followed suit. Thenceforth, Beijing, except the period of about 40 years before 1949, has always been the political, economic and cultural center of the nation.

466. 北京市有多少个区、县? 它们的分布状况如何?

北京市共辖 18 个区、县,其中在北京城区的有东城、西城、崇文和宣武 4 个区;近郊有朝阳、海淀、丰台和石景山 4 个区;远郊有门头沟、顺义、房山和通州 4 个区,还有昌平、大兴、平谷、怀柔、密云和延庆 6 个郊县。

How many districts and counties are there in Beijing? How about their locations?

There are 18 districts and counties under the administration of the Beijing Municipality, of which the four districts of Eastern City, Western City, Chongwen and Xuanwu are in the city proper; another four of Chaoyang, Haidian, Fengtai and Shijingshan are in the suburban areas and still another four of Mentougou, Shunyi, Fangshan and Tongzhou districts in the outer suburban areas and the rest six counties of Changping, Daxing, Pinggu, Huairou, Miyun and Yanqing are in the farther outskirts of Beijing.

467. 北京市劳保福利费用在哪些方面？

北京市劳保福利费用在医疗卫生、洗理、交通补助、福利事业补助、文娱体育、宣传费、计划生育补贴、丧葬和抚恤费等方面。

What aspects of life do the labor and welfare insurance funds cover in Beijing?

The labor and welfare insurance funds in Beijing cover the following aspects: medical and health care, personal cleaning, traffic subsidies, welfare allowance, expense for sports and recreational activities, expense on publicity and promotion work, subsidies for family – planning and allowances for death and burial as well as pensions for the disabled and the retired, etc.

468. 北京第一座民办公助性的现代艺术馆叫什么名字？何时落成？建筑面积是多少？

北京第一座民办公助性的现代艺术馆叫炎黄艺术馆,于1991年9月5日在北京亚运村竣工落成。总建筑面积为13,240平方米,内设展厅、画廊及多功能厅,是北京继中国美术馆之后的第二个大型艺术馆。

炎黄艺术馆是由已故国画大师黄胄联络海内外文化艺术界知名人士倡议并筹建的。

What's the name of the first modern art gallery in Beijing, which is privately run but subsidized by the state? When was it completed and what's the total floor space of it?

The first modern art gallery in Beijing privately – run but subsidized by the state is called the "Yan Huang Art Gallery". Completed on the 5th of September 1991, it is located in the Asian Games Village in Beijing. Covering a floor space of 13, 240 square meters and housing an exhibition hall, art galleries and a multi – function hall, it is a large – sized art gallery in Beijing next only to the Chinese Fine Art Gallery.

The "Yan Huang Art Gallery" was built at the suggestion of Huang Zhou, the late famous Chinese traditional painter in association with the celebrities of the world of arts and letters inside and outside China.

469. 北京首家京剧艺术剧场在哪里？是何时开张的？

北京首家京剧艺术剧场是北京前门饭店的梨园剧场,是1990 年 10 月 8 日开张的。

Where is the first theater for the art of Peking Opera in Beijing located? When was it opened to the public?

The first theater for the art of Peking Opera in Beijing is the Liyuan Theatre in the Qianmen Hotel in Beijing. It was opened to the public on the 8th of October, 1990.

470.京剧是如何形成的？它有什么特点？

京剧起源于安徽的徽剧和湖北的汉剧，形成于 19 世纪中叶清代的都城北京。

约在 200 年前清朝的康熙年间，北京盛行的是昆曲和戈阳腔。到了乾隆年间，秦腔（陕西梆子）也在北京打开了局面，与昆曲和戈阳腔并存。公元 1781 年（乾隆五十五年），安徽名艺人率徽剧入京，从此徽剧不断地发展，陆续兼收并蓄了昆曲、戈阳腔和梆子等剧种的长处，逐渐形成了唱、念、做、打俱全的剧种。到了 19 世纪上半叶清道光时期，流行于湖北一带的汉剧也传入了北京。由于当时徽剧和汉剧经常在一起演出，艺人间互相吸收对方的长处，再加上吸收北京口音这一必不可少的因素，这样，以二黄为基调的徽剧和以西皮为基调的汉剧，便自然地形成了一个有独特风格的剧种。起初有人称之为"皮黄"，也有人称其为"京调"，后来才叫做"京剧"。

京剧艺术是一种包括文学、音乐、舞蹈、美术和武术在内的综合艺术。它的表演形式和手法，总起来讲有程式化、虚拟化和节奏化三个特点。程式化：即根据不同的行当，把各行的唱、念、做、打用固定的格式方法形成程式；虚拟化：即用演员的表演体现出舞台上并不存在的东西，例如开门、关门的动作都是虚拟的，是以手势来表示从而给观众以门户存在的实感；节奏化：在演出中表演是十分鲜明的。京剧里的程式化、虚拟化的动作，都要在一定的节奏里才显得活跃、真实、有生气。

京剧在表演方面，具有多种多样的版式和曲牌，根据不同人物的思想感情，在曲牌的旋律上加以变化。表演方面，京剧有一套规格严谨的基本动作，演员可以根据剧情需要灵活运用。这种程式化的动作都有其生活依据，但作为艺术形象时，则动作夸张，节奏鲜明，虚实结合而又富于真实感。就舞蹈性的动作而言，无论是静止的亮相，还是运动中的一招一式，都富有艺术上

460

的造型美。京剧乐队以民族的管弦乐和打击乐为主,板鼓鼓师实际上承担着整个乐队的全局指挥,这也是京剧艺术的一个重要特点。京剧在美术上的特殊成就主要表现在服装和脸谱这两个方面。脸谱是中国古典戏曲中独具的高度夸张的化妆艺术;京剧在舞台艺术方面具有浓郁的中国民族特色和独特的艺术风格,在世界艺术宝库中,是一颗誉满全球的璀璨明珠。

How did the Peking Opera come into being? What are its special features?

The Peking Opera began to be formed on the basis of the Hui Opera from Anhui and the Han Opera from Hubei. It gradually came into being in Beijing by the middle of the 19th century during the Qing Dynasty. Around 200 years ago in the reign of Emperor Kangxi, there prevailed in the area of Beijing only Kun and Geyang melodies. By the time of Qianlong, the Qin Opera (called Shaanxi Bangzi) began to penetrate into Beijing and go along well with the former. However, in 1781, the 55th year of Qianlong's reign there came into Beijing a Hui Opera troupe headed by a famous actor and by taking in something good and essential from the Kun, Geyang and Qin operas it came to become an opera combining singing, narration, acting and martial arts. Up to the first half of the 19th century in the reign of Emperor Daoguang the Han Opera then in rife in Hubei also made its way into Beijing. As the Hui and the Han operas often went along well with each other in performance, many artists naturally learnt from one another, taking in the strong points from others to enrich ones own skill, and then by integrating the Beijing accent in singing, the indispensable factor into their own operas, an opera of a special art form naturally came into being on the basic melodies of Erhuang of the Hui Opera and Xipi of the Han Opera. It was then called "Pi-huang" or "Jing Melody" first but by and by it was called the "Peking Opera" finally.

The art of Peking Opera is a kind of composite one consisting of literature, music, dance, fine arts and martial arts. Its artistic forms and performing arts have the following three distinctive features, namely every action in a play is stylized, suppositive and rhythmical. To be stylized means to put singing, narration, acting and wrestling into a given form according to different roles played; to be suppositive means to suggest something which is non – existent on the stage by appealing to some suppositive actions. Take opening or closing the door for instance, it is suggested by a mere gesture of hands to give the audience a sense of reality; and to be rhythmical means that every action in a play is very distinctive in rhythm. The stylized and suppositive actions in the Peking Opera can be made lively and lifelike and true to life only when performed in a rhythmical way.

The performing art of the Peking Opera expresses itself in many forms and tunes. To keep pace with the changing feelings of actors and plots the strains of the tunes must be tuned to accordingly. So far as its actions are concerned, it has a strict set of basic formulas, upon which actors and actresses may act flexibly following the development of the plots. The formularized actions are all taken from real life. However, as an artistic form actions are exaggerated and clear – cut in rhythm, a sort of combination of something fictitious and substantial, which is able to suggest a sense of reality. Judging

462

from its dance movement, every single act whether in stillness or movement, is beautifully shaped. The band for Peking Opera is mainly consisted of the Chinese traditional orchestra and percussion music instruments. For instance, "Bangu", a small clattering drum for marking the time, is actually sounded to conduct the whole band. This is one of the important features in Peking Opera. The special accomplishment attained by the Peking Opera in fine arts manifests mainly in costumes and types of facial makeup, which stand out a kind of art unique and highly exaggerated out from among other Chinese traditional operas. Rich and unique in artistic forms and styles the Peking Opera of the Chinese nation has proved to be a renowned brilliant pearl in the treasure house of world dramas.

471. 北京能吃到全国多少种风味菜点？

在北京能吃到北京、四川、山东、广东、江苏、上海、天津、山西、福建、湖北、湖南、陕西、东北、江西、云南、青海和清真等 17 种全国各地的地方风味。

How many special local cuisines of the country can one have the chance to enjoy in Beijing?

In Beijing one will have chance to taste 17 kinds of local special cuisines. They are the dishes of Beijing, Sichuan, Shandong, Guangdong, Jiangsu, Shanghai, Tianjin, Shanxi, Fujian, Hubei, Hunan, Shaanxi, Jiangxi, Yunnan, Qinghai and that of northeast China as well as Hala food for Moslem people.

472. 北京烤鸭的来历如何？它是怎样制作的？

北京烤鸭有着悠久的历史,早在公元 10 世纪就有了。而到了元代,烤鸭就成了皇宫大内的御缮珍肴之一。烤鸭的制作方法如下:

制作北京烤鸭必须选用体重达 2.5 公斤左右的北京填鸭,这种鸭一般 50 天左右即能育成。北京填鸭色洁白,皮薄脯大,肉层红白相间,质地细嫩丰腴。

从填鸭制成烤鸭,主要有三个环节:一是烤制前对填鸭的处理;二是入炉烤制;三是片鸭上席。对填鸭的处理一般要经过打气、掏膛、洗膛、挂钩、烫皮、打糖和晾皮等 8 道工序。打气是将鸭身吹鼓,以使鸭皮绷紧无皱纹,烤出的鸭子外皮光亮,入口即酥;打糖是往鸭身上洒饴糖水,为的是使烤出的鸭子色泽枣红,味道香甜。填鸭入炉前还要从其体侧切口处灌入八成满的开水,这样,鸭子入炉烤制时鸭身被火烤燎,腹内开水沸腾,形成"外烤内煮"的情势,这就是北京烤鸭之所以外焦里嫩的决窍。烤时要掌握火候,火大了鸭子会变焦,火小了又会不酥,火候要恰到好处,一般四十分钟即可烤得。烤成了的鸭子重量一般比烤前减少三分之一。

What's the story about the Beijing Roasted Duck? How is it prepared?

The Beijing Roasted Duck has a long history, which can be traced back to the early days of the 10th century. During the Yuan Dynasty it was even presented to the royal court as one of the delicacies for the emperor.

The way of preparing the Beijing Roasted Duck is as follows: First you have to choose a forced-feeding Beijing duck of about 2.5 kilograms. Generally speaking it takes about 50 days to raise a duck to such a size as the duck raised like this has a full chest with white flesh and thin skin, and what is more, the meat is delicate and tender.

Basically it takes three steps to turn a forced − feeding Beijing Duck into a roasted one: first cleaning; secondly to be roasted over the fire in the oven and thirdly to be sliced into pieces and served at the table. A duck to be prepared must undergo the following steps: to be air − pumped, to get the insides out and washed, then the skin to be scalded and with sugar applied on it and finally to help cool the skin. Take the step of air − pumping for instance, it is to make the duck fully round by filling it with air so that the skin becomes smooth with no wrinkles and the skin thus roasted looks shiny and tastes crispy; To apply sugar onto the skin can help turn the duck out brownish − red, taste sweet and smell fragrant. However, before the duck is brought over the fire its cavity has to be filled with boiling water to the mark of 80% full from its side opening. In this way, when the outside skin is being roasted the inside flesh is being boiled. This is the very know − how that the Beijing Roasted Duck looks brownish − red outside, yet the flesh inside tastes delicate and tender. To roast a Beijing Duck you have also to control the temperature and the time over the fire properly so as to bring it to a turn. If the flame is too ablaze the duck will be over − roasted, whereas it won't become crispy should the temperature falls short. In short, it takes about 40 minutes to get a duck done and the roasted one weighs 1/3 short of the unprepared.

473."全鸭席"是怎么回事?

全鸭席的主菜是烤鸭,辅以用鸭的舌、胗、腰子、肠、心、肝、膀和掌等,用烧、炸、爆和焖等方法,做成的百余种风味各异的冷、热菜。摆放时,宴席中心为烤鸭,周围为冷热鸭菜,形如"众星捧月"之状,色彩绚丽,令人大饱口福眼福。

How does an "all – duck banquet" look like?

The main dish of an all – duck banquet is the roasted Beijing duck and the assorted dishes, made of the duck's tongues, gizzards, loins, intestines, hearts, livers, wings and webs. They are made into more than a hundred kinds of dishes either cold or hot by way of boiling, frying, stirring and braising. The table is set in a way with the roasted Beijing duck placed in the center of the table and around it are all kinds of assorted dishes hot or cold to suggest a pattern of "myriad of stars round the moon", thereby making the dishes on the table look more colorful and also very appealing to the taste, and pleasing to the eyes.

474.北京第一座全周影院何时开始接待游人?

位于八达岭山麓的北京长城全周影院是北京的第一座全周影院,1990 年 9 月 3 日正式开始接待游人。

When was the first spherical cinema in Beijing open to film – goers?

Located at the foothill of the Badaling, the Beijing Great Wall Spherical Cinema is the first of its kind in Beijing, which was opened to film – goers on September 3, 1990.

466

475. 北京有哪些园中之园？

在北京众多园林中,山环水绕,廊榭亭轩自成格局的园中之园有:

颐和园中的谐趣园,那是北京最有名的"园中之园",它是仿照无锡惠山的寄畅园而建筑的。

中南海的静谷,是一座闹中取静的"园中之园"。

香山公园的见心斋,是一座小巧玲珑,且十分雅致的"园中之园"。

此外,北海公园中的濠濮涧、静心斋,还有故宫里的乾隆花园,都是各具特色、名闻遐迩的"园中之园"。

Which gardens are the "gardens within the gardens" in Beijing?

Among various gardens in Beijing, the gardens within the gardens girdled by hills and waters and decorated with balustrade, water – side arbors or pavilions in their own styles and special features are:

Xiequyuan (Garden of Harmonious Delights) inside the Summer Palace: It is built in imitation of the Jichang Garden – a famous garden by the side of the Hui Hill in Wuxi, south of the Yangtze River.

Jinggu (Dale of Tranquility) in Zhongnanhai is a garden within the garden: a place for seeking tranquility out from hustles and bustles.

Xianxinzhai (Tranquil Heart Studio) in the Fragrant Hill Park is another small yet elegant garden in Beijing.

In addition, Haopujian and Jingxinzhai in Beihai Park and the Qianlong's Garden in the Imperial Palace are all typical "gardens within the gardens" of their own styles and features.

476.北京城仅存的箭楼在哪里?

经崇文门东行不远,直立着一座雄伟高大的城楼,这就是明永乐十五年(1417 年)始建、正统四年(1439 年)落成的北京内城东南角的箭楼,是北京仅存的一座比较完整的箭楼。

箭楼为重檐歇山顶,平面成曲尺形坐落在城墙上,通高 29 米。箭楼内并列有 20 根金柱,上铺楼板 3 层。箭楼墙体辟有 4 层箭孔,共有 144 个。

箭楼在古代是用于军事上的城防建筑,因其高大坚固,视野开阔,易守难攻而为历代帝王所重视,曾多次加以修茸。在最近一次修缮中,发现刻有明"嘉靖"、"隆庆"年款的城砖和琉璃瓦件;同时也发现了印有英文字母的炮弹壳及引信,这是箭楼历尽艰难,饱经沧桑的历史见证。箭楼被列为第二批全国重点文物保护单位。

Where is the only intact embrasure watch – tower over the city gate located in Beijing?

Not far away to the east of the Chongwenmen City Gate, you will find a watch – tower standing magnificently over the city wall. This is the only intact embrasure watch – tower on the southeast corner of the city of Beijing. First built in 1417, the 15th year in the reign of Emperor Yongle in the Ming Dynasty, it was completed in 1439, the 4th year of the reign of Emperor Zheng tong.

With a hip – roof of doubled eves, the tower, 29 meters in height, sits squarely right on the corner of the city wall. Supported on 20 gilt pillars in line, the tower has three floors with 144 shooting – holes in total built onto the 4 leveled embrasure wall.

In ancient times, the watch – tower over the city wall is a kind of defence works. Built high and strong with a view of wide – angles, it is easy to defend yet difficult to attack. Therefore, rulers of various dynasties have taken a great account of it with many a time of renovation and restoration done. In the restoration carried out recently we've discovered some bricks and glazed tiles made in the period of "Jiajing" and "Longqing" of the Ming Dynasty and at the same time some debris of shells and fuses of gun – shots with English words carved on were found there too. It is a vivid witness of the changes of history the watch – tower underwent. It is now listed as a unit of cultural relics under the protection of the state.

477.北京有多少个著名风景区？

北京现有 40 余处著名风景区，随着旅游业的发展和新景区的开发，数量还在不断增多。

How many famous scenic areas are there in Beijing?

There are so far over 40 famous scenic areas in Beijing. However, along with the development of tourism in Beijing and some new scenic areas to be tapped, more of them are to come in future.

478.自首都机场至市内(称为机场路)有多少公里？

自首都机场至市内有 27 公里，至市中心则有 30 公里，乘汽车约需 50 分钟左右。

How far is it from the Capital Airport to the city of Beijing?

It is 27 kilometers from the Capital Airport to the city and 30 kilometers to the city center. It takes around 50 minutes drive by coach to cover the distance.

479. 北京有几条地铁线路？何时建成？各有多长及多少辆机车？

北京是中国第一个修建地铁的城市。第一期工程是北京站至苹果园,始建于 1965 年 7 月,1969 年 10 月竣工,全长 23.6 公里,设 17 座车站和一座古城地面车辆段,试运营 12 年,至 1981 年 9 月正式运营。第二期工程为环城线,工程开始于 1971 年 3 月,1984 年建成通车,全长 16.04 公里,设 12 座车站和一座太平湖车辆段。第三期工程为贯穿东西长安街的东起八王坟、西至复兴门地铁,该项工程已于 99 年 9 月竣工,并正式投入运行。

地铁客车由全国 180 多个厂家协同制造,车辆设计构造为时速 80 公里,运行速度 35.4 公里,动力为 825 伏直流电。地铁建成后,客运量逐年增加,年载运量达 1.01 亿人次,日高峰运量为 47 万人次,从而大大地缓解了地面上的交通压力。目前有机车 300 多辆。

How many subway lines are there in Beijing? When were them completed? How many kilometers does each of them cover? And how many trains do they have?

Beijing is the first city in China, in which subways began to be built. The first section of the project is from Beijing Railway Station to Pinguoyuan (the Apple Garden). Started in July 1965 the project was completed in October 1969. The length totals 23.6 kilometers with 17 underground stations and another section — the Gucheng Rolling Stock Section on the ground. This section, through 12 years of trial running, was officially put into operation in September 1981. The second phase of the project is that for encircling the city of Beijing with the construction being started in March, 1971 and coming to a finish in September 1984. With 12 stations plus a Taipinghu Rolling Stock Station all along, the total length it covers is 16.04 kilometers. Starting from Bawangfen in the east the third phase of the project runs through the Chang'an Avenue to terminate at Fuxingmen in the west, the work has already completed and opened to the public in September 1999.

The subway trains are manufactured through the joint efforts of 180 factories and units in the country. The designed speed and structure of the train is 80 kilometers per hour, but the actual running speed is 35.4 kilometers, operated with an engine using D/C electricity of 825 voltages. With the completion of these subways, the passenger flow increases year by year and its carrying capacity reaches 101 million annually with the daily peak at 470,000, thereby greatly reducing the traffic pressure on the ground. The trains they use add up to over 300 now.

480. 北京最早的一条铁路始末站是哪里？是哪年建成的？

北京的第一条铁路是 1896 年英国将唐山至胥各庄的唐胥铁路延伸至丰台卢沟桥，始称津卢铁路。1901 年在北京前门设火车站，才形成了北京的第一条铁路。

Where are the starting and ending stations of the earliest railway in Beijing? **When was it built**?

The first section of the railway to Beijing used to be that from Tianjin to Lugouqiao (the Marco Polo Bridge) in Fengtai area, an extended section of the Tangshan – Xugezhuang Railway done by Britain in 1896, being called the Jinlu Railway. Later in 1901 only when a station was built at the Qianmen area did the first railway in Beijing come into being.

481. 北京最早的中外合资企业是哪个？ 哪年开始营业的？

北京最早的中外合资企业是与法国合作成立的马克西姆餐厅，它是 1983 年 9 月 27 日正式开始营业的。

Which is the earliest joint – venture enterprise in Beijing? **When was it put into operation**?

The earliest joint – venture enterprise in Beijing is the French Maxim's Restaurant. It was put into operation on the 27th of September 1983.

482. 北京最早安装的电灯在哪里？ 是哪年安装的？

北京安装得最早的电灯在颐和园的乐寿堂内，装于 1903 年，这是德国商人通过贿赂手段，买通总管太监李莲英后慈禧才准许安装的。

Where were the earliest electric lights installed? **And when was it installed**?

The earliest electric lights were those installed in the Hall of Happiness and Longevity in the Summer Palace. It was first done in 1903 by a German businessman, who first bribed the notorious eunuch Li Lianying and through him to get the approval of Empress Dowager Cixi for the installation.

483. 中国现存最大的坛庙在北京什么地方？建于何时？占地多少？

北京现存中国最大的坛庙是位于北京天桥南大街的天坛。建于明永乐十八年(1420年)，占地4,000余亩，比故宫的占地面积大3倍。

Where is the largest intact altar temple of China located in Beijing? When was it built and how large an area does it cover?

The largest intact altar temple of China is the Temple of Heaven located at the southern section of the Tianqiao Street, in Beijing. Built in 1420, the 18th year of Emperor Yongle's reign in the Ming Dynasty the temple covers an area of about 270 hectares, being three times larger than that of the Imperial Palace.

484. 北京市最老的涉外饭店是哪一个？请简述其历史沿革？

北京市最老的涉外饭店是位于市中心的北京饭店，它由3座楼构成。中间部分建于1901年，东西两楼是解放后扩建的。东楼最高18层，建于1974年，是70年代北京最大的涉外饭店，也是当时北京最高的建筑物之一。

1900年，八国联军侵入北京，在东城设置了兵营，酒店和妓院也就相机应运而生。那年冬天，有两个法国人在苏州胡同开了一家三开间门面的酒馆，这就是后来北京饭店的前身。随着小店生意日益兴隆,1901 年便迁到了今天的王府井南口的地方,正式取名为北京饭店。当时出入饭店的都是些洋人,他们为了在中国做买卖,赚大钱,便常在这里租借一席之地。

1945 年日本投降以后,国民党北平政府接收了北京饭店。继之,国民党战地服务团便把北京饭店辟为招待美国军队的住所,使这个饭店沦为士兵们寻欢作乐的场所。

1946 年 1 月,蒋介石为了赢得时间布置内战,在美国的授意下与中国共产党签订了停战协定,在北京成立了"北平军事调处执行部",北京饭店就成了它的第二招待所,当时共产党、国民党和美军三方面的代表就住在这里。

1949 年北京解放后,北京饭店回到了人民的怀抱,接着便进行了全面的修扩建工程,北京饭店开始以其崭新的面貌迎接着来自国内外的宾客。

Which is the oldest hotel in Beijing for overseas visitors? **Can you say something about it**?

Located in the center of the city of Beijing, the Beijing Hotel is the oldest one in Beijing for hosting overseas visitors. The middle part was built in 1901 and the eastern and western parts were done after 1949. Built in 1974, the eastern part towers 18 storeys high, the largest and the highest hotel in Beijing in the 1970s.

In 1900, the Eight Powers Allied Forces invaded Beijing and army barracks were then set up in the eastern part of the city, and with them cropped up the bars, restaurants and brothels as well. The same year in winter two French men opened a 3 – bay tavern in the nowadays Suzhou Lane, which turned out to be the predecessor of the Beijing Hotel. As the business in the tavern was booming with each passing day it was moved in 1901 to a place, the southern end of the present day Wangfujing Street and was since formally renamed Peking Hotel. At that time those who haunted the hotel were all foreigners. Renting a place to do business they were amassing great fortunes in China.

With the surrender of Japan in 1945 the hotel was taken over by the Beiping Municipal Government of the Kuomintang and it was later turned by the Battle Service Corps of the Kuomintang into a lodging for hosting the American army — men, thus reducing it to a pandemonium for doing things unspeakable.

In January 1946, instigated by the U.S., Chiang Kai — shek, in order to gain time for the preparation of the civil war in China, signed an armistice agreement with the Chinese Communist Party. With the set — up of a tripartite executive body for the arbitration of military affairs in Beiping the hotel then became the No.2 Reception House for the representatives of the CPC, the Kuomintang and the U.S. army.

With the liberation of Beiping in 1949 the hotel returned to the arms of the people. Then a work of renovation and expansion was carried out in an all round way, and the hotel turned over a new leaf for entertaining guests from at home and abroad.

485. 北京最著名、最热闹的街道是哪一条？

北京最著名、最热闹的街道是王府井大街。位于北京市中心，它是北京非常热闹的商业街，大街的东边有大型的东安市场，西边有百货大楼，在这条街上经营各色商品的店铺达 140 余家。

王府井大街的由来已久,约有 550 余年的历史。辽金时代,这里是旷野荒郊,元代开始有街,称丁字街。明永乐年间,在周围修建了 10 座王府,嘉靖时始称十王府街。到清代,十王府逐渐消失,但街名却延续了下来。又因街内有口甜水井,所以便叫王府井。

然而,王府井成为热闹的街道不过是四、五十年前的事。该街的柏油马路是 1928 年才修筑的,由于当时的中国是半殖民地半封建的国家,王府井的发展便反映出了当时的时代背景。王府井以往的繁华来自两个方面:从北方来的体现在东安市场,是地道中国式的货物与商场;而从南方来的则以座落在王府井南口、由西洋人开的北京饭店为首。这里以台基厂、崇文门一带为外围,是完全洋式的。

今天的王府井大街发展非常迅速,它已成了北京人和外地客人必游和购物的中心。尤其是从改革开放以来,开张了许多店铺,门面也进行了装修。新建的东安市场、穆斯林商厦、北京烤鸭店及东来顺分店等分列马路两侧,给前来购物、观光的中外客人提供了许多方便。

Which is the most famous and brisk street in Beijing?

The most famous and brisk street in Beijing is the Wangfujing Street. Extending from north to south in the center of the city it has over 140 shops of all kinds in business here with crowds of people shopping and visiting all along the street. Displaying on the eastern side is now the large - sized newly - built Dong'an Bazaar, while opposite on the west you'll see the Beijing Department Store.

The Wangfujing Street has a history of over 550 years. Tracing back to the period of Liao and Kin dynasties, here used to be a piece of waste - land but later in Yuan Dynasty a

T – shaped street came into being. During the period of Emperor Yongle's reign (1403 – 1424) in the Ming Dynasty, Ten mansions of the royal families began to be built in the area, hence the Ten Royal Mansion Street being named in the period of Emperor Jiajing's reign (1522 – 1566). In the Qing Dynasty the Ten Royal Mansions sunk gradually into oblivion, yet the name of the street was kept and passed on. As there used to have a sweet water well nearby the street was thus known as the Wangfujing Street ever since.

However, the street has seen its glorious days only in the recent 50 years. With the first asphalt surface road paved in 1928 the shaping of the street witnessed a vivid scene of the old semi – colonial and semi – feudal China. Unfolding itself in the following two ways, the Dong'an Bazaar from the north reflects something typical Chinese, while the area in the south, with the foreign owned Peking Hotel just at the entrance, and Taijichang and Chongwenmen in its surrounding areas, are something totally alien.

Seen a rapid development in recent years the street has become a must – see and shopping center for Beijing inhabitants and tourists to Beijing from elsewhere. Especially since the adoption of the policy of opening to the outside world in the late 1970s, many shops have been opened and renovated. With the newly – built Dong'an Bazaar, the Muslim Shopping Building, the Beijing Roasted Duck Restaurant and the branch of Donglaishun Restaurant cropping up one after the other along the street, it has offered a lot of convenience to visitors Chinese or foreign coming here for shopping and sightseeing.

486.北京一条古老文化街名叫什么？有什么特点？

北京古老的文化街叫琉璃厂，它有着悠久的历史，早在一千多年前的辽代，这里就已形成村落。公元1277年，元代官方在这一带建立琉璃窑厂，烧制供皇家使用的五色琉璃瓦件。琉璃厂便因此而得名。

清朝乾隆年间，这里开着30多家书铺，其它如古董、南纸、书帖、裱褙、笔墨、砚合、图章、印泥、胡琴以及折扇等文化行业的铺子也不少。总之，几乎当时文化人、读书人所需要的纸墨笔砚、琴棋书画等用品一应俱全，应有尽有。由于经营同一行业的铺子很多，但同时又各有特色，因而便于顾客选购和游览。

解放以后，尤其是最近二十余年来的改革开放，给琉璃厂的发展揭开了一个崭新的历史时期。为了适应文化艺术、旅游的发展需要，琉璃厂进行了全面的修改扩建。经过调整合并以后的琉璃厂，布局更为合理，但仍保留了各自的特色，从而得到了国内外广大旅游者的赞赏。目前的琉璃厂以经营珍贵的古旧书籍、文物字画、古碑拓本和纸墨笔砚而闻名遐迩，为中外的爱好者和鉴赏者提供了方便。

What's the name of the old cultural street in Beijing? What special features does it offer?

The old cultural street in Beijing is called the Liulichang Street. With a long history behind it, the place used to be a small village about 1,000 years ago during the Liao Dynasty. Towards the year of 1277 in the Yuan dynasty, some kilns for making glazed ceramics began to be built officially in this area and glazed tiles and objects were fired and to be used by royal families, hence the name Liulichang.

During the period of Emperor Qianlong's reign (1736 –

478

1796) in the Qing Dynasty, there appeared in the street over 30 book stores and in addition, there were also many such shops as selling curios and antiques, paper from south China, books of calligraphy models, book − cases, brushes and ink − sticks and slabs, seals, chops and pads, Chinese fiddles and folded − fans as well as painting and mounting shops, etc. One can say in a way that men of letters could find almost everything needed here. As there were many shops selling same articles along the street, yet with each having its own special feature, it proved very convenient for customers to buy or to feast their eyes on them over here.

After liberation and especially over the past 20 years since the adoption of the policy of opening to the outside world, the Liulichang Street has made much headway and entered an utterly new historical period of development. To cater to the needs of the development of art and culture and tourism as well, a work of complete renovation and adjustment has been carried out on a large scale by putting neatly together shops doing the same business while still keeping their own special features, thus winning appreciation from visitors both at home and from abroad. At present the street is renowned far and wide for dealing in old books, cultural relics, paintings and calligraphy, stele rubbings as well as the four treasures − paper, Chinese ink − sticks, brushes and ink − slabs used in a study, thereby offering great convenience to visitors there either for shopping or appreciation.

487. 北京古老繁荣的商业街是哪一条？

在北京许多重要繁华的商业街市中，大栅栏是一条古老的商业街。在封建王朝时代，皇城和紫禁城占去了北京内城的大半。早在明朝就有人在大栅栏地段开店设市，后来便逐渐形成了一个商业街市。但在八国联军进攻北京之时，这里被一场大火化为瓦砾，后又重建并恢复了其原来的面貌，这就是今天大栅栏街的前身。

这条街上的主要商店都有较长久的历史，资本也较雄厚。瑞蚨祥绸布店就是过去北京有名的"八大祥"之一，这家店铺原有4个门市部，除了垄断着丝绸布匹的买卖外，还兼营皮货和茶叶，占了这条街北面的绝大部分，它所拥有的资金占到了当时整个北京棉布业的一半以上。同仁堂药铺的开业是在康熙八年（1669年），距今已有330年了。

大栅栏以往的兴盛，除了那些店铺外，还与那里比较集中的娱乐场所有关。仅在这一条街上就有5家戏院：庆乐园、三庆园、广德楼、庆和园及同乐园。在这些戏院里，三庆园的历史最长，相传它是清初宴乐的地方；庆乐园和广德楼现旧址犹存，但均已改建，一个成了现代戏院，另一个则成了小型剧场；至于其它两家，则早在"庚子大火"时化为灰烬了。

在大栅栏里还有当时北京城里的第一家电影院，那便是于1913年首次上演电影的大观楼。这里原是一家两层楼的商场，楼上卖珠宝玉器，楼下售日用百货。到电影业开始兴起，便拆去二楼，加上座椅，成了一座影院。后几经扩建，便成了现在的甲级影院。

过去的大栅栏，还是北京的灯市。每逢元夜，家家店铺门口都用竹杆支起两盏宫灯；后来电灯代替蜡烛以后，还出现过一些奇异的灯彩。每年这一夜，大小店铺都是灯烛辉煌，通宵达旦，大街小巷挤满着观灯的人群，但今天这些都已成了历史陈迹了。

Which street used to be the old flourishing business street in Beijing?

Among many important and flourishing business streets in Beijing the Dazhalan Street used to be an old and renowned one. Under the feudal dynasties, the royal mansions and the Forbidden City occupied almost the major part of the inner city of Beijing. As early as in the Ming Dynasty, people began to set up stalls or have their shops opened in Dazhalan area and then a business street by and by came into being. However, in 1900, when the Eight Powers Allied Forces besieged Beijing the street was reduced to a heap of ashes and debris in a big fire. It was later rebuilt and restored to its original shape, this being the predecessor of the nowadays Dazhalan Street.

With a long history behind, all shops along this street used to be rich in capital. Take Ruifuxiang Drapery and Cloth Shop — one of the 8 famous draperies in Beijing for instance, it used to have a shop with a four – bay frontal, almost monopolizing at that time the drapery business in Beijing. In addition, it also dealt in leather goods and tea. Its shops almost occupied the most part of the street and the capital it owned at the time e-qualed to a total half of the drapery business then in Beijing putting together. Tracing some 330 years back in history, the Tongrentang Herbal Medicine Shop started its business in the year of 1669, the 5th year under the reign of Emperor Kangxi in the Qing Dynasty.

The past glory of the Dazhalan Street reflected not only in those shops but also in having 5 opera houses: Qingleyuan, Sanqingyuan, Guangdelou, Qingheyuan and Tongleyuan all a-

481

long the street. Said to have been a place for banquets and a-musements in early Qing period Sanqingyuan, enjoyed the longest existence in history. As to Qingleyuan and Guangde-lou, though you can still find some traces here, one of them has already been turned into a theatre with modern facilities and another a small opera house. The rest were reduced to cinders in that big fire in 1900.

In Dazhalan Street you can also find a Daguanlou (Grand View Tower), the first cinema in Beijing. Beginning to show films in 1913, it used to be a two-storied shop, selling jade and jewelry ornaments on the second floor and daily necessities on the first. However, when the film business began to show up and by and by came in vogue the place with the second floor dismantled was refurbished into a cinema and the repeated efforts later have turned it into one of modern style.

Renowned also for its lanterns on the evening of the 15th of every first month in lunar calendar, all shops along the Dazhalan Street would have two red lanterns put up on a bamboo-pole in front of the gate, presenting a scene so fantastic that everybody couldn't but feel like enjoying it. However, the street was rendered ever more beautiful when the candle-sticks were later replaced by electric bulbs. Every year on the very evening people, old and young alike were out on the street, enjoying the lanterns of various descriptions. What a spectacular scene! But alas, gone are the days! it is something historical now.

488. 北京市最老的天主教堂是哪个? 建于哪一年?

坐落在宣武门内路北的天主教堂是北京城内最老的教堂,

有 300 余年的历史,原名叫"圣母无染原罪堂"。因教堂位于北京市的南边,故习惯上称其为"南堂"。

明万历廿八年(1600 年),意大利传教士利玛窦从广州来京,得到了明神宗朱翊钧的赏识,同意他在城内购宅传教。该堂的前身是明东林党的首善书院,清顺治七年(1650 年),教士汤若望加以重新扩建,但后被毁,光绪后期又修复。现今所见的教堂即是 1900 年以后修复的教堂。堂内有圣母油画、耶稣圣像,以及受苦"十四路"的壁画等。现在这里是北京教友的宗教活动中心。

Which is the oldest cathedral in Beijing? When was it built?

Located at the north of the avenue inside Xuanwumen Gate, the cathedral with a history of over 300 years is the oldest cathedral in Beijing. As it's located in the south of the city it is usually called the Southern Cathedral or Nantang as local people put it.

In 1600, the 28th year under the reign of Emperor Wanli in the Ming Dynasty, Matteo Ricci, an Italian missionary came from Guangzhou to Beijing and greatly appreciated by the emperor. He was granted the right to buy his abode and do his preaching in the city of Beijing. In the Ming Dynasty, the location of the cathedral used to be the site for the best - chosen Academy of the Donglin Scholastic Society but was later expanded by a German Jesuit, Father Adam Schall in 1650, the 7th year under the reign of Emperor Shunzhi in the Qing Dynasty. However, it was destroyed and the present cathedral was rebuilt after 1900 during the late years of Emperor Guangxu's reign. What you can see in the cathedral now is an oil painting of the Blessed Virgin Mary, a sculpture of Jesus and some murals telling the stories of his sufferings. The place is now the center of religious activities for the believers in Catholicism in Beijing.

489. 北京城内最大的天主教堂是哪个？建于哪一年？

坐落在西城区的西什库教堂是北京城内最大的天主教堂，称为北堂。北堂原来位于府右街的蚕池口，光绪十六年（1890年），在扩建西苑时，慈禧太后担心近在苑西的教堂钟楼能窥视苑内，于是便和法国公使商量，在西什库拨地 20 英亩，并补偿拆迁费 7.5 万英镑，将蚕池口的教堂拆除迁走。

在中国近代史上，西什库教堂是很出名的。1900 年，义和团的反洋教运动蓬勃展开时，这里曾是激烈的战场，在反帝斗争的中国近代史上留下了光辉的一页。现在，这里成了北京市第三批重点文物保护单位。

Which is the largest cathedral in Beijing? When was it built?

Located somewhere near Xishenku in the western district of Beijing the Northern Cathedral (Beitang) is the largest of all cathedrals in Beijing. Situated formerly at Canchikou in the Fuyou Street, it was dismantled in 1890, the 16th year under the reign of Emperor Guangxu in the Qing Dynasty. At that time Empress Dowager Cixi wanted to enlarge her western garden but for fearing that her activities in the garden might be spied by someone from the bell – tower over the cathedral nearby, the problem was brought up and settled through a discussion with the French counselor on the condition that a piece of land measuring 20 acres and an indemnity of 350,000 taels of silver be paid for the removal of the old cathedral away from Canchikou.

The Xishenku Cathedral is quite a well – known one in the modern history of China. In 1900 when the Boxers Movement was in full swing against the foreign religion the place used to be a battle field for many battles, thereby left over a brilliant page in the struggle against imperialism in the modern history of China. Today the cathedral is listed as a piece of cultural relics under the protection of Beijing Municipal Government.

490. 北京市最大的、保存最完好的、最典型的喇嘛庙是哪个? 建于哪年?

雍和宫是北京市内最大、保存最完好和最为典型的喇嘛庙,建于 1694 年,已有 300 余年的历史。

Which is the largest, the most well – protected and typical lamasery in Beijing? When was it built?

The Yonghegong is the largest, the most well – protected and typical lamasery in Beijing. First built in 1694, it has a history of over 300 years.

491. 北京最早的道教庙宇是哪个? 何时建成?

北京的道教庙宇最早莫过于西便门外的白云观。该观最初建于唐开元二十七年(739 年),原名天长观,观址在现今白云观的西边,是供奉老子的地方。现在的白云观是清代光绪年间重修的,它现在是中国道教协会所在地。

Which is the earliest Taoist temple in Beijing? When was it built?

The earliest Taoist temple in Beijing is none other than the Baiyunguan Taoist Temple located outside the Xibianmen city gate. Started to be built in A.D. 739, the 27th year under the reign of Emperor Xuanzong in the Tang Dynasty, and first named Tianchangguan in consecration of Laozi, it was located just a little to the west of the present temple. This Baiyunguan was rebuilt in the period of Emperor Guangxu's reign in the Qing Dynasty. The temple is now used for the Taoist Association of China.

492. 北京市历史最久的清真寺在哪里？建于哪年？

坐落在宣武区牛街路东的牛街清真寺，是北京市历史最为悠久的清真寺，始建于辽统和十四年（996 年），明、清期间都曾进行过大规模的修缮，解放以后也曾几度作过油漆，从而使这个清真古寺焕发出了新的光彩。

寺内的建筑具有浓郁的阿拉伯风格，由于《可兰经》上有禁止使用动物形象作为装饰的说明，所以寺内建筑物上的彩绘，均为阿拉伯文字和几何图案组成。

Which is the mosque with the longest history in Beijing? When was it built?

Located at the eastern side of the Niujie Street in Xuanwu District, the Niujie Mosque is the one with the longest history in Beijing. Built in 996, the 14th year under the reign of Tonghe in the Liao Dynasty reparations had later been carried out on a large scale in the Ming and Qing dynasties and particularly after liberation, it has been repainted several times, thereby making it look shiny and bright ever more.

Refurbished in typical Arabic style and as prohibited in Koran that no animal designs should be used for decoration in the mosque, the paintings and murals on the buildings are all composed of colorful Arabic scripts and geometric designs.

493. 北京最大的图书馆是哪个？建筑面积是多少？藏书有多少？

北京最大的图书馆是首都图书馆,建筑面积为 0.6 万平方米, 共有藏书 157.4 万册。

Which is the largest library in Beijing? How large a floor space does it cover and how many books in collection does it have?

With a floor space of 6,000 square meters, the Capital Library is the largest one in Beijing, which has a collection of books totaling 1.574 million volumes.

494. 北京最大的博物馆是哪个？建筑面积、占地面积和藏品各是多少？

北京最大的博物馆是故宫博物院,占地面积为 72 万平方米,建筑面积为 15 万平方米,共有藏品 92.4 万件。

Which is the largest museum in Beijing? How large an area and a floor space does it cover? And how many pieces of relics does it have in collection?

The largest museum in Beijing is the Palace Museum. Covering an area of 720,000 square meters, it has a floor space of over 150,000 square meters with 924,000 pieces of relics in collection.

495.北京最大的展览馆是哪个？建筑面积是多少？

北京最大的展览馆是中国国际展览中心,建筑面积为 7.7 万平方米。

Which is the largest exhibition hall in Beijing? How large a floor space does it cover?

With a floor space of 77,000 square meters, the China International Exhibition Center is the largest exhibition hall in Beijing.

496.亚洲最大的神经外科中心在哪里？何时建成？

亚洲最大的神经外科中心是北京的天坛医院、北京市神经外科研究所新院,于 1990 年 11 月 10 日建成。

Where lies the largest neuro – surgery center in Asia? When was it completed?

Completed on the 10th of November 1990 the largest neuro – surgery center in Asia is the Tiantan Hospital, a newly – built Neuro – surgery Research Institute of the Beijing Municipality.

497.北京最早的戏院是哪个？

北京最早的戏院是前门大栅栏的三庆园,相传这是清初宴乐的地方。

Which is the earliest theater in Beijing?

The earliest theater in Beijing is the Sanqingyuan in Dazhalan Street. It is said to have been a place for holding banquets and performances in the early days of the Qing Dynasty.

498. 北京最早的电影院是哪个？何时开始营业的？

北京最早的电影院是前门大栅栏内的大观楼，是 1913 年开始营业的。

Which is the earliest cinema in Beijing? When did it begin to show films?

Beginning to show films in 1913, the earliest cinema in the city of Beijing is the Daguanlou (Grand View Tower) located in Dazhalan Street.

499. 北京"同仁堂"是何时建成的，其简历如何？

"同仁堂"是北京的老字号药铺，坐落在北京前门大栅栏，初创于清朝康熙八年(1669 年)，至今已有 330 年的历史。同仁堂的创始人乐尊育(1630－1688 年)，原籍浙江宁波府慈水镇，其祖上于明永乐年间迁居北京行医。乐尊育本为走街串巷行医卖药的"郎中"，后在清皇宫太医院任出纳文书。他博览历史方书，收集了大量古方和宫廷秘方，以后创办了同仁堂，致力于提高丸、散、膏、丹和药酒的质量。雍正年间(1723－1735 年)，同仁堂取得了向御药房供药的特权。

同仁堂之所以享有盛誉，是因为其成药配方独特，原料上乘，加工精细所致。1861 年慈禧太后当政后，同仁堂奉命直接为皇室制药，已实际上取代了御药房的作用。

北京的有些药铺，如永仁堂、怀仁堂、宏达堂、继仁堂等，都是乐家分号发展的产物。乐家药铺遍及全国。世界上大约有 20 多个国家和地区与同仁堂有着生意上的往来，其中成药的出口额居全国同行的首位。

When was the "Tongrentang Herbal Medicine Shop" brought into business in Beijing? Say something in brief about its history.

Located at Dazhalan outside the Qianmen Gate in Beijing the famous Tongrentang Herbal Medicine Shop was opened in 1669, the 8th year of Emperor Kangxi's reign in the Qing Dynasty.

The founder of this 330 - year - old business is Le Zunyu (1630 - 1688), whose ancestor used to be a native in a small town called Cishui in Ningbo Prefecture, Zhejiang Province and coming to Beijing in the period of Emperor Yongle's reign of the Ming Dynasty as a quack doctor while selling medicine. Later, when working as a cashier in the dispensary of the Royal Qing Court he read and collected a great many old and secret prescriptions of the court and on that basis he opened up Tongrentang Herbal Medicine Shop, devoting himself to raising the quality of its pills, ointments, pellets and powder as well as medicinal wine. During the period of Emperor Yongzheng's reign (1723 - 1735) the shop acquired the privilege of supplying medicine to the dispensary of the Royal Court.

Tongrentang attributes its success in medicine to the unique prescriptions with high quality materials, careful way in preparation and effectiveness in healing. When Empress Dowager Cixi came to power in 1861 the medicine used in the imperial dispensary was ordered directly from Tongrentang, which actually replaced the imperial dispensary of the Royal Court.

Many other such medicine shops as Yongrentang, Huairentang, Hongdatang and Jirentang in Beijing are actually all branches of the Le's shot up in its ensuing development. Now the Le's medicine shops have spread all over the country and Tongrentang has already established its business relations with more than 20 countries and regions in the world, its export of ready – made medicine standing preeminent from among the medical trade.

500. 北京有哪些在世界上享有盛名的特种工艺？

北京的特种工艺在世界上久负盛名，其中玉器、牙雕、景泰蓝、花丝镶嵌、地毯、宫灯和刻瓷等，曾获巴拿马国际博览会金质奖及伦敦、名古屋等地展览会的嘉誉。

What are the special arts and crafts in Beijing that are well – known in the world？

The special arts and crafts of Beijing which have long been known in the world are jade – ware, ivory – carving, cloisonné, filigree, rags and carpets, palace lanterns and porcelain carvings. Some of them won gold medals at the Panama International Fairs and were also highly appreciated at the fairs held in London and Nagoya.

501. 景泰蓝的名称是怎么来的？ 创于何年？

景泰蓝又称"珐琅"，是北京著名的特种工艺品之一。景泰蓝创于明代宣德年间（1426 – 1435 年），到明景泰年间（1450 – 1459 年）才流行开来。在此期间，这种工艺无论是在艺术水平的提高，还是在产品的数量和质量方面，均已达到了空前的水平,因而便由景泰帝的年号而获名。至于"景泰蓝"名称中的"蓝"字,则是因为当时这种工艺品多以晶莹的宝石蓝、孔雀蓝等蓝色釉料为主而得名。

景泰蓝的花式品种很多,从造型上来说,它既有传统的炉、鼎、薰和瓶类等制品,也有新的各种花瓶、灯具、烟具、文具、餐具及首饰等制品。在图案上,既有山水花鸟,也有古今人物。其色鲜艳,充满了珠光宝气,但有的则显得朴素淡雅,古色古香。

How did the name "Jingtailan"(cloisonné) come about? When was it created?

"Jingtailan"(cloisonné, or called enamel) is one of the famous arts and crafts in Beijing created first in the period of Emperor Xuande's reign (1426 – 1435) in the Ming Dynasty. It became popular in the period of Emperor Jingtai's reign (1450 – 1459), in which either its craftsmanship or artistry was greatly raised and the quantity and quality of the products were brought to an ever high level, hence the name derived from the emperor's reigning title "Jingtai". As to the word "Lan" (blue), this is because the artifacts produced at the time was mainly glazed with such color as sapphire blue, malachite or turquoise.

There are many varieties of cloisonné products. So far as its shaping is concerned it has traditional burners, tripods, sandal – wood burners and vases. In addition there are still some newly created ones as flower – pots, lamps and smoking sets, stationery, tableware and ornaments and in design they vary from landscape to birds and flowers as well as figurines of old and new. With colors bright and glistening as of pearls or precious stones some of the products look very splendid, while others simple yet elegant and still some very much archaic.

502.北京的市树叫什么名字?

北京的市树叫国槐和侧柏。

What are the symbol trees of the city of Beijing?

The symbol trees of the city of Beijing are known as the Chinese locust and cypress trees.

503.北京的市花叫什么名字?

北京的市花叫月季及菊花。

What are the symbol city flowers of Beijing?

The symbol city flowers of Beijing are the monthly rose and chrysanthemum.

504.东安市场是怎样形成的?

东安市场所在的地方,最初是明末叛将吴三桂的"王府"。后来又因吴三桂反清,清廷又毁掉了他的王府,改为"八旗练兵场"。后因日久而废止,这里就成了一个大广场,但普通平民百姓还是不能随便进入的。

光绪二十九年(1903年),当时的户部尚书那桐住在东城的金鱼胡同,为了上朝方便,就想从东安门到金鱼胡同修一条"马路"。当时东安门两旁有不少摊贩,既不便于过车过轿,也有碍观瞻。趁此修路之机,光绪便下令驱走这些摊贩。后经这些小摊贩的多次上奏哀告,才允许他们进入"八旗练兵场"的北头一角设摊做买卖,这就是后来东安市场的雏型。自1903年4月搬迁起,距今已有90多年了。

东安市场最初均为"地摊"摊贩,后来逐渐盖了些极为简陋的平房,经卖的都是些小吃、小百货和小玩具之类。

袁世凯1912年发动兵变,东安市场被毁。事隔一年以后,原来的一些摊贩又集资建房设摊,这才初步形成了市场的规模,行业和商户也逐渐增多,并先后建成了一些戏院、杂耍园等,也有一些看相的、算卦的混杂其间,可称五花八门,行行俱全。

从封建时代的北京直至解放前夕,北京的一些军阀、官僚、政客及资本家等大都集中居住在东城一带,于是这里便由出售一些低级商品发展到高档商品。一些"舶来品"到了北京以后也首先出现在东安市场上,以适应上流社会人士的生活之需,这里也便成了各行各业商人在商战中进行角逐的竞技场。

解放后,东安市场翻开了它历史上新的一页。1969年,政府将原来的东安市场全部拆除重建,形成了当时北京较大的百货商场之一。现在,随着改革开放的深入,东安市场已发生了翻天覆地的变化,以一座现代化商城的新貌屹立在王府井大街的东侧。

How did the Dong'an Bazaar come into being?

The Dong'an Bazaar is located at the site of a former palace for Wu Sangui – a treacherous general at the end of the Ming Dynasty. Later as Wu turned round against the Qing's rule his palace mansion was destroyed and changed into a "Drilling Ground for the Army of the Eight Banners" of the Qing dynasty. However as time went on, it was discarded and laid useless to be a mere open square, yet still no common people were permitted to get into it.

In 1903, the 29th year under the reign of Emperor Guangxu, a certain minister by the name of Na Tong who then lived in the Goldfish Lane in the eastern city wished to open up a road leading from his home to the Dong'anmen Gate so as to facilitate his going to the court for audience every day. But at that time there were many peddlers along both sides of the Dong'anmen Street. It was neither easy for chariots or sedan – chairs to pass by nor was it a pleasing sight to set eyes on. Taking the advantage of paving the road an edict was given to oust those peddlers. It was only by submitting in a repeated way the petitions to the court asking for permission of doing business that the peddlers were allowed to set up stalls at the north end of the "Drilling Ground". This is the Dong'an Bazaar in the shaping and it happened some 90 years ago in the April of 1903.

At the very beginning there were only some peddlers and stall – keepers. As time went on shacks were built for selling refreshments, small articles of daily – use and toys or suchlike.

In 1912, Yuan Shikai staged a mutiny and in the course the place was ruined. However, a year or so later peddlers began to come back for doing business again. By pouring funds together they started to build houses and set up stores and shops, thereby forming the Dong'an Bazaar in the initial phase. With shops and trades of various kinds increasing daily in the area, opera houses and jugglers began to join in and at the same time in flocked the fortune – tellers and geomancers and people of all walks of life. The place finally turned up to be a bazaar doing all sorts of business.

In days of old to the time before liberation as most of warlords, bureaucrats, politicians and capitalists lived in the eastern part of the city of Beijing, the bazaar changed from the one selling only goods of low quality to the one selling things of high grades so as to meet the needs of those living a luxurious life. Some imported goods also began to show first in Dong'an Bazaar and the place since then became an arena on which businessmen of all trades staged wars in making as much profits as possible.

With the liberation came the turning – over of a new leaf for the Dong'an Bazaar and in 1969 as decided by the people's government the old Dong'an Bazaar was pulled down and on its site replaced a new one. However, still greater changes have taken place since the implementation of the policy of opening to the outside world. The new Dong'an Bazaar is a highly sophisticated building towering magnificently opposite the Beijing Department Store on the eastern side of the Wangfujing Street.

505. 北京火车站是哪年建成的？总面积是多少？

北京火车站建于 1959 年,总面积为 46,700 平方米。现在北京新的火车站——北京西站已经落成,并已于 1997 年正式投入运营。

In which year was the Beijing Railway Station built and what is its total floor space?

Built in 1959, the Beijing Railway Station has a total floor space of 46,700 square meters. A new railway station – the Beijing Western Railway Station was completed and put into operation in 1997.